TIBET 2000

Environment and Development Issues

Environment and Development Desk, DIIR
Central Tibetan Administration
Gangchen Kyishong
Dharamsala, HP, India

2000

Published by the Environment and Development Desk, DIIR
Central Tibetan Administration
Gangchen Kyishong, Dharamsala, 176215 District Kangra, HP, India
ecodesk@diir.gov.tibet.net website: www.tibet.com
April 2000

ISBN 81-86230-29-7
Printed at : Archana, 787, Church Road, Jangpura, New Delhi
Ph.: 4311992, 4318937, 4322834, Telefax : 4322834

Tibet 2000: Environment and Development Issues Project Team

Project Director and Principal Researcher	Tsultrim Palden Dekhang
Researchers	Tashi Choedon Bidhartsang
	Khedup Waiser
	Judy Duncan
	Nick Schofield
	Lorne Stockman
	Laura Ziemer
Editorial Consultant	Jane Perkins
Production	Tsering Yangkey
	Dekyi Tsondue
Cartographer	Dr. Kunchok Tsundue

Acknowledgements
The Environment and Development Desk, DIIR would like to thank the following individuals and organisations for their contribution and support:
Anusha Fernando, Nicholas Schofield, Judy Duncan, Lorne Stockman, Laura Ziemer, Kunchok Tsundue, Susan Mizrahi, Gabriel Lafitte, Peter Raine, Catherine Moore, John Ackerly, Lodi G. Gyari, Tempa Tsering, Bhuchung K. Tsering, Tseten Samdup, Chris Rapaport, Leslie Dickout, Karin Tang, Markus Strumpel, Jordhen Chazotsang, Pema Dorjee, Rachel Fleming, Department of Security, Planning Council and Tibetan Reception Centre of CTA, Library of Tibetan Works and Archives, ICT, ICLT, TIN, TYC and the staff of DIIR. Our special thanks to Milarepa Fund for funding the research for this report.

Cover: *Tibet's Yarlung Tsangpo becomes the Brahmaputra as it flows into India and Bangladesh*

For further information on Tibet and its environment, please visit websites: www.tibetnews.com; www.tibet.com; www.savetibet.org; www.earthisland.org/tpp; www.milarepa.org; www.rokpa.org

DEDICATION

Dedicated to
His Holiness the 14th Dalai Lama
of Tibet whose concern for the future of this
planet and the message of non-violence
continues to inspire us all.

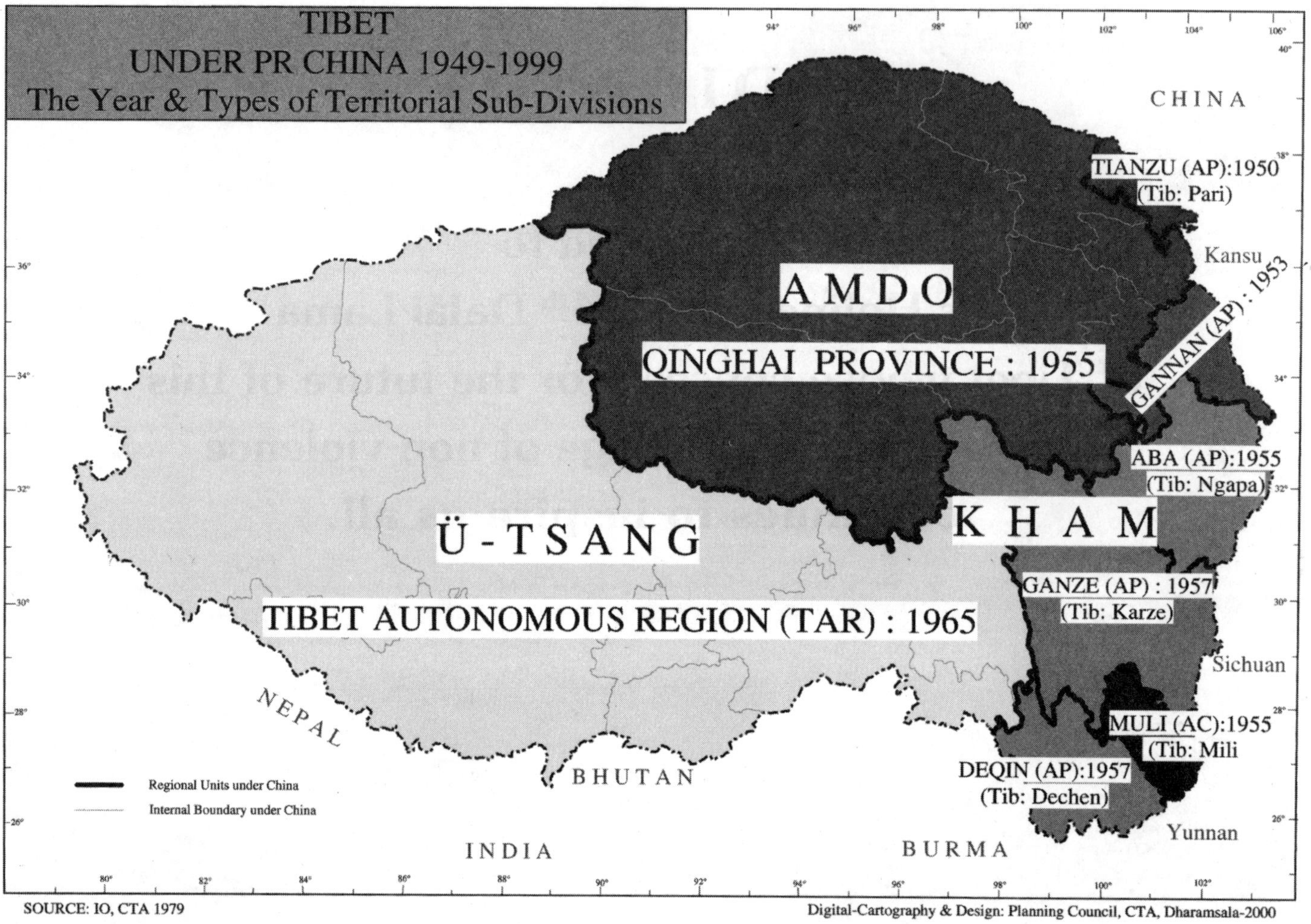

Note : See colour map at the end of the book

CONTENTS

PREFACE

WHY SAVE TIBET'S ENVIRONMENT?

TIBET, popularly known as the "Roof of the World", existed for over 2,000 years as a sovereign nation, with its three administrative regions, Kham, Amdo and U-Tsang, spanning 2.5 million sq. km. Communist China invaded the country in 1949. And today Beijing refers only to the so-called Tibet Autonomous Region (1.2 million sq. km) created in 1965 as "Tibet".

The Tibetan Plateau is the highest and largest plateau on earth and towers over the continent of Eurasia. It is home to over 5,000 higher plant species and over 12,000 species of vascular plants, 532 different species of birds, 126 identified minerals and has rich old growth forests.

It is also the source of many of Asia's major rivers whose tributaries are the lifeblood of millions of people in the Asian continent. Our research figures show that rivers originating from Tibet sustain the lives of 47 per cent of the world's population. Thus, the environmental issue of Tibet is not an inconsequential regional issue; it has a huge global significance warranting international attention.

Scientists have shown that the environment of the Tibetan Plateau affects the global jetstreams that blow over it. This in turn causes Pacific typhoons and the El Nino (warm ocean current) phenomenon, which stirs up ocean water causing disruption to marine food chains, affecting the weather patterns and the economy of Peru, Ecuador and the California coastline of USA, while New Zealand, Australia, India and Southern Africa reel under dreadful drought. It also has an important influence on the monsoon, which provides essential rainfall for the breadbaskets of South Asia to meet the food needs of millions of people. The monsoon contributes 70 per cent to India's annual rainfall. But excessive rain leads to flooding while little or no rain causes drought and famine in South Asia.

Ever since the Chinese occupation of Tibet, widespread environmental destruction has taken place due to logging of virgin forests, uncontrolled mining, water pollution and nuclear waste dumping, which has resulted in the degradation of grasslands, extinction of wildlife, desertification, floods, soil erosion and landslides. Also, the transfer of huge numbers of Chinese settlers into Tibet demonstrates the colonial nature of Chinese rule. Under such a system, Tibetans have been marginalised in the economic, educational, political and social spheres and Tibet's rich culture and traditions are rapidly disappearing.

Given the high altitude and the extreme climatic conditions of Tibet, the damage caused to the environment and the fragile mountain ecosystem is becoming irreversible. This is a cause of great concern not only for the Tibetan people; it has much larger ramifications. More than ever before, the need to save the Tibetan Plateau from ecological devastation is urgent because it is not a question of the survival of Tibetans, but half of humanity is at stake.

It is for this reason that His Holiness the Dalai Lama included the protection of Tibet's environment as one of the points in his Five-Point Peace Plan for Tibet, and spoke of Tibet becoming an oasis of peace and non-violence where man and nature will co-exist harmoniously.

Through extensive research this report details the destruction of Tibet's environment and the inherent dangers to our planet today. We hope this publication will fill a knowledge gap and help increase ecological awareness about Tibet to save its unique and fragile environment.

Kalon T.C. Tethong
Minister
Department of Information and International Relations

EXECUTIVE SUMMARY

BIODIVERSITY

Chapter 1: Pages 1-18

AN EARLY botanist-explorer perceived Tibet as "one great zoological garden". By remaining isolated and undisturbed until the mid - 20th century the plateau's vast landmass of 2.5 million sq.km is a storehouse of innumerable species which are necessary to the balance of life worldwide: "What takes place in Tibet also affects global biodiversity and the life of people throughout the world", asserts the World Wide Fund for Nature.

Although Tibet remains one of the few countries on the globe to have limited scientific research carried out on the biological aspects of its diverse species, scientists compare the plateau's known biodiversity to the Amazon Rainforest. Endemic flora and fauna abound — many currently endangered — and due to the variety and complexity of unique ecological niches across the massive landscape Tibet is still seen as a final sanctuary for some of the world's rare plant and animal species.

The statistics are staggering. Over 12,000 species of 1,500 genera of vascular plants are identified; fungi alone account for 5,000 species of 700 genera; of the more than 5,000 higher plant species in 280 families over 100 are woody plants of 300 species. There are altogether 400 species of rhododendron on the Tibetan Plateau, which make up about 50% of the world's total species. Of immense value and potential to medical science are the over 2,000 medicinal plants in the wild.

The animal world is equally rich. There are 210 species of mammals in 29 families; endemic animals are abundant and include the snow leopard, blue sheep, giant panda, red panda, golden monkey, Tibetan argali, takin, musk deer, Tibetan antelope, Tibetan gazelle, wild yak and the Himalayan marmot and Himalayan woolly hare. And although the plateau remains an ornothological paradise with 532 bird species in 57 families, at least 37 are endangered including the rare endemic black-necked crane, tragopan, Tibetan eared pheasant, Tibetan snowcock and Tibetan sand grouse. Today more than 81 animal species in Tibet are endangered.

The danger of extinction began with China's invasion in 1949. In an ethical reversal of Buddhism's respect for all living creatures, whereby man lives in an interdependent partnership with his environment, the Chinese have viewed all wildlife as an economic resource for human use and gain. This attitude is the underlying cause of today's rapid loss of biodiversity.

Most rare animal, bird and plant species are found in the more temperate forests of Eastern and Southeast Tibet — the very ancient, dense forests where China's clear-fell logging activities have been most intense. To settle and feed Chinese migrants, the species-rich rangelands of Northeast Tibet are being converted to farmland, depriving nomads of their traditional grazing pastures.

Mammals are largely endangered due to hunting and poaching — some for the commercial value of their wool, antlers, skins, fur, bones and inner organs; some gunned down as trophies to take home to China or sell as meat. Fish are dynamited in lakes and rivers. While wildlife conservation laws are in place in the legal system, their implementation is weak and barely enforced since wildlife is a state-controlled commodity and therefore categorised as a renewable and exploitable resource.

Because the loss of Tibet's unique flora and fauna would be irreversible, the potential impact on the fabric of the plateau's living system and on the evolutionary process is of grave global concern.

WATER RESOURCES

Chapter 2: Pages 19-41

THE MOST political commodity of the 20th century was oil. With environmentalists identifying water as the resource that will lead to wars this century, Tibet's pivotal importance in sustaining life on earth will spiral. The Tibetan Plateau is source to the world's 10 greatest river systems which flow downstream to feed the most populous region on earth: China, India, Nepal, Bhutan, Bangladesh, Pakistan, Vietnam, Burma, Cambodia, Laos and Thailand all depend upon Tibetan watersheds and rivers for their survival. That adds up to 47% of the world's population.

The headwaters of China's two great rivers — the Yangtze and the Yellow River — lie high in Tibet's northeastern and eastern provinces: downstream 1,250 million Chinese depend on their flows to supply four fifths of China's water. In

1998 and 1999 summers these flows brought catastrophe. The worst flooding of the Yangtze in 40 years left between 3,656 and 10,000 dead in August 1998, and a year later 66 million were affected and over 400 dead in a second deluge. In an environmental wake-up call, President Jiang Zemin advised his people to "understand the law of nature ...and follow it to facilitate our economic development".

China's policies of development, industrialisation, resources extraction and population transfer on the plateau have all led to massive intervention in Tibet's rivers and lakes. The most developed region, Amdo (Ch:Qinghai), is home to massive dams providing power to burgeoning cities in Western China and serving the growing Chinese settler communities in Amdo. Dams in Kham (Ch:Sichuan) have resulted in river fragmentation while wholesale deforestation is destroying hydro-ecology. U-Tsang (Central Tibet) — whose rivers flow to South and East Asia — is now facing increasing hydro-development, major dam projects and water pollution from industrial and agricultural waste. The largest hydropower potential in the world has been identified by Chinese scientists at the Great Bend of the Yarlung Tsangpo in U-Tsang — a gorge which could supply 70,000 MW of power. (China's Three Gorges Dam will have an 18,200 MW capacity).

Tibet's hydropower potential is among the highest in the world and China plans further largescale schemes to harness waterways to service the Mainland's growing shortfall of power and to provide for the further industrialisation and urbanisation of Tibet. The dams and reservoirs result in fragmentation and stagnation of rivers which in turn lead to destruction of ecology and fish species and finally extinction of already endangered plant and aquatic species. And by controlling flooding, dams deprive alluvial plains downstream of fertile soil for agriculture.

China has already suffered the devastating results of its interference in the Yangtze and Yellow River headwater regions. Now, with mining nominated as one of Beijing's "Four Pillar" industries in the 'TAR' ('Tibet Autonomous Region'), South and East Asia's Indus, Salween, Brahmaputra and Mekong rivers will face pollution from toxic mining wastes infiltrating soil and so contaminating downstream flows. Tailings from large-scale mining operations are a primary source of water pollution today in Amdo. Rivers around Lhasa already report mounting pollution problems from untreated sewage, industrial waste and salts and nitrates leaked from fertilisers used in intensive farming projects designed to meet the food needs of Central Tibet's expanding Chinese population.

China's unbridled economic growth, industrialisation and urbanisation has contributed to widespread water pollution and scarcity. China has some of the most extreme cases of water shortage in the world. Out of 640 major cities, more than 300 face water shortages, with 100 facing severe scarcities. Approximately 700 million people — over half of China's population — consume contaminated drinking water. The impact of water pollution on human health has been valued at US$3.9 billion annually. The 'TAR' 1996 Environment Report states that 41.9 million tons of liquid waste was discharged in the Lhasa River (Kyichu).

As well as its bountiful rivers, Tibet boasts lakes covering 25,000 sq.km of the plateau — many of them held sacred. Yamdrok Tso in U-Tsang has special spiritual significance. Yet its pristine ecology is being destroyed by a pumped-storage plant to supply Lhasa's electricity needs — a project whose design is now judged to be faulty and leading to lowering water levels, increased salinity, and habitat loss for the diverse and rich wildlife including birds and fish. Over-fishing, pollution, human intervention and shrinkage due to climate change are all endangering the purity and ecological survival of Tibet's legendary lakes.

China's mining and deforestation are obvious examples of colonist exploitation via resource extraction. But utilising Tibet's waterways for hydropower and irrigation — particularly where the energy is largely transmitted to industrial cities in China or serving Chinese migrants in Tibet — is equally as exploitative. Beijing's assumption seems to be that Tibet is an endless resource for China's economic development.

AGRICULTURE

Chapter 3: Pages 42-52

SINCE OVER 80% of Tibet's population still relies on primary sector agriculture for its livelihood, farmers and nomads are the major community to suffer under China's exploitative policies. A way of life which once rewarded hard work in a harsh environment with self-sufficiency, freedom and interdependence with nature is now threatened by a welter of economic and development controls. The very survival of nomadism is uncertain since their grasslands are degrading and dwindling through overstocking, conversion to agriculture, fencing and encroachment from Chinese industry and settlement.

Despite the unencumbered simplicity of their existence, Tibet's nomads were once wealthy in livestock, lifestyle and the rewards of barter and commercial trade from a range of primary products. But today China is intent on curbing nomad freedoms and in 1998 Beijing's vice minister of agriculture boasted that 67% of Amdo's herdsmen were now settled and housed and an end was soon expected to nomadic life.

Nomads - or *drokpa* - have moved their mixed herds across the grassy plateau, steppes and lower mountain slopes that characterise Tibet for over 4,000 years. Their rangelands total 70% of the plateau and today around a million nomads and semi-nomads tend up to 70.2 million head of livestock. Cropland — by contrast — accounts for only two percent of Tibet. Amdo (Ch:Qinghai) in the northeast is 96% grassland, central 'TAR' ('Tibet Autonomous Region') is 56.72% highland pasture and Kham (Ch:Sichuan) — the fertile eastern province — has superior pasture and grassland. By a complex system of cyclical grazing, nomadic inherited wisdom kept these grasslands healthy and viable for centuries.

The relatively small arable niches along river valleys in all three provinces of traditional Tibet were sufficient to more than meet the country's foodgrain needs until the Chinese invasion. Organic farming methods, crop rotation, fallow periods and mixed cropping sustained soil fertility in a fragile mountain environment. While the harvest was overwhelmingly highland barley, sizeable crops of rice, maize, mustard, millet, sorghum, buckwheat and rape-seed were also produced, plus a variety of vegetables which — thanks to abundant sunshine — were often massive.

China's destruction of the plateau's agro-pastoral economy began with communism's "Democratic Reform" of the 1950s and '60s which brought redistribution of livestock, bans on bartering, taxation and class struggles. Livestock numbers declined and foodgrain shortages emerged for the first time in history. The Cultural Revolution of 1996 — '76 introduced communes so that private ownership of land and animals ceased. Due to crippling taxation, production quotas, the export of meat and grain to China and shifting agricultural policies that ignored social and geographic reality, Tibet experienced outright famine and widespread death.

It was then that the marginal lands were first brought under cultivation to boost production to feed China and high-yield wheat introduced. This accelerated foodcrop and livestock production led to extensive destruction of fragile grasslands — an ecological setback that continues to this day.

The third phase in China's experimental agricultural policies in Tibet — the "Household Responsibility System" — disbanded communes after 1982, redistributed lands and livestock and allowed farmers to retain any surplus after quotas were met. But in 1989 this "liberal policy" was reversed and agriculture became controlled by a centralised system designed to intensify land use and produce grain surpluses for "the state". This central control continued throughout the 1990s. The result is that incentives for farmers are minimised by grain quota systems, a multitude of taxes, shifting state procurement policies and a move to intensive farming relying on monoculture. This requires heavy outlays on chemical fertilisers which lowers profitability and destroys the natural fertility of soil. Additionally Tibetans see Chinese settlers enjoying subsidised rice and wheat while their own staple grain, highland barley, is left to market forces.

Unlike the irreversible degradation from forestry, water and mining policies, China's damaging controls on foodcrop production can be rectified by decentralising agricultural policy, revising price reforms, changing land-use patterns and improving farming techniques through training and investment in modern implements. Nomads could benefit from education on maximising rangelands and grasslands, improving living standards and conserving biodiversity.

But experts and researchers should equally develop policies that respect the experience and ecological wisdom of nomads in dealing with their inhospitable environment. Consultation with Tibetans on all aspects of "development" and "modernisation" is essential to redress the wrongs of half a century of agro-pastoral mismanagement imposed by China.

FORESTRY

Chapter 4: Pages 53-69

IT WAS only when the Yangtze River floods of August 1998 caused a national disaster that Beijing finally focussed the blame on deforestation around the river's fountainhead in Tibet's Kham (Ch:Sichuan) and Amdo (Ch:Qinghai) provinces. Now China's scientists are slowly articulating and documenting the role of deforestation in the nation's more frequent and intense flood damage: China's Agenda 21 even lists soil erosion on the Tibetan Plateau as among the country's most serious environmental problems.

Until 1949 Tibet's forests were one of the oldest reserves in all Central Asia, located in the country's east, southeast and south and largely growing undisturbed on steep, isolated slopes. Regeneration was natural since logging and cutting trees for firewood were banned.

Having denuded its own forests — and being the world's third largest consumer of timber — China succeeded between 1950 and 1985 in reducing Tibet's forest cover from 25.2 million hectares to 13.57 million hectares. This 46% reduction had an estimated market value of US$54 billion. Between 1949 and 1998, the forests of eastern Kham have generated over US$241 million in taxes and profits for the Chinese state logging enterprises. Clear-cut felling continues on an unsustainable level in many regions today; in spite of a reforestation programme the ratio of planting to felling is still only one to 10. Deforestation and Chinese migration are today identified as the two major contributors to Tibet's environmental degradation.

Officially the intensive deforestation in Tibet is being reversed. In the wake of the 1998 floods government timber markets are closed and a blanket ban on logging imposed on 4.6 million hectares of forest land in Kham, southeastern Tibet. By December 1998 unofficial reports suggested a temporary shutdown of lumber processing mills in Southeast 'TAR' ('Tibet Autonomous Region') and the start up of reforestation projects employing former loggers as tree planters. However, recent reports from Tibet — in mid-1999 and January 2000 — indicate that deforestation is ongoing in the Kham and Amdo regions.

The purpose behind Beijing's improving environmental policies is seen to be foreign policy dictated: with the role of "good international citizen" a priority, "environmental diplomacy" is an easy image-builder. But prevention and policy enforcement are lacking. State-owned forestry enterprises, which control the majority of the timber resources, are obliged to fill annual quotas. But since these enterprises are forced to fell and sell a surplus to subsidise the low income produced from underselling their quota, the forestry sector is in effect destroying itself. Additionally, illegal felling is believed to exceed planned production in the 'TAR'.

Poor forest management is the major factor contributing to Tibet's dwindling cover: this includes timber poaching, high-yield industrial logging, lack of fire and disease control and conversion of forest land for agriculture and human settlement projects.

The domestic and transnational effects of China's rapacious forest felling in Tibet are widespread and severe. In addition to the siltation, pollution and flooding of the 10 major rivers that feed China and South Asia — sustaining 47% of the world's population — Tibet's vegetation controls the plateau's heating mechanism and this in turn affects the stability of Asia's monsoon. India receives 70 percent of its rainfall from the monsoon. Deforestation also heads irrevocably to desertification: in a reversal of flooding, this curtails water flows — a phenomenon already experienced during the 1990s by China's Yellow River which dried up several times and suffered an overall 23% fall in water discharge. In its upper reaches the Yellow River is Tibet's Machu which has its watershed in Amdo.

With 400 Chinese cities already experiencing water shortages, 108 facing water crises, and major crop losses resulting from lack of agricultural irrigation, Beijing is bracing itself for further ecological catastrophes caused by a history of official disregard for nature.

POPULATION PRESSURES

Chapter 5: Pages 70-85

ALL THE elements of discrimination against a distinct people — as laid down in international covenants — are present in China's population transfer to Tibet. There is clear-cut discrimination in housing, employment, education, health care, the use of native language and national customs and finally, in the lack of political rights. Tibetans are increasingly marginalised and outnumbered on their own soil. This, says the Dalai Lama, is the "most serious threat to the survival of Tibet's culture and national identity".

By skewing the demographic composition Beijing is relentlessly achieving its policy objectives to incorporate Tibet, irrevocably, into China. Lhasa is already a predominantly Chinese city with government administrators, business migrants, military and security personnel (the latter now estimated at 500,000 to 600,000) outnumbering Tibetans two to one. This trait is replicated in urban centres throughout Tibet and reaches the extreme in Amdo (Ch: Qinghai) where cities can be over 90% Chinese.

Beijing's population transfer policy is colonist, embracing needs to quash resistance to Chinese rule, exploit natural resources, solve domestic population and unemployment pressures and consolidate its hold over a militarily strategic zone in Central Asia.

Preferential policies favour Chinese settlers economically, from accomodation and "hardship allowances" boosting government cadre salaries to the ease of procuring licenses for industries and business ventures. Tibetans are disadvantaged and marginalised in the "development" and "modernisation" schemes currently transforming Tibet's economy and landscape. Owing to an education policy heavily weighted to Chinese literacy, few Tibetans can progress to higher education. This ensures discrimination favouring Chinese in subsequent employment opportunities, reinforces income disparities and sidelines Tibetans from any decision-making role in economic and social development. Admitting that 20.7% of Tibetans in 'TAR' ('Tibet Autonomous Region') live below the poverty line — although a 1997 report by the International Commission of Jurists claims a figure above 70% — the Lhasa administration attributes this to "inherent backwardness and remoteness".

Through its open door economic policy of the 1990s, to

attract foreign investment, and by incorporating Tibet in its economic development programme, Beijing is stepping up infrastructural and resource development on the plateau which in turn justifies an ever-increasing Chinese labour force. The expanding road and rail networks, easing of residency regulations, free market systems, relaxing rules on business licenses and exemptions from taxes have increased the accessability and attractiveness of Tibet for China's migrant or seasonal workers, petty traders and small-scale entrepreneurs.

With no independent census figures, and with Tibet's original boundaries redrawn to incorporate nearly half the plateau into Chinese provinces, accurate population data does not exist today. Statistics are concocted to suit political requirements and remain unreliable. What is certain, however, is that the official population transfer policy that absorbed Eastern Turkestan (Ch:Xinjiang), Inner Mongolia and Manchuria into China by massive migration is today being applied in Tibet.

Today Chinese outnumber Inner Mongolians by 10 to one: half a century ago Mao envisioned a similar equation for future Tibet.

MINERALS AND MINING

Chapter 6: Pages 86-101

TIBET'S stupendous mineral wealth was one of China's primary reasons for the invasion of 1949 and today — with thousands of geological maps plotting the discoveries of hundreds of scientific surveys — Beijing controls what is arguably the last truly great frontier of the mining world.

Over 126 minerals have been identified including some of the world's most significant deposits of uranium, chromite, lithium, boron, borax and iron. Oil, gas, gold, silver, copper and zinc reserves are also of global importance and additionally the plateau contains corundum, vanadium, titanium, magnesite, sulphur, mica, cesium, rubidium, arsenic, graphite, lepidolite and potash.

Since China's industrialisation is heavily dependent on a huge consumption of minerals and energy, and many of its own resources are near exhaustion, Tibet's rich deposits are now of paramount importance. A self-sufficiency in raw materials helps reduce China's foreign debt and any surplus produce is exported.

The consequences for Tibet's landscape and the quality of life for Tibetans has been deplorable. Unchecked mining practices have led to environmental degradation often permanently altering landscapes. Massive debris, slag heaps, abandoned mines and slope destabalisation blight the above-ground. Below, the soil is polluted with mining tailings and toxic wastes from materials used in extraction. These have led to mysterious illnesses, birth deformities and decreasing crop-yields around mining areas and, as tailings and toxic wastes leak into waterways, the health hazard to downstream Asia is of growing international concern.

Massive wastage is also recorded due to improper extraction methods, outdated technologies and low efficiency in recovery, production and utilisation. In addition to environmental despoliation, social problems have arisen as accelerated mineral extraction fuels a huge influx of Chinese migrant labour, attracted by high wages and subsidies. With a growing road and rail infrastructure opening up Tibet, illegal miners are also drawn to the benefits from random mining exploitation. The result is that in addition to Tibet losing its mineral wealth, mass Chinese settlement jeopardises the Tibetans' quality of life, dilutes their culture and traditions, and leads inevitably to social conflict.

China's revised mining law of January 1997 focuses more on encouraging foreign investment and further exploration and extraction rather than controlling illegal mining, corruption, hazardous wastes and inefficient mining operations. Sporadic environmental protests by Tibetans are at best ignored; at worst the result is torture and lengthy prison sentences.

Foreign investment from multinational companies and international aid agencies is now subsidising what has become the major economic activity in Tibet's industrial sector. Mineral extraction is the main contributor to Tibet's 30% annual economic growth over the past five years. Today China is investing US$1.25 billion in prospecting and developing mineral resources in Tibet's central and western regions alone — an area estimated by experts to contain US$81.3 billion in mineral reserves. Official figures certainly downplay the true extent of deposits, but the acceleration or extraction and investments indicate the certainty of mammoth returns.

Although the major resources are concentrated in Tsaidam Basin, Nagchu, Golok, Chamdo, Chang Thang, Kandze and Lhoka, mineral reserves are distributed throughout the plateau. Tsaidam Basin alone has immense and diverse reserves spread across its 220,000 sq.km region — an area almost the size of Britain. In addition to high-profile oilfields — estimated at 42 billion tons and currently producing up to two million tons annually — Tsaidam's natural gas reserves of 1,500 billion cubic meters are to become an important new clean energy source for China. At current consumption levels these reserves would meet China's total needs for seven years and the first phase of a massive pipeline network takes Tsaidam gas from Amdo (Ch:Qinghai) to Gansu's capital Lanzhou in 2001.

Among some of the world's largest mineral deposits Tibet counts the Norbusa Chromite Mine in U-Tsang (Central Tibet) with its estimated overall value of US$375 - 500 million. Current annual extraction revenues of US$1.5 million are expected to spiral to US$3.75 million from this top quality deposit. Yulong Copper Mine, near Chamdo, holds one of the world's largest copper reserves at over 6.5 million tons and current annual production levels of 20,000 tons — bringing in a profit of US$2.5 million — are projected to rise to 100,000 tons by 2010.

The Chinese word for Central Tibet is 'Xizang' meaning "Western Treasure House". China has always called Tibet "The Treasure Bowl Awaiting Development" and by promoting mining as a "pillar industry" to fast-track the plateau's economic development, Beijing is finally succeeding in draining Tibet of its once-dormant mineral resources.

NUCLEAR THREATS

Chapter 7: Pages 102-117

IT IS a karmic irony that Tibet — once governed to the last detail on Buddhist principles of non-violence and which functioned as the natural buffer state between the two Asian giants, India and China — is today a storehouse for Chinese nuclear weapons and the site for dumping radioactive waste.

With the arrival in Lhasa in September 1951 of the People's Liberation Army advance party, the militarisation of Tibet by Mao's China had taken its first step. Now the plateau is a frontline, militaristically, in Beijing's ambitions to dominate Asia and achieve superpower primacy.

By 1971 the first known nuclear weapon was brought to Tibet and installed at Tsaidam Basin in northern Amdo (Ch:Qinghai). Today the defence arsenal is believed to include 17 top secret radar stations, 14 military airfields — 11 of which are now being lengthened for new long-range combat aircraft — eight missile bases, at least eight intercontinental ballistic missiles, plus 70-medium range and 20 intermediate-range missiles.

China's own nuclear programme was partially pioneered on the Tibetan Plateau at the Northwest Nuclear Weapons Research and Design Academy (the "Ninth Academy") 100 kms west of Amdo's capital, Siling (Ch:Xining). The Academy worked on nuclear bomb prototypes from the early 1960s, and the first batch of nuclear weapons produced there were stationed at two nuclear missile deployment and launch sites at Tsaidam Basin by the early 1970s.

Today China's DF-4 intercontinental ballistic missiles with ranges of 4,000 — 7,000 kms are stored at the Tsaidam sites. Further DF-4 missiles are deployed 217 kms southeast of Tsaidam at Terlingkha (Ch:Delingha) — headquarters of a missile regiment with four launch sites. A fourth new nuclear missile station, located in southern Amdo bordering Sichuan, houses four CSS-4 missiles with ranges of 12,874 kms.

The 1970s also saw work on a missile base near Nagchuka in the 'TAR' ('Tibet Autonomous Region') where underground complexes now house intermediate and medium-range ballistic missiles at a site which was selected as an alternative to Xinjiang's Lop Nor for possible nuclear testing. Another underground complex close to Lhasa stores ground-to-air and surface-to-surface missiles which are paraded through the capital annually on Chinese Army Day. Further stockpiles of these missiles are kept at Kongpo in southeast 'TAR'.

With China rapidly expanding and modernising its defence arsenal, and continuing its programme of nuclear stock piling, Tibet's strategic value for military deployment and proliferation can only escalate this century.

However, grassroots concern is concentrated more on evidence that nuclear and other hazardous wastes are being dumped on the plateau. China's official *Xinhua News Agency* admitted in 1995 that radioactive pollutants had been discharged from the Ninth Academy near the shore of Lake Kokonor in a 20 sq.metre dump. A chemical industry institute in the Academy was established in the late 1970s and experimented with highly enriched uranium fuel. Radioactive wastes, liquid slurry and solid and gaseous wastes have been dumped by the Academy which is located in a watershed draining into the Tsang Chu River which becomes China's Yellow River downstream. Although it was decommissioned in 1987, the Academy is still guarded around-the-clock.

It is known that China still employs shallow burial techniques for nuclear waste — a method now obsolete in the West — and remote regions of Tibet are earmarked in Beijing's plans to trade in the profitable recycling of hazardous and toxic wastes from developed nations. Already an abnormal rate of childbirth mortality, birth deformities, unprecedented and mysterious illnesses in humans, and high death rates among animals and fish, are recorded from regions around two nuclear production departments in Amdo. Nomads and villagers around the Ninth Academy also experienced high rates of cancer in children — similar to findings of post-Hiroshima.

Similar reports of deformities and mysterious illnesses in humans and animals link to uranium mining which is prevalent in the 'TAR' and Amdo. Contaminated waste water from Tibet's largest uranium mine, near Thewo in southern Amdo, is reported to be released into the local river and victims — both human and animal — turned blue or blue-black after death.

With Asia so heavily dependent upon Tibet for its water, pollutants dumped on the plateau can have massive transnational implications for nations downstream. Deforestation exacerbates the possibility of nuclear-related waste from uranium mines in Tibet entering Asia's waterways; already only 32% of China's river water is rated drinkable. Nuclear proliferation on the Tibetan Plateau has become both drink and food for serious thought.

HUMAN RIGHTS AND THE ENVIRONMENT

Chapter 8: Pages 118-126

ENVIRONMENTAL human rights law is a concept of the late 20th century — a link first established in a UN Declaration in 1972 and further investigated and defined by the UN Sub-Commission on Prevention of Discrimination and Protection of Minorities in a series of four reports to the UN Commission on Human Rights, submitted between 1989 and 1993. These landmark reports established the legal basis and human need for environmental rights and recommended certain rights to be enshrined in international law through a Draft Declaration of Principles on Human Rights and the Environment.

This chapter focuses on defining how and when environmental violations have been perpetrated in Tibet and analyses their implications through the legal lens of the Draft Declaration. Principles of particular pertinence to Tibet include 5: "...the right of all persons to be free from pollution and all kinds of environmental degradation which may threaten life, health, livelihood, well-being or sustainable development" and 6: "...the grounding of human survival in healthy eco-systems and the maintenance of biological diversity".

Topics scrutinised include China's food production and compulsory purchase policies, destruction of agricultural rangelands and controls on nomadism, commercial logging and mining and the despoliation of sacred sites in the name of "development".

The right to be free from hunger is violated by China's institutionalised agricultural policies. The famine decades of collectivisation and communes have led to today's command economy in which the heavy reliance on state procurement and crippling taxation make farming and herding subsistence occupations. By increasing the commercialisation of rangelands and restricting their movements, China is denying nomads their "right to the sustainable use of nature and natural resources for cultural and spiritual purposes".

The cultural and spiritual component in deprivation of human rights is particularly applicable to Tibet's abundant sacred sites. Across Tibet today pilgrimage and religious places are being desecrated, polluted and despoiled by Chinese "development" projects. Mining, hydropower schemes and deforestation are irreversibly defiling the plateau's spiritual heritage.

In exploiting the nation's natural resources — leading to environmental degradation and pollution — China is also denying Tibetans their right to self-determination. "The environmental dimension of the right to self-determination lies at the heart of the economic exploitation that inures to the benefit of the dominating force", states the Declaration's Preamble. Additionally the internationally defined legal rights to freedom of expression, environmental information and participation in decision-making are all denied under China's colonial occupation. The situation is a vicious circle: "Human rights violations lead to environmental degradation and that environmental degradation leads to human rights violation" concludes the Preamble. ■

CHAPTER ONE

BIODIVERSITY

The centre of heaven, The core of the earth,
The heart of the world, Fenced round with snow,
The headland of all rivers, Where the mountains are high
And the land is pure.

Tibetan poem, eighth-ninth century

"THE ROOF of the World", "Shangri-la", "the Third Pole", "Lost Horizon" and other such terms express the fascination many earlier adventurers and explorers felt for Tibet. These pioneer travellers described the unique aspects of Tibet's culture and traditions with a sense of mystery and discovery. However, no extensive research was then carried out on the country's wildlife.

The word "wildlife", contrary to popular belief, not only refers to wild animals but also includes wild plants as well. Tibet is one of the few regions in the world where limited scientific research has been conducted on the biological aspects of its many species. Some species still have not been properly scientifically studied, and some are even yet to be discovered.

Senator Bob Brown of Tasmania, Australia, said at the Endangered Tibet Conference, held in Sydney on 28 September 1996, that the three greatest regions of our planet are the Amazon, Antarctica and Tibet. The first two enjoy a certain degree of global protection, public awareness and growing concern for their preservation. However, Tibet has to date attracted none of these safeguards.

Yet the Tibetan Plateau is the storehouse of innumerable species of unprecedented value to the balance of life worldwide. The plateau's distinctive geological evolution, landscape, climatic variation, hydrological systems, and unique atmospheric circulation patterns, have been scientifically proven to influence the health and wellbeing of the entire planet.

The biodiversity of Tibet is only presently beginning to be viewed as an important issue. The World Wide Fund for Nature states:

> **The conservation of biodiversity in Tibet will have a strong impact on China, South Asia, and Southeast Asia. What takes place in Tibet also affects global biodiversity and the life of people throughout the world.**

This chapter provides an overview of the biodiversity of the Tibetan Plateau.

Usually images of Tibet portray a barren, forbidding landscape, especially in the wintertime. However, visitors are often astonished to find various regions of Tibet covered with lush forests, teeming with countless species of birds, animals and insects; rolling meadows carpeted with wild flowers, and vast plains swaying with glistening fields of barley, mustard, and emerald alpine grass.

With its huge landmass, it is no wonder that Tibet's varied array of ecological niches possess such diversity making it the last sanctuary for some of the world's rare plant and animal species. This is primarily due to Tibet's long period of isolation and the centuries-old protection provided by its sky-tapering, majestic mountains. The natural protection is further strengthened by the Tibetan Buddhists' ethos of living in harmony with nature. In olden in days Tibet there were no specially-designed nature reserves or parks as the modern world today demands. Formal protection of wildlife was not needed in a land where Buddhist compassion for all living beings reigned supreme.

Captain C. Rawling in his book *The Great Plateau* published in1905 says, "Almost from my feet away to the north and east, as far as the eye could reach, were thousands upon thousands of doe antelope [Tibetan antelope] with their young...There could not have been less than 15,000-20,000 visible at one time."

British plant hunter and explorer, Kingdon Ward, who made several surveys in Tibet, wrote before the First World War, "I have never seen so many varieties of birds in one place, one great zoological garden."

In the forties, American adventurer Leonard Clark reported, "Every few minutes we would spot a bear, a hunting wolf, herds of musk deer, kiang [kyang], gazelles, big horned sheep or foxes. This must be one of the last unspoiled big game paradises."

However, after the Chinese occupation of Tibet in 1949, the eco-friendly belief system of Tibetans was trampled upon, monks and nuns persecuted and thousands of Tibet's monasteries were destroyed in the process of converting the peaceful land of Tibet into a zone of socialist zeal. Even the wildlife of Tibet didn't escape the Communist madness and was decimated with a vengeance. Today, the danger of extinction looms large for innumerable species as their native habitats fall prey to China's colonialist policies.

After spending over a millennium perfecting their ecological code, Tibetans have much to offer to the rest of the world.

An Evolved Environment

Tibet was for centuries distinguished by its isolation. It is that isolation and the harsh natural conditions of the country that forced Tibetans to evolve a way of life which protected their delicate homeland and its resources, at the same time providing sustenance for their survival. Survival meant unflagging attention and strict conservation, which Tibetans integrated into their religious rituals and every aspect of their lives.

> *On this highland humans and nature coexist harmoniously!*
> *The land where spiritual and human laws reign supreme,*
> *In the land where celestial powers are revered,*
> *Where animals are partners in life's struggle,*
> *Where birds fly without fear, Where fish swim in freedom,*
> *Where wildlife is protected,*
> *Where men and women cherish inner peace and outer freedom.*
>
> Tibetan folk song

> *Whatever joy there is in this world*
> *All comes from desiring others to be happy,*
> *And whatever suffering there is in this world*
> *All comes from desiring myself to be happy.*
>
> *But what need is there to say much more?*
> *The childish work for their own benefit,*
> *The Buddhas work for the benefit of others.*
> *Just look at the difference between them!*
>
> Shantideva, a Buddhist master
> from Nalanda University, India,
> eighth century

All living things, from insects to yaks, were recognised as threads in the web of life and were deemed worthy of respect and protection. Many Tibetans adopted vows of *ahimsa*, or "non-violence", as a lifelong practice. Consideration for all living creatures is the most visible manifestation of Buddhist faith and one which figures directly in the intimate equation linking Tibetans to their environment (Apte and Edwards 1998).

In fact, in the Tibetan language there is no equivalent to the word "environment" as it is understood in the modern-day world. This indicates that Tibetans did not separate the environment as an external physical resource, but rather treated their surroundings as part and parcel of human society and came to understand ecological principles naturally. They were already sensitised to the fact that exploiting the environment in essence means hurting human beings themselves.

In the Water Horse Year of 1642, His Holiness the Great Fifth Dalai Lama was appointed the spiritual and political mentor of a united Tibet. From this date onward, in the tenth month of every year, a Decree (*Tsatsig*) for the Protection of Animals and the Environment was issued in the name of the Dalai Lama. Decrees were declared by the Dalai Lama. Different provisions were applied to various areas with the objective of maintaining the tenuous balance of all life.

After spending over a millennium perfecting their ecological code, Tibetans have much to offer to the rest of the world. Unlike the western societies which sought to tame the "wild", Tibetans endeavoured from the earliest times to secure a kind of partnership with their "wilderness". Scientists are only now beginning to understand the necessity of such a relationship with the earth as a whole, which is today being recognised as a living, ever-changing organism, capable of causing harm to those who fail to treat it with respect. Through a viewpoint of the inter-relationship and interdependence of all living and non-living things, the scientific community has begun to make global connections of major importance. The land must continue to provide for its inhabitants, but the developmental relationship must be sustainable — meeting the basic survival needs of the present generation without compromising the ability of future generations to meet their own basic survival needs.

However, the impetus of industrialisation still prevails worldwide, bringing the global environment frighteningly close to breaking point. This reality has been clearly demonstrated since the 1949 Chinese invasion of Tibet.

© David Lawson

The endangered snow leopard, killed for its valuable pelt

WHAT IS BIODIVERSITY?

Biodiversity is a shortform which means biological diversity. In the broad sense, biodiversity encompasses the interrelations and interdependency of all species of plants, animals, micro-organisms, their genetic material and the ecosystems of which they are a part — many of which have developed over millennia of evolutionary history (Dekhang 1997). Biodiversity is usually divided into three fundamental categories; genetic diversity, species diversity, and ecosystem diversity. Within the scope of this chapter, species diversity will be the main focus.

The Tibetan Plateau

The Tibetan Plateau towers over the central part of the continent of Eurasia. It is bounded by the Himalayan mountain chain in the south and connected with the Altyn Tagh and Gangkar Chogley Namgyal mountains (Ch: Qilian Mts.) in the north. Its western region merges with the Karakoram mountains and its eastern reaches slope downward more gradually with the Minyak Gangkar and Khawakarpo mountain ranges.

The Tibetan Plateau is the highest and largest plateau on the earth, occupying an area of more than 2.5 million sq. km. Its average elevation exceeds 4,000 m (13,000 ft), and many of the peaks reach beyond 8,000 m, Mount Everest at 8,848 m being the world's tallest mountain. In fact, Tibet is home to all 14 of the world's peaks greater than 8,000 m (26,259 ft.) in elevation. The Tibetan Plateau consists of a variety of landscapes ranging from lunar vistas in some parts of Southern Tibet to lush and thick tropical forests in Eastern Tibet.

The plateau stretches from 500 m to 5,000 m from its edges to its hinterland; within the two extreme values lies an infinite combination of climatic elements. Factors such as the mean temperature which ranges from -8°C to 20°C, the annual rainfall which spans from 25 mm to 4,000 mm, and total solar radiation which varies from 110 cal/cm^2/year to 210 cal/cm^2/year are just a few variables that contribute to the myriad possibilities for life on the plateau.

Topography

In the mid-Cretaceous period, around 130 million years ago, the Indian subcontinent broke away from the southern continent of Gondwanaland and drifted northward. It finally collided about 40-50 millions years ago with the Central Asian landmass, forming the highest plateau on the earth — the Tibetan Plateau (Molnar 1989).

Based on natural topography, Tibet can be roughly divided into four parts; valley and drier regions in the south, plateau in the north, high mountains with river valleys in the southwest and wet forest regions in the east. Climatic zones vary north to south from the arid polar alpine ice-snow zone to a humid low montane tropical zone.

When speaking in ecological terms, Tibet can be di-

VERTICAL CLIMATIC ZONES OF THE SOUTHERN TO THE EASTERN EDGE OF THE TIBETAN PLATEAU

S.No.	Climatic Zones	Ecosystem Zones	Altitude (m)	Annual mean rainfall (°C)	Annual mean rainfall (mm)
1	Humid low mountain tropical	Low mountain evergreen, semi-evergreen monsoon rain forest	<1100	>18	2500 to 5000
2	Humid montane subtropical	Montane evergreen, semi-evergreen broad-leaved forest	1000 to 2400	8 to 18	1000 to 2500
3	Humid mid-mountain warm temperate	Mid mountain evergreen, needle leaved and broad leaved mixed forest	2200 to 2800	5 to11	1300 to 2500
4	Humid sub-alpine cold	Sub-alpine evergreen needle leaved forest	2500 to 4000	0.8 to 8	1500 to 2000
5	Humid alpine cold	Alpine shrub and meadow	3600 to 4600	-3 to 0.8	1000 to 1600
6	Humid alpine cold freezing	Alpine ice-edge	4400 to 5000	-5 to -3	<1500
7	Humid polar alpine ice-snow	Polar alpine ice-snow	4900 to 5000	< -5	<1500

Adapted from Dekhang 1997; Li 1995

vided into three broad zones:

1) humid tropical and subtropical southeast where the oriental and paleoarctic floras and faunas meet
2) broad valleys of the Yarlung Tsangpo and Indus which are bordered to the south by the Himalayas and to the north by the Mt. Tesi (Kailash) range and Nyenchen Thangla ranges
3) frigid alpine and desert steppes of the Chang Thang (Northern Plateau), much of which lies above 4,500 metres.

The unique geo-morphological configuration, the complex land conditions, the diversified climate and the unique geological evolution has created the Tibetan Plateau to become a crucial centre for the composition and differentiation of mountain species in the world, especially of high-altitude flora and fauna.

The Tibetan Plateau continued to form throughout the quaternary period, when a horizontal distribution pattern of ecosystems became established. These included zones of tropical rainforest, subtropical evergreen broad-leaved forest, sub-alpine evergreen needle-leaved forest, alpine shrub-meadow, high-cold steppe, and high-cold desert. In the mountains of each horizontal zone, ecosystemic vertical zones also developed. This resulted in an extremely complex landscape, containing unique niches found nowhere else on the planet. (see table above).

During the late 19th and first half of the 20th centuries, explorers and travellers, many of whom were scientists, collected general information on the animals and plants of Tibet. Amazed by the country's biodiversity, they gave accounts of a vast variety of flora and fauna — including golden monkeys, takin and red pandas — roaming the lower forests. At the higher reaches they recorded that blue sheep, snow leopards and wild yaks thrived. Tibet has a variety of bird species ranging from tiny finches to enormous bearded vulture, whose nine-foot wingspan enables it to hover over ice-capped pinnacles like a pterodactyl (Apte and Edwards 1998).

The hydrological net in Tibet is formed by inner and outer river systems. Both systems reflect an abundance of unique and varied biodiversity. The inner river systems usually run in specific seasons and form many lakes and ponds in the basins of the plateau. The Tibetan Plateau is dotted with more than 2,000 lakes with the largest and most important being Tso-Ngonpo (Lake Kokonor), Namtso (Lake Namtso), Yamdrok Tso (Lake Yamdrok), and Mapham Tso (Lake Manasarowar).

The outer river systems mainly rise in the west, south and central Tibet, the area that is the source of Asia's 10 major rivers: Yarlung Tsangpo (Brahmaputra), Sutlej, Indus, Yangtze, Salween, Arun, Mekong, Karnali, Manas, Yellow River, as well as their numerous tributaries. These rivers and their tributaries sustain the lives of 47 per cent of the world's population, or 85 per cent of Asia's total population. (See rivers map).

The Significance of Jet Streams

The jet streams, or high altitude winds in the innermost layer of the atmosphere up to about 15 km in elevation, travel rapidly and move the lower air over the landscape to bring changes in weather patterns. Terrestrial features such as the Tibetan Plateau affect these jet streams both by their bulk and by variations in their temperature. The plateau acts like a huge iceberg to deflect the high altitude winds. In winter, cold air settles on the plateau, whereas in spring and summer it heats up and the warm air gives rise to a high-pressure system to form an eastward-flowing jet stream which brings the June monsoon to the Indian subcontinent. If, however, the Tibetan Plateau is covered with snow, the heat absorption of the plateau is delayed and this, in turn, may delay the monsoon to affect the lives of millions of people in Asia.

The Tibetan Plateau's effect on the southwest monsoon by acting in this heat-island fashion also has great significance for the formation of flora and fauna. As the tropical monsoon climate extends northwards to the southern slopes of the Himalayas, and along the Yarlung Tsangpo River valley, it has moved through almost six latitudinal zones beyond the Tropic of Cancer. As a result, the plateau consists of two biogeographic regions: the pan-arctic and the paleotropical region for plants, and the palaeoarctic realm and the Indo-Malayan region for animals (Li 1995).

The Diverse Display

The distribution of plant and animal species on the plateau is extremely uneven due to differences in topography and climate. For example, the Chang Thang (Northern Plateau) occupies about a quarter of the Tibetan Plateau, but hosts only one-tenth of the total species found on the plateau. However, the Himalayan and Hengduan Mountains (i.e. the regions of Khawakarpo mountains in south and southeastern Tibet) contain less than one-fifth of the Tibetan Plateau, but are home to over 80 per cent of the total species living on the plateau.

The vast land surface of the Tibetan Plateau has wide climatic variations caused by the unique plateau atmospheric circulation system and the great difference in elevation. Such unusual natural conditions give rise to diverse natural habitats for complex species of flora and fauna. The areas of eastern and southeastern Tibet receive monsoon showers during the months July to September and have abundant plant and animal species, many of which are rare and endangered.

The plateau is the differentiation centre for *Rhododendron, Primula, Saussurea,* and *Pedicularis;* there are altogether 400 species of *Rhododendron* alone, which accounts for about 50 per cent of the world's total species. Many endemic plant species such as *Circaeaster, Himiphrogma, Chionocharis, Milula, Cyananthus, Leptocodon, Maharanga, Pegia, Chamasium* and various others are found on the Tibetan Plateau.

In fact, it is important to remember that some exotic flora now common in the West such as *Rhododendron, saxifraga, paeonia,* were brought from Tibet by early travellers such as British botanist Kingdon Ward, who made many large-scale explorations early this century in search of exotic plants. The American adventurer, Leonard Clark returned from Tibet in 1948 with valuable botanical samples. He wrote:

> **Surprisingly, our scientists estimated that among the basic foundation stones of this inherent Mongol power for war is grass, strong grass converted into excellent animal flesh — among the finest in the world. I was taking grass samples and seeds, hoping to transfer its power to the pastures of America and Europe.**

According to Wu and Feng (1992) the Tibetan Plateau is host to over 12,000 species of 1,500 genera of vascular plants, accounting for over half of the total genera found in China. There are over 5,000 species of 700 genera of fungi, accounting for 82.4 per cent of China; additionally, 210 species belonging to 29 families of mammals account for 65.90 per cent of the total families found in China.

There are also over 532 species of birds in 57 families on the plateau accounting for approximately 70.37 per cent of the total families found in China and 115 species of fish.

Though the scope of this chapter does not allow for an in-depth discussion of the ecosystemic side of Tibet's biodiversity, it is important to note its vastness. On the Tibetan Plateau, diversified ecosystems and complex, varied boundary surface conditions between them provide a favourable setting for ancient species, differentiation of new species, and exchange of geographic components. Under such conditions, the Tibetan Plateau has produced its own species diversity. Based on Ellenbeg's scheme (1973) for determining world ecosystems, the Tibetan Plateau contains all the large ecosystems for the macro-ecosystem terrestrial-ecosystem: forest, scrub, steppe, desert and aquatic formations. Such a diverse display is usually found only on a continental scale.

FORESTS

Forests on the Tibetan Plateau are largely found in eastern and southeastern regions. The lushest forest cover is found in the Namchakbarwa region, where the Yarlung Tsangpo river turns to flow into India as the Brahmaputra. In eastern and southeastern regions of Tibet receiving the monsoon — forest grows up to an elevation of 4,100-4,500 metres. A mixed coniferous and broad-leaved forest composing mainly of spruce, fir and oak with an understory of *Acer, Lindera, Rhododendron, Litsea* and other trees predominate. The forest of Eastern Amdo is patchy and mainly consist of junipers (*Sabina*). Tree species such as *Picea crassifolia* and *P. asperata* as well as *Betula* grow below an elevation of 3,500 metres in the Amnye Machen Range (Schaller 1998).

Tibetan Plateau contains all the large ecosystems for the macro-ecosystem terrestrial-ecosystem: forest, scrub, steppe desert and aquatic formations. Such a diverse display is usually found only on a continental scale.

Most of the rare animal and plant species make their home in the forests of Eastern and Southeast Tibet because of the variety of habitats the forest belts provide and the pleasant climate. Rare animals found in these forest regions are giant panda, white-lipped deer, takin, musk deer, goral and birds such as Himalayan monal, snowcock, satyr tragopan, Tibetan partridge and blood pheasant to name a few.

The forests of Southeast Amdo are known not only for their variety but also for their tremendous timber storage. For example, there are 200-year-old spruce forests in the valleys of Tramo (Ch:Bomi) county. The average diameter of the trees is 92 cm with a height of 57 metres; maximum storage per hectare is 2,000-2,500 cubic metres, and the average growth rate per year is 10-12 cubic metres per hectare. When one huge plum yew tree with a seven metre circumference fell across a road, it took more than a day for a squad of China's People's Liberation Army soldiers to cut it in half (Du 1987).

WILDLIFE

Chinese biological investigations in Amdo found that there are 10 million birds belonging to 200 species, which equals about one-third of the bird population of Europe (Chen and Zhang 1987). Tso-Ngonpo (Lake Kokonor) in Amdo alone boasts 10 out of 15 recorded duck families. It is also rich in fish species; according to Chinese statistics the total fish catch from the lake between 1957 and 1970 added up to some 128,500 tons.

The well-known Bird Island on Tso-Ngonpo is only 67,000 sq. metres in size, but it has four main breeding birds such as bar-headed geese, great black-headed gulls, brown-headed gulls and cormorants. If the number of other birds, such as tern and snipe, are added the total number of birds will exceed 100,000 on the island (Chen 1987).

In the 'Tibet Autonomous Region' alone there are 2,307 species of insects, 64 species of fish, 45 species of amphibians, 55 species of reptiles, 488 species of birds and 142 species of mammals. There are 163 rare, endangered and valuable species, consisting of 74 species of mammals, 79 birds, four reptiles, two amphibians, two fish and two insects.

There are over 5,000 higher plant species and 280 families. Among them woody plants total over 100 families and 300 species. Being rich in wild plants in terms of number of species and population, Metok, Tramo and Kyirong are called the rare natural plant museums.

Chamdo region in East Tibet has steep valleys and rich forest cover which provide good habitats for many wildlife species. This region is called "pheasant realm" with over 10 pheasant species plus golden monkey, sambar and black stork.

The southern Lhoka region has many rare species and has diverse topography including dry valleys and tropical and subtropical vegetation. The Tibetan sub-species of red deer (*Cervus elaphus wallichi*) thrive in this region.

The valleys of Kongpo in southern Tibet are covered by sub-tropical vegetation and are rich in species diversity. Long-tailed leaf monkey and Himalayan tahr are mainly distributed in this region. Nyingtri region of Kongpo, in the east part of the Himalayas, enjoys warm and moist climate, and has tropical and subtropical vegetation and is one of the richest areas for wildlife diversity.

ENDANGERED MAMMALS

Common Name	Tibetan Name	Scientific Name
Asiatic black bear	*Thom*	*Ursus thibetanus*
Assamese macaque	*Tay*	*Macaca assamensis*
Blue-sheep or bharal	*Naa*	*Pseudois nayaur*
Clouded leopard	*Goong-zig*	*Neofelis nebulosa*
Giant panda	*Thomtra*	*Ailuropoda melanoleuca*
Golden or snub-nosed monkey	*Ser-tral*	*Rhinopithecus roxellanae*
Goral	*Gyagora*	*Naemorhedus goral*
Himalayan tahr	*Ra-goth*	*Hemitragus jemlahicus*
Ibex	*King*	*Capra ibex*
Long-tailed leaf monkey	*Tay*	*Presbytis leucocephalus*
Lynx	*Yi*	*Lynx lynx*
McNeil's Deer	*Shawa*	*Cervus elaphus macneilli*
Musk deer	*Lawa*	*Moschus sefanicus*
Musk deer	*Lawa*	*Moschus fuscus*
Musk deer	*Lawa*	*Moschus cephalophus*
Oriental small-clawed otter	*Saam*	*Aonyx cinerea*
Otter	*Saam*	*Lutra lutra*
Pere David's deer	*Shawa*	*Elaphurus davidianus*
Red goral	*Gyagora*	*Naemorhedus cranbrooki*
Red panda	*Wob*	*Ailurus fulgens*
Rhesus macaque	*Tay*	*Macaca mulatta*
Shou or Red deer	*Shawa*	*Cervus elaphus wallichi*
Siberian Tiger	*Siberia Taag*	*Panthera tigris altaica*
Stone/beech marten	*Ogkar*	*Martes foina*
Snow leopard	*Saa*	*Panthera uncia*
Sumatra serow	*Gyara*	*Capricornis sumatraensis*
Tibetan antelope	*Tsod / Chiru*	*Pantholops hodgsoni*
Tibetan argali sheep	*Nyan*	*Ovis ammon hodgsoni*
Tibetan brown bear	*Dremong*	*Ursus arctos pruinosus*
Tibetan gazelle	*Gowa*	*Procapra picticuadata*
Tibetan macaque	*Tay*	*Macca thibetana*
Tibetan takin	*Bamen*	*Budorcas taxicolor tibetana*
Tibetan wild ass	*Kyang*	*Equus hemionus kiang*
Tibetan wild yak	*Drong*	*Bos grunniens*
Takin	*Bamen*	*Budorcas taxicolor*
Takin	*Bamen*	*B.t. taxicolor*
White-headed langur	*Pa* or *Tralkar*	*Presbytis entelus*
White-lipped deer	*Shawa chukar*	*Cervus albirostris*
White takin	*Bamen*	*B.t. whitei*

Sources: Li 1995; Dekhang 1997.

RICH RANGES AND PASTURES

A major portion of the Tibetan Plateau is under pastures and rangelands. The rangelands' ecosystems are important in that they are the headwaters' environment for major rivers in Asia, so what takes place in these watershed areas has far-reaching effects on the downstream regions. Pastures and rangelands are rich in biodiversity, are a storehouse for valuable medicinal resources and also provide habitats for rare and endangered species. In addition rangelands are home to millions of Tibetan nomads with their livestock and wildlife, and are thus fundamental for the survival of their unique way of life.

The principle pasturelands are in Chang Thang in the north and in Amdo and Kham in the east. The Chang Thang rangelands as a whole are in good condition. However, the total plant cover is only 25 per cent consisting mainly of grasses, sedges and a few herbs. Species variation is small with no more than about 20 species in a 20 sq. metre plot and the biomass is also low (Schaller 1997). The challenge now is to keep these grasslands in healthy condition and to prevent the spread of plant diseases, especially exotic ones, in the future.

ENDANGERED BIRDS

Common Name	Scientific Name
Black-necked crane	*Grus nigricollis*
Black-tailed godwit	*Limosa limosa*
Blood pheasant	*Ithaginis cruentus*
Blyth's tragopan (grey-bellied tragopan)	*Tragopan blythii*
Brahminy kite	*Haliastur indus*
Demoiselle crane	*Anthropoides virgo*
Golden eagle	*Aquila chrysaetos*
Himalayan monal (monal pheasant)	*Lophophorus impejanus*
Himalayan snowcock	*Tetraogallus himalayensis*
Kalij pheasant	*Lophura leucomelanos*
Koslow bunting	*Emberiza koslowi*
Lammergeier (bearded vulture)	*Gypaetus barbatus*
Long-billed calandra lark	*Melanocorypha maxima*
Long-legged boteo	*Buteo rufinus*
Pallas's fishing eagle	*Haliaetus leucoryphus*
Red-breasted hill partridge	*Arborophila mandellii*
Red-headed trogon	*Harpactes erythrocephalus*
Rufous-necked hornbill	*Aceros nepalensis*
Rufous-throated partridge	*Arborophila rufogularis*
Saker falcon	*Falco cherrug*
Satyr tragopan	*Tragopan satyr*
Sclater's monal pheasant	*Lophophorus sclateri*
Snow partridge	*Lerwa lerwa*
Spoonbill	*Platalea leucorodia*
Temminck tragopan	*Tragopan temminckii*
Tibetan eared pheasant	*Crossoptilon crossoptilon*
Tibetan partridge	*Arborophila rufpectus*
Tibetan sand grouse	*Syrrhaptes tibetanus*
Tibetan snowcock	*Tetraogallus tibetanus*
Woodsnipe	*Capella nemoricola*

Sources: McCue 1991; Li 1995; Dekhang 1997.

ENDEMISM ON THE TIBETAN PLATEAU

Since animals have a wider area of activity their endemism is less obvious than that of plants. The endemic distribution of animal species on the plateau is abundant, boasting 40 endemic mammals which constitute 60 per cent of China's total; 28 endemic birds, two endemic reptiles and 10 endemic amphibians.

The endemic animal species of the Tibetan Plateau mainly consist of those species of the moist eastern and southern fringes and the Chang Thang. The former includes mammals such as giant panda, red panda, takin, musk deer and various species of birds such as tragopan, Tibetan eared pheasant, Himalayan monal and others.

The Chang Thang region hosts a number of endemic animal genera such as Tibetan antelope, Tibetan gazelle, wild yak, *kyang*, Himalayan marmot, Himalayan mouse-hair or Pika, Tibetan woolly hare, vole and birds like Tibetan snowcock, Tibetan sand grouse and others.

Ngari region situated in the western part of Tibet, is a major distribution range of endemic wildlife species such as wild yak, Tibetan wild ass, black-necked crane, snow leopard, blue-sheep and others.

There are now 81 endangered animal species on the Tibetan Plateau, which includes 39 mammals, 37 birds, four amphibians and one reptile (DIIR 1998).

PUTTING A VALUE ON BIODIVERSITY

The comprehensive uses of various plants and animal products and by-products on the Tibetan Plateau cannot be outlined and justified in a brief article. However, the following is a general introduction to their scope and utility:

The basic needs of the people in Tibet are provided by plants and animal products or their by-products. The main food crops are barley, wheat, maize, mustard, millet, sorghum, buckwheat and rice, with *tsampa* (roasted barley) forming the staple diet of most Tibetans.

The main vegetables that grow well are cabbage, cauliflower, lettuce, radish, turnip, peas, celery, carrot, potato, spinach, chive, kidney bean, tomato, squash, coriander and others. The abundant bright sunshine is good for growing vegetables and it is not unusual for a radish or cabbage to grow to a dozen kilograms, and a potato to half or even one kilogram. These days people grow vegetables in greenhouses to provide fresh nutrition throughout the four seasons, especially in the Lhasa areas.

Orchard trees that grow well in Tibet are apple, chestnut, orange, walnut, apricot, peach, plum, cherry, banana and pear. Strawberries, grapes, rhubarb and mushrooms also grow in abundance.

Tea is cultivated in Metok, Zayul, Tramo, Nyingtri and certain areas of Amdo and Kham. The main species under cultivation are black tea, green tea, reddish-bracted, small-clustered, rape-flowered, large-leaved and small-leaved tea (Dekhang 1997).

Clothing is also provided by animals and plants. Much of the traditional Tibetan wardrobe is derived from animals such as yak, sheep and goat. Indian hemp can be woven into materials to produce first rate clothing.

Trees and bamboo, which are used for building houses of all shapes and sizes, are derived directly from the forests. The forest products are also fashioned into a variety of items for daily use such as furniture, tools and in paper production. China sells Tibetan timber in the international market and uses it domestically in building bridges, ships, boats, railway sleepers, furniture and other commodities.

Tibet has 400 species of rhododendron, half of the world's total

There are now 81 endangered animal species on the Tibetan Plateau, which includes 39 mammals, 37 birds, four amphibians and one reptile.

A Medical Fountainhead

According to Dr. Tenzin Choedak, senior personal physician to His Holiness the Dalai Lama, there are over 2,000 medicinal plants in Tibet. These plants have an immense potential to cure various chronic and common ailments such as asthma, hepatitis, diabetes, anaemia, tuberculosis, malaria, cancer and many other deadly diseases. For example, *Taxus wallichiana*, a tree found in the forests of Tibet, is the source of the allopathic drug taxol — today regarded as one of the most effective remedies for certain kinds of cancer.

Examples of common medicinal plants growing on the Tibetan Plateau which are widely used in allopathic, homeopathic, Tibetan, and Chinese pharmacy includes *Gastroda elata*, *Angelica sinensis*, *Coptis tectoides*, *Picrorhiza scrophulariiflora*, *Rheum officinalis*, *Magnolia officinalis*, *Terminalia chebula* and *Liolyophora phalloides*.

The *angong-niu-huang* pill, a traditional Chinese medicine prescribed to relieve critical cases, is made from the grass stones formed in the gall bladder of yaks. Musk has very high medicinal value — being an essential component of some traditional Chinese drugs, like *liushen* (six-gold) pills and musk ointment — and is also a fundamental ingredient in perfumery world-wide.

From 1987 to 1992, in the region of Amdo Golok in eastern Tibet alone, China extracted medicinal plants such as *Rheum palmatum* (*chumtsa)* to the tune of 1,017.5 tons; *Frittilaria sp.*(*abhika*) over 30 tons; *Cordyceps sinensis* (*yartsa gunbu*) 9,105 kg; *Gentiana robusta* (*kiche*) 36 tons. Over a period of 30 years Chinese have extracted 6,105 tons of *chumtsa*, 180 tons of *abhika*, 54.9 tons of *yartsa gunbu* and 28.5 tons of deer antlers from Amdo Golok alone (Palbar 1994).

Various food grains and berries are used in brewing industries such as wines, beer, whisky and others, while the government of China has also produced a new market-oriented Tibetan barley beer in Tibet on a commercial scale.

> *All beings tremble at punishment,*
> *To all, life is dear.*
> *Comparing others to oneself,*
> *One should neither kill nor cause to kill.*
>
> Milarepa, 11th century Tibetan poet – hermit.

Spiritual, social and cultural value

Tibetans believe that there is an intricate and primal relationship between the natural world and human beings. This belief in the sanctity of living beings has encouraged them to become effective stewards of their environment. To Tibetans every life is precious and they believe that one should refrain from harming other living beings down to the tiniest creatures. One Tibetan spiritual text, the Pungsang Sutra says, "Taking your body as an example, don't harm other living beings."

China's official approach to wildlife can best be illustrated by statement such as, 'wildlife is a renewable natural resource. The final purpose of protecting and rescuing endangered animal species is to protect a natural resource that can be constantly used'

Tibetan Buddhist scriptures explain that the earth is the *noe* (container) and all the things on this earth — biotic and abiotic elements — are the *chue* (contents). Thus if the container is broken and destroyed it cannot protect the contents. Mother Earth is the container sustaining the existence of countless living creatures including the lives of human beings (Dekhang 1997).

His Holiness the Dalai Lama writes in his poem on the environment in 1993:

In the remoteness of the Himalayas
In the days of yore, the land of Tibet
Observed a ban on hunting, on fishing
And, during designated periods, even construction.
These traditions are noble
For they preserve and cherish
The lives of humble, helpless and defenceless creatures.

The endless verdant grasslands, snow-capped mountains reflected in turquoise lakes, meandering rivers and abundant wildlife in Tibet never fails to impress visitors, filling their minds with inspiration and joy. This soul-soothing environment invests flora and fauna with an immense aesthetic value.

THREATS TO WILDLIFE

Hunting and Poaching

Hunting and poaching of wildlife for commercial gain is one of the principle threats to the survival of various wildlife species in Tibet. Rare animal skins and other parts such as deer antlers, Tibetan gazelle heads, leopard skins and other endangered animal parts and plant are sold in the open market by those with connections and money to pay bribes without the fear of legal penalties.

Many Tibetan refugees have been eye witnesses to the People's Liberation Army (PLA) brigades venturing out in hunting parties to machinegun down herds of wild animals across the plateau without any consideration for the sanctity of wildlife. This "sport" was especially popular after the final occupation of Tibet in 1959. The heads and skins of slaughtered animals were either taken to China as trophies or their meat was exported or consumed locally by the Chinese army.

China's PLA soldiers stationed in Tibet often dynamite rivers and lakes to catch fish; this not only kills the fish, but also poisons the whole aquatic ecosystem where dynamite is being detonated.

China's official approach to wildlife can best be illustrated

> *Tibetan Antelope Poaching*
>
> *On 16 January 1994, Gisang[Kalsang], a Tibetan and three police officers detained a gang of poachers with more than 1,300 Tibetan antelope skins in Kokoxili Nature Reserve (45,000 sq. km) in Amdo (Qinghai) region on the Tibetan Plateau. The officers loaded the 15 poachers onto the back of a truck and began the four-day drive to Golmud, the nearest town. Two days later, the poachers overpowered them. They shot Kalsang to death, bound the other officials, stole a jeep and fled, leaving the pelts behind. Kalsang's predecessor, Sonam Thargay died five years ago in a gun fight with 18 poachers. Kalsang's brother-in-law, Zhaba Duojie [Dakpa Dorjee] joined to form the Wild Yak Brigade in 1995 to save the antelope. However, Dakpa was found dead in his home on 8 November 1998. Qinghai provincial government decided to close the reserve from 1 January 2000 to protects its wildlife*
>
> China Daily 1999c; Forney 1999; Lowe 1998

by statements such as, "Wildlife is a renewable natural resource. The final purpose of protecting and rescuing endangered animal species is to protect a natural resource that can be constantly used" (NSP, 1994). "Rich wildlife resources of Qinghai (Amdo) provide important exports for China. Each year, 130,000 marmot skins are exported" (Du 1987). According to Chinese scientist Wu Ning three decades ago herds of hundreds of wild yaks could be found on the rangelands in Ngaba (Ch: Aba) Tibetan Prefecture in Amdo. Due to hunting and degradation of their habitats they have become almost extinct in most of their range (Wu 1997).

> *Destruction of nature and natural resources results from ignorance, greed and the lack of respect for earth's living things.*
>
> H.H. the 14th Dalai Lama, 1993

Commercial Exploitation

Trophy hunting of wildlife by foreigners on the Tibetan Plateau began in Amdo, Xinjiang, and Gansu during the 1980s. The government of 'Tibet Autonomous Region' is now considering commercial hunting as it is a quick way of making money. Usually trophy hunting benefits the hunters and the government, not the animals and local people (Schaller 1998).

In a country where the per capita income is US$30 it is perhaps hard to resist the temptation of selling rare animal parts for hard cash. A snow leopard coat can fetch US$20,000 on the black market. Agenda 21 for Sustainable Agricultural Development in the 'Tibet Autonomous Region', which the government of China issued in 1996 states, "Hunting is prohibited, but few local governments have not given enough recognition to this issue and their measures for protecting wildlife are ineffective."

George Schaller, the eminent American wildlife scientist who has conducted several wildlife studies on the Chang Thang, writes in the August 1993 issue of *National Geographic*, Tibet Forest Bureau has tried to curtail the illegal Tibetan antelope wool trade. For example, one truck driver was taken to court for killing 300 antelopes. However, control is extremely difficult, in part because officials, instead of upholding the laws, themselves often hunt. One Tibetan herdsman in the area said that Chinese officials from Gerze [Gyertse] come in winter to Chang Thang to hunt yaks and antelope with modern weapons. He said, "If the officials obey the law and stop hunting we will too."

In his book, *Tibet's Hidden Wilderness*, Schaller recalls the party secretary of Shuanghu, Suolang Gongbu, who sent trucks to the far north to shoot wild yaks for winter meat, even though the species is fully protected in China. In 1991 he handed several rifles to his staff for a *kyang* (wild ass) hunt as meat was needed to feed Chinese labourers on a local construction project...Ironically in 1993 Suolang was named National Wildlife Protection Model by the so-called Tibet Autonomous Region government for his 'contribution' to conservation.

Wildlife authorities in China on the whole are poorly trained and wardens and patrol teams are ill-equipped to stamp out illegal hunting (Cai 1997). Many poachers now hunt with automatic weapons due to the lucrative nature of the illegal trade in rare animal parts.

Contrary to the high-sounding rhetoric of the Chinese government over protecting Tibet's wildlife, a state-run company called China National Native Produce and Animal By-products Import and Export Corporation sends its agents into the countryside to trap or kill wild animals of all kinds (Schaller 1994). Since deer antlers, musk, tiger bones, bear gall bladder and leopard bones, and other parts of animals are used in traditional Chinese medicine, there is a huge illegal operation to poach these rare species of wildlife. In many areas musk deer populations have vanished (Wangdu 1998).

There is also widespread commercial hunting of Tibetan wild animals. A permit to hunt an endangered Tibetan antelope is issued for US$35,000, and an argali sheep permit is US$23,000. The plateau's endangered species, such as snow leopard, giant panda, black-necked crane, wild yak, and Tibetan antelope, enjoy protection in word only on Chinese government paper.

Political Pandering

There are now only about 1,000 giant pandas left in the wild, which means that the species is threatened with extinction. However, pandering to international curiosity, China exploits the giant panda to earn hard cash through zoo rental programmes as well as to gain political leverage from influential countries. Beijing presented two giant pandas to Hong Kong on July 1, 1997 to celebrate the change of sovereignty! Earlier China had presented two giant pandas to the then British prime minister, Edward Heath, a pair to the Japanese prime minister in 1972 and a pair to the Washington's National Zoo after then US President Richard Nixon's visit to China in 1972, plus a pair to London Zoo.

Tibetan gazelle head selling as a souvenir in Amdo

China sold two giant pandas to the San Diego Zoo on 10 May 1999. Again two giant pandas arrived in the US on 5 November 1999 for a ten year loan to the Atlanta Zoo. The Zoo will pay China US$ 1 million a year for the loan of the cubs (*Inside China Today* 1999c). These endangered animals should not be used as official souvenirs to be sent overseas at the whim and fancy of China.

The Population Factor

The late Panchen Lama said on 8 March 1987 at the National People's Congress Conference held in Beijing, "The expenditure on a Chinese in Tibet is four times more than that in China. Why should Tibet pay so much to sustain this Chinese population in Tibet? The government of China's policy of sending Chinese into Tibet is harming Tibet. In the beginning a few thousand Chinese migrated, but now several thousand more are pouring into Tibet."

Human population growth obviously increases the pressure on the natural resource base. Tibetan wildlife habitat is falling prey to intruding Chinese settlers and many animals and plants suffer from habitat loss. Rare animals like the giant panda and golden monkey are some animals which are threatened with extinction. The production of furs and pelts in Central Tibet has reached 5,360,000 each year on an average. Most of these furs come from Himalayan marmot, musk deer, blue sheep, Tibetan gazelle, Tibetan antelope, stone marten, foxes, lynx, leopard cat (*Felis bengalensis*), common otter, oriental small-clawed otter and wild red dog (*Cuon alpinus*).

A 1988 report by the Convention on International Trade in Endangered Species (CITES) found that China's export of large cat skins totalled 89,650, which is the highest export number in the world; ironically China is a signatory to CITES. By 1996 China had a total of 213 threatened species, including 75 mammals, 90 birds, 15 reptiles, one amphibian, 28 fishes and four invertebrates (IUCN 1996b).

Deforestation

Since many diverse flora and fauna thrive in the forest regions of Tibet, deforestation leads to the loss of biodiversity. Tibet's total forest cover declined from 25.2 million hectares in 1950 to 13.57 million hectares in 1985 alone, which means 46 per cent destruction. According to Chinese official statistics from 1950 to 1985 Tibetan timber worth US$54 billion was felled and sold in the international timber market by China. (see forestry chapter).

Tibetan forest regions of Nyingtri, Gyalthang, and Drago were ravaged between 1965-1985 and a total of 18 million cubic metres of timber was transported to China. The state of Tibet's forest can best be illustrated by Tenzin, a middle-aged farmer of Markham village in Kham, Eastern Tibet, who told *The New York Times* correspondent, Nicholas Meysztowics, in April 1990, "In the time it takes to drink one cup of tea, 15 Chinese trucks loaded with Tibetan logs pass by."

The chaotic commune-period (1956-1981) initiated by the government of China caused an unprecedented destruction of Tibet's forest. During this period local villages became production brigades during which mountains in Tibet were stripped of their forests to feed inefficient steel furnaces in the madness to produce enough steel for China to advance rapidly to the ranks of the advanced nations.

According to Tenzin Palbar, who escaped from Tibet into India in 1987, in the Ngaba Tibetan Autonomous Prefecture from 1955-1991 the Chinese government extracted 50.17 million cubic metres of Tibetan timber, which is worth US$ 3.1 billion in Tibet itself when calculated at the average price of 50 yuan per cubic metre. In the Ngaba region there were 340 million cubic metres of forest in 1950 and in 1992 it reduced to 180 million cubic metres, of which only 34 million cubic metres could be used. Therefore, Ngaba lost 47 per cent of its forest cover between 1950 to 1992 alone (TIN 1999a).

Deforestation in Tibet is still continuing at a fast rate. Tibetan refugees arriving in Dharamsala in 1999 from Gonjo in Kham reported that at least 300 Chinese logging trucks leave Tibet to China loaded with timber every day.

The major reason behind the clear-cutting of forest is to 'develop' the local economy. But the loss that is incurred by over cutting is more than the gain (Wangdu 1998). One case in point is the Yangtze flood in August 1998 in China, which resulted in an economic loss of US$ 37.5 billion and 3,656 people died (DIIR 1999a). The President of China, Jiang Zemin, admitted that the flood was mainly due to rampant deforestation upstream on the Tibetan Plateau.

Forsake wastage
Pollute not the clean,
Clear nature of the four elements
And destroy not the well-being of people
But absorb yourself in actions
That are beneficial to all.

His Holiness the 14th Dalai Lama, 1993.

Grassland degradation

Tibet is 70 per cent grassland and the health of these extensive grasslands are fundamental to the survival of about 1 million people consisting mainly of nomads and about 70 million population of domestic animals such as sheep, goat and yak and countless number of wildlife.

The principle pasture lands of Amdo regions of Tibet before 1949 [before Chinese occupation of Tibet] grew to an average height of 20 cm, covering 75 to 90 per cent of the area. Today, the grass grows to a maximum height of only 10 cm. while the percentage coverage of pasture lands has fallen considerably and grass yields are estimated to have fallen by up to approximately 50 per cent (Wang and Bai 1991).

In the Tibetan Plateau the rate of biomass (fuel) consumption is greater than naturally-occurring replacement rates. Unsustainable conversion of grassland into farmland during the Great Leap Forward and the Cultural Revolution seriously damaged the grassland in some areas. Herd structure and composition are far from optimal. Better herd management techniques and promotion of solar energy may provide opportunities for simultaneous grassland recovery and economic growth (US Embassy 1996b).

In 1991, the State Council established the China Council for International Cooperation on Environment and Development (CCICED) to facilitate cooperation between China and the international community in the fields of environment and development. The Biodiversity Working Group of CCICED concluded in 1995 that China's grassland resources, which cover two thirds of China's land mass, deserve special attention. The reasons are: They support unique ethnic groups meeting their nutritional, clothing, fuel and medicinal needs; and, significantly, their degradation could very adversely affect neighbouring environments that house one-fourth of the world's population.

China's White Paper on Population, Environment and Development of the 21st Century, which the State Council approved on March 1994, delivers a similar message — the grasslands are far more important to China and the world environment than the value of their economic output. The U.S. National Academy of Sciences also reached this conclusion when it appointed its Grassland Review Panel to engage Chinese grassland specialists in developing a broad view of China's pastoral frontier (US Embassy 1996c).

CONSEQUENCES OF BIODIVERSITY LOSS

The various benefits of wildlife such as medicinal, industrial, educational, aesthetic, spiritual and cultural values, will vanish altogether with the extinction of wildlife on the Tibetan Plateau. This will not only be an irredeemable tragedy for Tibet, but for the whole world as well.

With the disappearance of flora and fauna the environment of the plateau would be irreversibly disturbed. Felling trees, for instance, threatens to not only wipe out a number of species but is also shown to upset the complex ecological balances which regulate the amount of rain and heat a given region receives to cause soil erosion, landslides, silting, floods, drought and other perils.

Because of its immense geographical extent and height, Tibet considerably influences global weather patterns by affecting the flow of jet streams over its plateau. As a huge land surface, the plateau affects the path of jet streams as an enormous iceberg would dramatically change the navigational routes of ships in oceans.

Loss of forest and grassland cover on the plateau will affect jet stream patterns, which will in turn influence the Pacific typhoons and also cause the El Nino effect. Taken together this controls the weather patterns across Europe, the USA, Mexico, Peru, India, China and other adjoining areas and will affect their ecology and economies.

PRIORITIES FOR FUTURE ACTION

The conservation of biodiversity differs from traditional nature preservation in that it is less of a defensive mechanism than a proactive effort — seeking to meet human needs (not greed) from biological resources and at the same time sustainably managing these resources for future generations.

The phrase "East or West home is the best" holds true for plants and animals. The destruction of their habitat ultimately means the destruction of many species of plants and animals, so wildlife habitats on the Tibetan Plateau need to be protected proactively. Wherever possible the niches of wildlife regions must be restored so that some now-silent habitats will once again teem with wildlife and bird songs.

One way of conserving habitats for species survival is to set up more effective nature parks and reserves for wildlife. Today there are in total 21 "nature reserves" on the plateau on government paper; in actuality they offer no practical protection since there are no adequate wildlife wardens or reserve managers to oversee the species in these "reserves". Therefore there is a pressing need for more sustained and active involvement by the government and local people through financial and human resource mobilisation.

Policy reforms at all levels should consider the basic needs of local inhabitants and provide direct economic incentives towards conserving biodiversity.

The Tibetan antelopes has been decimated from nearly two million in 1900 to barely 75,000 now. Some 20,000 Tibetan antelope on the Tibetan Plateau are killed every year.

Legislation and Effective Enforcement

It is not a case that there are no laws for the conservation of wildlife on the Tibetan Plateau. It is simply that these laws are too weak to stamp out the illegal activities of seasoned poachers and hunters. Wildlife criminals and black-marketeers get away without paying fines or serving jail sentences by invoking the many loopholes in the legal system.

The 1988 National Wildlife Law of China declares that it is a state policy to promote and perpetuate wildlife, and prohibits the killing of endangered and some non-endangered species, but does little to address wildlife habitat loss and fails to set up an infrastructure which can monitor and enforce such laws and regulations (Harris 1995-96).

In January 1995, China's State Councillor, Chen Junsheng, said in a *Xinhua* report that more effort is needed to protect forests and rare wildlife, including revising the existing forestry laws and drawing up new laws to crack down on illegal logging and hunting.

The indiscriminate hunting and poaching of Tibetan antelope was brought to the attention of international audiences in 1999. Several organisations, including Friends of Nature in China, campaigned to stop the slaughter of these gentle and endangered creatures for their wool — popularly known as *shahtoosh* (king of wool) — which is woven into expensive shawls fine enough to pass through a wedding ring. It is also warm enough to hatch a pigeon's egg, and can fetch up to US$ 75,000 per shawl in the world's fashion capitals (O'Donnell 1999). *Shahtoosh* shawls are currently a high fashion item and sell at inflated prices in exclusive boutiques around the world. About three antelopes are killed to make a single shawl. The Tibetan antelope has been decimated from nearly two million in 1900 to barely 75,000 now. Some 20,000 Tibetan antelope on the Tibetan Plateau are killed every year. (*The Times of India* 1999; Clark 1999)

On April 13, 1999, an accused of Indian origin, Bharati Ashok Assomull, was fined US$39,000 and sentenced to a three-month suspended jail term in Hong Kong for selling 130 *shahtoosh* shawls worth US$65,000 (*South China Morning Post* 1999a). This punishment sent a clear message to poachers and smugglers that this kind of illegal activity will not be tolerated by the global community.

According to *Xinhua's* 30 April 1999 issue, a team of Chinese police and wildlife enforcement rangers arrested 42 poachers in the Hol Xil [Kokoxili] Nature Reserve in Amdo after a successful crackdown on the poaching of Tibetan antelope and other rare animals. They also confiscated more than 1,000 Tibetan antelope furs, 300 antelope heads, four wild yak furs, 26 wild donkey hides, a number of bear paws and heads of wild yaks, nine rifles, 8,000 rounds of ammunition and 12 vehicles.

The Chinese government's state departments plan to continue to cooperate with its northwestern provinces to tighten protection of wild animals in this reserve, which is home to more than 20 rare species under state protection including yaks and Tibetan antelopes. Such successful enforcement campaigns are exemplary and need to be replicated elsewhere.

Ecological Ethic

Modern consumerism which acquires, pollutes, and throws away is regarded by the Chinese government and populace — and unfortunately by some Tibetans — as a sign of prosperity and social status. Ironically, this modern western disease is already shown to be responsible for many of the environmental ills of this century. This consumerist disease should be transformed to a more responsible, compassionate, caring, and universal consciousness as championed by His Holiness the Dalai Lama. In other words, before we go on to clean the external environment, it is an urgent task to clean the inner environment i.e our mind of its greed and selfishness (Dekhang 1997).

The Chinese character for animal translates as "moving things" and the Chinese consider wild animals as an economic resource to be used for human purposes. This utilitarian view of wildlife is the main cause behind the loss of biodiversity on the Tibetan Plateau as well as in China. Therefore, the Tibetan Buddhist ideology of respecting wild animals as equal partners in an interdependent natural ecosystem should be given prominence and not looked down on as "backward" as most Chinese still tend to do.

Conservation Education

Holistic grassroots conservation education and extension services should be provided to the younger generations. These education and training schemes can easily be built upon the rich resources of Buddhist ecological ethics. Such an education will convey the spiritual and economic benefits of good resource management and may involve monks, nuns, biologists, economists, environmental educators and others.

Conservation education and training should include wildlife management, wildlife research, conservation training, conservation workshops and education, conservation extension work, designing nature parks and reserves. Chinese scientist Li Bosheng, who has done extensive research on the plateau's biodiversity, says that one of the biggest stumbling blocks in the path of conserving biodiversity in Tibet is the shortage of talented personnel and lack of funds and materials. Tibetan and international bodies as well as the government of China can play an active role in such avenues.

Growing Respect for Tradition

The "we know what is good for you" approach of China and some international donor agencies usually doesn't work in other regions — and so is the case in Tibet. One self-evident fact that must be understood is that Tibetans have successfully lived in harmony with nature for centuries.

Tibetan Buddhists' earth-friendly value system should be at the core of any conservation agenda or programmes initiated either by China or international agencies. Fortunately many Chinese scientists are now beginning to recommend this concept. Professor Zhang Rongzu, a Chinese geographer, noted in 1989:

> **It is worth considering the significance of this tradition (Tibetan). It must be treated as a sound background for any kind of economic development initiatives, rather than simply presuming that it is backward. Many experiences of inner China and its conventional models have a limited relevance here (Tibet).**

Another Chinese scientist, Wu Ning (1997) of the Chinese Academy of Sciences, admits that Tibetan nomads have accumulated a wealth of experience in the use of rangelands. He finds seasonal migration management systems well adapted to local conditions and suggests that modern and scientific approaches of managing grassland and animals on the Tibetan Plateau should take advantage of the wealth of traditional Tibetan knowledge accumulated through centuries.

George Schaller in his 1997 book, *Tibet's Hidden Wilderness*, found the general attitude of officials toward traditional grazing practices was dismissive, based on the notion that nomads are inefficient and backward. But they did admit that a combination of the traditional and new scientific systems could perhaps lead to viable range management.

One of the biggest stumbling blocks in the path of conserving biodiversity in Tibet is the shortage of talented personnel and lack of funds and materials.

Sensitive Research

More research on the biodiversity of the plateau could shed light on the habits and habitats of the region's rare and rich plants and animals. Here the call is for sensitive research which respects Tibetan culture and traditions to sustainably manage the biological resources. Research on the carrying-capacity of pastures, forests, lakes and other natural resources should be conducted for the longterm environmental management of the plateau.

The domestic and international scientific network on biodiversity should be strengthened to improve communication and information flow among scientists and researchers in developing and developed countries to share experiences or learn lessons from each other. International agencies should support longterm ecological research in Tibet so as to provide a baseline for understanding natural ecosystems and learning how to modify them most effectively, consistent with the development needs of the Tibetan people.

The magnificent black-necked crane, endemic to the Tibetan Plateau, is listed as an endangered species

Gene Pools and Seed Banks

The genetic pool of wildlife and domestic animals and plants provides the survival needs for human beings. They are the storehouse of genetic resources to improve livestock, develop new crop varieties, cure diseases and bring numerous other benefits yet undiscovered. The rich biodiversity of the Tibetan Plateau must therefore be preserved. Government — and internationally funded gene pool centres and local seed banks should be set up in some selected areas to store genetic resources. Seed bases need to be established in pasture areas below 3,000 metres to improve rangelands. New varieties of seeds such as common oats (*Avena sativa*) were successfully introduced in Zamthang and accepted by herdsmen as a successful means of supplementing fodder for animals (Wu 1997).

Scientific research should be conducted to assess the value of these resources. These centres not only become academic in nature, but also share their knowledge with Tibetan farmers, foresters and nomads to improve their living standard and to help in conserving genetic diversity.

Remote Sensing

The data gathered by remote sensing techniques, coupled with the data management capacity of Geographic Information Systems (GIS), offer unprecedented opportunities to assess and monitor ecosystem processes. Training opportunities for Tibetans must be made available through international development assistance.

Check Population Transfer

The single and most serious threat to the plateau's environment, especially to its wildlife, is the transfer of a huge number of Chinese settlers who open up new regions for agriculture, industries and small factories.

According to Xu Chengshi and Zhong Bu some of the 1.2 million Chinese who will be evicted by the massive Three Gorges Dam being built on the Yangtze River may go to Tibet. Sources within Tibet say at least one million Chinese will move to Tibet's southern Kongpo region because of its climatic similarity with the Yangtze region from where they are being displaced.

Moreover, the increased number of Chinese settlers pouring into the lower valleys of Tibet (the winter pastures of nomads) have disrupted the traditional migration pattern of nomad herds, thereby pushing them to marginal areas leading to overgrazing. The conversion of marginal lands for agriculture for Chinese settlers has devastated the vast grasslands in Amdo (DIIR 1996c).

There is an urgent need for stricter laws on issuing residential permits to outsiders entering Tibet and effective enforcement to be introduces when checking illegal immigrants.

Curbing Corruption

Guanxi is the Chinese character for a "personal connection" — a social disease that is rampant in China and is fast overtaking Tibet. For example, to log Tibet's forests one only needs a "license" which can be easily obtained if the right "personal connections" are in place. Thus some officials treat the resources of the Tibetan Plateau as their private property and give permission to cut down trees, and mine, kill or hunt animals as they fancy.

Mr. Gonpo, a Standing Committee member of Tibet People's Political Consultative Conference, said during the committee's meeting in Lhasa, 16-22 May 1995: "Citizens of Lhasa and Nyingtri (in Kongpo region) have expressed serious concern over the destruction of forests by timber poachers on the excuse that they have an official license from the various government forest departments to fell trees."

Involving People

Wildlife in China is a state-controlled commodity and due to ineffective enforcement of wildlife laws in many cases becomes a common property resource to be exploited. And the maxim "whoever hunts it, gets to keep it" becomes a reality. The people who live alongside wildlife receive no incentives for wildlife protection beyond the vague sense of helping to preserve some national treasures (Harris 1995-96).

Works in the development field by domestic, international, bilateral and multi-lateral agencies show that "top-down" development projects are no longer the trend. For successful realisation of projects a "bottom-up" strategy is preferred — that is, giving more decision-making power to locals and involving local people in project appraisal, implementation and evaluation. This trend is obvious because local people have lived, sustained and survived in their native regions for thousands of years. The field biologist George Schaller says any projects in the Chang Thang Wildlife Reserve will have to consider the cooperation and participation of Tibetan nomads to ensure the protection of wildlife (Schaller 1997).

Participatory approaches to development remain virtually non-existent in China. Thus, developing multi-use management plans on the Tibetan Plateau will require more attention to the needs and aspirations of Tibetans; without the adequate understanding, interest and participation of the people, even the best conservation plans have little chance of success.

A Regional Experts' Meeting from November 5-7, 1996 in Kathmandu, Nepal on Rangelands and Pastoral Development in the Hindu Kush-Himalayas, came up with recommendations for the conservation of rangeland biodiversity listed in the table on next page.

GLOBAL ACTIVISM

On 19 July 1993, the government of 'Tibet Autonomous Region' passed the resolution to establish the Chang Thang Nature Reserve. It is the second largest reserve in the world, exceeded only by one in northern Greenland which consists mostly of ice cap. It is almost as large as Germany (Schaller 1998). This reserve was established with the assistance and encouragement from the Wildlife Conservation Society of New York.

In 1980 the Wolong Nature Reserve in Kham, the main habitat of giant panda, was designated an international biosphere conservation area by UNESCO's Man and the Biosphere Program. Such UNESCO actions should be further extended through international participation, pressure, and activism, to include major regions of rich forest resources on the eastern Tibetan Plateau and the Chang Thang Wildlife Reserve as world heritage sites and international biosphere reserves (Dekhang 1997).

CONCLUSION

In terms of richness the biodiversity of the Tibetan Plateau could be compared to the rainforest of the Amazon basin. To date it has not received the recognition and attention it deserves due to the paucity of information and restrictions imposed on travellers and scientists. The plateau is a storehouse of unique flora and fauna found nowhere else in the world — especially its extraordinary high-altitude species.

Many rare, endemic and endangered plants and animals continue on the roller coaster towards extinction under the current regime. In the Chang Thang region of Tibet wildlife has been unsustainably hunted so that in the past decades numbers have decreased by as much as 90 per cent (Schaller 1998). The loss of these biological resources will not only lead to the extinction of certain species; drastic changes will occur to the food chains and food webs of the

CONSERVATION OF RANGELAND BIODIVERSITY

MAJOR ISSUES

- decrease in biodiversity/loss of species
- habitat loss
- illegal hunting
- lack of data/knowledge/awareness
- overgrazing
- wildlife-livestock competition
- climatic changes
- cultural diversity problems
- medicinal plants-lack of knowledge
- inappropriate government policies
- lack of monitoring

PRIORITY ACTIONS

Research on:

- wildlife movements/grazing systems
- wildlife habitat
- wildlife and range ecology
- wildlife-livestock interactions
- indigenous pastoral management systems
- awareness campaigns, education
- establish biosphere reserves
- create monitoring teams
- control illegal hunting
- manage stocking rates/sell unproductive animals
- establish a biodiversity database
- rehabilitate overgrazed ranges
- introduce improved forages
- incorporate indigenous knowledge into development plans
- create off-farm and alternative employment opportunities
- promote appropriate land ownership rights/legislation for tenure

ecosystem network in which they play a vital role in building the web of life and maintaining the delicate balance of fragile ecosystems. It is therefore important to take concrete **action**, not mere register **reaction**, to conserve the biodiversity of the Tibetan Plateau. This can be done by focusing on achievable results through working on joint projects with Tibetan and international NGOs, government organisations and — last but not the least — the People's Republic of China.

The loss of Tibet's unique flora and fauna has consequences far more profound than more widely-recognised environmental dilemmas. Because the loss is irreversible, the potential impact on the human condition, on the fabric of the plateau's living system, and on the process of evolution is immense.

Whatever geographical, political or imaginary lines we may draw on the globe, the fact is that all the inhabitants of this world — irrespective of race, nationality and sex — share the same planet. Therefore, the conservation of biodiversity on the Tibetan Plateau is undoubtedly a global responsibility.

Conserving the biodiversity of Tibet could be a symbol of global human strength and commitment to saving other plant and animal species in peril elsewhere. This would not only guarantee the long-term survival of rare and endangered wildlife on the plateau, it will ensure the survival of the roof of the world — one of the most enchanting, mystical and sacred landscapes on earth — for the enrichment and enjoyment of future generations. ■

CHAPTER TWO

WATER RESOURCES

Though people lack not wealth,
They cannot afford to breathe clean air,
Rains and streams cleanse not,
But remain inert and powerless liquids

His Holiness the 14th Dalai Lama, 1993

THE MOUNTAINS of Tibet constitute the headwaters of many of Asia's major rivers. Tibet's high altitude, huge landmass and vast glaciers endows it with the greatest river system in the world. Tibet's rivers flow into the most populous regions of the world, supplying fresh water to a significant proportion of Asia's population (see Table 1).

Tibetan rivers are distinguished by their high silt loads resulting from the largely desert landscape from which they originate. In the Zachu (Mekong), Gyalmo Ngulchu (Salween) and Drichu(Yangtze) watersheds, as well as the eastern reaches of the Yarlung Tsangpo, deforestation is steadily increasing these high silt loads.

Net hydrological flows in Tibet total 627 cubic km per year. This comprises roughly six per cent of Asia's annual runoff and 34 per cent of India's total river water resources. Historically, negligible utilisation rates in Tibet meant that nearly all of this water was transferred to countries in downstream basins including India, Nepal, China, Bangladesh, Pakistan, Bhutan, Vietnam, Burma (Myanmar), Cambodia, Laos and Thailand. Today, hydrological transfers from Tibet to other countries total 577 cubic km from a gross basin area of 1.1 million sq. km. This excludes internal and landlocked rivers. Transnational flow thus accounts for 92 per cent of net hydrological flows.

The availability of fresh water in Tibet — 104,500 cubic metres per year — ranks fourth in the world after Iceland, New Zealand and Canada, and is 40,000 times higher than in China. Given the low precipitation in Tibet, a higher proportion of river flows originate from glaciers which have a total area of 42,946 sq. km and groundwater sources. Perennial sources like these result in what are called stable or base flows. Because they are independent of seasonal precipitation patterns they are an important factor in sustaining hydrological regimes (DIIR 1992).

The quantity of water flowing from the plateau, and the steep gradients, mean the hydropower potential of Tibet's rivers is among the highest in the world. Over two thirds of China's hydropower potential is located in, or directly surrounding, Tibet. The hydropower potential of this area has been calculated at 1305 TWh (Cheng 1994). The Great Bend of the Yarlung Tsangpo in Southeast Tibet is estimated to have the largest hydropower potential of any place on earth at 70,000MW (Verghese 1990). The gorge where this potential exists has become the focus of recent exploratory expeditions. Currently, the exploitation of hydropower resources in Tibet is mainly concentrated on the Upper Drichu (Yangtze) and its major tributaries the Yalong and Dadu Rivers in Kham. The Upper Machu (Yellow River) in Amdo is also the focus of largescale hydropower exploitation.

Tibet is endowed with more than 2,000 natural lakes. The major ones include Tso Ngonpo (Kokonor), Nam Tso, Yamdrok Tso — the largest fresh water lake in the North Himalaya — Mapham Tso and Panggong Tso. The largest lake in Tibet is Tso Ngonpo, which has an area of 4,460 sq. km. The combined area of Tibet's lakes is over 35,000 sq.km

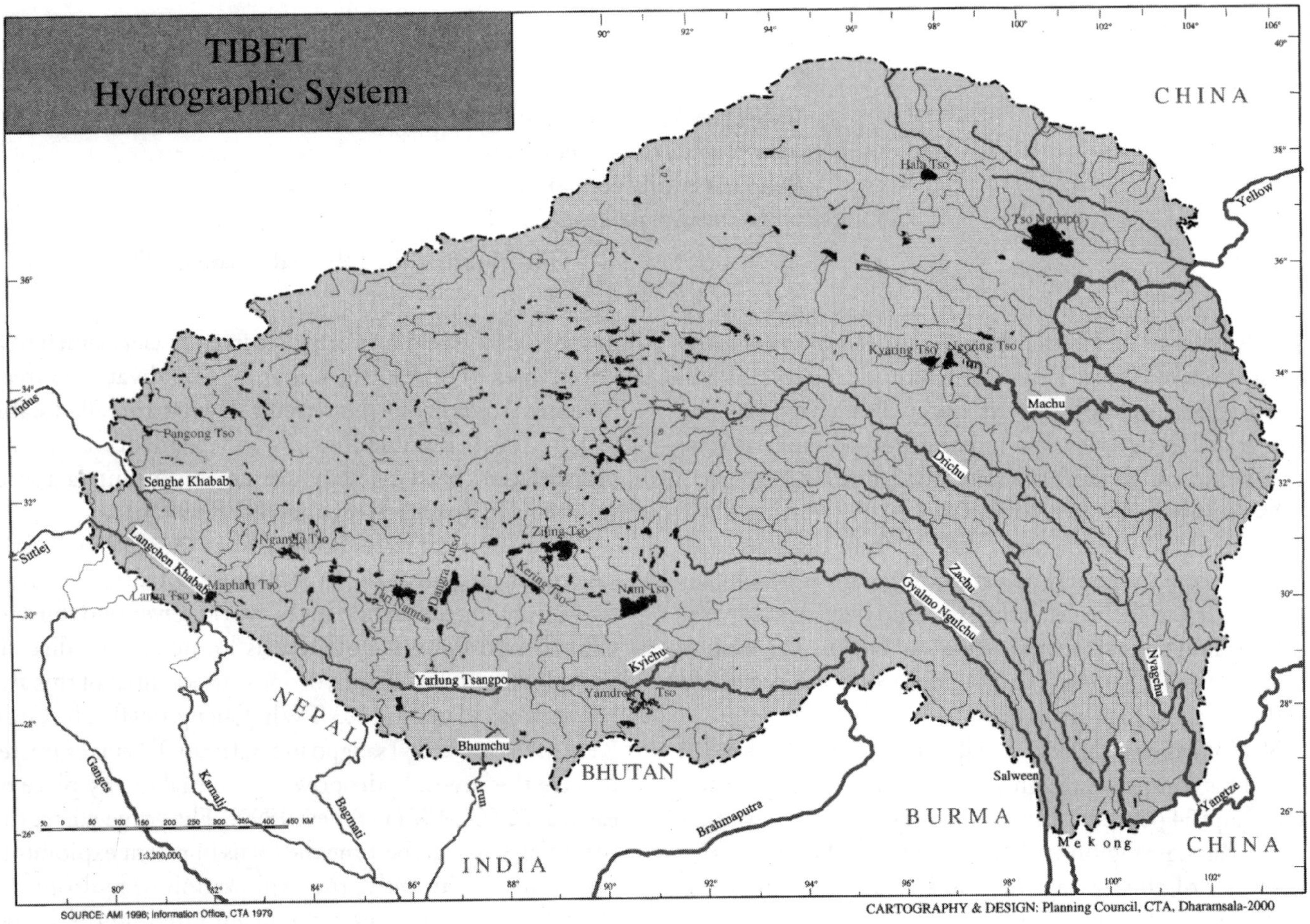

Note : See colour map at the end of the book

TABLE 1 THE MAJOR RIVERS OF TIBET AT A GLANCE

Tibetan	Other	Chinese	Source (ht. in metres)	Length (km)	Watershed regions	Outflow
Machu	Yellow River	Huang he	Amdo Bayanhar Mountain (5266)	5,464	Tibet, China, Inner Mongolia	Yellow Sea
Drichu	Yangtze	Chang Jiang	Mt. Thangla (6328)	6,380	Tibet, China	East China Sea
Zachu	Mekong	Lancang Jiang	Mt. Thangla (Ch. Tanggula)	4,500	Tibet, China, Vietnam, Laos, Cambodia, Thailand,	South China Sea
Gyalmo Ngulchu	Salween	Nu Jiang	Mt. Thangla	2,800	Tibet, China, Burma, Thailand	Andaman Sea
Yarlung Tsangpo	Brahmaputra	Yarlung Zangbo	Mt. Tesi range	2,900	Tibet, India, Bangladesh	Bay of Bengal
Macha Khabab	Karnali	Maqa Zangbo	Mt. Tesi range	1,609	Tibet, Nepal, India	Bay of Bengal
Langchen Khabab	Sutlej	Langquen Zangbo	Mt. Tesi (Kailash)	1,450	Tibet, India, Pakistan	Arabian Sea
Senge Khabab	Indus	Senge Zanggbo	Mt. Tesi (6638)	3,100	Tibet, India, Pakistan	Arabian Sea
Bhumchu	Arun		Mt. Shishapangma (8012)	1,207	Tibet, Nepal, India	Bay of Bengal
Lhodrak Sharchu	Norbu Lakchu or Manas		Mt. Zholchen (6106)	380	Tibet, Bhutan, India, Bangladesh	Bay of Bengal

Sources: Dorje 1996; DIIR 1995; DIIR 1992; Science Press, Beijing 1990.

Tibet's high altitude, huge landmass and vast glaciers endows it with the greatest river system in the world. Tibet's rivers flow into the most populous regions of the world, supplying fresh water to a significant proportion of Asia's population.

accounting for about 1.5 per cent of the country's total surface area (DIIR 1992). The catchment area ecology of most of the lakes is relatively unknown and utilisation of their waters has remained low until recent times. Many of these lakes have been receding slowly due to natural processes for thousands of years.

According to Chinese surveys, there are 71 species and sub-species of fish in the 'Tibet Autonomous Region' ('TAR'). This constitutes 63 per cent of the species and sub-species on the entire Tibetan Plateau. Among these are various species of: Schizothoracinae, Nemacheilinae and Sissoridae (Zhang 1997).

There were no cases of Tibetan rivers being diverted, polluted or extensively fished before 1949. A small hydropower station was built in 1928 in the Togde Gully on the Kyichu with an installed capacity of 92 kw (Yan 1998). Diversions for irrigation were also minimal. In this period, Tibet's agriculture was dependent on monsoon rains and small-scale river diversions organised on a village basis. These would have had a negligible impact on the flows of Tibet's rivers. The absence of any modern industry at this time, and the low population density, meant that it was unlikely that wastes entering Tibet's rivers caused any significant pollution.

For devout Tibetan Buddhists eating fish is a sacrilege. There is a saying: "Because a fish is without a tongue, killing is unforgivable" (Duncan 1961). Fish were not an important part of the Tibetan diet. Therefore, few people engaged themselves in fishing. The fishing activity around Yamdrok Tso in southern Tibet was regulated by the central government in Lhasa as the lake is of great spiritual significance. The *Kashag* (Cabinet of the Tibetan Government) regulated the size of fishing net holes so that young fish and other non-edible creatures were protected (Tsering 1996). Therefore the exploitation of fish resources prior to 1949 was minimal and harvests were sustainable.

WATER FOR THE MILLIONS

As mentioned above, rivers originating in Tibet flow into various regions in Asia. In some cases the distance traversed by these rivers through Tibet is short, while for many of them Tibetan terrain constitutes a large proportion of the rivers' total length and contributes largely to the rivers' perennial flow. Since Asia is dominated by monsoon patterns of rainfall, bringing rain for only a few months (usually three months) of the year, the perennial flow of its rivers relies upon the constant flux of glaciers on the Tibetan Plateau. Tibet's high altitude causes extreme diurnal variation in temperature, so that every day, winter or summer, glaciers can partially melt and refreeze. This daily snowmelt feeds the river systems.

Since Asia is dominated by monsoon patterns of rainfall, bringing rain for only a few months of the year, the perennial flow of its rivers relies upon the constant flux of glaciers on the Tibetan Plateau.

From Tibet's Rivers Flows Asia's Survival

For 1,600 km of its total 4,500 km length, the Mekong traverses through Tibetan territory (Lafitte 1996). Beginning in Amdo, the Mekong passes through the eastern side of Tibet near Sangang and Chamdo and flows near the Tibetan town Jol and then Balang to the Chinese town Lajing in Yunnan Province. It then continues in a south southeasterly direction through Yunnan and on into Southeast Asia. After leaving China, the Mekong flows through Laos, Thailand, Cambodia and Vietnam.

The Salween begins in Thangla Mt. (Ch. Tanggula) in Tibet and flows east towards the Mekong. It then travels in an almost parallel gorge just west of the Mekong in the Khawakarpo Mountains. Once in Kham, the two river valleys diverge and the Salween heads southwest into Burma, where it becomes the country's primary river.

The two great rivers of China, the Yangtze and the Yellow, originate high up on the plateau in Amdo. The Yellow River travels northeast through Amdo before entering the Loess Plateau and the North China Plain. This region of China supports 550 million people and two thirds of the country's cropland. However, the watershed only supplies one fifth of the country's water. The Yangtze watershed and the region to its south supports slightly more people (700 million), accounting for four fifths of China's total water yet only one third of the country's cropland (Brown & Halweil 1998). The imbalance of water resources to cropland between these two major watersheds of China is emerging as one of the Beijing's biggest ecological problems. As groundwater and river water is becoming exhausted in the north, Chinese engineers are contemplating massive inter-basin water transfer projects.

In the southwest of Tibet, four major rivers originate around Mt. Tesi (Kailash). One is the Yarlung Tsangpo which travels for over 2,200 km within Tibet. Its easterly course skirts north of the Himalayan divide before turning sharply south into the plains of Arunachal Pradesh, India, where it becomes known as the Brahmaputra. After flowing through the Assam Plain in India, the Yarlung Tsangpo enters Bangladesh to irrigate the fields of the country's 128 million people, before joining the Ganges and the Meghna to form the great delta of northeastern India known as the Sunderbans.

The Senge Khabab (Indus) has its source north of Tesi mountains (Kailash). It then passes west into Ladakh as the Senge Tsangpo and then to Kashmir and continues to become Pakistan's principle river. The Langchen Khabab (Sutlej) begins west of Tesi mountains, crossing the Himalayas into Himachal Pradesh in northwest India, passing through the Punjab region before joining the Indus in Pakistan. The Macha Khabab (Karnali) originates from Mt. Tesi Range (Kailash Range), crosses the Himalayas into western Nepal and then into India where it joins the River Ganges.

Fertile River Valleys

Every year the major rivers flowing out of Tibet flood when the spring sun melts the winters' snow and then again when the monsoon rains arrive — mostly between July and September. At times these floods are severe, often wreaking havoc downstream as they did in China and Bangladesh in 1998 and 1999. Nevertheless, a regular annual flood can be a beneficial function of a healthy river. As these rivers cascade down into the foothills and plains of Asia they bring with them more than just water. The silt loads of Tibet's rivers deposit millions of tons of silt and sediment to create fertile river valleys and flood plains in the downstream regions in Asia. This is the key to maintaining the viability of downstream ecosystems. The fertile river valleys of

Brahmaputra, Yellow and Mekong are cases in point.

As the floods recede they leave behind silt which replenishes the topsoil with vital trace elements such as silica and iron. This sedimentation process also maintains the deltas of major rivers. The annual flood also facilitates the breeding of freshwater fish. While the floods are at their peak, fish swim into the shallows and lay their eggs in still waters where they can develop without disturbance. As the floodwaters recede, the hatchlings find their way into the main streams. These benefits are not always appreciated by agro-scientists and developers and, perhaps not surprisingly, by those affected by the floods. Catastrophic floods appear to be becoming more regular and more severe. This is a possible consequence of the interference in hydrological systems, climate change and continuing deforestation.

It is becoming increasingly clear that rivers have more ecological functions than just the provision of water. The interaction of flood plains and rivers is one such vital function. The Tibetan Plateau — with its weather patterns, hydrological system, glacial conditions, forest, and soil functions — has an essential influence over Asia (with high population densities) and which also provide sustenance to some of the world's most productive agricultural zones.

China's unbridled economic growth, industrialisation and urbanisation have contributed to widespread water pollution and scarcity. China has some of the extreme cases of water shortage in the world. Out of 640 major cities, more than 300 face water shortage, with 100 facing severe scarcities.

CURRENT SITUATION

Water Pollution and Scarcity

It is obvious that there would be catastrophic consequences to the billions of people downstream if Tibet's rivers were to become severely polluted. In many of the reliant regions water treatment facilities are very basic, and many people rely on the rivers for drinking water as well as for irrigation and for other daily needs. In China water pollution is already a serious problem. Up to 45,000 million tons of untreated wastewater currently enters China's rivers every year (Edmonds 1994). Approximately 700 million people — over half of China's population — consume drinking water contaminated with animal and human waste (Cai 1993). In many Chinese cities today, rivers are biologically dead and are little more than a toxic soup of human and industrial wastes. One half of the ground water in the cities of China is contaminated (Zhang 1994).

China's unbridled economic growth, industrialisation and urbanisation have contributed to widespread water pollution and scarcity. China has some of the extreme cases of water shortage in the world. Out of 640 major cities, more than 300 face water shortage, with 100 facing severe scarcities (NEPA 1997). Water shortages in cities cause a loss of an estimated US$ 11.2 billion in industrial output each year. The impact of water pollution on human health has been valued approximately at US$ 3.9 billion annually (The World Bank 1997).

Until China deals with this problem in its industrial centres, it seems unlikely it will devote significant attention to the quality of water flows outside its borders. In Lhasa, plastic waste and oil waste from mechanical workshops can be seen dumped on the banks of rivers. During the flood season these get washed into rivers. A 'TAR' government report on the state of its environment in 1996 reported that 41.9 million tons of waste liquid were produced that year. The report also noted that the trend for rivers in the Lhasa area was towards increasing pollution (*Tibet Daily* 1997). Lhasa, therefore, appears to be following the path of Chinese cities.

For rivers such as the Indus, Yarlung Tsangpo (Brahmaputra), Sutlej, Karnali, Bhumchu (Arun), Lhodrak Sharchu (Manas), Salween and Mekong which all originate from the Tibetan plateau to flow into various regions in Asia, the threats of Chinese development on the Plateau are far-reaching. While industrial development is still relatively small-scale in the upper reaches of these watersheds, and population density also relatively low, the main sources of severe pollution can be traced to mining activities. Mining is one of the "Four Pillar" industries in the 'TAR' and it is a considerable threat to the purity of rivers in Tibet. Tailings from copper, gold, chromite and other mines on the plateau pollute rivers with sulphuric acid, cyanide and heavy metals. These are carried downstream where they infiltrate soils as well as the water supply of millions of people. Other major pollution threats can be attributed to increasing levels of untreated sewage, increasing nitrate run-off as a result of the intensification of agriculture and increasing levels of animal wastes due to the increase in meat production.

Development Disasters

Additional threats to Tibet's rivers depend upon the level to which China allows the mountains surrounding the Yarlung Tsangpo, Mekong and Salween watersheds to become deforested as well as the strategy China chooses for developing hydropower and irrigation resources on these rivers. By controlling Tibet, China controls the ecological viability of a massive section of South and Southeast Asia's river systems. To date, China has most extensively affected its own principle rivers — the Yellow and the Yangtze — with its current development strategies on the plateau. The Yellow River is suffering dramatically from a shortage of water in its lower reaches, partly due to the huge dams in the upper reaches in Amdo. The Yangtze has suffered from deforestation in its upper reaches which triggers to turn the annual flood into a disaster scenario. In March 1999 the Director of China's State Environment Protection Administration, Xie Zhenhua, suggested that "ecological reserves should be developed in source areas of the Yellow and Yangtze rivers" (*Xinhua*, 14 March 1999).

Mekong and Salween are threatened by increased deforestation in the upper reaches in Tibet as well as by hydropower development. The Yarlung Tsangpo is becoming increasingly interrupted by medium-sized dams in Tibet and may one day host the biggest dam in the world. If this scheme were implemented it would impede the downstream flow of the primary resources — water and alluvial sediment — that India and Bangladesh depend on. These issues demand an urgent and unprecedented degree of regional and international cooperation if Tibet's resources are to continue to benefit the billions of people who live downstream.

The Yarlung Tsangpo is becoming increasingly interrupted by medium-sized dams in Tibet and may one day host the biggest dam in the world. If this scheme were implemented it would impede the downstream flow of the primary resources – water and alluvial sediment – that India and Bangladesh depend on.

Since the occupation of Tibet, the Chinese government has embarked upon unsustainable development schemes in the region which have adversely impacted most of the rivers and some of the lakes in Tibet. The level of industrial and other development in the region is not geographically balanced. The northeastern province, Amdo, has far more industry than U-Tsang — or Central Tibet — so pollution problems are higher there and dam-building is on a much larger scale. In the southeastern province, Kham, the main issue is deforestation as well as increasing river fragmentation caused by extensive dam-building. In U-Tsang pollution and dam construction is only recently on the increase. Water utilisation is set to increase as agricultural intensification is stepped up. Decreasing levels of precipitation in U-Tsang and shrinking glaciers could multiply the impact of new water-intensive developments. Lakes, which are also experiencing accelerated shrinking due to human interferences and partly due to climatic change, are also being increasingly exploited for water, fish and power production within the last five decades. These issues will be examined on a watershed basis in order to assess the specific impact of developments on each watershed's ecological function. Currently the watersheds of concern are the Yarlung Tsangpo, Mekong, Salween, Yellow and the Yangtze river basins.

YARLUNG TSANGPO WATERSHED

The Yarlung Tsangpo watershed drains most of the southern part of Tibet except for the area just north of Chomolungma (Mt. Everest). It originates from Western Tibet just southeast of Mapham Tso (Lake Manasarover). The Yarlung Tsangpo flows east through the most densely populated region of Tibet, irrigating most of the agricultural land in the historical Yarlung valley. Then it passes through Shigatse City and, flowing south of Lhasa, it drains the Kyichu river. East of Lhasa it flows through the once forested and now degraded Kongpo region before turning abruptly near Mt. Namchakbarwa to the south, cutting straight through the Himalayan divide to flow into India as Brahmaputra and then to Bangladesh.

The Yarlung Tsangpo and its two major tributaries, the Nyangchu and the Kyichu, have become the foci of development plans in the 'TAR'. The Three Rivers Development Project (TRDP), also known as "One River Two Streams" was first announced in May 1991. It refers to the area encompassing the Yarlung Tsangpo, the Nyangchu and the Kyichu and is bordered in the north by Nagchu and in the northeast by Chamdo. It includes 18 cities, 231 towns and 1,890 villages (Yan 1998a). It is a comprehensive infrastructural development plan concentrating principally on agricultural development but also on communications, transport and energy sectors.

In conjunction with the TRDP, a further list of "62 Aid Projects" for the 'TAR' was announced in 1994. The term "Aid" in the title of this plan refers to the funding for the project, which comes from individual cities or provinces in China as an "aid gift" to support the development of the 'TAR'. The "62 Aid Projects" and the TRDP include the largest irrigation projects to be built so far in the 'TAR'. The plans also involve a significant increase in energy generation capacity in the 'TAR', most of which is derived from hydropower.

Aiding Who?

Under the recent development plans encompassed by the TRDP and the "62 Aid Projects", increased exploitation of the Yarlung Tsangpo watershed's resources is a major feature. The main emphasis has been on increasing irrigation capacity, particularly in the Gyangtse and Shigatse areas where the Nyangchu is especially exploited. This is to increase the production of rapeseed, potatoes, vegetables, winter wheat and other crops. This is in itself a controversial policy, as these crops are primarily preferred by the Chinese population. The Shigatse and Gyangtse region has the largest available agricultural land area in the 'TAR.' Most other regions are also increasing their irrigation capacity.

Until recently, Central Tibet has had sporadic electricity supplies. These were based on a few key stations around Lhasa and some 400 small hydropower plants, most of which have been badly planned and maintained, making many of them inoperable (Wang and Bai 1991). The new developments are likely to change this dramatically with a number of large hydropower stations recently being put into operation and additional ones under construction, or at the planning stage. Many existing small stations are being upgraded and improved, such as the Tongchu power station northwest of Shigatse.

Improved power generation is probably welcomed by Tibetans, rural and urban alike, and the smaller hydropower stations will be relatively environmentally friendly. However, the inclusion of a number of bigger plants, and the dual facility of some of these for intensive irrigation, may have an increasing impact on the environment. Sacrificing environmental security to provide irrigation for exotic species of food crops for the Chinese population in the region is a price many Tibetans do not wish to pay.

Reservations About Reservoirs

The creation of reservoirs behind dams often results in the flooding of prime agricultural land. The poor record of dam builders and governments in relocating populations ousted by reservoirs is well documented. Resettlement has been involuntary in Tibet and has often disenfranchised the oustees (see Manlha Water Project).

The impact of a reservoir on the hydrology of the river is well-documented. A reservoir transforms a flowing river into a semi-stagnant body of water. Although there are outflows and inflows these are nothing like the natural functions of a river, especially as water releases into the river below are governed entirely according to the needs of electricity generation. The reservoir remains a still body of water most of the time. This affects the chemical, thermal and physical characteristics of the water. Therefore, the temperature and chemical composition of the water released from the dam into the river below is often quite different to the natural flow. For example, in summer the sun can heat the surface of the reservoir while the lower depths will remain cold. Releases of water from the top of the reservoir will be too warm and likewise those from the lower depths too cold. This can have serious consequences for aquatic life. Considering the high level of solar radiation in Tibet, and the extensive hours of sunshine, surface heating of reservoirs is likely to be high in the summer. Reservoirs also encourage certain breeds of fish well adapted to lakes to thrive while many species uniquely adapted to the river environment may die out thus affecting biodiversity.

Tibetan sacred lake Yamdrok Tso in Central Tibet

Another feature of reservoirs is that they cause river sediments and silt to settle to the bottom. This can cause problems over the longterm with the reservoir's capacity to hold water being reduced by the build-up of these sediments. A further ecological concern is that this causes the water released from the reservoir to become what is termed as "hungry". The sediment-free waters seek to recapture their sediment load, which causes the water to be more corrosive, eroding the bed and banks of the river at a far greater rate than normal. This can remove all the erodible material from the riverbed below the dam, destroying the habitat of benthic inverte brae such as insects, molluscs and crustaceans that live in the gravels on the riverbed and provide food for fish and waterfowls (McCully, 1996). The longterm effects on the morphology of the river are also far reaching. Patrick McCully (1996), commenting on this problem, notes:

> **In the long run, the major impact on the downstream river channel will often be to make it deeper and narrower, turning wide-braided, meandering rivers with gravel bars and beaches and multiple channels into relatively straight single channels. Reducing a braided river to a single channel will greatly diminish the diversity of plants and animals it can support.**

Fragmented and Stagnant Rivers

The overarching consequence of damming rivers is the resulting fragmentation of each river as an integral ecosystem. This has a devastating effect on many of the species that migrate up and down the river with seasonal changes, as well as on the morphology and ecology of the river and its adjacent flood plains. Fragmentation isolates groups of fish species and other aquatic organisms so that breeding within a small group causes genetic problems. In cases of already endangered species this can lead to an insufficient gene pool for breeding and leads to subsequent extinction (McCully 1996).

Nearly all dams restrict seasonal flooding by storing floodwaters and this is often seen as a benefit of the dam. However, seasonal flooding performs a function which is highly beneficial to soil fertility, groundwater recharge and aquatic species regeneration. As floodwater covers the flood plain it brings with it rich nutrients which are left on the soil when the floodwaters recede. This is one of the reasons why flood plain lands are often prime fertile agricultural lands.

Fish populations have declined severely in many dammed rivers due to fragmentation of their habitat. Sediment build-up in river estuaries is also greatly reduced causing similar problems of soil viability and fish species decline. This has had a severe impact on the breeding grounds of 80 per cent of the world's fish catch. Mitigation efforts, which involve attempting to release waters in a manner that mimics the natural flow of the river, are rarely successful (McCully 1996).

Given the highly erodible and fragile soils of the Yarlung Tsangpo valley and its tributaries, this is of major concern in light of the increasing hydro-development in the area. Silt build-up in reservoirs in the Yarlung Tsangpo watershed is also likely to be reducing the overall life of the hydropower stations. Additionally, freezing for long periods in the winter will reduce the benefits of these developments.

There are over 400 hydropower stations in the 'TAR' (*Tibet Daily*, 27 June 1997). Many of these are concentrated in the Yarlung Tsangpo watershed. These are generally small run-of-the-river schemes generating less than 500kw, which individually have little environmental impact on the river as long as they are operated properly. Wang and Bai reported in 1991 that of 816 small hydro stations set up in U-Tsang, 23.3 per cent were scrapped and 15.7 per cent were malfunctioning. Given that recent Chinese news sources quote figures of just over 400 stations since then, many more have been scrapped. Since 1991, larger-scale projects have been emphasised, including at least five projects over 10,000kw (see Table 2). The measure of environmental impact of these plants is generally linked to the size of the dam and reservoir and the proportion of the natural flow of the river that is interrupted.

Yet other important factors are the amount of water used for irrigation, and the degree of intensive irrigation. The number of medium-to-large-scale power plants and reservoirs created for irrigation in the Yarlung Tsangpo watershed suggest the beginning of a breakdown of the river's ecological integrity. This could manifest itself in a number of ways. The course and condition of the river beds may change, becoming less supportive to aquatic wildlife to affect the biodiversity of fish and aquatic organisms in the river. Sediment transportation may be reduced, affecting downstream agriculture. Water transfers downstream from irrigated areas may contain higher levels of salts and nitrate contamination from chemical fertilisers. Over time, the river may become like the majority of rivers in the developed world today, less of a natural and wild feature supporting biodiversity and flood plain vitality, and more of a stagnant water body simply carrying water from one utilisation point to another.

This is additionally worrying given the changing climatic pattern in the Yarlung Tsangpo watershed. In Western Tibet, near the source of the river, decreasing precipitation has caused the county seat in Dongpa (Ch. Zhongba) County to be relocated. According to Yang Yong — a geologist working in the area — there is the possibility of the Yarlung Tsangpo becoming a seasonal river in its upper reaches. He attributes this to global warming causing glacier reduction and falling rates of precipitation in what is already the most arid part of the region (*Xinhua*, 17 September 1998). If the sources of the Yarlung Tsangpo dry up, and the trend of falling precipitation rates in south-central Tibet continue, the impact of major diversions on the river will be greatly increased.

Tibet's mighty Drichu becomes the Yangtze River as it flows into China

Saline Soil From Irrigation

Large-scale irrigation projects are known to be notoriously wasteful and inefficient in their water use. China's record of efficiency in this respect is far from adequate. According to Dong (1990), inefficiency in agricultural irrigation in China results in the use of an estimated 66 per cent more water to produce the same amount of wheat as in an average developed country. China's irrigation projects, have a long-standing reputation for wasting water and causing erosion and salinisation — especially in arid and semi-arid regions.

About one-sixth of China's irrigated cropland suffers from salinisation. By 1990, 50.4 per cent of the cropland of the North China Plain had reached this degraded condition (Edmonds 1994). In 1991, salt-affected areas in Northwest China were estimated at three million hectares (Umali 1993).

Salinisation is the accumulation of highly soluble sodium, magnesium and potassium salts in the soil. This process is greatly accelerated by the excessive and inefficient use of irrigation waters. All waters contain some dissolved salts and irrigation facilities such as reservoirs and extensive canals expose water to unnaturally high levels of evaporation. When water evaporates the dissolved salts are left behind. Reservoir and canal waters carry slightly higher levels of dissolved salts as a result. Water used for irrigation is returned to the atmosphere through transpiration from plants and evaporation from the soil surface. The amount of salt taken up by plants is negligible and this leads to accumulation of salts in soils (Umali 1993).

In arid and semi-arid areas of Tibet this problem is likely to be compounded by the already naturally high levels of salts in the soil. Additionally, the more arid a region is the more irrigation water is likely to be applied and correspondingly less rainfall is available to leach away some of the accumulated salts. Some farmers are aware of salt accumulation in their soils and attempt to wash these out from the root zone by applying extra water between crops. This tends to elevate the water table, which may already be rising due to irrigation. When the water table reaches within two metres from the surface, groundwater is drawn up to the surface by capillary action. This saline groundwater sits on the soil surface, evaporating under the sun and leaving behind a deadly crust of salts. Once soil has reached this condition it is extremely difficult to rehabilitate (Umali 1993).

Saline soil affects the ability of crops to utilise water and make biochemical adjustments necessary to their survival. Therefore it can greatly reduce yields and in extreme cases renders land uncultivable. On the Sarda-Sahayak canal irrigation project, in the Indian state of Uttar Pradesh, it was found that farms with salt-affected land were yielding 41-56 per cent less than non-degraded land in the area. Consequently net incomes were reduced by 82-97 per cent. At the Menemem irrigation and drainage project in Izmir, Turkey, average incomes on salt-affected paddy lands were reduced to 35 per cent of the average earned from unaffected lands (Umali 1993).

The disposal of saline water into rivers can have adverse downstream impacts. This will compound problems for downstream irrigation, municipal and industrial users and can also affect wildlife (Umali 1993).

As the Yarlung Tsangpo watershed is arid to semi-arid, with unreliable precipitation and high ambient salt levels in the soil, irrigation-induced salinity is a serious threat to the sustainability of the new agricultural programme being implemented by China. Further, if salinity does occur on a large scale, as it already has in many parts of China, the Yarlung Tsangpo will be exporting salinated water to the densely populated downstream environments.

MANLHA WATER PROJECT

Just off the road to Lhasa via Yamdrok Tso, 20 km east of Gyangtse, is a huge construction site. This project, the largest of the "62 Aid Projects", involving an investment of 1 billion yuan (US$125 million), will irrigate 16,000 hectares of land and will have an installed capacity of 20MW (*Xinhua*, 6 October 1998). According to eyewitnesses, in 1997 a huge town had sprung up around the site to house Chinese workers. This had also spurred a wave of urban growth on the eastern side of Gyangtse town, a region which used to be known for retaining its Tibetan character (ICT 24 July 1997).

The Yarlung Tsangpo enters a canyon that has been recently recognised as the longest and deepest canyon in the world.

The dam for Manlha Water Control Works is the largest currently under construction and the largest ever built in Central Tibet. Built on the Nyangchu, a major tributary of the Yarlung Tsangpo, it has already displaced the inhabitants of six villages including its namesake, Manlha (Tenzin 1998). There may be further displacement to make way for the reservoir when it is filled. The dam wall is reported to be complete and stands at 75.3 metres tall and 287 metres wide. The reservoir will hold an estimated 157 million cubic metres of water. Construction of the power station and water tunnels should be finished in 2000 (*Xinhua*, 6 October 1998). A Manlha villager Gedhun Tenzin now in exile recalls:

> After some time, the Chinese told six villages north of the site ... that they had three years to evacuate the place ... During that time the Chinese issued a form for people to complete. The Tibetans had no idea what the form stated (as it was in Chinese) and they were just told to sign it ... the form said that the public had been asked to move from this site and that they had signed in agreement. The land they were given to relocate to is totally flat and has no water supply...people downstream are worried the dam will not be operated properly and they will get flooded by excessive releases of water...local people don't see any benefit from such projects (Tenzin 1998).

A recurring complaint voiced by exiled Tibetans is that small hydropower projects around the area are not benefiting local people. Farmers complain of having their land suddenly inundated by large and unexpected releases of water. Concerning the number of small projects in Lhundrub county, north of Lhasa, one interviewee said:

> There are many small dams around there, but they are useless for the common people; they don't provide any benefit. All the benefit is taken by the government offices. There is a shortage of water in Tibet because they have changed the courses of many rivers, a lot of farmers are not getting water.

This was the disturbing theme of many interviews, especially with people from Amdo where dams are generally larger in scale:

> My family were farmers in the area and when they released the water our fields were washed away. We only got a little electricity from the dam. Some people have been washed away when they release water because they do not give any warning and people working by the river get washed away. Many children have died because of these accidents.

Since the late 1970s, extensive waterworks have been built on the Nyangchu. Prior to the Manlha water project, 55 irrigation ditches totalling 399 km, eight small, and medium-sized reservoirs, 39 ponds and two medium scale pumped storage power plants were built up to 1992 (Xiao 1992). All of this development is on a 90 km river in an area with only 400 mm average annual rainfall. With the implementation of Manlha it appears that the Nyangchu will be utilised to its maximum potential. Its course has been changed and most of the river is diverted into a series of canals. The benefits from this are highly dubious. More land is being irrigated and a more diverse range of crops are being cultivated. However, the sustainability of these practises and the benefits for local Tibetans are questionable.

Plans for The Great Bend of Yarlung Tsangpo

At Mt. Namchakbarwa (7,756 metres) near the Tibetan village of Jodong in Southern Tibet, the Yarlung Tsangpo enters a canyon that has been recently recognised as the longest and deepest canyon in the world (Ciu Bian in *Beijing Review,* 30 March - 5 April 1998). The Yarlung Tsangpo Gorge is eight times as steep and three times as large as the Colorado in the Grand Canyon (McRae 1999). The river descends over 3,000 metres in approximately 200 km (Alford 1992) and this constitutes one of the greatest hydropower potentials anywhere in the world. Where the river emerges from the canyon it enters India's northeastern state, Arunachal Pradesh.

At a July 1986 conference in Alaska, in which projects under the Global Infrastructure Fund (GIF) were discussed, the "Himalayan Hydropower Project" was short-listed. This envisaged a series of 11 dams around the "Brahmaputra loop" and included a tunnel through the mountains bringing water to a powerhouse projected as having a capacity of 48,000 Megawatt. The overall capacity of the "loop" was speculated to be 70,000 Megawatt (Verghese 1990). It is unclear what has happened to this ambitious plan; the GIF certainly no longer publicises it. However, Chinese engineers may be pursuing the idea of a single mega power station with an installed capacity of around 40,000 Megawatt. By comparison the largest power station in operation today is Itaipú in Brazil, with a total installed capacity of 12,600 Megawatt. Three Gorges Dam, currently under construction on the Yangtze River, will have a capacity of 18,200 Megawatt. It would become the world's biggest dam.

An increasing amount of publicity about the dam proposal, and about the Yarlung Tsangpo Gorge in general, indicates that the plan may not be entirely shelved. In September 1997, *AFP* in Beijing reported that "Three experts propose construction of giant dam in Tibet". In this short report quoting an article in a Chinese newspaper, the *Guangming Daily,* it was stated: "After a long experience of exploration on the site, we believe that the project could begin to be included in the agenda of the concerned department." Electricity produced was claimed to be available for export to Bangladesh, Burma and India, (a feature of the GIF plans) and "the diverted water could irrigate the northwestern deserts of the country". Since then the project has been mentioned in news briefs in the *China Daily Business Weekly* (21 September 1997) and the *International Water Power & Dam Construction Monthly* (November 1997).

This project has also been associated with plans to divert water from the Yarlung Tsangpo to the northwestern deserts of China using so-called "Peaceful Nuclear Explosions" (PNEs) to drive an underground tunnel through the mountains (Horgan 1996). China signed the Comprehensive Nuclear Test Ban Treaty in 1996, which disallows PNEs. Further, there are serious doubts as to whether this is even possible.

On January 7, 1998 ZDF television reported on its programme "Die Welt" that indeed a large dam twice as big as Three Gorges was proposed on the Yarlung Tsangpo and interviewed the Chief Planner, Professor Chen Chuanyu. Chen described the plan to drive a 15 km (9.3 miles) long tunnel through the Himalayas to divert the water before the bend and direct it to the end of the bend. This would shorten the distance of the roughly 3,000 metres altitude drop from 200 km to just 15 km. The hydropower potential was given as 40,000 Megawatt. He further describes using the power to pump water to Northwest China over 800 km (497 miles) away.

No more details have been forthcoming since the ZDF television piece. However, throughout 1998 the Chinese launched expeditions, rafting trips and other exploratory forays into the gorge. They have been discussing the expansion of tourism in the area and an American kayaker, Doug Gordon died in October 1998 in an expedition down previously unexplored parts of the gorge (McRae 1999). These trends would suggest an opening up of the area, which

Yarlung Tsangpo bend at Drachu in Southern Tibet

could lead to the development of the big Yarlung Tsangpo dam becoming more feasible.

The Yarlung Tsangpo, before it emerges from the great canyon onto the Indian plain, constitutes 33 per cent of the total flow of the Brahmaputra, based on mean annual flow (Alford 1992). It may constitute a larger proportion of stable flow from glacial sources. The implications of a huge storage dam on the Yarlung Tsangpo for India and Bangladesh would be far reaching. These countries would be at the mercy of China for adequate releases of water during the dry season, and for protection from flooding during the rainy season. A massive diversion of this water to China's northwest would be even more devastating. Nutrient-rich sediments that enrich the soils of India and Bangladesh would be held back in the reservoir. The river's delta will become deprived of silts; thousands of fish species which rely on the delta for breeding and raising young will be affected, as well as the maintenance of the delta itself.

Protest against the plant at Yamdrok Tso has been strident from both within, and outside, Tibet. The late Panchen Lama protested strongly and construction was stopped for a while in the mid-eighties. Shortly after his death in 1989 work was resumed.

The reservoir for such a huge dam could stretch hundreds of kilometres up the Yarlung Tsangpo well into the Kongpo region. This would inundate vast areas of virgin forest within the canyon and beyond. And as much of the flora and fauna within the canyon is undocumented, rare species of flora and fauna which have yet to be scientifically studied could be lost. It is said to be home for more than 60 per cent of the biological resources on the Tibetan Plateau (*China Daily* 1998b).

Although the population in the canyon is small, the people that do live there would suffer great hardship in being forced from their ancestral lands. Tibetans in Tibet would not benefit from the power produced as it is targeted for export to earn foreign currency. The water diversion scheme is likely to be a highly inefficient and wasteful exercise with billions of cubic meters of water being lost to evaporation in the 800 km-long canals. If these plans are implemented, it would mean the grave loss of a world heritage. The Yarlung Tsangpo canyon is a unique and magnificent natural phenomenon with diverse plant and animal life which should be considered as an UNESCO World Heritage Site or similar preserved site of international significance.

Water Pollution

According to the 1996 'TAR' environment report published in the *Tibet Daily* in June 1997, the trend in the Kyichu (Lhasa River) basin is towards increased pollution. The report stated that a total of 41.9 million tons of waste liquid was discharged in 1996, 25.4 million tons was from industrial sources. Pollutants included cyanide, arsenic, sulphides and nitrates. The Toelung River, a small tributary of the Kyichu was reported to be lightly polluted with arsenic and fluorine. Despite this, water quality was said to be generally good (*Tibet Daily*, 27 June 1997). Increasing pollution from industrial, domestic and agricultural sources are a major concern considering the predicted increases in industrial and agricultural activities in future years. With increasing use of chemical fertilisers throughout the Yarlung Tsangpo watershed, prospects for the maintenance of the river hitherto clean waters are not good. This should be of major concern to all downstream users.

Flood Deaths

At a time when nearly half the deaths from nature are caused by floods, the summer of 1998 saw severe flooding in the Yarlung Tsangpo watershed, all over Tibet. At least 53 people were killed in heavy flooding across 40 counties of the 'TAR'. Water levels were apparently at a record high level in the Yarlung Tsangpo and Kyichu Rivers. It was reported that at least 400 yaks and sheep were killed and that 80,000 people were affected by the flooding. Tourists returning from Tibet at the time said roads between Lhasa, Gyangtse and Shigatse were impassable. Boulders and rocks were strewn around the valley floors where flash floods had washed them down from mountainsides (TIN September 1998). The causes of the extreme flooding are difficult to assess, and were probably the result of a mixture of factors.

YAMDROK TSO

Yamdrok Tso (Yamdrok Lake) is situated 100 km south-west of Lhasa at an elevation of 4,441 metres. It has a catchment area of 6,100 sq. km and a surface area of 678 sq. km. The lake is almost a closed system with only a small tributary of the Yarlung Tsangpo River flowing out from it. Inflow is from precipitation and snow melt from surrounding mountains.

The lake, a resting place for many migrating birds crossing the Tibetan Plateau and then the Himalayas, is also a habitat for many native species including the endangered black-necked crane. In addition it is one of Tibet's four most sacred lakes and the famous Samding monastery is situated on its shores. The Tibetans regard it as a "life power lake" and the resting place of the spirit of the Tibetan nation. A legend holds that if Yamdrok Tso should dry up then the whole population of Tibet will meet their death (*Free Tibet Campaign*, 1996).

A 90 Megawatt pumped-storage hydropower plant has been constructed; it began trial operations in 1997 and was officially reported to be fully operational in September 1998 (*Xinhua* , 19 September 1998).

Tibet's extraordinary topography has enabled the designers to use Yamdrok Tso as a reservoir to generate hydroelectricity without having to build a dam. Instead, six km-long tunnels have been bored through the sides of the lake to a powerhouse situated next to the Yarlung Tsangpo River 850 metres below. Elsewhere in the world the theory behind pumped-storage is primarily that the reservoir can be replenished by pumping water back. This is usually done by building two reservoirs; one from which water is drained to create electricity and another to catch that water, store it and pump it back up to the initial reservoir. The economics of this are usually based on the extreme differences in demand and price of electricity between peak and off-peak hours. Therefore, the station is generating electricity during peak hours and consuming power for pumping water back during off-peak hours when there is a surplus of cheap power.

On the face of it, Yamdrok Tso would appear to be a reasonably low-impact station for producing power and making more efficient use of the grid. However, there are two main design inefficiencies to be explored — in addition to the social and cultural concerns of Tibetans over the use of a sacred lake in this fashion.

First, there is no reservoir to catch the water pumped out of Yamdrok Tso. The water from the lake drains into the Yarlung Tsangpo River and when water is pumped back, it is Yarlung Tsangpo water that is used. The lake's water, which is oligotrophic (high in minerals and low in nitrates), is very different to that of the river's and the mixing of the two could have adverse ecological impacts. The pH in the lake is 9.11 while in the river it is 8.13, indicating that the river is slightly more acid than the lake. The total mineralisation in the lake is 1941 mg per litre as compared to only 174 mg per litre in the river. The nitrate concentration in the Yarlung Tsangpo in 1983-84 was found to be 0.65 mg per litre, which may have increased since and may increase further given the rising population upstream and increasing intensification of agriculture. In the lake, the nitrate concentration is only 0.16mg per litre. The replenishing of Yamdrok Tso water with Yarlung Tsangpo water could increase acidity and nitrate levels.

The lake, which has been a closed system for centuries, will begin to change in its basic properties. The aquatic organisms in the lake have adapted to the unique conditions over millennia. In a very short time that ecosystem, which has never been properly studied, will alter radically (Stockman and Seibert 1997).

A second contention with this project is that the installed capacity of the plant (90 Megawatt) is the largest on the grid. This is very unusual in the light of pumped-storage requiring base load stations to provide off-peak power for return pumping. The installed capacity of the Lhasa grid is increasing with new stations coming on line in the near future.

Mekong is currently the focus of a massive international development plan involving China, Thailand, Laos, Vietnam and Cambodia. Despite the fact that 1,000 km of the river's 4,500 km total length runs through Central Tibet and Amdo, only the downstream Yunnan Province is represented at these negotiations.

Nevertheless, on 19 September, 1998 *Xinhua* news agency reported that the addition of Yamdrok Tso "trebled the capacity of the Lhasa grid". This implies that the rest of the Lhasa grid has only 45 Megawatt installed capacity. The addition of stations forecast to go on line in the near future, such as Manlha and others, would still not raise the rest of the grid's capacity to the equivalent of Yamdrok Tso. The energy needed to pump water back up to Yamdrok Tso is equivalent or greater than that which it produces, so the station cannot produce any net gain of power unless it does not pump back equivalent quantities of water used (Stockman and Seibert 1997). This indicates one of two things. Either the authorities do not plan to return water to the lake for a long time, if at all, or the power capacity of Yamdrok Tso is far above the current demand. If the latter is the case, they may utilise less of the plant's potential power and therefore require less electricity to pump back water but still not gain any net production of power.

The utility of such a large and expensive plant is thus called into question. If it is to be used as a pumped-storage plant, it appears to provide no gain for the Lhasa grid, which the plant is supposed to service. But if not the lake will be drained to provide a net gain of power. This will cause a water level drop of between six centimetres to 60 centimetres annually, depending on the rate of utilisation (Stockman and Seibert 1997). This too would have a devastating effect on the lake, reducing the area and quality of shallows around the edges which are necessary for the nesting of waterfowl. Shrinking the lake area could also increase salinity, which may affect wildlife adversely.

The Yamdrok Tso station appears to have been built with either an expectation of a huge increase in power demand and capacity installation in the Lhasa area, or with no intention of using it as a pumped-storage facility but instead as a base load station. Either way, it seems to be a huge and inappropriate investment in Lhasa's potential industrial development and a no-win situation for ecological maintenance of the lake. Large quantities of earth have been moved, a sacred feature of the Tibetan landscape has been defiled and the economics of the project do not appear to make any sense.

Protest against the plant at Yamdrok Tso has been strident from both within, and outside, Tibet. The late Panchen Lama protested strongly and construction was stopped for a while in the mid-eighties. Shortly after his death in 1989 work was resumed. After much lobbying from The International Committee of Lawyers for Tibet and the Free Tibet Campaign and others, the International Union for the Conservation of Nature (IUCN) passed a resolution at its World Conservation Congress in 1996 which called upon China to "strengthen their effort of co-operation with the international community in exchange of information, including that related to the local environment at Yamdrok Tso... consider establishing a nature reserve at Yamdrok Tso ...[and] ...calls upon the IUCN commissions to work with China in identifying areas of collaboration on maintaining the ecological health of Yamdrok Tso" (IUCN 1996). So far little progress has been made between the IUCN and the Chinese government. Meanwhile, the waters of Yamdrok Tso are draining into the Yarlung Tsangpo River.

Over-Fishing

The Chinese have described Yamdrok Tso as the "Fish Barn of Tibet". In 1960 the reported catch was 255,000 kg. In 1994 it was 1.04 million kg. A fish-powder factory was set up in Ngari in 1993 with an annual output of 70 tons (Zhang 1997). Restrictions have also been placed on catches in the Lhasa River, in which fish over 250 grams can apparently no longer be caught due to previous over-fishing. Carp has been introduced from China and is generally bred in ponds in Lhasa (Zhang 1997). Concerns have been expressed by Tibetans, and more recently by China, about the sustainability of the catch and practises such as the use of explosives and electric fishing have recently been banned.

MEKONG AND SALWEEN WATERSHEDS

The Mekong has its sources in Amdo in a remote part of the Thangla Mountains. The Salween has its sources around the town of Nagchu in the northern part of the 'TAR'. The Salween travels east until it nears the eastern town of Chamdo where it starts to head south towards Khawakarpo Mountains to flow into the Tibetan town of Tseka, running nearly parallel with the Mekong. The two rivers continue this south, southeast direction into Yunnan Province and then separate their courses, the Gyalmo Ngulchu running into Burma to become the Salween and the Zachu later joined by Ngomchu entering Laos to become the Mekong.

The Mekong is currently the focus of a massive international development plan involving China, Thailand, Laos, Vietnam and Cambodia. Despite the fact that 1,000 km of the river's 4,500 km total length runs through Central Tibet and Amdo, only the downstream Yunnan Province is represented at these negotiations. This ignores the role of the Tibetan Plateau in the hydrology of the river and enables China to have the Mekong River Commission overlook the developments it carries out on its upper reaches. In his paper on the Upper Mekong Gabriel Lafitte argues that the Mekong River Commission should pay heed to the Tibetan people's preference for conservation of the upper-reaches of the Mekong i.e. to convert the Tibetan Plateau as a Zone of Peace as expressed in His Holiness The Dalai Lama's Five Point Peace Plan for Tibet in 1987 (see Appendix 4)..

A 34 metres high dam at Chalong in Nagchu Prefecture is the largest dam on the Salween in Tibet according to our information. The Chamdo-Jinhe Power Station on the Mekong was originally completed in the 1970s. The dam was recently upgraded as part of the "62 Aid Projects" with new equipment to increase efficiency and new power lines running to the Yulong Copper Mine. The next stage in the development of the Chamdo-Jinhe Power Station is to install a 60,000 kW generation set.

There is no available information on the size of this dam but the future installed capacity of 60,000 kW suggests it is large. In the Chinese propaganda magazine *China's Tibet* Vol.7 No.2, Li Mingsen reports that, "efforts are being made to construct more power plants for the formation of a power grid centred around the Mekong in the 21st century". There are no details of these plans as yet, but it is known from proposed mining activity in the area that the focus of this

The world's muddiest river cradles China's civilisation

The Machu as it is known in Tibetan, or Yellow River is often regarded in its lower reaches as the cradle of Chinese civilisation. The world's sixth longest river, it flows 5,464 km from its source in the Bayanhar Mountains in Amdo region of Tibet to finally drain into the Yellow Sea. It has a drainage area of 745,000 sq. km (77,249 sq. km are within Tibet). From its source, the river flows east, traversing Kyaring and Ngoring Lakes, then turning westwards to cross the Amnye Machen Ranges, and flows northwards from Rabgya, descending in a series of rapids to Lanzhou. From here it flows through Ningxia, Mongolia, Shanxi, Henan and Shandong Provinces of China. The river has an average flow of 1,530 cubic metre per second, an average annual volume of 48.2 cubic km, and an average precipitation of 470 mm (mostly snow melt from the Tibetan Plateau). As affirmed by its name, the Yellow River is the world's muddiest river carrying an annual silt load of 1.52 billion tons (Dorje 1996).

development will be mining, which has its own adverse impact for the Mekong.

Toxic Metals In Rivers

Mining poses a significant pollution threat to water bodies but the severity depends upon the degree of care taken to mitigate such impacts. The main problem is the threat posed by the careless disposal of tailings which contain heavy metals, ores and leaching agents. Waste materials from mining are often piled up outside the mine and can contain pyrite and sulphide minerals which, when exposed to the atmosphere and water, may produce sulphuric acid. Sulphuric acid in the tailings can leach out other heavy metals left behind in the process. These can pass into the water table or become washed into water bodies during storms.

In addition to sulphuric acid, these solutions may contain heavy metals such as silver, cadmium, cobalt, copper, mercury, manganese, molybdenum, nickel, lead, zinc, arsenic, antimony, and selenium. Some of these are highly toxic to humans and wildlife alike. Improper storage of mine tailings and ineffective containment of contaminated waters can lead to these pollutants entering water bodies and decimating life in rivers for hundreds of miles. Dilution depends on the quantity and quality of water supply and concentration of the pollutants (US EPA 1994).

China's record for implementing pollution control at mines, especially in Tibet, is lax and has led to severe pollution of water bodies. At the International Symposium on the 'Qinghai Tibet Plateau' [Tibetan Plateau] in Xining, 24 July 1998, two Chinese scientists from the Commission for Integrated Survey of Natural Resources reported of mining operations in Amdo:

> There are few measures taken to prevent pollution, with the result that wastes pour into the rivers, endangering livestock, contaminating lakes downstream. Existing laws regulating mineral resource extraction are not implemented, so there is no planned exploitation leading to extensive rather than intensive mining. This kind of extraction is focused on the quick extraction of the most readily accessed and highly concentrated portion of the deposit, often rendering the rest uneconomic, even despoiled (Song and Yao 1998).

Amdo has experienced intensive industrialisation and population transfer since the Chinese invasion. A former pastoral heartland of Tibet, it has been transformed into a landscape of factories, dams, big cities, large mechanised farms, *laogais* (forced labour camps), mining operations and oil wells. Towns have sprung up in places where only nomads once camped, and the new population is predominantly Chinese.

This is often the typical procedure at mines in Tibet, and it constitutes a serious waste of resources and an equally serious risk to the health of people and wildlife, both locally and downstream.

Clear-Cutting In Eastern Tibet

Forest erosion on the Tibetan Plateau has a history of at least 5,000 years (Winkler 1999). A thousand years ago, juniper forests existed in the Lhasa valley but they have largely disappeared due to natural and human factors (Miehe 1998).

This would suggest that there would have been a steady increase in the silt load of Tibet's rivers, particularly the Yarlung Tsangpo, over this period. It is unclear how quickly the landscape may have changed during that period. However, the barren state of the upper reaches of the Yarlung Tsangpo is a contributing factor to the river's extraordinarily high silt load.

The Chamdo area of Kham province, which includes significant portions of the Mekong and Salween watersheds, was once home to extensive cold-temperate forests, largely of juniper, pines and spruce. It is relevant to state that in the Chamdo area logging practises have been unsustainable and this may pose a threat to the hydrology of these vital Asian rivers.

Clear-cutting has been the norm in these areas and associated soil erosion correspondingly high. Countries downstream planning hydro-development on the Mekong or Salween should be aware of the threat of increasing siltation.

On top of this the dam brought over 100,000 Chinese workers to Amdo, many of whom lived there, thereby increasing pressure on the dwindling natural resources.

Yellow River Watershed

The headwaters of the great Yellow River — known as Machu to the Tibetans and Huanghe to the Chinese — lies entirely within the Amdo region of Tibet. From Amdo the river flows into the arid North China Plain. Heavy utilisation is creating an emerging water shortage in North China and developments along the Yellow River may be to blame.

The Yellow River has run dry each year with the dry period becoming progressively longer; in 1996 it was dry for 133 days and in 1997, a year exacerbated by drought, it failed to reach the sea for 226 days and its 1998 annual dry period was 137 days (SEPA 1999; Brown 1998). The amount of water flowing down the Yellow River in Amdo at present is 23 per cent less than that in the 1970s, which is one of the main factors causing drying up of the river in its lower reaches (*China Daily* 1999a). For long stretches it did not even reach Shandong Province, the area growing one-fifth of China's corn and one-seventh of its wheat, depends on the Yellow River for half of its irrigation water (Brown 1998).

Unconstrained development in Amdo on the upper reaches of the Yellow River is exacerbating the situation in China as well as causing widespread environmental degradation in Amdo. The deteriorating environment and lack of rain are reported by *Xinhua* to have caused more than 1,000 lakes to dry up in a region of Amdo around the Yellow River's source (*Xinhua*, 7 April 1999). Amdo has experienced intensive industrialisation and population transfer since the Chinese invasion. A former pastoral heartland of Tibet, it has been transformed into a landscape of factories, dams, big cities, large mechanised farms, *laogais* (forced labour camps), mining operations and oil wells. Towns have sprung up in places where only nomads once camped, and the new population is predominantly Chinese.

While many areas retain the designation of "Tibet Autonomous County" the reality is that the burgeoning Chinese population dominate most counties and Tibetans have little or no say in "the development plans".

The focus of industrial development in Amdo (Ch.Qinghai) is on mineral extraction and processing. Amdo boasts China's biggest potash fertiliser plant, the biggest asbestos production base, and the second biggest lead and zinc mine.

The impact of this industrial development came to light in 1996 when authorities announced the desperate state of the Huangshi River valley, a tributary of the Yellow River. The area contains 60 per cent of Amdo's population, industrial and agricultural output on only 2.2 per cent of the province's total landmass. The report stated that:

> **hundreds of thousands of litres of polluted water have been poured into the river each day, untreated. Dozens of ferrosilicon, iron, steel, aluminium and silicon carbide plants are releasing thick smoke every day. Experts say 76 per cent of the 16,000 sq. km valley suffers soil erosion and water loss. An estimated 19 million tons of soil is washed into the river...(FBIS 27 March 1996).**

This is an example of how industrial development in Tibet has been carried out in an uncontrolled and careless fashion resulting in severe environmental degradation. The rivers are choked with eroded soil and industrial pollutants. They are also being destroyed by massive dams and diversions.

In order to power the industrial drive in Amdo, an extensive network of major hydroelectric power stations has been built, some of which are amongst the largest in China. Vast areas of pastoral and agricultural land have been inundated by reservoirs. Nomads have been disenfranchised by the fragmentation of their rangelands. The main focus of this development in the coming years will be the

"Upper Yellow River Cascade". This consists of 15 major dams which are projected to generate 13,462MW. Five of these were supposedly completed in 1992 and two more were under construction (Cheng 1994). It would appear that the two major dams discussed below are part of this scheme, as well as many of those under construction or planned (see table 3).

The two biggest projects operating on the Upper Machu (Yellow River) in Amdo — and some of the abuses reported by Tibetans that have resulted from the construction and operation of these plants — are discussed here. The environmental impact of these dams is far-reaching. In general, these huge projects are turning the Machu into a series of semi-stagnant water bodies. The release of water into the river is largely dependent on the demand for electricity generation and follows no natural pattern. The river's ecosystem is breaking down, causing a sharp drop in biodiversity. Conflicting needs along the basin — between electricity generation, irrigation and water supply for industrial and domestic use in cities — are pushing the Yellow River to crisis point.

Tsanga Gag

Tsanga Gag or Tsanga Dam (Ch. Longyangxia) is located to the south of the Tso Ngonpo in Tsolho (Ch. Hainan) County between Chabcha (Ch. Gonghe) and Trika (Ch. Guide) on the Machu (Yellow River) and was completed in the late 1980s and stands a staggering 178 metres high. This makes it the largest dam in Tibet and the second biggest in China after Ertan in Sichuan, which will remain the biggest until the Three Gorges project is complete. Tsanga Gag reservoir can store the entire flow of the Machu for three whole months (Tsering 1998). This creates a reservoir covering a surface area of 393 sq. km (Wang 1984).

The powerhouse has an installed capacity of 1280 Megawatt producing 5.8 billion kWh annually. It took 30,000 Chinese workers to construct the dam which cost 1.769 billion yuan (US$221.12 million). Around 10,000 people who were displaced from prime agricultural land to make way for the reservoir were allocated land in formerly pastoral areas which they had to convert to farmland. They were supported by the government for two years after which they had to achieve self sufficiency (Tsering 1998). On top of this the dam brought over 100,000 Chinese workers to Amdo, many of whom stayed there, thereby increasing pressure on the dwindling natural resources (ICT 1992).

Tibetans have seen little benefit from this project as much of the power goes to military bases and cities dominated by Chinese inhabitants and state-owned industries.

The provision of power spawns development that has, in turn, consumed ever-increasing quantities of Tibetan land and resources, caused pollution and excluded Tibetans from the economy. The Longyang Gorge where the dam is located is 1,688 km from the source of the Yellow River. It is the first in a series of 15 dams to be located downstream of Longyang, between Longyang and Qingtong. Upstream from Longyang, which is all Tibetan territory, there are future plans for a chain of 12 more power stations between the source and Longyang. These are expected to be installed with a total of 6,330 Megawatt capacity (Bian 1987).

> *On 27 August 1993 the Gouhou dam burst in Tsolho (Ch. Hainan) Tibetan Autonomous Prefecture in Amdo unleashing cascades of water that wiped out several villages and killed at least 223 people. Thousands were injured and many were missing after the dam broke. The economic losses were estimated at more than 100 million yuan (US$17 million). This disaster has severely affected the lives of nomadic herders and farmers on the arid and high plateau.*
>
> International Herald Tribune, *30 August 1993*

Ngogyai Gag

Ngogyai Gag or Ngogyai dam (Ch. Lijiaxia) went into full operation early in 1998 (*International Water Power & Dam Construction*, March 1998). The 165 metres high and 420 metres long dam wall holds back 1.65 billion cubic metres of water and is the third of the 15 plants planned as a cascade between Longyang and Qingtong. It is situated 109 km downstream from Tsanga Gag on the borders of Chentsa Tibetan Autonomous County and Hualong Hui Autonomous County in Amdo.

The reservoir inundated at least 430 hectares of land and involved the relocation of at least 4,012 people. To give an idea of the level of earthworks and construction at such large dams, Ngogyai Gag construction involved 4.5 million cubic metres of rock and earth excavation; 3.25 million cubic metres of concrete placement; 4.8 million cubic metres of earthworks; 144,000 metres of consolidation grouting; 47,000 metres of drilling for curtain grouting; and 10,000 tons of metal works (Huang 1996). More than 20,000 Chinese workers worked at the dam site and many settled permanently afterwards (Tsering 1998).

Tsanga Gag and Ngogyai Gag are the largest dams currently operating in Amdo. According to *Xinhua* in 1992 there were 156 medium and small hydropower stations operating in Amdo with a combined annual output of 236 million kWh.

The damming of the Machu River and its tributaries in Amdo has uprooted tens of thousands of people from their homes and is expected to move thousands more. The loss of agricultural and pastoral land has uprooted Tibetan communities from their traditional economic base. The environmental impacts associated with the economic development accompanying these projects are far reaching. Mining and associated processing industries are the main benefactors of power from these dams as Amdo Province has become a major centre of the metallurgic industries. A lack of regulations has led to severe water and atmospheric pollution in the province while power has facilitated the expansion of major cities, consuming more and more land in a region that used to be occupied by nomads and their temporary camps.

In interviews with recently-exiled Tibetans in Dharamsala in July 1998, refugees from Amdo told of how water was released from dams in the region without warning, posing great dangers to people living downstream. People working in fields by the rivers are drowned in flash floods and houses and farm buildings are often washed away. Many claimed they have never received any compensation for these losses. One man spoke of how his family had to give up farming and become road labourers as their land was so often washed away by these sudden releases from dams that it became unusable.

The worst Yangtze flood of August 1998 in China resulted in an economic loss of US$37.5 billion and death of 3,656 people (DIIR 1999a). At a rally on 28 September 1998, held in Beijing by the Communist Party to declare "victory" over the disastrous summer floods, President Jiang Zemin admitted — in a significant ideological departure — that Communist governments had too often tried to impose their will on nature.

The utilisation of the Machu River and its tributaries in Amdo appears to be taking place at a rate that implies maximum exploitation. There seems to be no consideration of sustainable development, no consideration of the wishes and aspirations of local people, and no consideration of the long-term survival of the river's ecosystem. Tibetans in Amdo express concern for the future viability of such development and equal consternation over the safety of people living around these projects who suffer frequent inundation from rising reservoirs and flash floods associated with dam releases.

The Upper Yangtze Watershed

The source of the Drichu (Yangtze River) lies deep within Amdo in the Thangla Mountains (Ch. Tanggula) and it runs through Tibet for more than 2,000 km of its 6,380 km length. It is the longest river in Tibet and the third longest river in the world after the Amazon and Nile (DIIR 1995). The catchment area of the Yangtze and the regions to its south contain 82 per cent of China's total volume of water flow, but only 36 per cent of its cultivated land (Chen and Edmonds 1989). While the river and its main tributaries, the Yalong Chu and Daduchu, rise from Amdo, the Yalong and Dadu lie east of the main channel and enter Kham (western Sichuan) before joining the Yangtze in the Chengdu Plain.

In Sichuan and beyond the Yangtze is extensively dammed, as are some of its main tributaries such as the Dadu and Yalong. China's biggest dam in operation, the massive World Bank-funded Ertan Dam (240 metres) is located on the Yalongchu just before it meets the Yangtze.

The construction of the projects themselves incurs a large toll on the local environment, involving massive earthworks and road building. Further, it attracts migrant labourers, who become established in new towns with new transport links, and facilitate industrial development and settlement upstream.

In Kham, where forests and wildlife are coming under increasing pressure, dam-building is the next step on the path to increasing environmental destruction. The establishment of a power source in one place attracts new settlements and new industries (such as resource-intensive paper and pulp mills), and upstream areas become the focus of further development.

Among the schemes to build many major dams on the Upper Yangtze and its tributaries there is also a plan to divert water from the upper reaches to supplement the ever-decreasing flows in the Yellow River. This plan envisages taking water from the main stream and the Yalong River from a point on the Tibetan Plateau (Zhang 1989).

Forest Loss and Water Loss

While the development of a network of hydropower projects in the Upper Drichu watershed is supposed to include flood protection facilities, this has been severely frustrated by massive deforestation which increases the impact of flooding greatly. In the summer of 1998, the Yangtze reached record flood levels, yet actual flows were not at a historical high. This was analysed as a sure sign that deforestation activities upstream were causing floods to be more severe, despite lower actual water quantities (see Forestry chapter).

Forested hillsides along the banks of major rivers provide various ecological functions which affect the river. Firstly, forests act as a kind of sponge, absorbing water and releasing it back into the atmosphere through the process of transpiration. Therefore, where there is no forest water will travel on or through the soil without being taken up by the roots of trees. This increases the overland flow of water into the river. Another function is soil protection. An area with no forest will lose a lot of soil during a storm from the kinetic action of the rain falling on the soil, which is then washed into the river. This soil will eventually settle to the riverbed, especially downstream in the flood plain where the river may become wider and slower.

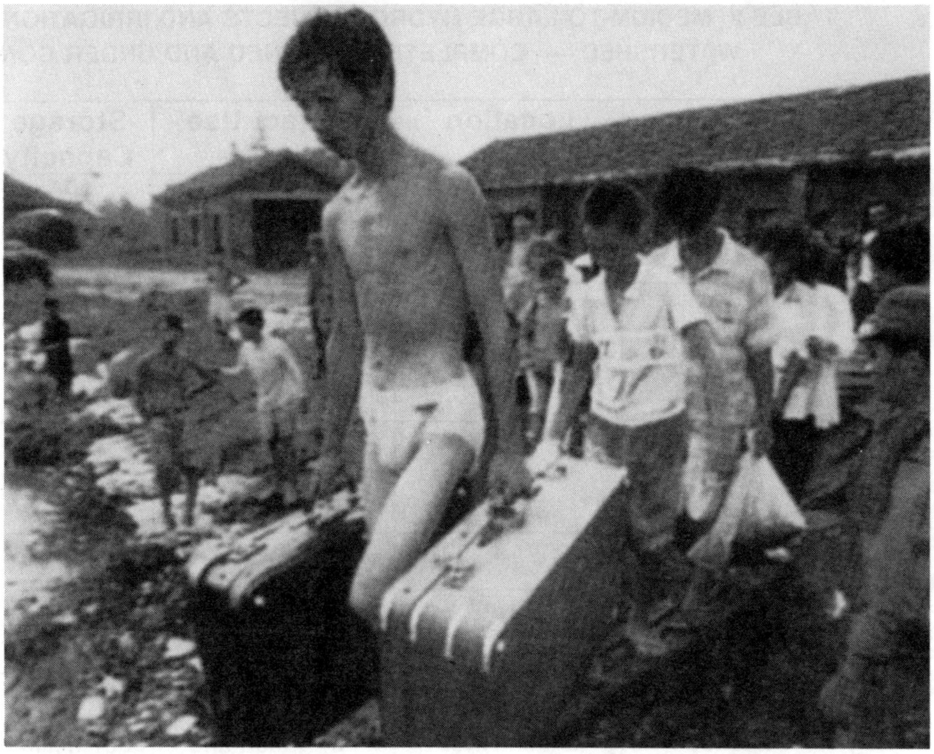

Catastrophic flooding along the Yangtze left 66 million Chinese affected in August 1999

If soil and silt content increases, the riverbed in these low-lying areas will rise as more and more soil settles to the bottom. This may have been the main reason less water caused greater flooding in the Yangtze in 1998. The riverbed is slowly being raised by decades of increasing soil loss into the river. Thus there is actually less room in the main river channel to absorb large flows.

Zhuang Guotai, a member of China's State Environmental Protection Agency, told a Chinese newspaper that for every 70,000 hectares of forest lost, a natural reservoir that can store one million cubic metres of water is also lost (US Embassy in Beijing, August 1998). This gives a vivid insight into the potential flood protection provided by leaving forests intact.

Much of the deforestation in the Yangtze watershed has taken place in Tibetan areas, with little benefit to the local people as most of the wood is trucked out. Only recently are the Chinese authorities beginning to realise the true value of the Tibetan Plateau and its environs in relation to the ecological protection of much of China.

Flood Deaths

The worst Yangtze flood in China of August 1998 resulted in an economic loss of US$37.5 billion and the death of 3,656 people (DIIR 1999a). At a rally on 28 September 1998, held in Beijing by the Communist Party to declare "victory" over the disastrous summer floods, President Jiang Zemin admitted — in a significant ideological departure — that Communist governments had too often tried to impose their will on nature. It was important now, he said, "to understand the law of nature, correctly manage it and learn how to follow it to facilitate our economic development and other social undertakings" (Lawrence 1998).

The International Red Cross on 4 August 1999 said that more than 400 people have been killed and 66 million affected by disastrous summer flooding along the Yangtze river in August 1999 and an international appeal for emergency aid was launched (*Inside China Today* 1999b).

Amdo's Shrinking Lake

Tso Ngonpo (Blue Lake) as it is known to the Tibetans, more familiarly known by its Mongol name, Lake Kokonor,

TABLE 2 MEDIUM-TO-LARGE HYDRO PROJECTS AND IRRIGATION DAMS IN THE YARLUNG TSANGPO WATERSHED — COMPLETED, PLANNED AND UNDER CONSTRUCTION (PARTIAL LIST)

Project Name	Location	Project Use	Storage Capacity	Size of Plant	Construction Status
Yamdrok Tso Pumped - Storage Power Station	Yamdrok Tso	Power and Power Regulation	N/A	90,000 kW	Completed 1997
Manlha Water Works	On the Nyangchu between Nagartse and Gyangtse	Irrigation and Power	157 million cubic metres	20,000 kW	Expected 2000
Chonggye	Near Chonggye Township	Irrigation	11.58 million cubic metres	N/A	Completed 1997
Nyingtri-Payi	Nyingtri, Kongpo	Power	—	84,000 kW	Completed 1995
Wolka (Ch.Oiga)	Chumo Gully - Sangri County, Lhoka	Power	—	20,000 kW	Completed 1998
Drikong	Lhasa River Basin	Irrigation and Power	—	30,000 kW	Planned
Pangduo	Lhasa River Basin	Irrigation and Power	687 million cubic metres	120,000 kW	Planned
Yangjingshi	Lhasa River Basin	Irrigation and Power	81 million cubic metres	4,500 kW	Completed
Pingco	Lhasa River Basin	Power	—	—	Completed
Tago (Tiger Head) Reservoir	Lhasa River Basin -	Irrigation	12 million cubic metres	—	Completed (date unknown)
Changsuo Basin irrigation Project	Chomolungma Reserve	Irrigation	—	—	Proposed 1991
Chongba Tso	Drongpa County - Shigatse	Irrigation	—	N/A	Completed
Chun Sun	Tributary of Nyechu - Panam County	Irrigation	24 million cubic metres	—	Possibly completed
Suo Chang	Trib. of Nye Chu - Panam County	Irrigation	18 million cubic metres	—	Possibly completed
Gyantse Pumped -Storage Power Station	Nyangchu upstream from Manlha	Power and Irrigation	—	1,100 kW	Completed 1979
Kamai Pumped-Storage Power Station	Nyangchu	Power and Irrigation	—	800 kW	Completed 1987

The International Commission on Large Dams, defines "large dams" as those above 15 metres from foundation to crest. Dams of 10-15 metres are defined as "large" if they have a crest length of at least 500 metres, a reservoir capacity of one million cubic metres or more, or maximum flood discharge of at least 2,000 cubic metres per second. "Small-hydro" refers to plants with an installed capacity of 10MW (10,000 KW) or less.

is the largest lake in Tibet. It has a size of 4,460 sq. km and is situated at an elevation of 3,197 metres above sea level (Chang 1987). It has in recent decades been intensively fished, mined for salts and the heavy utilisation of the rivers flowing into it may be causing a decline in the water level. In May 1998, *World Journal* reported that the level of the lake had dropped three metres. It is anticipated that within 30 years the sandy region of the lake will increase from 450 sq. km to 700 sq. km. This is expected to have a major impact on birds nesting in the area and on other wildlife (*World Journal* 14 May 1998).

PRIORITY ACTIONS FOR THE FUTURE

Conservation of watersheds

Much of the development in Tibet described above reveals a pattern focusing mainly on natural resource extraction. Mining and deforestation are the most obvious examples of this; the utilisation of rivers for hydropower and irrigation is another facet of the same focus. The Upper Yellow River is primarily utilised for the generation of large quantities of power that either facilitates natural resource extraction in Amdo or is transmitted out to burgeoning Chinese cities. Major dams on the Upper Yangtze and its tributaries either transmit power east into China or provide power for logging, mining and other associated industries. On the banks of the Upper Mekong and Salween, power is generated for mining and for meat processing. In the Yarlung Tsangpo watershed, dams are mainly used for irrigation, although power is also generated in areas where mining activity or urbanisation is prominent.

Increasing utilisation of the Yarlung Tsangpo watershed poses many dangers for the sustainability of a fragile ecosystem. The Three Rivers Project, with its programme of agricultural intensification, threatens the Yarlung Tsangpo with pollution from fertilisers and fragmentation from multiple dams and diversions. The associated effects on the soils in the valley will also affect the river in the long run because as soil erosion and salinisation increases so does the salt and silt content of the river.

The primary solution for improving the sustainability of water resource utilisation in Tibet — as well as preserving a unique and important watershed ecosystem — is to bring about a fundamental change in the paradigm in which these resources are viewed. The current emphasis in Tibet is on resource extraction. This reduces the value of resources for their long-term ecological function — a function that is similar to many upper riparian environments which provide stable downstream flows of freshwater and sediment.

This does not exclude development in the Tibetan Plateau per se. However, it does exclude development that is primarily focused on over exploitation through resource extraction and commercialisation of agricultural and pastoral production. More importantly, it also excludes development that is primarily planned by a central government operating thousand of kilometres away in Beijing.

Water Conservation

Given the acute shortage of water resources in many industrial regions of China, water conservation, especially upstream on the Tibetan Plateau is vital for the livelihood of millions of people downstream. Zhu Dengquan, Vice-minister of Water Resources of China said, "At current rates, a preliminary tackling of the country's soil and water conservation problem could take as much as 60 to 70 years" (*China Daily* 1999b).

In Tibet irrigation schemes should be planned in consultation and cooperation with local populations and should be scaled down to less ambitious production targets. Local seed varieties that are better adapted to the local environment with less demand for water and artificial fertilisers should be prioritised. Traditional water harvesting techniques should be studied and developed in cooperation with local users. These traditional techniques are often ignored by planners who prefer a top-down centralised know-all approach.

Tibet possesses great potential for the generation of power by micro-hydro, solar and wind power. These small power plants can provide villages with a reliable source of electricity with minimal impact on the environment.

Traditional small-scale techniques of irrigation are bound to be more efficient as the systems are based on the participation of users in all aspects of planning. Conversely, the centralised approach relies on the knowledge of a few "expert" technicians alienating farmers from the process.

These techniques involve smaller-scale dams and diversions that do not interfere with the river's natural course and functions. Preference should be given to methods of rainwater catchment and storage and techniques aimed at minimising water consumption such as drip irrigation should be studied. Crops that are well adapted to local conditions should be planted. In Nepal, for example, indigenous

TABLE 3. LARGE-TO-MEDIUM DAMS COMPLETED UNDER CONSTRUCTION AND PLANNED ON THE YELLOW RIVER AND ITS TRIBUTARIES IN AMDO (PARTIAL LIST)

Project Name	River	District	Dam Size	Storage Capacity	Capacity of Plant	Construction Status
Tsanga Gag (Longyangxia)	Yellow	Chabcha	178 metres high	24.70 billion cubic metres	1280 Megawatt	Completed in 1986
Ngogyai Gag (Lijiaxia)	Yellow	Chentsa	165 m high 458 m crest length	1.65 billion cubic metres	2000 Megawatt	Completed 1997
Gongboxia	Yellow	—	133 m high	550 million cubic metres	1500 Megawatt	Expected completion 2000
Heiquan	Baoku	Datong	124 m high	—	41.5 Megawatt	Expected completion 2000
Gouhou	trib. of Yellow	Chabcha	70 m high	3.1 million cubic metres	—	Completed 1988 Breached Aug. 1993 1,257 deaths
Nina	Yellow	—	45.5 m high	—	200 Megawatt	Expected completion 2004
Laxiwa	Yellow	—	250 m high	1 billion cubic metres	3720 Megawatt	Planned
Jishixia	Yellow	Yazi (Ch. Xunhua)	100 m high	272 million cubic metres	1000 Megawatt	Completed
Dragkhung Nakha (Zhiganglaka)	Yellow	Between Chentsa & Huolong	—	—	192 Megawatt	Planned with AES Corp. USA
Kangyang	Yellow	Chentsa	—	—	—	Planned
Xionghou	Yellow	Xionghou	—	—		Completed 1995
Qushi'an	Confluence of Bachu and Yellow	30 km west of Gepasumdo (Ch.Tongde)	—	—	—	Completed late 1980s
Shawo Gag (Amixia)	Yellow	Downstream from Lijiaxia near Yazi Dzong	—	—	—	Under construction
Dananchuan	Dananchuan	Near Dianzhong City	46.5 m high 460 m length of crest	13.10 million cubic metres	—	Completed 1974
Dashitan	Luobagou	Drotsang (Ch. Ledu)	43 m high/ 396.5 m	4.24 million cubic metres	—	Completed 1978
Yunguchuang	Yunguchuan	Dianzhong	43 m high / 393 m	7.65 (106m)	—	Completed 1978
Golmud	Golmud	Golmud	48 m high/ 60.4 m	24 (106m)	32 Megawatt	Completed 1979

irrigation still accounts for three-quarters of irrigated land. (McCully 1996). India has a long tradition of highly-efficient water management which is currently being rediscovered and promoted, due to the failure of many modern centralised techniques. Some of these good and effective practises could be studied and adapted for use in Tibet.

Renewable Energy

Tibet possesses great potential for the generation of power by micro-hydro (up to 100 kW per unit), solar and wind power. As discussed above, the maintenance of small hydro plants in Tibet has been lax and a high proportion have fallen into disrepair. These small power plants can provide villages with a reliable source of electricity with minimal impact on the environment so they should be encouraged rather than left to fall into disrepair.

Where micro-hydro is not feasible, solar and wind generation should be considered. A mixture of these techniques should be the focus, rather than relying on any single method, and needs should be calculated on a local scale so that an appropriate solution for each location can be found. The provision of solar powered equipment such as solar ovens and water heaters should be increased so that there is less need for burning wood or manure, which can be put to better use as fertiliser.

Due to its high altitude the Tibetan Plateau has one of the highest solar radiation values in the world at 140-190 Kilocalorie per sq. centimetres per year (Zhao 1992). In the Yarlung Tsangpo valley 70-80 per cent of precipitation occurs at night giving the area an extraordinarily high quantity of sunlight. Lhasa averages 3,400 hours of sunshine annually (Zhao 1992). This potential should be fully utilised before resorting to extensive damming of rivers to provide power.

Preventing Pollution

The threat of pollution is one problem that can be easily assessed and resolved, given the will and co-operation of the Chinese government. Control of tailings and wastes from mines could mitigate many of the impacts on watersheds; sewage treatment and control of wastes can also be improved. However, so far mining in Tibet has been carelessly regulated resulting in unnecessary waste production and inefficient use of resources (Lafitte 1998). Other influences on the hydrological regime of Tibet may be far more difficult to address as they require China to adjust short-term and long-term patterns of economic development.

The Chinese government should enforce existing laws and regulations to ensure the safe and efficient operation of mines. As an area that contains the headwaters of so many of Asia's major rivers, Tibet is the last place on earth where pollution regulations can be relaxed or ignored. Preferably there should be no large scale mining at all in an area in which the highest value should be placed on the ecological function of the upper riparian environment. Surveys should be carried out immediately to discover how much pollution has occurred and to prevent further occurrence.

About 70 per cent of China's wastewater is dumped into rivers with the Yangtze river receiving 41 per cent of the country's sewage. The figure is expected to rise in the future. Fifteen out of China's 27 major rivers are considered to be seriously polluted (Zhu,1990). China planned to increase its spending on controlling pollution from the current 0.8 percent of its GNP to more than one percent at the turn of the century or approximately US $ 17.5 billion (The World Resources Institute 1998).

In urban areas, sewage treatment should be developed immediately and industrial pollutants must not be dumped in rivers. Public education campaigns should focus on informing people how to avoid polluting rivers with household wastes and non-biodegradable garbage such as plastics.

Sustainable Development

Tibet, with its huge variety of natural resources and its unique high altitude situation, demands careful location-specific planning to utilise its resources sustainably. Over exploitation in a fragile mountain environment can lead to long-term ecological consequences.

The assumption that Tibet can be an endless resource for China's economic development should be abandoned. With the use of appropriate technologies, Tibet's resources can be developed in a way that draws upon traditional knowledge of the land and its potential.

International agencies, as well as countries situated downstream from Tibet, should consider targeting any aid to Tibet that encourages in sustainable development and public participation. Continued unsustainable resource-stripping — and its associated deleterious effects on waterways — is of grave concern to the billions of people dependent upon these valuable water resources for their livelihood and for the gift of life itself.

■

CHAPTER THREE

AGRICULTURE

Ancient cultures which have adapted to their natural surroundings can offer special insights on structuring human societies to exist in balance with the environment. For example, Tibetans are uniquely familiar with life on the Himalayan Plateau. This has evolved into a long history of civilisation that took care not to overwhelm and destroy its fragile ecosystem.

His Holiness the 14th Dalai Lama, 1995

AGRICULTURE has traditionally been the foundation of the Tibetan economy. The three major forms of occupation in Tibet are pastoral nomadism (*drokpa*), grain farming (*shingpa*) and semi-nomadism (*sama-drok*). Over 80 per cent of the total population of Tibet is still engaged in primary sector agriculture (TIN 1999a). Farmers are mainly concentrated in valleys where they utilise fertile soil for crop cultivation, while pastoral and semi-nomads are found on plateaus and mountains suitable for raising animals.

Natural rangelands abound in Tibet, accounting for 70 per cent of the total territory supporting an estimated population of 70.2 million domestic animals and about one million pastoral nomads (DIIR 1992). The rangelands are mostly concentrated in the Chang Thang (Northern Plateau) which has long been regarded as one of the best grazing regions in Asia. Cropland accounts for only two per cent while forest accounts for five per cent.

Desert, rocky and permanently barren lands, settlements, lakes and rivers account for the remaining 23 per cent of the total territory (*ibid*).

According to Chinese sources, grasslands in the north-eastern province of Amdo (Ch: Qinghai) account for 96 per cent of the province, while in 'TAR' 56.72 per cent of the region constitutes highland pasture (*Tibetan Bulletin* 1992a). The vast rangelands of Kham produce superior quality grass.

MAJOR OCCUPATIONS

Pastoral Nomad Migration

Tibet's pastoral nomadism represents a unique example of the sustainable pastoralism that was once common in many parts of the world. The pastoral nomads manage their grazing lands with a combination of traditional knowledge, instinct and sensitivity to environmental conditions; skills that have ensured the productivity of these pastures for millennia.

Tibetan nomads migrate with their herds of yaks, sheep and goats and their movements are designed in such a way that the herds are moved to various pastures during different seasons of the year. Different pastures were used for summer and winter grazing allowing the land to recover and retain its fertility. The staple diet of the nomads is *tsampa* (roasted barley) supplemented by butter, cheese, yoghurt and meat; their drinks are butter tea and a beer called *chang*, which is usually made from barley.

The milk products such as butter and cheese are bartered with farmers for food grains. *Dri* (female yak) milk is churned every day using a wooden churner called *dongmo* and the butter that is collected is then pressed into a hard circular cake from which all liquid is removed and then packed into skin and wooden storage containers. The butter is prepared so well that it can be stored for long periods

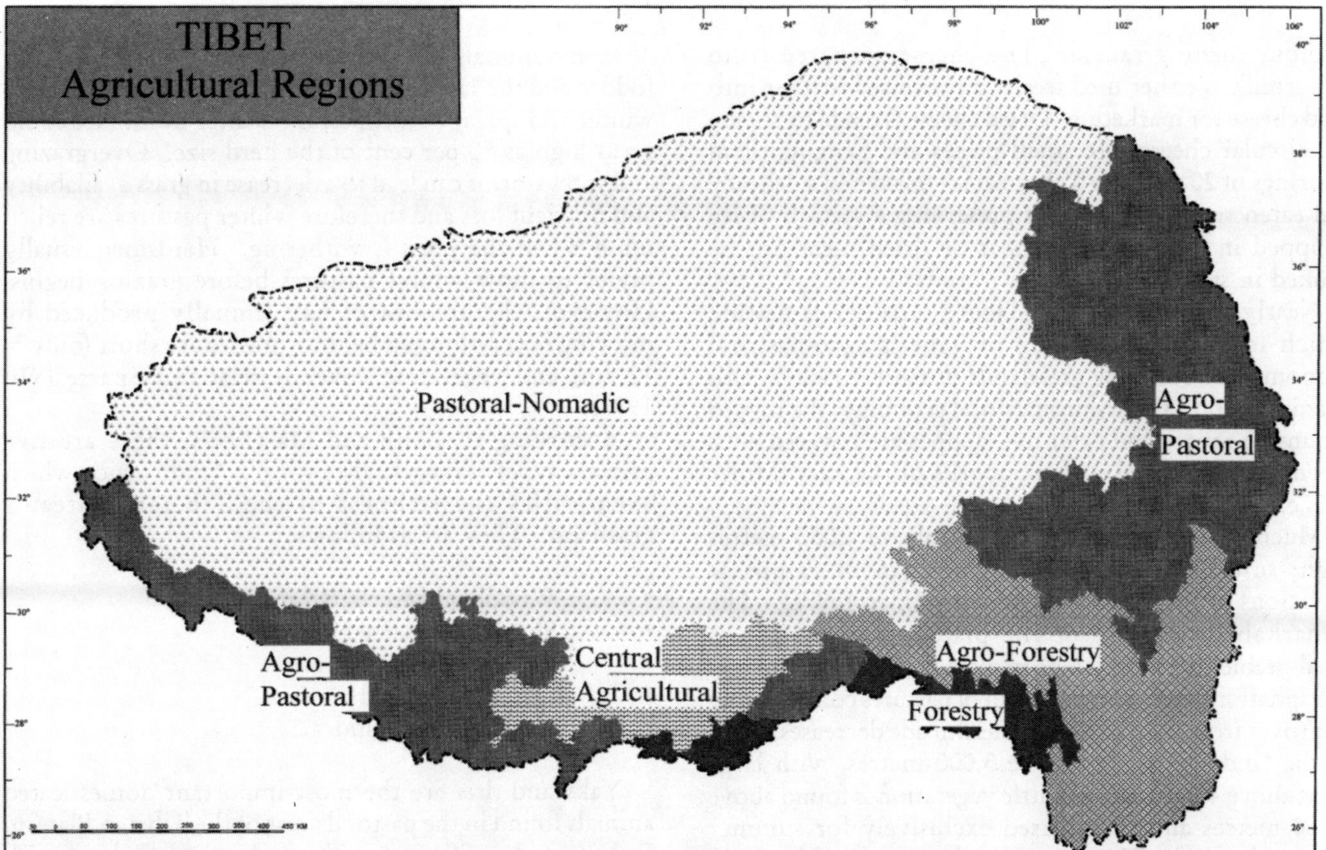

SOURCE: Statistical Year Book 1994; 1998

CARTOGRPAHY & DESIGN: Planning Council, CTA-2000

Note : See colour map at the end of the book

Fencing in wide, open rangelands

Rangelands are defined as "those areas of the world which by reason of physical limitations, low and erratic precipitations, rough topography, poor drainage, or cold temperatures are unsuited for cultivation and which are a source of forage for free ranging native and domestic animals, as well as a source of wood products, water and wildlife" (Stoddart et al 1975). This definition includes grasslands as well as shrublands and forest areas often used by grazing animals. The term "range" implies broad, open, unfenced areas in which grazing animals roam; but as rangelands are more intensively managed, fences — once useful for distinguishing range from pasture lands — are to be found increasingly on rangelands.

without turning rancid. The cheese prepared from buttermilk is either used fresh or processed further into hard cheese for marketing. Dried cheese is made by slicing the circular cheese into small pieces and hanging them in strings of 20 squares. Yak meat is considered a delicacy and eaten raw (red meat) by preserving a section of leg wrapped in cloth. Fresh meat or dried meat can be cooked in stews.

Nearly three quarters of Tibet's territory is pasture which forms the backbone of Tibet's agro-pastoral economy. Though the grasslands nurture a rich wealth of animals and a flourishing pastoral economy, the rugged mountain ranges and extensive steppes are covered with green grasses for only a few months of the year (Miller 1997c).

Much of the Tibetan Plateau is above 4,000 metres high; some nomads maintain permanent camps at elevations as high as 5,100 metres (Miller 1997c). The remarkable variation of the plateau's vegetation is attributable to its variations in altitude, temperature and precipitation. The natural growth of pastures consequently improves from west to east as the altitude decreases. Most of the landmass stands above 3,000 metres, with large areas above 4,000 metres. Little vegetation is found above 5,000 metres and this is used exclusively for summer pasture (*yar-tsa*). The vegetation between 4,000 - 5,000 metres altitudes is called spring pasture and the winter pasture (*gun-tsa*) is mainly found in valleys around 3,000 metres high.

These nomads remain in their winter and spring season pastures for seven months, moving north to their summer and autumn pastures in the middle of May. This seasonal migration involves the movement of all livestock and humans alike. Nomads pack up their belongings — including the yak hair tents which are their homes — and move to new campsites. Summer and autumn grazing lasts from June through September in the pastoral areas of Northern Tibet. In the south, this grazing period begins two weeks earlier and lasts until the end of October. In most of Tibet's pastoral areas the winter-spring grazing season lasts from October to May.

Many animals die every year due to the shortage of fodder and the fact that grasses are buried under snow in winter and spring. At times, the winter death rate could go as high as 50 per cent of the herd size. Overgrazing and snowstorms can lead to a decrease in grass availability and nutrient loss and therefore winter pastures are relied upon when the grass is withering. Herdsmen usually prefer to mow winter pastures before grazing begins. However, the amount of hay annually produced by mowing is very limited because grasses are short (only 5-12 cm) and vegetation cover is relatively sparse (Wu 1997).

According to Long and Ma (1997), there are five primary types of rangeland existing in Amdo region which exemplifies the richness of the Tibetan Plateau's grassland. They are as follows:

- Woodland and coarse grass
- Shrub and coarse grass
- Dry rangeland
- Desert rangeland
- Meadow rangeland

Yaks and dris are the most important domesticated animals found in the pastoral areas of the Tibetan Plateau. Dris provide milk and milk products, and along with yaks yield meat, hair, wool and hides. They are also used as pack as well as draught animals and for riding. Their dung is an important source of fuel on the plateau where firewood is scarce. They make life possible for people to live in one of the world's harshest environments.

Sheep and goats are also very important animals on Tibet's rangelands. Although yaks characterise Tibetan pastoralism, sheep and goats are often more economically important in many areas. Sheep and goats provide wool, meat, hides and in some areas of Western Tibet, sheep are also milked. Sheep meat is preferred among nomads and agricultural people throughout Tibet. Tibetan wool is well known for its quality and is highly prized in the carpet industry for its great elasticity, deep lustre and outstanding tensile strength. Tibetan goats produce cashmere; some of the finest cashmere in the world comes from Western Tibet and much of it is exported to Europe. Goats are also milked as they lactate for a longer period of time than sheep. Nomads spin sheep and yak wool and yak hair. Women weave wool into material for tents, blankets, bags and clothing and men braid ropes. These items are still used in everyday nomadic life.

Grain from Productive Niches

Croplands of Tibet are located at very high altitudes compared to croplands in other parts of the world. Croplands account for only two per cent of Tibet's total area and yet this supplies the essential food grain needs of the populace, despite its extreme altitudes, weather conditions and a short growing season. The principal croplands are arable niches along the Drichu, Zachu and Gyalmo Ngulchu river valleys of Kham, the Yarlung Tsangpo valley in U-Tsang and the Machu valley in Amdo. Kham province is the most fertile cropland region, accounting for 85 per cent of the country's arable land (DIIR 1992).

The traditional agricultural system naturally embodied organic farming principles. The principles of crop rotation, mixed crops and periodic fallows were sustainable and appropriate to the fragile mountain environment. Traditionally the principal Tibetan crop was highland barley used for making *tsampa*; and under Chinese government directives, wheat is increasingly being planted to suit the Chinese migrant diet. However, in one *mu* (15 Mu equals 1 hectare) of land, the barley yield has decreased from 1300-1500 *gyama* (1 *gyama* equals 500 grams) to about 900 *gyama* in Rebkong, Amdo(*Tibet Times* 1999). Other major crops include rice, maize, mustard, millet, sorghum, buckwheat and rape-seed. The main vegetables that grow well are cabbage, lettuce, radish, turnip, peas, carrot, potato, spinach, kidney beans, tomatoes and others. The abundant sunshine is good for vegetable production and it is not unusual for a radish or cabbage to grow to a dozen kilograms, or a single potato to weigh half or one kilogram. These days fresh vegetables grown in greenhouses are available throughout the four seasons, especially in the Lhasa area (Dekhang 1997).

Normally much of the farm work is done by family members, but during the sowing and harvesting seasons — which extend for only a few days and have to be completed according to climatic conditions — they hire people who are paid in kind or they exchange labour. Any harvest surplus is traded for animal products with nomads in pastoral areas.

Semi-Nomadism

A third agro-pastoral category is semi-nomadism — a mixture of nomadic lifestyle and farming in productive niches, which involves the raising of livestock and at the same time engages in agricultural practices.

TRADITIONAL AGRICULTURAL SYSTEMS

Over the centuries, the pastoralists of the Tibetan Plateau have been immensely successful not only in using their vast rangelands but also in conserving the grazing capacity of these areas. Wildlife also coexisted with nomadic populations on the plateau (Schaller and Gu 1994). Over thousands of years nomads adapted to their environment, learning to live with what it offered instead of trying to change or mould the landscape to suit their own needs (Miller 1997c).

Nomads have been herding livestock on the grazing lands of the Tibetan Plateau for nearly 4,000 years, but pastoral production strategies and practices vary widely across the rangelands, depending on altitude, environmental conditions and rangeland types (*ibid*).

For centuries, trade was based on a barter system of exchanging nomadic products like wool and salt for the grains of farmers. Traditionally, the Tibetan pastoral nomads did not involve themselves in the practice of commercial meat production. This is because most Tibetans are religious and believe in life-after-death which could mean being reborn as the animals killed and therefore they seldom slaughtered. Although Chinese nomads can earn 10 times more per animal, Tibetans do not show much interest in monetary rewards or in changing their behaviour to maximise returns, especially when it means increasing

LANDSCAPE IN TIBET

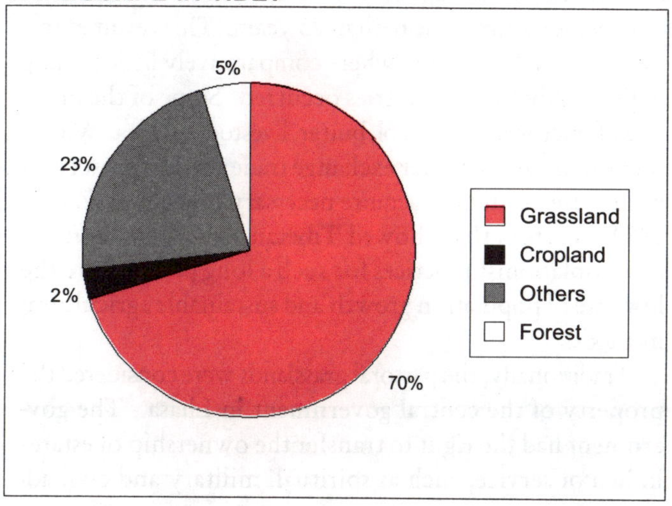

the accelerated slaughter of their herds.

Prior to the Chinese invasion, nomadic herdsmen kept "pasture book" records which regulated the permitted number of animals on every pasture to save pasturelands from overgrazing and erosion. Herdsmen exceeding the established grazing limits or regulations were penalised (Goldstein and Beall 1990). A livestock census was taken every three years to avoid overgrazing of pastures (Atisha 1991).

Tibetan nomads lived in yak hair tents — called *ba* in Tibetan — made from the long, coarse outer hair of the yak and dri called *tsid-pa*, which is spun and woven by the nomads themselves. The tents suit the nomadic lifestyle because they can be easily taken down and packed on yaks when moving camp. These tents help to keep out the rain yet let in light. Sections of old and frayed tents can be easily replaced with new strips of woven yak hair. The tents are ingeniously designed to stand up to the fierce winds that blow across the high Tibetan plains in winter.

Pastoralists on the Tibetan Plateau often raise a mix of different animal species as each species has different characteristics and adaptations to the grazing environment. The multi-species grazing system, like raising yaks, sheep, goats and horses together, is commonly practised by Tibetan nomads and maximises the use of rangeland resources. Different species of animals graze on different plants and, when herded together on the same range, make more efficient use of rangeland vegetation than a single species (Miller 1997c).

In Tibet, grain constitutes over 80 per cent of total crops by value. Yields per hectare vary widely. Tibet's croplands were traditionally farmed using methods that were both efficient and environmentally sound and Tibetan society used to be self-sufficient with respect to food supplies. The dry climate allowed storage of surplus harvests for long periods of time, sometimes more than 25 years. This resulted in a mainly closed economy, where comparatively little trading with neighbouring countries occurred. Some of the products of trade were salt, wool, butter, livestock and tea. Within the communities, barter exchange trade was the most commonly used system to acquire necessary provisions (Zhang 1989). Factors that allowed Tibetan society to maintain these isolationist practices for such a long period were the low rate of population growth and sustainable agricultural methods.

Traditionally, the pastoral grasslands were considered the property of the central government in Lhasa. The government had the right to transfer the ownership of estates in lieu of service, such as spiritual, military and civil administration, rendered by different sections of the society. The grasslands were not demarcated, allowing a natural form of transhumance. Spiritual service was rendered by monastic institutions whereas the military and civil administration came from the lay population. Land use was restricted to three major estate-holders: local administrative officials, the nobility and upper-ranking lamas in monasteries (Goldstein 1989). These groups accounted for less than five per cent of Tibet's population, but controlled most farmland, pastures, forests as well as most of the livestock, of which 30.9 per cent was owned by officials, 29.6 per cent by nobles and 39.5 per cent by monasteries and upper ranking lamas. Farmers and nomads made up 90 per cent of old Tibet's population (Geography of Tibet 1991).

In accordance with popular teachings of Confucianism, most Chinese believed that human beings were the centre of the universe and that it was their mandate to control nature. It is not surprising that the continued deforestation and colonisation of virgin soil in China have been going on for thousands of years (ICJ 1997).

PHASES OF CHINESE AGRARIAN CHANGE

Ever since 1951, immediately after China occupied Tibet, a series of changes were imposed. These agrarian changes can be studied under three different phases. The first stage, Democratic Reform (1951-1965), was short-lived and the implementation of the second stage began half way through the 1960s. By 1975, the major objective of the second stage of establishing communes was 93 per cent completed (Grunfeld 1987).

Phase I: 1951-1962

The first phase was marked by the distribution of estate livestock among nomad households and the formation of nomad "Mutual Aid Teams". Soon class-struggles began because the whole community was divided on the basis of an "exploitation index" into five categories of nomads— lord, rich, middle, lower middle and poor. Changes in cultural freedom, trade and transport were also taking place in pastoral areas (Tsundue1999a). However, despite these changes, the situation instead of improving worsened due to political instability, heavy taxation, the ban of the traditional barter system,inexperienced leadership and more so due to curtailing cultural freedoms. The result was that, like in many farming areas, the pastoral community experienced food grain shortages and declining livestock heads which encouraged the agrarian resistance movement.

Phase II: 1965-1982

Mixed herds maximise the use of plant life on the rangelands

In the midst of the Cultural Revolution (1966-1976), communes were radically imposed and land, animals and even properties which had been distributed during the "democratic reform" of Phase I were taken back by the communes. Livestock were owned by communes, without any private ownership, and net income was distributed according to the labour contributed by an individual in the form of work points (Tsundue 1999b). Agricultural planning and decision-making was made at a high level of organisation and plans were implemented by farmers and nomads through a multi-tiered hierarchial system. The agricultural policy changed frequently and production growth-rates and net returns remained low. Because the economic reality was often disregarded and surpluses were appropriated, farmers lacked enthusiasm for the methods of increasing production (ICIMOD 1988). Most of the produce was forcibly collected as patriotic grains tax, compulsory livestock sales tax, military tax and famine protection tax. The remaining harvest was "purchased" at a nominal price by the Chinese government; this was rarely paid, the claimants being told the money had gone towards maintenance of the communes (Choephel 1976).

Failure of harvests and the export of grain and meat to China led to famines in the early 1960s. The late Panchen Lama specifically identified the cost of feeding Chinese immigrants as one of Tibet's main problems and wrote in a lengthy report to Mao Zedong:

> **The grain of about five kilos per month was not enough to feed Tibetans, even those with the lowest requirements, who in some places didn't receive anything at all. To dispel the daily hunger, Chinese officials gathered tree bark, leaves, grass roots and grass seeds, which really were not edible. After processing this, they mixed it with bits of food stuffs, made it into a thin gruel like pig food and gave it to the people to eat, and even this was limited in amount and couldn't fill their stomachs. He further added, "Anguish of such severe hunger had never been experienced in Tibetan history and was such that people couldn't imagine it even in their dreams. The masses could not resist this kind of cruel torment and as a result, colds and minor infectious diseases developed which caused a percentage of people to die. In some places, many people starved to death and in some cases, there was a phenomenon of whole families dying out" (TIN 1997c).**

During this phase, impossible quotas were imposed to increase crop yields and multiply the number of livestock in total disregard to the carrying capacity of arable land and grazing pastures. Carrying capacity is defined as the maximum density of domesticated livestock that a particular pasture can support without the risk of degradation (Aggarwal et. al 1993). Farmers, at that time in communes, increased the cultivation of marginal lands and grew high yield wheats which were unsuitable for local conditions or needs. These wheats were unable to tolerate severe highland winters and affected the traditional barley cropping system.

Inappropriate Chinese methods of increasing foodcrop and livestock production during the late 1950s and early 1960s resulted in the widespread destruction of Tibet's fragile grasslands. The increased number of livestock on limited grasslands led to overgrazing of Tibet's pastures

(Zhang 1989). This was one of the major ecological disasters generated by the Great Leap Forward policy of late Chinese leader Mao Zedong (US Embassy 1996b).

Phase III: 1981-1989

After the death of Mao in 1976, the much-awaited liberal policy of "Household Responsibility System" (HRS) was introduced. This third phase of agricultural experimentation was implemented in 1982 in Tibet. Under this policy communes were disbanded, every able-bodied person received an equal share of livestock and land, each household was entitled to be rewarded in the case of over-quota production, decisions were given to farmers, taxes exempted, people could retain part of their surplus produce and private ownership flourished.

The HRS provided opportunities for farmers to return to traditional crops and their methods of agriculture, based on socio-economic demands was supported by technical improvements (Zhang 1989). Unfortunately this phase lasted only around seven years.

In 1989 the policy was reversed and restrictions were imposed once again by bringing agriculture under a centralised system of intensification of land use to produce grain surpluses for the benefit of "the state".

Grain quota systems, a multitude of taxes and intensive farming have all contributed to a loss of freedom and incentive for Tibetan farmers.

AGRICULTURE IN TODAY'S TIBET

In Tibet, planning and development of agriculture has remained centralised in the 1990s and there is no freedom of land-use. Grain quota systems, a multitude of taxes and intensive farming have all contributed to a loss of freedom and incentive for Tibetan farmers. High altitude overgrazing and intensive agricultural production has resulted in the loss of many medicinal herbs and food plants, and has destroyed much of the winter food supplies for wildlife. Overgrazing has also caused wind and water erosion which has led to further desertification of the Tibetan Plateau. For example, 272 million hectares of land which is 17.03 per cent of 'TAR' has been turned into desert (*Tibet Daily* 1998a). Desertification is caused by a variety of factors; mainly from conversion of land for agricultural purposes, clearfelling of forests and overgrazing in grassland areas.

According to Beijing, development means raising productivity, capital accumulation and investment. Thousands of skilled and unskilled Chinese workers are being transferred into Tibet in the name of "development". Tibetans see development projects simply as a case of misguided aid applied by the Chinese government designed to benefit only Chinese migrants. Wheat and rice which China had to import that fed the growing Chinese immigrant population in Lhasa were subsidised by the Chinese government at a staggering cost.

Resistance still exists in rural areas against intensified monoculture, heavy taxation, the livestock compulsory slaughter quota, the inappropriate state procurement policy, lapses in price reform and other policies. For the agriculturists, these issues reach to the heart of food security and sustainable rural life.

ECONOMIC ISSUES

Widespread Taxation

A huge amount of tax is charged from the nomads to graze animals on the land. The amount of the tax depends on the size of the land and family. Each year, US$5 is collected from every individual between 15 - 60 years old which is supposed to benefit them during their old age. An education tax of one yak and two sheep is collected even from nomads who have never attended schools — for which the price they get is less than half the market price (Bidhartsang 1998).

Rigid Quota System

Since the reversal of the HRS policy in 1989, China has once again imposed a rigid quota system, whereby farmers must adhere strictly to the government's policy of cropping system with the risk of food security. They are forcibly required to sell 250 kilogram of grain and mustard oil seeds irrespective of the size of the family. Nomads are forced to sell their animal products like *khulu* (soft fur) and slaughter cattle. Some families, however, do not possess enough livestock to fulfill the quota and are forced to purchase sheep and goats from others.

Under such policies, in order to fulfil their grain quota, farmers are forced to buy grains at the market price for which they are paid a compulsory purchase price by the state or at times do not receive any compensation at all (Bidhartsang 1998).

Fencing and Privatisation

Although the policy of reform since the late 1970s has led to nomads being able to re-establish some features of their traditional economy, policy measures are increasingly focusing on "modernisation" which drive a process of dividing up land by fencing it and settling nomads has been under way since the mid 1980s in Qinghai. The Ninth Five Year Plan (1996-2000) for the 'TAR' includes provisions for the development of five million mu (335,000 hectares) of enclosed pastures. However, *Xinhua News Agency* has reported that fenced pasture exceeded 10 million mu (Dorje and Tsering 1999).

In 1998 Qi Jingfa, China's vice minister for agriculture, said that all herdmen were expected to end the nomadic life by the end of the century and that in Qinghai province 67 per cent of herdsmen have already settled into houses (*Xinhua* 1998i).

Although the introduction of fencing helps to some extent in the recovery of degraded pasture, it often leads to disputes over boundaries and resentments over its cost (Xinhua 1998i). Commercialisation of pastoral-nomadism is a serious issue. The World Bank and policymakers approve further commercialisation of pastoral nomadism through "scientific management" of grasslands and present strategies to overcome local cultural "obstacles" (Lafitte 1998b).

Documented interviews with Tibetan refugees in Dharamsala verify that there is widespread concern over the policy of fencing and the permanent settlement of nomadic communities. Natural movement of livestock has been practiced by the nomads for centuries but this policy change has caused social conflicts among Tibetan herding communities leading to regional instability and sometimes even the loss of life. At least 29 Tibetan nomads lost their lives due to a series of armed clashes over pasture lands (TIN 1999c).

STATE AND MARKET PRODUCE PRICES (US$ per kilogram)

ITEM	STATE PURCHASE PRICE	MARKET RETAIL PRICE
Wool	0.36	1.20
Butter	0.26	3.20
Meat	0.50	2.00
Whole Yak	38.00	500.00
Whole Sheep	10.00	76.00
Yartsa Gunbu	376.00	1,000.00

Adapted from Bidhartsang 1998

This deterioration has reached a point where if conservation measures are not taken soon, the longterm continuity of nomadic Tibetan civilisation is threatened.

SOCIAL ISSUES

Feeding Chinese settlers

The inequality of food subsidies makes living in 'TAR' more attractive to Chinese settlers while making it harder for poor Tibetans to survive in the way to which they were traditionally accustomed. Most of the subsidised items are foodstuff that is preferred by Chinese settlers rather than Tibetans. The staple diet of Tibetans is barley; however, it is only the two grains forming the staple diet of the majority of Chinese immigrants — rice and wheat — that are subsidised.

Shifting Policies

The Chinese government's frequent changes in policy have severely affected the livelihood of Tibetan pastoralists. Since 1949, ill-conceived policies were enforced which ignored local conditions and were aimed at growing crops — particularly grain crops — in all regions regardless of climatic and land conditions. Traditional production systems suited to local conditions were abandoned (Bidhartsang 1998).

Compulsory Fertiliser Purchase

New regulations require farmers to increase wheat production, especially winter wheat, which requires heavy applications of chemical fertiliser that Tibetan farmers believe depletes the soil (Grunfeld 1987). However, they are compelled to purchase fertiliser at fixed state prices, as part payment for grain procured by state trading companies.

This reduces their income, their power to pay for health and education benefits and discourages organic farming.

Increasing Human Pressure

According to Qu, Chairman of the Environment Protection Committee of the Chinese National People's Congress, and Li, an advisor to the Chinese National Environment Protection Agency:

> **A delicate balance exists between human population density and biomass productivity. By internationally accepted standards, a typical grassland area may support five persons per sq.km. On an average, Inner Mongolia's population density is home to 15 persons per sq.km. If that density is taken as a standard, the eastern regions of Tibet, which have absorbed the Chinese influx, now mostly support excessive numbers.**

ENVIRONMENTAL ISSUES

Overgrazing

The stocking rates on the Tibetan grasslands are today being pushed to the limit as a result of the 36 per cent increase in China's herds (ICJ 1997). As a result, pastures are overgrazed in many areas and livestock have difficulty in finding nutritious pasture and have consequently lost weight. For example, in Amdo, the average weight of an adult yak dropped from 112 kilograms in 1965 to 40 kg in 1981 (64 percent decrease).

Specific cases of grassland degradation are related to extensive areas being enclosed for Chinese settlers and farmers. Such interventions affect the nomads' traditional migration patterns and restrict them to ever-smaller areas which leads to conditions of irreversible damage. This deterioration has reached a point where if conservation measures are not taken soon, the longterm continuity of nomadic Tibetan civilisation is threatened.

Degradation of Grassland

The most significant threat to the herders is the increasing level of grassland degradation as the pastures are no longer able to produce sufficient cover to feed livestock. Although there are no reliable figures for the extent of the degradation of grassland, some reports have quoted percentages of a loss of between 17.2 per cent (*Xinhua* 1998j) and over 30 per cent (US Embassy 1996d) of grassland in the 'TAR'.

Official Chinese literature blames it on the grazing traditions of the nomads. But it is an irrefutable fact that nomads' traditional pasture strategies have allowed them to survive and prosper for centuries on the high plateau. So

AVERAGE ANIMAL CARCASS WEIGHT IN AMDO, 1965 - 1981 (in kgs)

ANIMAL	YEAR			WEIGHT DECREASE
	1965	1977	1981	1965-1981
Adult yak	112.0	50.0	40.0	64 per cent
Adult sheep	22.5	15.0	14.0	37 per cent

QUANTITY AND DISTRIBUTION OF DEGRADED RANGELANDS (x 10,000 hectares)

REGION	AVAILABLE RANGE	PERCENTAGE OF DEGRADED RANGES	
		1980s	1990s
'TAR'	6, 636.12	18.12	30.00
Amdo	3,161.03	28.29	31.82
NW Sichuan	1,416.04	27.31	33.00
Gansu	1,607.16	44.36	49.00
Total	**12,820.35**		

Adapted from Long and Ma 1997

MAJOR ISSUES IN RANGELAND MANAGEMENT, PASTORAL DEVELOPMENT AND PRIORITY ACTIONS

MAJOR ISSUES	PRIORITY ACTIONS
• fodder shortages, especially in winter • lack of trained manpower • rangeland degradation • land tenure problems • settling of pastoralists • lack of community participation in development efforts • lack of knowledge of both the traditional systems and pastoralists knowledge • poor government commitment to pastoral communities • lack of data/knowledge/awareness • overgrazing • inappropriate government policies • lack of monitoring • fencing of grassland • conversion of rangeland to agricultural lands • lack of traininng	• train professionals and locals • create opportunities for two-way exchange of information between pastoralists and professionals • develop programmes to study traditional systems and perceptions of pastoralists' problems • improve forage/fodder resources, especially in winter • improve people's participation and community organisation • determine the extent and severity of rangeland degradation • develop appropriate land tenure, legislation and policies • research on the herds' movement/grazing systems, pastoral management systems • awareness campaign, education • create monitoring teams • introduce improved forages • create off-farm and alternative employment opportunities, promote appropriate land ownership rights/ legislation for tenure

Adapted from Miller 1997c

inappropriate goverment policies are to blame for grassland degradation..

Seasonal Pasture Shortages

Even though the Tibetan nomads have accumulated a wealth of experience in the use of rangelands and seasonal migration management systems are well adapted to local conditions, many problems like shortages of pastures have arisen from uneven distribution of seasonal pastures. This shortage of such pastures has led to overstocking in winter areas and, therefore, insufficient nutritional provisions for the livestock during the winter (Wu 1997).

FUTURE PROSPECTS AND NEEDS

Tibet's population will continue to grow through Chinese migration at a relatively high rate and the consumption level of the population will increase, while the availability of land suitable for agriculture remains limited. But the prospect will not be so bleak if policy correction is embarked upon to redress the problems now.

The degradation of agricultural resources can no longer be regarded solely as a localised problem since the implications are widespread, affecting regional, national and international interests. Intensive use of land through changing land-use patterns should be encouraged, provided the interests of Tibetans and environmental conditions are taken into consideration. Also there is the need to encourage diversification of income for farmers through off-farm activities.

The Chinese government's centralised agricultural policy should be decentralised since it entirely ignores Tibet's local conditions, environment and the habits of the people. Increases in agricultural yields also depend upon improved agricultural techniques and not only on bringing more land under agriculture. This will require considerable new investment in the land and people skills. Training should be provided for Tibetans to use better agricultural tools and techniques. Studies on farmers' behaviour also should be made as this plays an important role in agricultural and rural development.

Protection of grassland is vital to the survival of Tibetans. There is a need for educational conservation programmes which convey the spiritual and economic benefits of good resource management. Such programmes should involve Tibetans, natural resource experts and others. Issues of overgrazing and degraded ranges can be addressed through joint efforts of herders and researchers, so that rangeland ecosystems and pastoral production systems will be better understood and conserved in the future.

Tibetan pastoralists' experience and deep understanding of the environment should govern policy decisions about grassland management. Policy reforms at all levels should consider the basic needs of local people and provide direct economic benefits to them. Incentives for rural development must be oriented towards improving living standards and conserving biodiversity.

Studies on the environment and development of the Tibetan Plateau are essential not only to fill the enormous gaps of knowledge on these dynamic, millennia-old ecosystems, but also to provide data that will enable the evaluation, by rational methods, of sustainable development strategies.

The preservation of nomads' extensive traditional knowledge of their natural environment, as well as the breeding and management skills of domestic and wild animals, remains vital. This knowledge should be fully investigated and integrated into the planning and implementation of development projects.

Herd diversification should be practised as an insurance against major outbreaks of disease, since different domestic species are generally not susceptible to the same pathogens. Strengthening a sense of community and personal responsibility is the key to the conservation of biodiversity and the rehabilitation of degraded ecosystems. The use and conservation of rangeland ecosystems should be the exclusive responsibility of Tibetan people.

CONCLUSION

Agriculture has historically been the primary source of livelihood for over 80 per cent of the total population of Tibet. Until the late 1950s, Tibetans survived on the principle Tibetan crop, barley, plus vegetables, meat and animal bi-products. Trade was based on a barter system where the nomads exchanged their products like wool and salt for grains from farmers. The systems of agriculture and trade prior to the Chinese occupation sustained both humans and nature to a much greater degree.

Due to the Chinese occupation, Tibetans are now facing many hardships like food scarcity, heavy taxation, centralised and frequent changes of policy, lack of Tibetan participation in "development projects" and the transfer of thousands of Chinese settlers. All changes were introduced in the guise of "modernisation" and "development of Tibet and Tibetans".

Although the Chinese government forced the cultivation of winter wheat on marginal lands, coaxing Tibetans away from their staple crop of barley, this crop change failed as it was unsuitable for local conditions. All the agricultural planning and decision-making in Tibet today is imposed from above. Production growth rates and net returns remain low because farmers receive no incentives for increasing production. Most of the produce is forcibly collected as taxes in various forms.

The issue of grassland in Tibet is centred around the sustainability of pastoral-nomadism which hitherto depended on the policies that would support restoration and preservation of a sound grassland ecosystem. Over 60 per cent of pastoral-nomadic counties in the 'TAR' are faced with extensive rangeland degradation caused by overgrazing, imbalances in the grassland food chain and the Chinese policy encouraging commercial exploitation of rangelands.

For the future it is important that the present arable land and pastures are conserved and utilised by following appropriate cropping patterns and grassing systems, as Tibet has the potential to meet future demands for food self-sufficiency and other basic needs. The most fundamental requirement is that there must be clarity and consistency on land policies so that farmers and nomads feel secure about their land rights. Agricultural sectors should be gradually decentralised while drastic revisions are needed in the areas of cropping patterns and price reforms. The active participation of both the farmers and nomads in all aspects of the development process is necessary. ■

CHAPTER FOUR

FORESTRY

At the global level, trees and forests are closely linked with weather patterns and also the maintenance of a crucial balance in nature. Hence, the task of environmental protection is a universal responsibility of us all.

His Holiness the 14th Dalai Lama, 1995

IN SUMMER 1998, the worst flooding of the (Drichu) Yangtze River to ravage China since 1954 killed between 3,656 and 10,000 people and left 240 millions affected by its waters. As well as devastating 64 million hectares of farmland and destroying 4.8 million hectares of crops, 5.6 million homes were destroyed and *Xinhua* (1998h) reported that over 0.5 percentage points were shaved off from the economic growth resulting in a direct financial loss of US$37.5 billion. Epidemics followed due to the spread of sewer and latrine contents. According to *China Daily* the flood was expected to shift one million citizens' incomes to below the poverty line of US$75 a year (Pomfret 1998b; *Tibetan Review* 1998b).

The Chinese government was slow to confess that a major cause of the Yangtze flood was extensive deforestation at the river's source, which lies deep inside the Tibetan provinces of Amdo and Kham. While the flow rates of the Yangtze at that time were below historic highs, water levels exceeded previous records due to increased silting. Chinese statistics state that the Yangtze then peaked at approximately 55,000 cubic metres per second, a rate it had exceeded 23 times since 1949. It has been estimated that the Yangtze now discharges 500 million tons of silt a year into the East China Sea, a volume equivalent to the total discharge of the Nile, Amazon and Mississippi Rivers combined (Pomfret 1998b; He 1991).

Only after the national disaster level of these flood in late August 1998, did Beijing acknowledge the deforested areas on and around the Tibetan Plateau as the fountainhead of tributaries of the Yangtze River. Finally taking remedial action, the government closed timber markets and placed an unconditional logging ban on an area of 4.6 million hectares covering 54 counties in Kham (Western Sichuan) according to a *Xinhua* (1998d). As of 9 December 1998, unofficial reports stated that the 'TAR' government also ordered the temporary shutdown of operations of all lumber processing mills in southeastern 'TAR', announcing that reforestation projects should begin immediately by employing former loggers as tree planters (Winkler 1999). These steps may be seen to signify a shift towards a more preventive and effective approach to environmental management.

Traditional Conservation

Situated at the centre of the Asian continent, the Tibetan Plateau not only contains the world's highest mountains and a vast arid plateau, but also fertile river valleys and ancient forests. The major forested areas on the Tibetan Plateau are in the south (Dram, Kyirong, Pema Koe, Kongpo, Nyingtri, Tawu, Metog and Monyul), the east (Chamdo, Drayab, Zogong, Kandze, Potramo, Dartsedo, Nyarong and Ngaba), and the southeast (Dechen, Balung, Gyalthang, Mili, Lithang, Zayul, Markham and Dzogang). These forested regions are primarily located on steep isolated slopes and prior to 1950 covered over 25.2 million hectares representing about nine per cent of the region (DIIR 1992).

The plateau possesses one of the oldest forest reserves in Central Asia and a wealth of over 100,000 species of

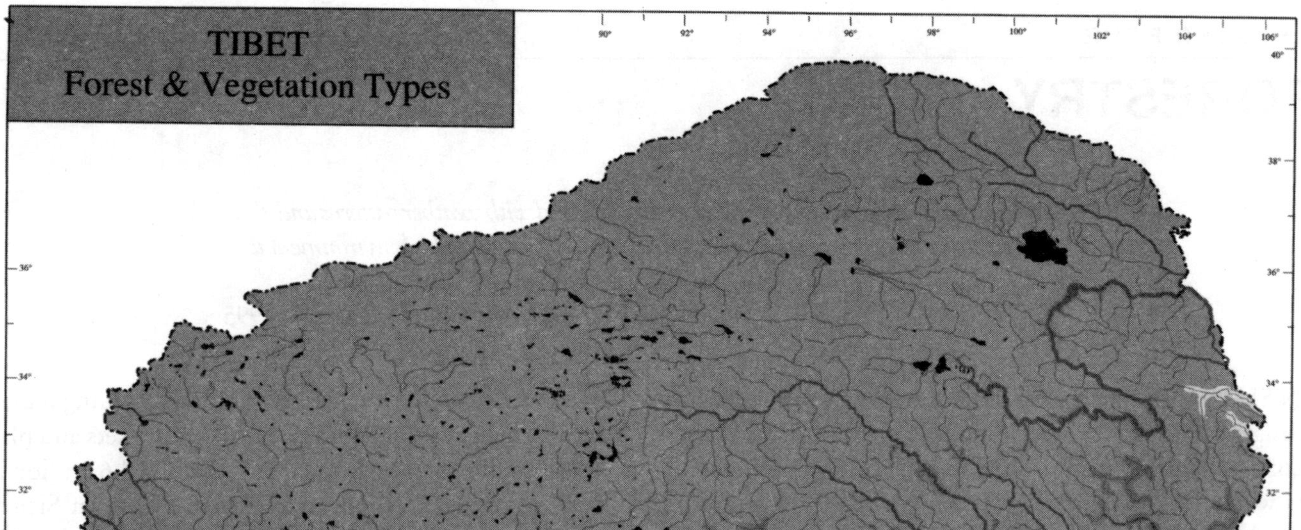

Note : See colour map at the end of the book

Logging ban ignored, reports recent escapee

A recent escapee from Tibet reported extensive clearcutting of forests being carried out in Thewo county, Amdo region by the Chinese government. Dorjee Tsering, who reached Dharamsala, India on 12 January 2000, described the dramatic rate of forest loss in his homeland. He provided the Central Tibetan Administration with several pictures he had taken. Dorjee said around the Tibetan towns of Tara, Yewa, Wapa and Zerongkha in Thewo county there is widespread clearcutting of forests.

Every day about 500 logging trucks loaded with Tibetan timber travel from Thewo county to the Chinese city of Kachu (Ch. Linxia) and some trucks go directly to Lanzhou city in Gansu. This mass transfer of logs to China has been taking place ceaselessly since the Chinese arrival. Dorjee added that in Kham region of Tibet, logging is still going on, despite the government logging ban announced in September 1998 after the Yangtze flood.

He said Thewo county has lost about 80 per cent of its forest cover. The logging is haphazard; even young trees are cut down. Most of the impenetrable forest regions seen during Dorjee's childhood have become bald and barren. The deforested Tibetan regions receive no compensation and are very poor. Dorjee said he was often in tears on witnessing the destruction of his homeland. Tibetans have to seek permission to cut trees for building houses, but the Chinese government continues commercial felling. He reports that Tibetans are frustrated and are saying, "If we don't cut the trees, the Chinese will take away everything and we will become even poorer".

Dekhang 2000

higher plants, 532 species of birds, and many rare wild animals such as giant panda, golden monkey, takin, and white-lipped deer (DIIR 1998a). These forests provide a variety of fruits, nuts and vegetables, including apple, pear, orange, banana and walnut. Given the remote and restricted conditions of the plateau, several of its botanical species have yet to be adequately studied and classified.

Alongside the diverse ecology of the Tibetan Plateau resides an ancient and endangered civilisation and at the very heart of this unique culture is the Buddhist ethos: "To hold all of nature in trust for all sentient beings".

The practical integration of this ethical belief allowed a symbiotic relationship to develop between the Tibetan people and their environment. Tibetans have adapted to their natural surroundings realising that their fragile environment provides a unique life-support system. By co-evolving with extremely harsh environmental conditions, the Tibetans developed a self-sufficient, intricate and responsive land use system. And so a tradition evolved and formed a rich source of knowledge necessary for human habitation within the fragile ecosystems of the Tibetan Plateau.

Tibet's small population lived primarily on sheep- and yak-herding and barley cultivation, leaving fields fallow for long periods which maintained fertility and helped prevent leaching and erosion. Wildlife was protected in accordance with Buddhist principles, while timber was harvested on a controlled and selective basis (Winkler 1996). Alak Tsayi, a senior lama from Tsayi in Amdo, explains how the Tibetans took care of their forests before 1950:

> **The forests in each region would be the property of the people of that region. If there were forests near a monastery, they would be under the monastery's control. If one was near a village, the villagers would have authority over that forest ... [We were] told that if [we] cut a lot of trees, the value, the fertility of the land would decrease ... You could not simply go and cut trees. If you wanted to construct a house or something, you had to write an application explaining why you needed the wood. The authorities would then see if you really were constructing a house, and then the permission to cut the trees would be granted. If you were not really building you would have to pay a fine (Apte and Edwards 1998).**

The traditional methods of fuel utilisation represent indigenous knowledge that worked with environmental realities to maintain a healthy ecosystem. Dung was predominately used as fuel for cooking and heating. Alternatively, when wood was used as fuel it comprised only dead branches and fallen trees which minimised the impact on the delicate regeneration patterns of the forests.

Many forest products, not just trees, were utilised for domestic purposes. Bamboo shoots remain a favourite ingredient in the cuisine of Eastern Tibet while grapes and other berries have been used to produce alcoholic drinks. Many plant species in Tibet such as walnut, camellia and tallow produce oils. Some species such as the *Pinus Griffithii* produce oil for food and also provide materials for paint, while pines and other plant species are a good source of gum and latex (Dekhang 1996).

There are over 2,000 plants used in Tibetan and allopathic medicines which can be collected in the Tibetan Plateau. Tibet's ancient medical system is highly respected throughout Central Asia and has a remarkable record of success in healing (Burang 1974). In direct contrast to the standpoint of allopathy, Tibetan medicine mirrors the principles that operate in nature, preferring a slow and gentle treatment that places great emphasis on natural remedies, treating humans and each medicine as an integral part of the environment (Badmayew et al 1982).

Each geological and climatic region on the Tibetan Plateau is home to an ecosystem endowed with distinct natural resources, each embodying its own unique form of wealth. In forested areas, for example, many surplus products were traditionally harvested and bartered locally or with neighbouring regions.

Despite Tibet's active role as a trading partner, it is critical to note that the Tibetan Plateau was a self-sufficient region. Tibetan traders were mainly dealing in surplus goods, creating a commercial activity that became a fundamental cultural pillar; Tibetans were able to enjoy goods from neighbouring regions without ever developing a dependency on this exchange for their basic needs.

Deforestation in China's History

Compared with the Tibetans, China's inhabitants have suffered a long history of ecological crisis and ancient documents show that the deterioration of Chinese forests has been taking place over thousands of years. The pace of deforestation accelerated ever since the 14th century, setting the precedent for a destruction that continues today. Starting from China's Ming period (1368-1644), all the forests in the central region of the Huang River valley, as well as the Xiang River valley were seriously denuded (Edmonds 1994).

Despite the lessons of history, timber remains a key commodity for economic exploitation in China and deforestation continues as a common phenomenon. The forestry sector plays a critical role in the Chinese economy, providing 40 per cent of rural household energy, almost all of the lumber and wood products for the large construction sector, and material for domestic pulp and paper industry.

The forest cover in China amounts to only 0.11 hectares per capita which is significantly below the world average of 0.77 hectares per capita. China is also the third largest consumer of timber in the world and faces an amplified imbalance between demand and supply for wood products. The present annual consumption level of approximately 300 million cubic metres of round wood exceeds the combined annual forest growth increment and total imports by about 50 million cubic metres per year. As a result, an estimated 500,000 hectares of forest area is lost each year; this is equivalent to 0.5 per cent of total forest area (Ministry of Forests 1997).

Tibet's Shrinking Forests

China now sees the Tibetan Plateau as its largest forest zone as industrial timber extraction penetrates deeper into Tibet's borders. Some 70 state logging enterprises have cut a total amount of 120 million cubic metres of wood from the

Logging trucks in Kachu (Ch: Linxia) waiting to haul Tibet's timber to nearby Lanzhou and other Chinese cities. November 1999

forests of eastern Kham (Sichuan), generating over 2 billion yuan (US$ 241 million) in taxes and profits between 1949 to 1998 (TIN 1998d). It is said that forest

> *We can share the earth and take care of it together rather than trying to possess it to destroy the beauty of life in the process*
>
> His Holiness the 14th Dalai Lama 1995

exploitation in western Sichuan is 2.3 times more than forest productivity (ICIMOD 1986). According to Tenzin Palbar, who escaped from Tibet into India in 1987, in the Ngaba Tibetan Autonomous Prefecture from 1955-1991 the Chinese government extracted 50.17 million cubic metre of Tibetan timber, which is worth US$ 3.1 billion in Tibet itself when calculated at the average price of 50 yuan per cubic metre. In this region there were 340 million cubic metres of forest in 1950 which reduced to 180 million cubic metres in 1992, of which only 34 million cubic metres could be used. Therefore, Ngaba lost 47 per cent of its forest cover between 1950 to 1992 alone (TIN 1999a). Income from the forestry industry is the main source of cash income in many of the poorest counties in Sichuan. Concern among the officials about the loss of this income amount to 70-95 per cent of revenues for many poor counties (Beijing Review 1998b). As reported by refugees arriving in Dharamsala in 1999 from the Tibetan Plateau, a predominant cause of environmental degradation on the plateau is the mass influx of Chinese settlers and the mass exodus of Tibetan timber.

There are inherent deficiencies in the Chinese system that create gaps between policy and practice and nullify optimistic goals, which in turn perpetuates high deforestation rates.

In the region of Kham absorbed into Sichuan, forest cover decreased from 30 per cent in the 1950s to 14 per cent in the 1980s. In the late 1980s and early 1990s the momentum has continued (Li 1993). In Ngaba (Ch:Aba) and the Tibetan and Qiang Autonomous Prefecture forest cover shrank from 29.5 per cent in the 1950s to 14 per cent in the 1980s (Yang 1986). This has left eight out of 11 forest factories in Ngaba district with exhausted resources. Similarly, in the Kandze district, five of seven forest reserves have been depleted (Zhao 1992). Reports from the World Watch Institute estimate the heavily-forested area from the Tibetan Plateau to the Yangtze River basin has lost 85 per cent of its original forest cover (Brown and Halweil 1998).

The extraction of non-timber resources within Tibetan forests is also a growing concern on the plateau. Approximately 3,000 of the species growing in Tibet's forests have considerable economic value in both the domestic and world markets.

According to the 1991 Social and Economic Annual Report of 'TAR' from 1975 to 1990 the Chinese government exported rare medicinal plants from Tibet amounting to 1.3 million kg of *yartsa gunbu* (*Cordyceps sinensis*) and 5.5 million kg of *honglen* (*Picrorrhiza*). Meanwhile, Chinese radio broadcasts from Lhasa reported that 1,100 tons of *thangchu* (gum) and another 30 tons of a thicker variety were collected between 1966-76.

Forest herbs have immense value in China and Chinese timber factories in Tibet claim to have culled up to eight million cubic metres of herbs, with a value of US$17.2 million (Dekhang 1996). This confirms that exploitation of Tibetan forests is not restricted to timber alone.

Treasure and Treasury

Recognition of the "natural" world's interdependent values is fundamental to creating a healthy relationship with one's environment. When forests are understood only in a utilitarian context many other values are disregarded and consequently sacrificed and harmed.

It is undeniable that timber resources extracted from forests are indispensable to human life. Additionally, a forest contains abundant plants and animals, complex stratified structures, many biological products and immense capabilities to exchange substance and energy, which play important roles in maintaining the life-support system of this planet.

Forests are not only a treasure but also a treasury of plant and animal resources. In brief, the concept of "forest" means not merely timber, but also a simultaneous consideration of intrinsic, ecological, social and economic values.

Fuelwood and Land Cultivation

It has been suggested that the traditional use of forests for fuelwood by the inhabitants of the Tibetan Plateau is a major contributing factor to deforestation of the area. However, upon closer examination it becomes clear that

TYPES OF VEGETATION ON THE TIBETAN PLATEAU

Types of Forest	Ecosystem Variant	Dominant Vegetation Community
Coniferous Forest	Sub-alpine coniferous forests	Sub-Alpine Fir Forests *Abies delavayi, A. spectabilis, A. squamata* Sub-Alpine Juniper forests *Sabina recurva, S. tibetica, S. wallichiana* Sub-Alpine Larch forests *Larix himalaica, L. potaninii, L. speciosa* Sub-Alpine Spruce forests *Picea balfouriana, P. likiangensis, P. spinulosa*
	Temperate coniferous forests	Temperate Hemlock forests *Tsuga dumosa* Temperate Pine forests *Pinus armandi, P. gerardiana, P. griffithii* Temperate Spruce forests *Picea asperata, P. brachytyla, P. smithiana*
	Sub-tropical coniferous forests	Subtropical Cypress forests *Cupressus ducloxiana, C. torulosa* Subtropical Pine forests *Pinus yunnanesis, P. roxburghii*
Broad-leaved Forest	Sub-alpine broadleaved forests	Broad-leaved Deciduous Forests *Betula albo, B. platyphylla, B. utilis* Evergreen Oak forests *Quercus semecarpifolia, Q. pannosa*
	Sub-tropical broad-leaved forest	*Alnus nepalensis, Betula alnoides, Populus ciliata*
	Tropical monsoon forest	*Shorea robusta, Ficus, Castanopsis spp,*
Bamboo Forest	Temperate bamboo forests	*Sinarundinaria spp*
	Sub-tropical & tropical bamboo forests	*Bambusa intermedia, Phyllostachys spp.*
Scrub Forest	Alpine scrub	*Potentilla fruticosa, Salix lindleyana,*
	Sub-Alpine scrub	*Rhododendron, Caragana, Sabina, Salix* spp.
	Temperate scrub	*Gauteria yunnanensis, Lyonia, Myrica spp.,*
	Sub-Tropical and tropical scrub	*Sophora, Bauhinia, Dodonaea, Vitis, Terminalia* spp.

Sources: Dekhang 1996; Li 1995 and Li 1993.

despite the large demand for fuelwood, traditionally Tibet's population was small and most fuel was derived from shrubs, branches and predominantly agricultural residues such as dung (DIIR 1992). This fact was also reconfirmed in December 1998 by a majority of the newly-arrived Tibetan refugees interviewed in Dharamsala. Furthermore, in Lhasa fuelwood is now sold at a price per cubic metre that exceeds the average annual per capita income (Richardson 1990). Hence, the traditional use of forests for fuelwood on the Tibetan Plateau accounts for a negligible part of the pressure on forest cover.

However, with the mounting flow of Chinese settlers into Tibet, the total population has increased from six million to approximately 13.5 million, the population density more than doubled to 5.4 persons per sq. km. With China's population expanding by 14 million a year, Beijing provides incentives for Chinese workers to migrate to Tibet.

For the Chinese who settle in rural Tibet over 80 per cent of their energy is supplied by fuelwood (Li 1993). Consequently fuelwood pressure on forests is now a growing concern in Tibet. In a 1998 refugee interview, a farmer from Kham reported, "Before, our fuelwood was right outside the door, but now to get the wood we have to go off in the morning with two to three donkeys to carry it, and don't return until evening."

As illustrated by Winkler's research, Tibetan traditions were not completely without effect and have slowly altered the environment over several millennia. One example is the reduction of forest cover through grazing. "Full utilisation of the south-facing slopes for winter grazing enables herders to keep their store of winter fodder which is a time- and energy-consuming necessity in any environment with harsh winters to an absolute minimum" (Winkler 1998). However, unlike the consequences of commercial timber extraction and uncontrolled resource liquidation, the impact of the past was not a short-sighted destruction of resources, but rather a logical consequence of developing various regions of Tibet as grazing land. But in today's Tibet, as in many places around the earth, processes of land alteration that evolved over thousands of years can now happen within decades or even years.

Faulty Forest Enforcement

While deforestation on the Tibetan Plateau is a complex issue and its causes are difficult to isolate, Tibetan, Chinese and foreign researchers maintain that the dwindling forest cover is primarily caused by poor forest management. Forest management in this context is an inclusive term that refers to human-created changes in environmental conditions ranging from random timber poaching and various inefficiencies to high-yield industrial logging.

A host of administrative dilemmas face China in its forest practices. This predicament is embedded in faulty enforcement rather than in a crisis of insufficient forest laws. For example, Article 25 of the (Forestry Law(s) of the People's Republic of China 1985) further states that: "The state, acting on the principle that consumption of the timber forest should be lower than its growth, imposes strict control on the annual forest cut" (Richardson 1990). Recent government planning is targeting reforestation with the intention of increasing the forested area to a level of self-sufficiency.

Unfortunately, there are inherent deficiencies in the Chinese system that create gaps between policy and practice and nullify optimistic goals, which in turn perpetuates high deforestation rates.

The volume of illegal felling equals legal felling, and it has been estimated that in areas of the plateau such as Central Tibet (U-Tsang) illegal felling significantly exceeds planned production.

Ineffective Reforestation

Reforestation is a priority built into the Chinese constitution and large afforestation programmes have been conducted since 1950 (He 1991). However, the government's reforestation efforts are losing ground to the attack on forest cover. It is estimated that the ratio of trees felled to trees planted is 10:1 (*ibid*) and the total reforested areas in the southwestern mountain region is as low as 12.7 per cent of the actual deforested area. There is a huge discrepancy between the impressive attempts and the meagre results of China's reforestation campaign with the overall survival rate for new plantation at only 30 per cent (Li 1993).

Losses result from inadequate management procedures in fire control, disease control, pest infestation, poaching, urbanisation, reclamation for agriculture and water resource development projects (Li J. et al 1988). Environmental changes such as extreme temperature fluctuations reaching up to 51° C, caused by clear-felling large areas, further hinder successful regeneration (Yang 1986).

The Quota Factor

According to Vaclav Smil (1984), even though it may

contradict Chinese policy, planned commercial extraction has been the leading cause of the 50 per cent reduction in Tibetan forest cover. The inconsistency between policy and practice can be further demonstrated by examining the state's quota-based system. State-owned forestry enterprises, which control the majority of timber resources, are obligated to fulfill annual quotas. The state purchases timber from its forestry enterprises at only one third of the market price. These prices do not even meet production costs, let alone include afforestation fees or scarcity values.

At a Tibet People's Political Consultative Conference's general meeting held in May 1995, Mr Gonpo explained that the Chinese government pays US$22 per cubic metre for timber and then sells it in Beijing for US$963 or for US$1,204 in Japan (Dekhang 1996). Hence the state-owned enterprises are forced to produce and sell a surplus on the free market in order to subsidise the quotas imposed on them. These quotas alone are double or triple the annual growth increment. With these quota systems in place the forest sector is slowly destroying itself. This is one of the major challenges facing the infrastructure of the forestry industry.

Logs waiting to be pushed into the Dharto River in eastern Tibet when waters rise

Loss Via Inefficiency

According to then vice-minister of the P.R.C.'s Ministry of Forests, another debilitating aspect of Chinese forest management is the loss due to negligence (Dong 1985). Estimated losses from fire and rotting wood in China

A rich harvest of non-timber resources are also extracted from Tibet's forests

are extremely severe, especially in the inaccessible forest reserves of Tibet. It has been estimated by Chinese experts that efficiency in forest management throughout China is on average 60 per cent (Li 1993). With Tibet's inherent transportation problems, operations are even more inefficient and due to poor coordination between cutting and hauling agencies US$2 billion of lumber is left to rot each year (Dekhang 1996).

Fires and Disease

Inadequate prevention and control of fires, pests and diseases have resulted in further forest degradation. During 30 years of high-yield logging in 'TAR' there have been 240 forest fires destroying more than 10,000 acres of forest (Dekhang 1996) and over 100,000 forest fires have blazed through regions of Kham lying in Yunnan Province. This amounts to a five per cent or 1.3 million cubic metres loss of forest cover which almost equals the commercial extraction of the national forest enterprises.

In 1996 there were nine forest fire disasters burning 179.56 hectares of forest land in 'TAR' (*Tibet Daily* 1997).

Corruption

Lin Xinshu — who spent time in detention for his involvement in China's 1989 pro-democracy movement — was again detained for writing a letter on 20 August 1998 to President Jiang Zemin and Premier Zhu Rongji. In it he accused corrupt officials of using inferior materials on dikes and of worsening soil erosion by ordering intensive logging in order to pocket money, stating that, "A one-party dictatorship has no means of controlling its own corruption" (Jiang and Zhu 1998).

Concern over poaching was expressed by citizens of Lhasa at the Tibet's People's Political Consultative Conference held in Lhasa in 1995. Illegal felling occurs partly due to the issuing of counterfeit timber licences, and the problem is further exacerbated where environmental administration is coordinated by the same local officials who are also responsible for goods production (Bohm et al 1998). As a result of a governmental hierarchy with no independent environmental monitoring authority, inspectors and officials often have an incentive to overlook violations.

An article entitled "Some People Dare Disobey Orders from the Party Central Committee" appeared in the Communist Party's internal distribution of the journal *Banyuetan*. According to the article a local official explains, "It doesn't matter what the central or provincial leaders say. What counts is what the regional committee secretary and the township party secretary say" (US Embassy 1998c). In China the volume of illegal felling equals legal felling, and it has been estimated that in areas of the plateau such as Central Tibet (U-Tsang) illegal felling significantly exceeds planned production (Richardson 1988). Furthermore, of the few cases of poaching that go to court only 10 per cent actually result in some kind of indictment (He 1991).

According to a US Embassy Report (1998a), many local governments in China depend on forestry for as much as 90 per cent of their revenue, so the fabrication of annual growth rates to increase the extraction rate is a tempting way to increase revenue which in turn further increases pressure on Tibet's forest cover.

Deteriorating Economics

Over-harvesting of forests on the Tibetan Plateau is reinforced and intensified by the deteriorating economic conditions of the Chinese forest industry. In the early 1980s output of the Ngaba district's forest industry accounted for 70 per cent of the region's total industrial output, and in Kandze output equalled 55.5 per cent. Yet, in 1987 only five out of 15 forest companies were continuing to make a profit and by the 1990s output in the Ngaba district had declined by 58.6 per cent.

As the number of forestry jobs decreases and the number of retired forest workers increases, the ratio of individuals receiving pensions has now surpassed the active labour force. Shelter and protection forests are slowly liquidated to support the escalating number of retired forest workers (Zhao 1992).

As resources decline, Tibetan communities are pushed further into social and economic instability. Whilst the majority of timber workers are Chinese, the percentage of Tibetan loggers is slowly growing. Although forest rights were delegated in 1981 between the state-owned timber companies, county timber factories and village collectives, the borders are not clear. These ill-defined boundaries lead to further over-cutting and ethnic disputes (*ibid*).

In the area of Dokhar county in Gyalthang, Yunnan, 112 million cubic metres of timber was felled between 1958 and 1986 which would have a current market value for China of US$ 908 million. A great percentage of this extracted timber does not benefit the Tibetan population of the area but is transported east to benefit and help fuel the Chinese economy (DIIR 1998b).

The once-stable Tibetan economy is now facing a predicament. The introduction of a modern industrial economy into Tibet's traditionally subsistence culture has radically transformed the relationship of Tibetans with their environment:

> **In the past it was generally believed that a carpenter, no matter how successful he is in his business, cannot become rich. This is based on the belief that to trample upon or cut even a small plant is an unwholesome deed, not to mention big trees that are cut down for his business (Choephel 1983).**

Tibet's traditional system of trading, done mostly through bartering encouraged small volumes of trade while maintaining a high degree of self-reliance. This level of self-sufficiency is a fundamental aspect of the Tibetan traditional land use system that supported a non-exploitative relationship with the environment.

Slowly, through Chinese-imposed development, Tibetans are becoming dependent on imported goods and services and losing their tradition of self-reliance. As "free market" economics and globalisation encroach on the Tibetan way of life, a growing number of young Tibetans seek wage-earning employment. To earn a now-necessary wage, or to meet new financial demands imposed by the Chinese government, Tibetans often supplement their income by privately harvesting trees or working as loggers. It can be assumed that the reliance on intense resource liquidation, such as deforestation, to produce exchangeable goods to ensure survival would not have emerged under the traditional system.

China has experienced a 614.1 billion cubic metres decline in precipitation as a result of excessive deforestation contributing to 56 per cent of the cause of arid and semi-arid land.

The various tax structures imposed by the Chinese regime further undermine Tibetan traditions by encouraging the exploitation of resources. Article 9 of the Chinese Constitution provides that "The state protects the right of citizens to own lawfully-earned income, savings, houses and other means of livelihood." In contradiction to its constitution the Chinese government is denying the rights of the Tibetan people to own their own income by imposing alarmingly high taxation rates. A variety of taxes have been imposed on land, animals, wool and fur, hides, meats, grains, butter, milk, cheese, hay, fertiliser, medicinal plants, old age, education and a human tax (TCHRD 1997c).

In December 1998, Tibetan refugees who escaped to Dharamsala from Dawachan village in Central Tibet reported that a tax had even been imposed on individuals whose property contains more than one tree. These irrational and unreasonably high taxes often pressure Tibetans into harvesting timber and selling it back to Chinese officials to raise the tax payments.

CONSEQUENCES OF DEFORESTATION

The Tibetan Plateau has become a diversified gene pool containing varieties of wild and domesticated animals that have co-evolved with the special conditions of the Tibetan Plateau. Diminishing forest cover, especially through clear-cut logging, is resulting in a major loss of biodiversity and consequently an increased rate of species extinction (DIIR 1992). In 1995 Tibet contained a total of 81 endangered animal species (Li 1995). In many areas of Tibet there are a significant number of invertebrates as yet unclassified (Fleming 1998).

It is this rich biological diversity that has enabled human inhabitants to sustain themselves in such harsh, fragile environments. Consequently, as deforestation on the Tibetan Plateau continues, the biodiversity of the plateau slowly erodes, washing away with it the plateau's capabilities to sustain human and other lives.

Erosion and Landslides

The Tibetan Plateau contains the sources and upper reaches of 10 major Asian rivers; the Indus, Sutlej, Karnali, Arun, Manas, Brahmaputra, Salween, Mekong, Yellow River and Yangtze. These rivers flow into ten different countries in Asia. Consequently, about half of the world's population live and sustain themselves along rivers which originate from the Tibetan Plateau (DIIR 1992).

Soil erosion on the Tibetan Plateau is listed in China's Agenda 21 as among the most serious of its environmental problems (UNDP 1997). Geologically speaking the Tibetan Plateau is young (40-50 million years old) and possesses thin topsoil and fragile vegetation cover. The high altitude and steep mountain valleys accelerate potential destruction that results from deforestation. Trees often function as an anchor, helping the soil to store rainwater and holding and supporting the earth that may otherwise be washed into rivers. With the mass extraction of trees follows a corresponding loss of soil. With no roots to hold the soil together, and no needles or leaves to fertilise the ground cover, deforestation produces inevitable, and in the medium term, irreversible soil erosion. This loss of soil then results in landslides and huge silt deposits in nearby rivers.

A spokesperson from Yunnan Province told *AFP* (1998) that landslides alone had killed 477 and injured more than 7,000 people in the mountainous provinces in and around the Tibetan Plateau. Similarly, in late August 1998, 239 people were presumed dead when landslides ravaged the Himalayan mountain districts near India's border (WTN 1998), while in Tibet several districts in the northeast were paralysed due to landslides triggered by unseasonal weather. S.P. Banerjee, a soil expert and visiting fellow at the Tata Energy Research Institute in New Delhi, stated that an overriding factor behind these landslides was deforestation (*ibid*).

Flooding Asia

In building an infrastructure to transport timber, erosion becomes intensified by a growing number of roads carving up the sides of the steep, unstable mountains. In the past 50 years, as a result of deforestation, soil erosion in China has increased from 360,000 sq. km to more than 800,000 sq. km (Jiang and Zhu 1998). As a result, riverbeds have dramatically risen, increasing the frequency of severe floods downstream in several Asian countries.

Tibet: On the Tibetan Plateau itself officials admit that floods have been severely intensified by deforestation and have hit 40 of 70 regions, destroying 2,000 houses, killing livestock and ruining crops (*AP* 1998). In late August 1998, at least 53 people were killed in 'TAR' (BBC 1998) from heavy flooding.

India: It was reported that in 1996 the Yarlung Tsangpo (Brahmaputra) River, flowing from Tibet to India, erupted more extensively than at any other time this century (Dekhang 1996). However, officials have since claimed that the 1998 floods in India rank among the worst inundations of the century (Tewari 1998). By September 1998, these floods, intensified by the extensive deforestation on the Tibetan Plateau, had claimed 1,218 lives in the Indian state of Uttar Pradesh, 299 in Bihar and 130 in West Bengal. In Assam, due to the floods, road traffic was paralysed affecting over 300,000 people (*ibid*).

Laos and Bangladesh: BBC reported on 26 September 1995 that the Mekong River overflowed in Laos affecting the lives of 0.5 million people and the disaster was compounded by a subsequent epidemic. Some scientists have blamed the floods that devastate annually in Bangladesh, affecting thousands of people, on the loss of forest cover in Tibet (Dekhang 1996).

China: Over the last few decades China has been plagued with escalating flood damage. The role of deforestation in increasing the frequency and intensity of flood damage is slowly being articulated and documented by scientists. In Kham (West Sichuan) deforestation has been linked with the frequency of flood disasters rising from once in 15 years to once in five years (Zhao 1992). In the summer of 1991 floods killed over 2,000 people in China and in 1983, an overflow of the Yellow River affected 12 million people (He 1991).

The Water Crisis

While reports of China's record of floods in 1998 captured the news headlines, experts warn that China's lack of water is actually a more serious environmental, social and economic threat (Brown and Halweil 1998). Tibet nourishes the fertile plains of Asia through flows from the upper reaches of the ten main Asian rivers. This creates a link between the environmental health of the Tibetan Plateau and the stability and survival of a mammoth percentage of the most important and productive agricultural areas in the world.

A correlation has been established between high and extended snow cover on the Tibetan Plateau and high winter sea temperatures over the North Atlantic, bringing on sunny summer weather in Europe and typhoons in the Pacific.

While many factors contribute to the gradual reduction of water resources in a geological region, the focus here is on a factor which is subject to human control—primarily timber extraction. If the Eastern Tibetan Plateau was as well forested as in the past, water molecules originating in distant water bodies falling on these forests as precipitation would eventually evapotranspire back into the atmosphere and return repeatedly as precipitation. Further, deforestation increases overland flow in the form of increased runoff and decreases regional humidity thereby affecting local rainfall patterns. Deforestation intensifies desertification processes and exacerbates water crises in China (Wang 1993). A Chinese government inquiry commission has blamed continual deforestation as the major cause for drastic reduction in the water flow of the Gyarong Gyalmo Ngulchu (Ch:Min Jiang) and Upper Yangtze rivers in Kham between January and May. Research by Richard Louis Edmonds (1994) demonstrated that China has experienced a 614.1 billion cubic metres decline in precipitation as a result of excessive deforestation contributing to 56 per cent of the cause of arid and semi-arid land in China, reconfirming the connection between the Chinese water crisis and deforestation.

China now has 400 cities suffering from water shortages, and 108 cities are considered to have a serious water crisis (Pomfret 1998a). Rivers and lakes are running dry. In the last nine years the quantity of water discharged from the Yellow River has fallen by 23 per cent, and on several occasions the river has dried up completely. In 1972, for the first time in the history of China, the Yellow River dried up before reaching the sea. In 1997 dry stretches have lasted for periods up to 126 days (*People's Daily* 1998) totalling 226 days (Brown and Halweil 1998). Some areas of China are so desperate for water that farmers have taken to tearing off manhole covers and pumping raw sewage onto their fields (Pomfret 1998a).

In China water has always been an extremely precious resource and increased pressure on water resources due to deforestation is magnifying irrigation problems, causing crop losses totalling hundreds of millions of dollars each year (Wang 1993). Scientists have been quoted in *China Daily* predicting that, "There is a possibility the Yellow River will become nothing more than a seasonal river" (Rennie 1998).

Global Weather Patterns

The Tibetan Plateau has a fundamental impact on both regional and global climatic patterns. As the various causes of the widespread destruction of Tibet's forests are slowly unveiled, the effects continue to trigger environmental, social and economic crises. Ecosystems do not exist in isolation and consequently these effects are not confined to the Tibetan Plateau. In fact, these ecosystem disturbances have the potential to destabilise environmental, social and economic patterns around the globe.

The adoption of the Kyoto Protocol calling for a reduction of greenhouse gas emissions at the United Nations Conference on Climate Change in December 1997 demonstrates a consensus emerging among scientists and policy makers that climate change is one of the most serious environmental challenges facing the world today. Another factor affecting both Asian and global climatic patterns is vegetation cover on the Tibetan Plateau (Derbyshire and Gasse 1996).

The Indian Monsoon

The Tibetan Plateau towers at the centre of the Eurasian landmass and consequently deflects jet streams of the upper atmosphere influencing the atmospheric circulation of the entire northern hemisphere. The plateau is a critical player in global climate stability and has an especially important influence on the Indian monsoon. In the summer the air above the plateau becomes hotter than the air above India. This enables the plateau to act as a heating mechanism. Consequently an anticyclone is formed over the Southern Himalayas, drawing in the Indian monsoon, until the plateau cools in the winter when the winds are reversed.

Through the help of computer modelling it has been estimated that there are approximately 15 to 29 major indicators which help predict the formation of monsoons. The pattern of jet stream winds in the upper atmosphere and the snow cover on the Himalayas and the Tibetan Plateau are amongst these indicators. The amount of snow cover on the plateau is partially determined by the amount of vegetation, forest and grass cover (Reiter 1993). More specifically, the amount and type of the vegetation influences the rate at which the snow cover recedes during the spring.

Green forest cover absorbs 95 per cent of solar heat; clear-cut areas and grasslands absorb only 80 per cent while barren land and bare rock absorb even less. Forested areas also break up snow cover and consequently help retain an even greater amount of heat (*ibid*). Hence, as the plateau's ability to absorb solar heat is crippled by incessant deforestation, the snow cover retreats at a decelerating pace.

As the tree cover decreases, the heating mechanism of the plateau diminishes, and through a series of interconnections the pressure systems are altered which either delay or reduce the Indian monsoon. This lingering snow cover disrupting the Indian monsoon (Zheng and Wu 1995) has the potential to foster disasters for Indian agriculture (Reiter 1993), thus establishing a link between the stability of the Asian monsoon and loss of vegetation cover on the Tibetan Plateau.

The monsoon rains contribute 70 per cent of India's total annual rainfall. Referred to as the lifeblood of Indian farming, its stability determines whether millions of Indians meet their basic food needs or not. In the latter half of 1998 the destabilised monsoon with unexpected rains and droughts caused extensive damage to many crops such as onion, potato, peas, cauliflower and cabbage. Even though threat to food security has been magnified by over-cautious policies and high inflation rates, according to agriculture specialist S.D. Saravanan, erratic monsoon behaviour is mostly responsible for escalating food prices (Anandan et al 1998). Som Pal, Indian Minister of State for Agriculture, has also blamed unseasonal heat and rains for rising onion prices (Rekhi and Singh 1998). This caused extreme hardships for people in India.

Clear-cut slopes littered with felled trees in Dragyab region, Kham, May 1999.

GLOBAL JET STREAMS

Among the earth's ecosystems, mountain regions have been identified as having a unique global importance. This is evident in Agenda 21, which is one of the major action plan that emerged from the 1992 UN Conference on Environment and Development (Stone 1992). The report emphasises that the present rate of deforestation is not only of regional or national importance but is a global issue demanding urgent attention. The scientific data is piling up to indict human activity as the source of the current phase of global warming. One example is the relationship between the deforestation on the Tibetan Plateau and global weather patterns. As explained above the snow melt on the plateau, delayed by shrinking forest cover, modifies the plateau's systematic heating. As the heating capabilities of the plateau are delayed, jet stream patterns that affect the entire northern hemisphere are altered.

The Tibetan Plateau is a significant contributor to global weather patterns, deflecting and compressing wind currents over thousands of kilometres (Reiter 1981). For example, a correlation has been established between high and extended snow cover on the Tibetan Plateau and high winter sea temperatures over the North Atlantic, bringing on sunny summer weather in Europe and typhoons in the Pacific. This relationship is partially explained by abnormal fluctuations in jet stream patterns above the Tibetan Plateau (Reiter 1993). These weather alterations also intensify floods and rain in Eastern China. The Yangtze basin may well be one of the areas receiving additional rainfall (Brown and Halweil 1998).

These Pacific typhoons further result in the interruption of trade winds off the West Coast of North and South America, which is responsible for El Nino. The El Nino stirs up ocean water causing disruptions of the marine food chain and affecting the entire economy of Peru and Ecuador. Storms causing damage on the California coastline and droughts in New Zealand, Indonesia, Australia, India and southern Africa are also part of this phenomenon. Recent studies have indicated that alterations to the Tibetan Plateau's vegetation cover play a role in generating regional climate disruptions which have the potential to dovetail into global climate change (Longrigg and Rowe 1991).

While there is no way of conclusively connecting global warming with specific weather events, the likelihood that they are linked has grown with each passing year. Even though to declare a cause-and-effect relationship between deforestation and certain climatic abnormalities around the globe is a simplification of a very complex fabric of many interwoven relationships, all evidence points to the fact that the Tibetan Plateau plays a major role in many of these relationships.

CAN CHINA LIVE UP TO ITS PROMISES?

Global consciousness is slowly awakening to the dire and inevitable consequences that arise from habitat destruction. Chinese attempts to scientifically manage forest cover on the Tibetan Plateau to ensure regeneration have so far failed miserably. The resulting environmental consequences have triggered and reinforced international pressure on the Chinese government. International environmental organisations such as The World Watch Institute have exposed various global threats caused by China's environmental crisis (Brown and Halweil 1998). This has raised global awareness and consequently increased international pressure on China to undertake reforms.

China is home to one fifth of humanity and within a decade its Gross Domestic Product (GDP) will probably match that of the United States. If China wants to be accepted as one of the world's great powers it must recognise that such power also brings with it responsibility. China will have to adapt to international rules and responsibilities that surround environmental management and social justice issues.

This opinion is supported by many Chinese scientists and academics. In fact, Chinese academics have long been aware of the potentially catastrophic environmental, social and economic impacts of industrial high-yield logging (Dong 1985) and have produced several papers quantifying deforestation during the 1983-87 policy reform. Calculations have estimated China's losses from excessive deforestation amount to US$66.2 billion a year, which is 12.1 per cent of China's total national income (Mao 1998). It has become obvious that China cannot environmentally, socially or economically afford to continue mismanaging its forests. Even though an increasing amount of energy is slowly being reallocated towards needed solutions, as the consequences ripple through China and the world solutions still lack a necessary sense of urgency.

Even ordinary Chinese citizens have started voicing their discontent over the destructive effects resulting from the dramatic difference between policy and practice. On 26 August 1998, in one of the most populist petitions since 1989, 309 democratic and human rights Chinese activists from 19 provinces signed "An Open Letter to the Chinese People: Protect the Yangtze, Our Mother River". The letter clearly states:

> **In the mountainous areas along the upper and middle reaches of the Yangtze River, all the farmland should be reverted to forest. We must abandon the plundering development plan which "drains the pond to get the fish." So-called high growth economics that waste resources and pollute the environment come at too high a price.**

These Chinese have appealed to the government for an end to the destructive forestry practices which have contributed to the devastating extent of 1998's flooding. They have accused their country of being "Guided by blind arrogance in thinking that man can conquer nature." The group reconfirms that the floods were caused in part by decades of bad environmental management in the Yangtze River Basin. The letter also contains several suggestions on changing the policies of rampant deforestation and land reclamation, demanding greater government accountability and better laws to protect the environment (Jiang and Zhu 1998).

In reaction to accumulating international and domestic pressure reforms, such as the codification of environmental crimes, were introduced in China's recently-amended criminal code for the first time. Sections 344 and 345 state that individuals who illegally cut trees or groups of trees shall be punished by imprisonment for up to three years or, in extreme cases, over seven years (US Embassy 1997). In August 1998, at a lawmakers' meeting in Beijing, officials called for stricter environmental protection policies (TIN 1998b). However, to alleviate pressure on forest cover, promised solutions must run deeper than policy creation. Policy formulations must be backed by effective enforcement and compliance.

As the consequences of failed attempts to ensure forest regeneration are increasingly understood and felt by China and its people, the inconsistencies between forest policy and practice are only partially addressed. Following many years of rapid growth at the expense of the environment, China is being forced to acknowledge the costs of ecological devastation.

The State Council orders placing an unconditional logging ban on 54 counties in Kham (Western Sichuan) on 1 September 1998, demonstrates that China's leaders have observed a clear connection among deforestation, the 1998 floods and the escalating political, social and economic crisis. On 9 December 1998 unofficial reports suggested that the 'TAR' government ordered all operations of lumber processing mills in southeast 'TAR' to shut down. The ban applies to all of Chamdo and Nyingtri prefectures, an area that contains over 85 per cent of

Given that the objective behind the opening of the Tibetan Plateau to foreign investment was to help fuel China's growth rate, it is highly unlikely that the favoured investment will consider environmental and cultural implications.

standing timber volume in 'TAR' (Winkler 1999). This announcement included an emphasis on reforestation projects to begin immediately by employing former loggers as tree planters. However the 9 December ban has not been confirmed and the degree of permanence of both bans has yet to be determined.

The danger remains that the bans are temporary and the forests in the newly-restricted areas will continue to be logged. Tibetans coming into exile from Tibet in the year 2000 corroborate that logging still continues in Kham, Thewo and Ngaba regions in Amdo and 'TAR'. Even though this shift in policy has the possibility of longterm benefits for the Tibetan areas, the potential benefits will only be realised if there is implementation behind the policy.

When the motivation behind many Chinese environmental policies is revealed, the conflict between policy and practice becomes understood and environmental degradation persists. An integral part of China's foreign policy interest is "to be a good international citizen" and includes participation in 126 international conventions and membership in all Inter-governmental Organisations (IGOs) in the United Nations system (Yufan 1992). However, much of the increasing environmental diplomacy practised within Chinese policy represents, as in many countries, an attempt to be seen as an active and constructive participant and a responsible member of the world community.

Environmental protection has thus become an available means of coping with the multiple problems it faces in its foreign policy agenda. Unlike human rights, arms sales and trade issues, environmental protection is less sensitive and affordable for Beijing leaders (*ibid*).

Ambitious Chinese environmental policy created in the last decade can be partially comprehended as a response, aimed at alleviating international criticism, to the political upheaval in Beijing in the spring of 1989. As a result little energy has actually been invested in effective enforcement, proactive policies and preventive environmental management.

Once the public relations purpose of China's new environmental policy is unmasked, a priority to economic growth is exposed. When the economic objectives behind the forest industry are revealed a bleak environmental future is painted. Since China launched its economic reform programme in 1978, its transition from a command to a market-based economy has helped fuel one of the world's highest growth rates (World Bank 1997). While the impact of China's rapid economic growth has made great strides in improving short-term social welfare (*ibid*), the effect on the environment has become a serious concern for China and the international community.

Despite the escalating number of environmental problems leading to developmental setbacks, the Chinese government remains convinced that social and environmental salvation lies in growth-based economics and an ever-increasing Gross National Product (GNP). The government has demonstrated its priority of economic growth over environmental protection on several occasions. At the UN Framework Convention on Climate Change in December 1997, China resisted international pressure to commit to emissions restrictions that would impede its growth. Chinese President Jiang Zemin commented at the Asia-Pacific Economic Cooperation Forum in Vancouver on 23 November 1997 that China wants to maintain its robust growth (Ming 1998).

China hopes to generate enough financial capital through unbridled economic growth to address environmental protection and social justice issues. Unfortunately the accompanying increase in energy use, natural resources depletion and pollution-producing activities that coincides with capital generating capabilities cannot be ignored. If the trend of environmental degradation continues at the present rate, by the time China is financially capable to invest more thoroughly in the environment and the future, the accumulated destruction of its life-support system may be beyond rehabilitation.

Tibet, when included under the Beijing umbrella, becomes incorporated into the Chinese government's quest for economic growth. Chairman of the 'Tibetan Autonomous Regional People's Government', Gyaltsen Norbu, stated that "the main direction of economic work in our region is to accelerate the development of the four pillar industries in 'TAR'" (Norbu 1997). These industries, which include forestry, were said by Gyaltsen Norbu to "play a big stimulating role and to produce such products on a large-scale as soon as possible so that they will become new economic growth outlets in our region". The Ninth Five-Year Plan for the Tibetan Plateau, 1996-2000, institutionalises the Chinese agenda of unrestrained growth: "With the strengthening of the region's ability to develop itself and on the condition that the economic structure is optimised, and economic efficiency raised, we will strive to have the 2000 per capita GNP quadruple the 1980 figure".

Although the plan recognises the need for active protection to overcome the phenomenon of over-logging in individual areas, it maintains a commitment to "increase the harvesting of wood year by year". In the eastern area of Tibet, including the Nyingtri and Chamdo regions, Tibet's largest forest area, the Five-Year Plan advocates,

Every day about 500 trucks loaded with Tibetan timber travel from Thewo, Amdo, to Linxia and Lanzhou in China. October 1999

"We will vigorously develop processing industries with the stress on processing timber." However, these two areas fall under the subsequent 9 December 1998 logging ban, reinforcing the rift that exists between China's environmental and economic policies and magnifying the complications that surround China's "promises".

Reform has also led to rapid integration with the world economy. In 1997 China was the tenth largest trading nation in the world and attracted more direct foreign investment than any country except the US (World Bank 1997). Foreign investment is one example of a tool used to fuel China's GNP. In pursuit of economic growth through direct foreign investment the Chinese government has created what it calls "Preferential Policies for Foreign Investment" ('TAR' Economy Coordination Committee). This is a legal guarantee that the regional government will give foreign-financed projects priority through each step of the formation process in planning, project approval, provision of capital, construction start-up, establishment of the business itself and registration.

Through various mechanisms such as tax rebates and incentives, foreign business people interested in a wholly foreign-financed enterprise or a joint venture are encouraged to invest in Tibet. Given that the objective behind the opening of the Tibetan Plateau to foreign investment was to help fuel China's growth rate, it is highly unlikely that the favoured investment will consider environmental and cultural implications.

LOOKING TOWARDS THE FUTURE

Tension between indigenous or local knowledge and "scientific" knowledge is nowhere more evident than in mountain regions like the Himalayas (Berkes et al 1998). The mountain communities on the Tibetan Plateau have survived and overcome natural constraints to satisfy their basic needs for centuries, while the emerging number of barren landscapes and devastated ecosystems on the plateau is the ultimate expression of Chinese-imposed industrial consciousness. Modern industrial society has tried, consciously and unconsciously, to break its ancestral traditions so as to control nature and human development through science and technology, thus selectively eliminating deeper values and rich sources of knowledge in the process (Drengson 1993).

One possible solution lies in the implementation of participatory land use practices. There is considerable research to suggest that a reactive approach with an emphasis on controlling access to forest resources may be less effective than a proactive mechanism that provides incentives for communities to manage them (Menzies and Peluso 1991). There is also growing evidence to support the fact that indigenous knowledge or local resource use plays a significant role in determining the longterm sustainability of those resources (Berkes et al 1998). This suggests that the most effective means of enforcing environmental sustainability comes from within the local communities themselves. This encourages the utilisation of detailed local knowledge gained from the community's co-evolution with its natural surroundings as opposed to attempting to enforce a predefined homogeneous policy against the natural diversity of each specific region.

Members of a "community-managed forest" will depend on subsequent benefits of the resource for their future welfare and consequently will have a vested interest in the forest's long term sustainability (Netting 1997). Policies that focus on a participatory approach to forest management can then be understood as an opportunity to utilise and cultivate indigenous, traditional and sustainable land use practices. For this to happen, policy makers must look beyond conventional economic theory to enable local communities to evolve environmentally and culturally appropriate forest management practices.

Another possible opportunity for the Chinese government to mitigate environmental, social and economic decay resulting from industrial logging resides with a refined look at investment. To offset the likelihood that foreign investment will remain consistent with a growth-oriented agenda and focus on high-yield profit maximisation, investment guidelines for the Tibetan Plateau should be created to ensure a preventive approach to sustainable land use practices. Towards this end Tibetan Government-in-Exile has issued guidelines for international development projects and investment in Tibet (see Chapter 9).

Mechanisms must be installed, and policies created, that encourage environmentally and culturally appropriate investment choices. For instance, an Environmental Impact Assessment (EIA) should be completed, at the expense of the investor, prior to the project approval. The EIA should not only determine the short- and longterm environmental effects of a proposal but the impacts on Tibetan culture and tradition.

Guidelines should be created providing incentives for environmentally and culturally appropriate investment, including fundamental restrictions and incentives supporting the following ideals:

- the assessment of an investment project should include representation from the affected community and all interest groups
- a standard level of community participation within the investment project should be defined to ensure that the allocation of the benefits derived from the invesment include the Tibetans
- an appropriate level of foreign investment should be determined in each region and investment in education, health and environmental regeneration should be given top priority.

Investment in social or community forestry is a good example of a type of development that effectively maintains environmental sustainability. These programmes provide incentives for local people to cultivate conservation practices and prove to be an excellent example of proactive forest management. Social forestry programmes, such as those in India, attempt to integrate indigenous knowledge with forest management in an attempt to improve rural welfare and reverse environmental damage.

Forest preservation is an intricate and longterm process. If it is done well, habitat preservation and economic development will begin to reinforce one another.

There is some evidence to suggest that China is shifting toward a forest use plan that stretches beyond policy statements and may be consistent with sustainable forest practices. For example, the World Bank-funded China-Forestry Development in Poor Areas Project is implementing programmes designed to develop forest resources. These projects are based on sustainable and participatory approaches to help reduce poverty and improve environmental management of forest resources (Ministry of Forests 1997).

Supporting and respecting Tibetan land use practices is an obvious direction to enable China to mitigate environmental, social and economic problems which have resulted from unbridled forest liquidation. With changing circumstances on the Tibetan Plateau, such as a doubling of population pressure, it is important to note that it is neither feasible nor desirable for Tibet to live as though it were in the past. However, this does not in any way negate the need or importance for restoring and maintaining the traditional knowledge and land use practices of the Tibetan people. The application and encouragement of projects that work on a participatory basis, respecting traditional knowledge, represents one possible design model. The decision to use, preserve and respect the immeasurable source of wealth residing within the Tibetan traditions through such projects will reveal to the world the level of sophistication and readiness of the Chinese government to peacefully and sustainably enter the 21st century.

By utilising the Tibetan knowledge and land use practices that have proven to be sustainable over the last 2,000 years on the Tibetan Plateau, China has not only an opportunity but also an obligation to alleviate pressure on forest cover and to rectify the local, regional and global catastrophes — both actual and potential — that have been slowly manifesting themselves as a result of deforestation on the Tibetan Plateau. ■

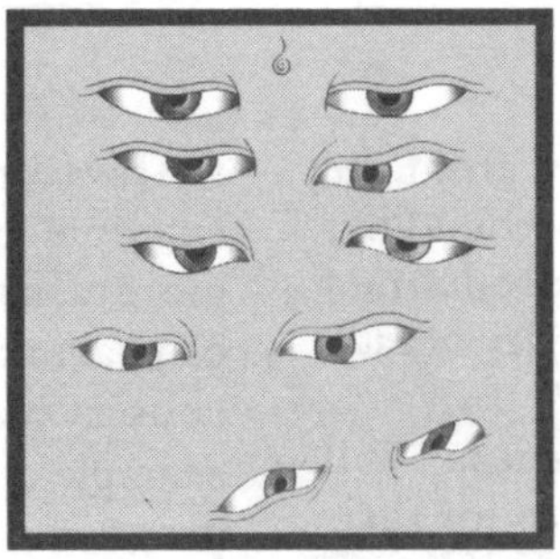

CHAPTER FIVE

POPULATION PRESSURES

The most serious threat to the survival of Tibet's culture and national identity is presently China's population transfer programme, which is reducing the Tibetans into an insignificant minority in their own land at an alarming rate.

His Holiness the 14th Dalai Lama, 1995

IN 1997, film maker Tenzing Sonam travelled to the northeastern corner of Amdo, one of the three traditional regions of Tibet, to visit the birthplace of his father which was also close to the home of the present Dalai Lama. The account of this very personal journey was recorded in the documentary *A Stranger in my Native Land* in which the Indian-born narrator discovers the reality of Tibet's — and therefore his — loss:

> **... It is ironic. In India my father devoted his life to the cause of Tibetan independence. I was brought up with a strong sense of my Tibetan roots. Yet it is here in my father's home I discover that our very identity is under threat...for more than two centuries Chinese settlers and Asian Muslims have outnumbered all Tibetans in this area... My father's extended family is one of only three Tibetan families in this village of nearly a hundred households. Even when my father was a child the Tibetans there had already lost their language. But they still maintained a distinct Tibetan identity, especially in their dress. Now there is no sign of even that...I am taken by surprise to find the graves of my grandparents, since Tibetans usually cremate their dead and offer their remains to vultures. But the Tibetans here have adopted the Chinese custom of ancestor worship. I feel a welter of contradictory emotions. I am moved by this family ritual which reaffirms my own consciousness. And yet I am also saddened because it confirms the decline of Tibetan culture here in my father's native region.**

Since 1950 there has been an undeniably large influx of Chinese into Tibet. This has resulted from a number of factors:

- The need for military forces and assorted security personnel;
- Government policy and programmes to transfer Chinese, particularly cadres and professionals, to the 'Tibet Autonomous Region' ('TAR') and other Tibetan regions;
- Government encouragement of voluntary migration;
- Work units bringing Chinese labourers to Tibet for construction projects;
- The market-driven migration of individual Chinese entrepreneurs and craftsmen.

Towns such as Gormo (Golmud) in Amdo have been created which are predominantly populated by Chinese (96 per cent). Tibetan urban centres have been sinocized and in Eastern Tibet's Kham province and in Central Tibet lands have been appropriated for agriculture. Where Chinese have settled they dominate commerce and are at the centre of development strategies. Education facilities increasingly

World Bank supports transfer of more than 60,000 Chinese into Tibet

The Chinese government's population transfer programme received a tremendous boost in 1999 with the World Bank funding of the controversial Western Poverty Reduction Project in Dulan, Tsonub "Tibetan Autonomous Prefecture" in Amdo despite heavy opposition from the United States, Germany and Tibet Support Groups. The World Bank's contribution of US$ 160 million out of US$ 311 million project is aimed to meet the needs of 1.7 million poor people in Northeastern Tibet. But the project involves bringing more than 61,775 non-Tibetans into the area and if this population transfer goes ahead the percentage of Tibetans in Dulan will reduce from 19 per cent to 10.1 per cent. Besides, the project has serious ecological implications in the form of land degradation, desertification, and loss of biodiversity.

DIIR 1999b

support the urbanised Chinese population to the disadvantage of Tibetans. In 1994 the Central Committee of the Communist Party's Third Work Forum on Tibet outlined official Chinese policies on population transfer, endorsing and encouraging the accelerated movement of Chinese to the 'TAR'.

POPULATION TRANSFER

"Population transfer" is defined by the UN Commission on Human Rights' Sub-Commission on the Prevention of Discrimination and Protection of Minorities as "the movement of people as a consequence of political and or economic processes in which the State government or State authorised agencies participate (ICJ 1997).

The definition is further explained:

> The term "transfer" implies purpose in the act of moving a population...The State's role may be active or passive, but nonetheless contributes to the systematic, coercive and deliberate nature of the movement of population into or out of an area... the State's role may involve financial subsidies, planning, public information or other judicial action, and even the administration of justice (UNDP 1994).

Population transfer has been conducted with the effect or purpose of altering the demographic composition of a territory in accordance with policy objectives or prevailing ideology, particularly when that ideology or policy asserts the dominance of a certain group over another.

Population transfer policies often single out specific ethnic, racial or religious groups in clear violation of the anti-discrimination principles laid down in the International Convention on the Elimination of All Forms of Discrimination, to which the People's Republic of China (PRC) is a party. Population transfer can lead to discrimination against the original inhabitants in the spheres of housing, employment, education, health care, and the use of native languages and national customs.

An influx of settlers into inhabited territory can present grave economic consequences for the original inhabitants. The imposition of an alien economic structure often disrupts original trading patterns upon which local inhabitants depend. New goods are introduced to meet the needs of settlers, with new business opportunities structured to favour the new arrival.

Poverty, homelessness, illiteracy and increased mortality rates can be the direct results of population transfer programmes. In this way, peoples may be systematically reduced to a powerless minority who are treated as second-class citizens in their own country and denied opportunities to actively participate in social and political processes. Famine, flooding and desertification can result from the introduction of inappropriate crops and harvesting methods, and the environmental burdens placed on natural resources by an increase in population.

The Fourth Geneva Convention of 1949 states that the transfer of civilians by an occupying power into territory it occupies is a violation of international law. However, it is a practice which many occupying powers, colonial administrators and totalitarian rulers have used and still use to break resistance to their rule and consolidate control over a particular territory.

COLONISATION

Beijing partly claims official legitimacy for colonising Tibet from its professed "advanced stage of civilisation". This rhetoric resembles the language of the "sacred trust" principle used in Article 22 of the Covenant of the League of Nations:

> The best method of giving practical effect to this principle is that the tutelage of such peoples should be entrusted to advanced nations who by reason of their resources, their experience or their geographical position can best undertake this responsibility.

The PRC claims to "assist" Tibet, politically, economically and culturally, to overcome its "backwardness". Chinese literature tends to present China's policies in Tibet as self-sacrificing efforts to help a poor and backward area and protect it from "western imperialism".

On 25 July 1959 the International Commission of Jurists (ICJ) published *The Question of Tibet and the Rule of Law.* The "preliminary" report examined the PRC's violations of the 17-Point Agreement (signed between China and Tibet in 1951, after China invaded Tibet) violations of human rights, the question of genocide and Tibet's legal status. It concluded that:

> Evidence points to a prima facie case of a systematic intention...to destroy in whole or in part the Tibetans as a separate nation and the Buddhist religion in Tibet.

The Tibetan people's participation in government is little more than a 'rubberstamp' function, with all real decision-making and executive authority exercised by the Chinese, particularly through the Communist Party and the army.

The Secretary-General of the ICJ stated that the report made it clear that:

> From the present report there emerges...a prima facie case of the worst type of imperialism and colonialism, coming precisely from the very people who claim to fight against it.

CHINESE COLONISERS

In 1962, the 10th Panchen Lama presented Chinese Premier Zhou Enlai with a 120-page report on Tibet known as "The 70,000 Character Petition" which was a detailed account of the tragedy facing Tibet. The secret report, which only came to light in 1997, written in 1962 (four years before the start of the Cultural Revolution), argues that China's policies were leading to the eradication of religion, the decline of Tibetan culture and potentially to the elimination of Tibetans as a distinct nationality (*TIN* 1997c).

A 1997 report entitled *China's Tibet: The World's Largest Remaining Colony* prepared by the Unrepresented Nations and Peoples Organisation (UNPO 1997) concludes that Tibet is a de facto colony of the PRC. It asserts that the present Chinese rule over Tibet was established in the way most colonial powers establish control: by military action and a treaty (the 17 Point Agreement of 1951) that bears all the characteristics of an "unequal treaty".

This is supported by the International Commission of Jurists' Legal Enquiry Committee on Tibet who in 1959 concluded that prior to the 1950 Chinese invasion Tibet had achieved de facto independence and all the requirements of de jure independence:

> Tibet demonstrated from 1913 to 1950 the conditions of statehood as generally accepted under international law. In 1950 there was a people and a territory, and a government which functioned in that territory, conducting its own domestic affairs free from any outside authority. From 1913-1950 foreign relations of Tibet were conducted exclusively by the Government of Tibet and countries with whom Tibet had foreign relations are shown by official documents to have treated Tibet in practice as an independent state (ICJ 1959).

The UNPO report adds that the administration of Tibet now has all the characteristics of a colonial regime. The Tibetan people's participation in government is little more than a "rubberstamp" function, with all real decision-making and executive authority exercised by the Chinese, particularly through the Communist Party and the army. The most senior Tibetans in the Chinese government are former aristocrats who have been co-opted, as was the case in European-owned colonies. The report further concludes that despite trying to give a semblance of autonomy, China mostly governs Tibet by direct, as opposed to indirect, rule.

Colonial rule superimposes national borders. The current division of Tibet into the 'TAR' and the 'Tibet Autonomous Prefectures/Counties' runs counter to the Tibetan concept of Tibet as consisting of one unified territory divided into three provinces of Amdo, Kham and U-Tsang.

The Chinese government presents and explains its policies in terms of a "civilising mission". Intercultural exchange is asymmetrical: the Chinese residents in Tibet adopt hardly any aspects of Tibetan culture, while the influence of Chinese culture on Tibetans, in particular those living in urban areas, is strong.

Economic development is planned and imposed by the colonial power and often benefits the metropolitan state at the expense of the satellite region. Resources located in the colony are transferred to, or used for the benefit of, the metropolitan state and for further processing and marketing by that state. China exhibits all these traits in Tibet where natural resources are exported to China or used for industrial and construction sites which primarily benefit Chinese settler communities. Chinese "development" projects in Tibet are imposed and Tibetans have little or no say in the planning and implementation of these projects.

Colonial authority is maintained by eliminating dissent within colonised populations. Tibetan protest against Chinese rule, or any aspects of it, in Tibet is systematically silenced. In order to maintain control the Chinese government maintains a large and permanent military presence in Tibet. The maintenance of authority is often strengthened by a policy of population transfer. There is a clear pattern of continuous and intensifying Chinese settlement in Tibet.

REASONS FOR COLONISATION

Although the Chinese claimed to be liberating the Tibetans from the oppression of "feudal serfdom" and introducing a "new era of prosperity", there were strong economic, strategic and demographic reasons for the occupation. His Holiness the 14th Dalai Lama believes that originally there were three reasons why China coveted Tibet. With control of Tibet, the Chinese would:

- Gain access to a variety of untapped natural resources
- Secure their southwestern borders
- Secure huge new areas of sparsely populated land in which to settle the growing Chinese population (Lama 1962).

This is supported by a statement made in 1960 by Premier Zhou Enlai who in the aftermath of the invasion said:

> Chinese are greater in number and more developed in economy and culture but in the regions they inhabit there is not much arable land left and underground resources are not as abundant as in the regions inhabited by fraternal nationalities (*Beijing Review* 1980).

More recently, Ragdi, chairman of the Standing Committee of the 'TAR Party Congress', admitted in a speech reported by *Tibet Daily* on 29 July 1998 that the wider aim of the intensified anti-Dalai Lama campaign was to protect the "unity and security" of the whole of China.

For the Beijing leadership, Tibet is the "southwestern gate of China" and its stability is essential for defence and strategic purposes. Tibet holds a crucial status in the overall order of China's political, economic and cultural development, being one of China's key defence outposts and strategic points, with the Himalayas being a natural defence.

So speeding up the economic and social development of the Tibetan region, to preserve its united and stable order, is of key significance to national security.

Even more important to China's leaders is the expectation that the Chinese will provide a powerful model of modern thinking and behaviour which Tibetans will perceive and eventually emulate. Based on the history of other minority areas, Beijing's leaders are partially banking on a process of acculturation in which the more "advanced" Chinese will open Tibetans up to new ideas and attitudes and create a new "modern" Tibetan in the process who will not be so easily influenced by religion.

Tibet holds a crucial status in the overall order of China's political, economic and cultural development, being one of China's key defence outposts and strategic points, with the Himalayas being a natural defence.

While Beijing realises that its open-door policy will likely create much pain and inhumanity to Tibetans in the short-run, it feels that this is the price which must be paid for modernising Tibetan society. The Beijing administration believes that in the long run its policies will triumph.

CHINESE POLICY ON POPULATION TRANSFER BECOMES OFFICIAL

The highest ruling body in China, the Central Committee of the Communist Party (CCCP), in 1994 officially and publicly lent its support to a policy of facilitating Chinese migration to Tibet as part of an economic development programme to counter the region's "separatist" movement. While a variety of government agents have in the past provided incentives for Chinese to work in Tibet, this was Beijing's first admission of such policies at a national level.

More significantly, the 1994 Third Work Forum on Tibet provided the first public confirmation of the assimilation of Tibet into the Chinese economic structure. The CCCP said that Chinese are "encouraged and supported" to move to Tibet, and that they will offer "preferential conditions" to attract more Chinese to the remote plateau. This lends support to a leaked

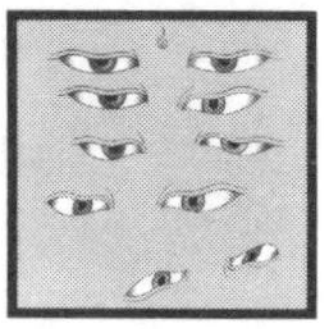

Lhasa: an answer to 40 years of alien rule

Lhasa City's sensational increase of Chinese population over the last 40 years has marginalised the Tibetans and created problems such as unemployment, alcoholism, prostitution, domestic violence, rising divorce rates and crime. In 1949 there were only 2,000 Chinese in Lhasa City but at present 60 to 70 per cent of the total population in Lhasa is estimated to be Chinese. This seven-fold increase of Chinese population—from 30,000 in 1959 to an estimated 200,000 today—outnumbers the Tibetans in the city by about three to one. The size of the city has also expanded from less than three square kilometres to more than 51 square kilometres, with the traditional Tibetan quarter of the city squeezed into less than five per cent of the urban area today. *TIN 1999b, ICJ 1997*

report of an earlier top secret meeting held in Chengdu on 12 May 1993 at which it was decided that to meet the growing political resistance in Tibet, China should intensify its population transfer policy.

Prior to this such policy statements only appeared in provincial and lower level regulations. Before 1994 the Chinese had always denied that there was any policy of moving Chinese to Tibet. A review of Chinese history provides evidence that refutes such claims. The first public indication of Chinese population transfer to Tibet came as early as 1952 in the Directive of the Central Committee of the CPC on Policies for Work in Tibet issued by Mao Zedong. Proposing a five-fold increase in the population of the western half of Tibet, later to be named the 'TAR', Mao said:

> **Tibet covers a large area but is thinly populated. Its population should be increased from the present two or three million to five or six million, and then to over 10 million (Tharpa 1968).**

The 1956 "rustication" programme known as *xiafang* (downward transfer to the countryside) in its quest for industrialisation sought to transfer millions of people from the urban areas of eastern China to the remote and sparsely populated regions in the north and west of the PRC. In Tibet the rustication system created an alien economic system which had little connection with traditional practices and methods of production.

For example, between 1954 and the mid-1960s, there was a large-scale resettlement of Chinese into the Tibetan province of Amdo to provide labour for construction of state farms and reclaim land for agriculture. The 1956-67 Beijing draft of the National Programme for Agricultural Development stated: "...wherever conditions permit, land reclamation should be carried out by organised new settlers". The demographic movement included peasants attracted by agricultural opportunities, compulsory relocated exiled cadres as well as prisoners and those sentenced to "reform through labour". Released prisoners were encouraged to have their families join them and thus became permanent residents. Hundreds of thousands of Chinese settled in Amdo during this period, including 200,000 in Siling (Xining) its capital.

According to Chinese sources, by 1984 Amdo had a population of 3.8 million, of which more than 2.5 million were Chinese and only 750,000 were Tibetan. Less than one year later, the total population had increased by almost 150,000, while the number of Tibetans remained the same (ICLT 1992). The resulting urbanisation may be seen as a precursor to the economic reforms of Deng Xiaoping's regime in the 1980s.

At the 1984 Second National Forum on Work in Tibet, the initiative to reduce the number of Chinese in Tibet, as promised by the Communist Party's then General Secretary Hu Yaobang in 1980, was effectively reversed. The movement of workers was facilitated under the guise of achieving "economic development" in Tibet through 43 development projects which were all contracted to provincial and municipal firms in the Chinese interior and employed Chinese personnel (Hessler 1999b). In 1984 and 1985 an estimated 60,000 Chinese workers associated with these "development" projects arrived in the 'TAR', primarily in Lhasa. All of the Chinese workers were on temporary contracts, but many eventually remained in the 'TAR' to pursue other economic opportunities (*Tibet Daily* 1994).

Under Deng's leadership the debilitating ideological and political campaigns of the Cultural Revolution were pushed aside in favour of economic reform. The "Four Modernisations" unleashed an economic fervour that swept the country. The four guiding principles were to include the:

- Reform of agriculture
- Reform of urban areas
- Decentralisation of control over state-run enterprises
- Reform of price structures to reflect the emerging market system (Grey 1995).

A statement by Deng on 29 June 1987, during a meeting with former US President Jimmy Carter, has been described as a "guiding principle" for Tibet policy:

> Tibet is a region with a sparse population and has a vast expanse of land. More than two million compatriots of the Zang [Tibetan] nationality alone are not sufficient for construction. There is no harm for the Han [Chinese] people to go and help them. Some more Han [Chinese] people there will be conducive to the development of the local nationality economy. This is not a bad thing (Hessler 1999a).

Deng's 'Spring Tide' campaign which began in 1991 initiated programmes throughout China to "deepen" and "speed up" economic reform. In Tibet this was to be framed as an "open-door" policy designed to open up Tibet to foreign investment and workers.

The effects of Deng's 'Spring Tide' campaign were felt in Tibet in 1992 when Lhasa was made a "Special Economic Zone", leading to an increase in both skilled and unskilled Chinese moving to the 'TAR'. Official statements referred explicitly to increasing migration to Tibet. For instance, on 5 September 1992, Chen Lianchang, executive vice-minister of the Ministry of Personnel, stated:

> All provinces, municipalities and other autonomous regions must unconditionally guarantee the supply of party and government cadres as well as specialised technicians needed by Tibet for its economic construction... In addition, various methods must be adopted, such as drawing up preferential policies, to attract scientists, technologists and students from the hinterland to work in Tibet.

DRIVERS OF POPULATION TRANSFER

Road-building Programme

Road-building policies in Tibet comprise two main elements: improving and upgrading existing roads and expanding the road network into the hitherto isolated countryside. These construction activities encourage population transfer. Road and rail construction in Gansu led to the emergence of a group of industrial cities along newly-created transport corridors. The Sichuan-Tibet Highway is one of about 20 transportation projects outlined in the 1998 list of 117 key state construction projects. The Sichuan route is a crucial one; it provides direct access to China's industrial heartland and is convenient to export resources from mineral-rich Eastern Tibet.

Relaxing Controls on Migration

Alongside these new economic policies which are encouraging migration to Tibet a number of administrative measures controlling the movement of the population were revoked from August 1992. The justification for this was that the existing system of checkpoints was an unnecessary restriction on the emerging free market system. "Unnecessary checkpoints and outposts" were abolished, and travel restrictions between the 'TAR' and neighbouring regions were eased.

Thus, by the end of 1992 economic and administrative reforms in Tibet had given people both the right to move around and access to an expanding road and rail network. Government policies favouring the rapid development of a free market system were an added impetus to population transfer. The significance of the earlier reform of the *hukou* (residence registration system) now became apparent. In the new relaxed atmosphere, traders from outside were able to move into and around Tibet without restriction. Since they were no longer dependent on the state for work, food, housing and other services, they were able to remain as long as their business was successful.

Freeing Up Private Enterprise

Having set up a framework within which population transfer could take place, the authorities then began to promote preferential policies to attract Chinese to Tibet and enable them to set up private enterprises in the country. Regulations governing the acquisition of business licences were relaxed and simplified in November 1993. Since then, licences have been available on provision of just an identification card and a letter of recommendation from the appropriate authorities. Official Chinese media has reported a huge increase in the number of individual and private enterprises in the region.

A substantial proportion of enterprises registered in the 'TAR' are run by Chinese, and official sources recognised that more than 25 per cent of new industrial and commercial enterprises set up in the 'TAR' in 1991 came from outside the region. In one monitored estimate of small business ownership in Lhasa, it was revealed that, from 1991 to 1992, of a total of 31,493 business establishments only 5,706, or less than 20 per cent, were owned by Tibetans.

Field research by Tibet Support Group-UK in *Tibet: Human Rights and the Rule of Law* (ICJ 1997) reveals that 756 of 1,061 individual businesses in old Lhasa's main market-hall were Chinese, as were 1,357 of 1,458 salespersons in Lhasa's vegetable markets. The same TSG-UK report says that the same situation is occurring in other towns around the 'TAR'. Of the 397 businesses in the centre of Tsethang, 277 are owned by Chinese. Of significance is the fact that little evidence of permanent Chinese settlement in the surrounding rural areas was found.

In addition to measures promoting the retail trade in Tibet, and between Tibet and neighbouring Chinese provinces, the government has also begun to develop a framework for increasing international trade through Tibet. Thus, reform of the retail trade and service sector combined with the active promotion of international trade have encouraged migration into Tibet, with Chinese and Chinese Muslim entrepreneurs quick to take advantage of the preferential policies.

A Swathe of Incentives

There are a series of benefits made available to "skilled personnel" and "technical experts" working in Tibet. Most of these are of a financial nature:

- Higher wages (Chinese migrant earnings are 87 per cent higher in Tibet than in China)
- Hardship allowances for people living in a remote mountainous region
- Reduction of, or exemptions from, taxation
- Improved pension opportunities.

This is confirmed in *China's Cadre Transfer Policy Toward Tibet in the 1980s* by Huang who quotes Tibet as being in the highest "salary zone" where income supplements for cadres in Tibet can be as high as 71.82 per cent of the original salary. A Chinese engineer agreed to relocate to Tibet because he was unemployed and would receive more than double the pay he was earning in Beijing (ICJ 1997). Such financial benefits are further increased should Chinese employees elect to remain in Tibet beyond their contracted term of service.

Also significant are a series of social benefits. Chinese cadres and staff living in the 'TAR' are eligible for better housing, enhanced access to education and medical facilities and longer periods of leave. For every 18 months of work in Tibet, Chinese employees are awarded a three-month leave package including pre-paid travel arranged by the government.

In relation to housing, there are strong indications, as cited in (Leckie 1994) *Destruction by Design, Housing Rights Violations in Tibet*, that official Chinese migrants are guaranteed accommodation as a matter of policy upon arrival in Tibet, something increasingly hard to obtain in China. Such housing assurances are not known to be in place elsewhere under Chinese jurisdiction.

In Kandze in Kham, preferential birth control regulations allow Chinese farmers who have lived in a "high, cold and remote mountainous area" in the region for more than eight years to have two children rather than the mandatory one.

SOCIAL CONSEQUENCES OF POPULATION TRANSFER

The United Nations General Assembly has on three occasions passed resolutions condemning the PRC's record in Tibet. In 1959 the UN called for "respect for the fundamental human rights of the Tibetan people and for their distinctive cultural and religious life". In 1961 and 1965 the Assembly again lamented "the suppression of the distinctive cultural and religious life" of the Tibetan people. In 1991 the Sub-Commission on Prevention of Discrimination and Protection of Minorities of the UN Commission on Human Rights was: "[c]oncerned at the continuing reports of violations of fundamental human rights and freedoms which threaten the distinct cultural, religious and national identity of the Tibetan people".

Social Isolation by Marginalisation

In his "70,000 Character Petition," written some 36 years ago, the 10th Panchen Lama already voiced concern about the possible loss of the Tibetan culture:

> **... once a nationality's language, costume, customs and other important characteristics have disappeared, then the nationality itself has disappeared too — that is to say, it has turned into another nationality (TIN 1997c).**

Marginalisation shows itself in a number of ways: people are disadvantaged in a system that is alien to them. Depending upon their formulation and implementation, education, welfare and health policies can all contribute to social isolation. There is sufficient evidence to show that Chinese policies in Tibet favour the growing Chinese population and, this encourage further migration of Chinese into the region.

Politics Over Education

Chinese rhetoric on education invariably refers to Chinese education as the path towards modernity and socio-economic progress:

> **The results [of Chinese education policies] helped free the [Tibetan] people from ignorant and backward conditions created by serfdom, and enabled them to**

walk along the glorious path of modern civilisation.

The education system is seen by many as an instrument of sinocization. Chinese educational policies minimise Tibetan language, Tibetan culture and Tibetan history. Chinese law demands Mandarin as the medium of teaching in all secondary schools with a few limited exceptions. The UN High Commissioner for Human Rights, Mary Robinson, noted during a visit to a school in Lhasa in 1999 that the children were reading a Chinese language storybook. When she asked the Chinese authorities about this, she was told that there were "no good story books in Tibetan".

Beijing's educational policies in Tibet have gone through a series of changes. After the Cultural Revolution, during which manifestations of Tibetan cultural traditions were virtually outlawed, Tibetan language education underwent a revival. This revival was mainly a result of Chinese concessions to the late Panchen Lama, who continuously promoted the Tibetan language as the language of education and administration. Since the late Panchen Lama's premature death in 1989, the political mood has changed considerably.

Chinese rhetoric on education in Tibet reflects a return to the primacy of politics over education standards. Most of the measures promoting the Tibetan language have now been reversed. Four Tibetan language secondary school classes, initiated by the late Panchen Lama in 1989 in three schools in Central Tibet, have now been dissolved, even though they were extremely popular and successful. As most Tibetan children attend Tibetan language primary schools, they score well below national averages at Chinese language secondary schools and so inevitably, the dropout rate among Tibetan students is high.

At the same time, the system is geared toward the urban population. Well-equipped schools established by the Chinese government are to be found in Tibetan cities and county headquarters with a predominantly Chinese populace. Local schools administered by Tibetans are desperately short of resources, frequently without furniture or trained teachers. Thus the vast majority of Tibetans have no access to adequate schooling or are unable to attend due to prohibitively high admission fees.

The implication of China's population transfer is also profound for the preservation of Tibetans' strong religious traditions, language and customs. As they become increasingly marginalised in their own country, the role of education becomes vital to the future of the Tibetan people.

Marginalisation is built into the system. Many Tibetan students enter secondary school with no background knowledge of Chinese language. As a result of this language handicap, Tibetan students are often grouped into "lower stream" classes and assigned inferior facilities with less qualified teachers.

Statistics suggest that approximately 33 per cent of school age children in Tibet continue to receive no education at all (Amnesty International 1995), compared with just 1.5 per cent of Chinese children (TCHRD 1997d). China often argues that physical remoteness is the cause of low education standards among Tibetan children. But in reality it is the high school fees which act as a barrier to Tibetan school admissions. This is exacerbated by general discrimination by authorities towards Tibetan students. Many bright Tibetan children are keen to go to China for further studies, citing the low level of education in Tibet as the reason.

In 1995, China's official news agency *Xinhua* reported that 13,000 Tibetans had enrolled in educational institutes in China since 1985, and that 10,000 Tibetans are currently enrolled, representing 28 per cent of all Tibetans in secondary education. This policy of sending Tibetan students to China rather than sending teachers to Tibet or training teachers in Tibet results in a number of negative effects including loss of language and cultural identity, problems of family relations and reduced funding for education in Tibet.

The 1997 report by the International Commission of Jurists suggests that if international measures of poverty are applied, the number of poor in the 'TAR' rises from China's figure of 20.7 per cent to over 70 per cent.

Under the provisions of the UN Convention on the Rights of the Child, education should include teaching a child respect for his or her own cultural identity, language and values. Yet Chinese authorities have for some time linked Tibetan language to Tibetan nationalism and thus to a propensity for "splittist" activities.

By repressing the use of Tibetan language and the knowledge of Tibetan culture and history it seems China hopes to completely integrate the next generation of Tibetans into China. This even extends to the policy of recalling Tibetan children who are currently in India for education. A report by Tibet Information Network suggests a further strengthening of China's already hard-line policies aimed at eradicating support among Tibetans for the Dalai Lama. This new campaign has led to the homes of Tibetan officials in Lhasa being searched for shrines and religious objects and a renewal of the requirement for Tibetan cadres to withdraw their children from exile schools in India.

The withdrawal of these children was first ordered in 1994; the latest ban threatens workers whose children are still in schools in India with expulsion from their jobs if the children are not brought back to Tibet. One such incident reported by the Tibetan Centre for Human Rights and Democracy (1999) states that in March 1998 the head of Lhasa Middle School asked three parents to bring their children back from India to attend school in Tibet within six months:

> **The parents were unable to travel immediately due to the difficulty in obtaining travel documents quickly and arriving in India during the hot weather. Six months later, in September, they were asked by the school authorities to explain why they had not been to India to collect their children... and were suspended from their work until they complied with the order.**

Employment Excludes Tibetans

As a signatory nation, the Chinese authorities under Article 5(e)(i) of the UN International Convention on the Elimination of all forms of Racial Discrimination (CERD) State Parties undertake to guarantee the right of everyone, without racial discrimination, to equal enjoyment of:

> **The right to work, to free choice of employment, to just and favourable conditions of work, to protection against unemployment, to equal pay for equal work, to just and favourable remuneration.**

There is increasing evidence to suggest that the latest campaign against the Dalai Lama is using the threat of unemployment against "non-compliant" Tibetans. A report by the Tibet Information Network dated 13 November 1998 states that "...if cadres are found in possession of altars or pictures of the Dalai Lama they will be regarded as having voluntarily resigned from their work units" (TIN 1997c).

The International Commission of Jurists (1997) contends that China has been unable to industrialise the processing of the agricultural commodities of Tibet, or to provide industrial employment for rural Tibetans. Despite massive Chinese State investment in infrastructure, very little has resulted in viable enterprises which employ Tibetans. Chinese investment has concentrated on state-owned enterprises in urban areas, which are largely reserved for Chinese employees. Only 2.5 per cent of rural Tibetans in 'TAR' are employed outside the traditional Tibetan agricultural economy.

Chinese authorities admit that a disproportionate number of public officers in Tibet are Chinese. At the private level, Chinese are also likely to make up a considerable proportion of company employees. In the private trading and natural resources Jinzhu Group — a spin-off of the Government's export-import agency — only 60 per cent of its 400 employees are Tibetan.

In 1997 the PRC issued a "White Paper" on its human rights in which it claimed to attach major importance to the protection of workers' rights. This report admits that while a minimum wage has been introduced in China this has yet to be implemented in the 'TAR'. There is further evidence to suggest that workers rights are seriously violated within the 'TAR' through the use of compulsory and unpaid labour. It is reported that in Lhoka County, (in Yartoe and Yarlung) each resident is forced to "offer" his services for between eight and 12 days per month for nine months of every year. If workers do not appear for the unpaid work, they are fined. In this situation the term "resident" includes monks and nuns.

In an editorial dated 16 October 1997 on the Chinese economy, the Kazakh-based Uighur émigré newspaper *Golos Vostochnogo Turkistana* reported:

> **Like any dictatorship, the Chinese Communist dictatorship uses gratis forced labour in its planned economy. For example, in Xinjiang in the 1980s-1990s the peasants of the Autonomous Region performed 36 million units of forced labour (each unit being from three days to three months forced labour). China reaps an enormous profit from the exploitation of the public, which continues to this day. The deaths of many thousands of peasants from 12-15 hour stints of forced labour in the deserts and mountain regions are not widely advertised.**

Tibetans are clearly at a considerable disadvantage both ideologically and financially in the economic sphere in Tibet. They face increased competition in the job market and in the agricultural sector. Their traditional skills and experience are generally undervalued and undermined. International lawyer Michael C. van Walt van Praag cites a case where 30,000 Tibetans employed under 16 labour units of Lhasa Municipality lost their jobs to Chinese workers. The Tibetans were simply told to go to the villages to look for work.

When official reference is made to the role of Tibetans within the economy it is generally in negative terms.

The *Tibet Daily* on 15 December 1997 stated:

> One of the most important reasons why Tibet lags behind the rest of China in development is because Tibet has not shaped a social environment favourable for development, and has not correctly solved problems existing in the spiritual sphere.

Poverty's Growing Gulf

It may be argued that China's strategy for poverty alleviation is economic growth rather than programmes specifically targeting the poor. The Australian Agency for International Development concludes from its work with the Chinese poverty alleviation system in Amdo:

> This approach to poverty alleviation places emphasis on activities that are project oriented in nature and not necessarily on the participation of the poor in identifying and developing solutions to their poverty. It also places emphasis on large enterprise activities and does not target poor households (Lafitte 1999).

There is ample evidence of the growing income disparity between urban Chinese and rural Tibetans in the 'TAR'. The 1997 Policy Paper for the 'TAR' reported that in 1996 urban incomes rose by over 25 per cent to reach US$628 per person. This makes residents of Lhasa wealthier on average than town dwellers in China, where the average income for 1996 was only US$537.

Urban incomes are now over five times the size of rural incomes, and growing at twice the rate. Rural incomes increased by 11 per cent in 1996 but still reached only US$121 per person, half the average rural income in China. A strong indication of the rapidly growing gulf between the Chinese and Tibetans.

The World Bank defines poverty as an income of less than US$1 per day, using purchasing power parity — in other words, exchange rates adjusted to local currency.

Poverty can also be defined in broader terms than by income alone. The Human Poverty Index, developed recently by the United Nations Development Programme (UNDP), defines poverty as an aggregate index that measures other forms of deprivation, including low life expectancy, illiteracy, and measures of access to health services, safe water and adequate nutrition. Figures available from *The World Resources* (1999) state that in China, for the period 1990-1996, only seven per cent of the rural population had access to adequate sanitation and 56 per cent to safe drinking water.

On 26 November 1994 local officials reported in *Xinhua* that 20 per cent of the total population in Tibet, "the poorest region in China", was living below the poverty line. The Tenth Five Year Plan for Economic and Social Development in its long term target for 2010 for the 'TAR' acknowledges that many Tibetans live below the poverty line and attributes this to inherent backwardness and remoteness. China, however, defines poverty as an income of US60 cents a day. The 1997 report by the International Commission of Jurists suggests that if international measures of poverty are applied, the number of poor in the 'TAR' rises from China's figure of 20.7 per cent to over 70 per cent.

Furthermore, the Chinese government often violates original inhabitants' right to an adequate standard of living by restricting their freedom of movement. For example, the level of affluence of pastoral nomads, historically higher than agriculturists, is dependent upon their ability to move freely to the best pastures. In a desire to increase output, the Chinese have divided pastoral lands into agricultural plots, increasing pressure on nomads to settle in one place. In this case the future of the pastoral economy, the nomads' way of life, and ultimately, self-determination, rests with the Chinese.

If this mode of large-scale development continues, the accompanying transfer of the Chinese population into Tibetan regions seriously jeopardises the survival of the Tibetan people.

ENVIRONMENTAL CONSEQUENCES OF POPULATION TRANSFER

Agriculture

Fears of a national grain shortage have led the Chinese authorities to promote agriculture in Tibet to feed an ever-growing Chinese population. In Tibet these strategies have one of two forms:

- Boosting yields on existing farmland through mechanisation and chemical fertilisers
- Increasing the area of land under cultivation.

Both of these actions have grave consequences. The first in terms of possible environmental damage to fragile soils and ecosystems and the second in its impact on traditional land use patterns, particularly in regard to

Tibetans begging in Lhasa: in 1997 the International Commission of Jurists reported over 70 per cent of Tibetans in the 'TAR' as poor

conversion of pasture lands to cropping farms.

The Panam project is part of the comprehensive "One River Two Streams" agricultural programme which was developed with a long-term economic focus of introducing a market economy into Tibet. The aim of the Panam project is to increase grain production in the allocated 1,001 sq. km area by installing a complete irrigation system, but the EU has since amended the plan to provide for education, afforestation, health and sanitation initiatives. There are concerns that these secondary aspects will be all but forgotten in practice. The Panam Integrated Rural Development Project was again approved in 1998 despite the controversy surrounding the project. In August 1998 the European Union (EU) granted China ECU 7.6 million aid for the programme and the remaining ECU 14.2 million was to be borne by China (TSG 1995).

The project is being implemented in an area that already possesses a basic infrastructure with a subsistence economy and is self-sufficient in food, rather than in one of the many poorer areas in Central Tibet that could benefit more from such a scheme. It promises to introduce a full market economy into the area and this threatens the livelihood of many of the locals. It appears that the project was conceived not for the benefit of Tibetans but to reduce the grain deficit and resulting economic strain induced by the influx of Chinese into Panam and surrounding areas.

The project aims to increase grain production by 78 per cent with the majority of this being accounted for by wheat. 1991 statistics indicate a wheat consumption rate of 10 per cent in Panam County, which suggests that the programme is not designed for the benefit of the local population but to create stability for the new, Chinese population (TSG 1995).

The stated long-term objective of the Panam project is "to establish a viable model for self-help development activities which can be replicated in other parts of Tibet". If this mode of large-scale development continues, the accompanying transfer of the Chinese population into Tibetan regions seriously jeopardises the survival of the Tibetan people.

If the similar UN World Food Program (WFP) #3357 is any indication of the outcome, Tibetans will have minimal input into the project. The UN WFP was essentially discredited "due to the lack of technical cooperation with unethical behaviour from the Chinese authorities".

In an interview, Jamyang Thargay is less than complimentary about the project. As the former accountant of Taktse Work Group, (WFP #3357), he had first-hand experience of the project. While the Chinese claim to have offered comprehensive training, Jamyang states that Tibetans were employed in menial tasks such as hauling boulders and clearing land – in other words, they were used as a source of cheap, unskilled labour. The WFP provides for a minimum wage of six to eight yuan per day but "Tibetans get less than five yuan per day" (DIIR 1997a).

Jamyang's Taktse Work Group of 40, of which the leader was Chinese, consisted of 30 Chinese and only 10 Tibetans. He cites examples of Chinese Muslims who bribe Chinese project officials to get good jobs on the project. He further adds that Tibetans who participated in the project did not receive the allocated ration of 1.925 kg of wheat flour nor the 45 grams of butter oil sanctioned by the WFP. Chinese officials are reported to sell such items in the markets of Lhasa (DIIR, 1997a).

Forestry

As population pressures increase so do the pressures on land. Deforestation is a result of urbanisation and commodification. As new roads are constructed to bring in new settlers and military personnel, the rate of deforestation increases.

In its simplest form, trees are felled as land is cleared to support increased Chinese workers and the construction of worker compounds. As these areas become urbanised, more land needs to be cleared to support agriculture. And so the cycle continues.

Although a substantial reduction in forest cover has occurred due to new population pressures and consequently a substantial increase in firewood gathering, and the clearing of forests for grazing and cultivation, it is the planned commercial timber extraction that is mostly responsible for the 46 per cent reduction in forest cover on the Tibetan Plateau (DIIR 1998).

> **Since the modern world made its way into the Tibetan Plateau via Chinese modernisation the forests have been reduced nearly by half (Winkler 1998a).**

According to Yang and He, the rate of destruction is by various estimates three to four times faster than the forests can regrow, a practice that results in a renewable resource becoming non-renewable. Vaclav Smil terms this extraction the "planned destruction" of the portion of Tibet annexed to Sichuan

Given that China's development strategy in Tibet also serves to alleviate population and employment pressure elsewhere in China many jobs are created for Chinese workers in factories and projects in Tibet. According to He Bochuan, in *China on the Edge*, the greatest single threat to the Chinese nation is population growth. Because over two-thirds of the population is under 30, creating employment opportunities is the first priority of government policy. Chinese officials at the Forestry Bureau in Trango, Kham, for example, candidly admitted to a fact-finding team in 1991 that the Forestry Bureau only serves Chinese settlers, providing them with 1,100 jobs, including housing, meals, laundry and long vacations. And paid transport back to their hometowns (ICT 1991).

Water

The Yamdrok Tso hydro-electric plant, located 120 km south of Lhasa, began in 1985 amid promises to "enhance development of industry, agriculture and animal husbandry". While mired in controversy — the project was halted at one point after Tibetan officials, including the late Panchen Lama, vigorously opposed it — of significance are the 4,000-5,000 Chinese military personnel brought in to build the hydropower plant. This is indicative of many Chinese infrastructure projects: Tibetan involvement is either zero or minimal.

Minerals

With regard to mineral resources, evidence from the unpublished 'TAR' Specialist Plan and other official sources indicate that China is planning to develop mining as one of the five pillars of economic development in Tibet.

Figures given for the Specialist Plan suggest that potential output is seen as an inseparable component of China's own mineral availability. *Xinhua* (1997c) reported that potential oilfields in the Chang Thang plateau in northern Tibet comprised the "last and largest oil belt" in the inland area.

Advanced preparations for full-scale development of a large copper-mine in Chamdo, the Yulong copper mine, were also announced. Executive vice chairman of the 'TAR' Yang Chuangtang has said that there are plans for this mine to be one of the biggest in Asia.

In April 1996, it was reported that some 500,000 ethnic Chinese were to be moved into Tibet to work on copper mines and that the Beijing authorities planned to build several mining towns to house about 100,000 migrant workers (DIIR 1997b). In the same month, 2,000 Chinese were sent to the Chang Thang Basin area where a "Geological Prospecting Team" is being led by Zhao Huan, chief engineer with the Geophysical Bureau of China National Petroleum and Natural Gas Corporation. Zhao and his team of workers have been exploring for oil and natural gas reserves since 1995. Over the past two years, China has sent many officials to Tibet under the pretext of surveying the progress of the various developmental projects initiated in Tibet, but according

Above: People's Liberation Army soliders policing the Minority Games in Lhasa. Right: A policy of intimidation - Tibetan prisoners are paraded in trucks through the streets of Lhasa.

September 1999

to sources in Tibet these officials seldom leave Tibet after their "survey" has been completed.

The prospect of gold has lured many to the region of Amdo. An estimated 80,000 licensed prospectors were in place at the beginning of the 1990s with many more applications to be processed. There are likely to be many more unlicensed gold prospectors. These miners are frequently outnumbering local Tibetan villagers. For example, in Chumarleb (Ch. Qumarleb) County 17,000 Tibetan herders are outnumbered by between 50,000 and 60,000 miners. Much of the mining activity is reportedly done in a haphazard way, causing destruction and waste.

TIN (1996) reported that in Shentsa County in Nagchu prefecture, the mining area is known to contain 10.1 tonnes of alluvial gold, forming one of the largest deposits in China. Local prospecting is encouraged. The term "wild mining" has developed, which reflects the fact that in many cases gold prospectors do not need a license. They are required to sell a certain ratio of their find to the government at a fixed low price.

Population Figures

There are a number of difficulties in assessing the true extent of Tibet's population. This is due to the extremely inaccessible terrain and general absence of fixed settlements such as nomadic communities which represent a sizeable proportion of the community. The Tibetan Government-in-Exile has estimated the Tibetan population inside Tibet at 6.1 million (DIIR 1992). This figure was reaffirmed in 1988 by Huan Xiang, Director of the Centre for International Studies of the State Council in Beijing, when the *Beijing Review* quoted him as saying:

> ... of the present population of six million Tibetans, only two million are living in Tibet ('TAR') while the remaining four million are in other provinces of China.

In addition, the Tibetan Government-in-Exile has suggested that there are upwards of 7.6 million Chinese settlers in all Tibetan regions.

In contrast, Chinese 1990 census figures from *The Present Population of the Tibetan Nationality in China* (Zhang & Zhang 1994) claim the total non-Tibetan population to be approximately 4.2 million and the total Tibetan population to be 4.59 million. With the impossibility of conducting a comprehensive, independent census in Tibet, it is extremely difficult to give any precise picture of its population profile. Difficulties are compounded by the manner in which China concocts its own statistics regarding Tibet, as exemplified above.

REGIONAL VARIATIONS

The military and civilian occupation of the Kham and Amdo regions (whose borders are contiguous with China's) occurred very early in the history of the occupation. Initially, following the invasion by the PLA in Tibet's easternmost border, the Chinese established military garrisons at every strategic point. During the 1950s, state-prompted migration policies brought the first civilians into Tibet, especially Kham and Amdo. Chinese settlers were sent to the Kham area and those from Gansu to Amdo. They were allotted plots of farming land by the Chinese authorities. Then road builders and workers came into the region to construct the network of highways that would permit the transportation of military supplies throughout Tibet. Government administrators and cadres began to arrive in significant numbers in the 1960s.

Amdo

Today in most cities and towns in Amdo Tibetans are the minority. This is a claim supported by population statistics from both the Tibetan Government-in-Exile and China. As of 1990 Chinese outnumbered Tibetans by more than two-and-a-half times.

Kham

Given its fertile land and proximity to China, Kham was the first region to suffer mass migration from the earliest days of the Chinese occupation. Population figures are scant. But according to Chinese sources there are approximately 1.5 million Tibetans in Kham. This number is contested by the Tibetan Government-in-Exile which believes the number to be closer to three million. The Chinese statistics fail to include those Tibetans living in areas now incorporated into non-Tibetan prefectures, and has underestimated the nomadic population.

As much of Kham was incorporated into Sichuan, China's most populous province, it can safely be concluded that problems of overcrowding in Sichuan have been alleviated through population transfer. Some observers suggest that there is approximately a 1:1 ratio of Tibetans to Chinese, with the Chinese outnumbering Tibetans in urban areas.

U-Tsang

The 'TAR' had, until recently, the lowest concentration of Chinese civilians in Tibet. Historic sources account for just 500 foreign traders in Lhasa before 1949, a figure that included Muslims, Nepalese and Chinese. It is to this region (and Lhasa in particular) that the Chinese are being encouraged to migrate. The announcement of an "open-door" policy in Tibet in June 1992 has led to significant changes in the last few years. This policy has encouraged Chinese settlers, opportunists, fortune seekers and vagrants to move to the area. A rising Chinese population needs, in turn, to be supported by government workers, cadres and craftspeople. A never-ending destructive cycle.

Chinese government sources give the Tibetan population of the 'TAR' as two million and the number of registered Chinese in 1990 as 81,200. But independent observers report that at least 100,000 Chinese live in Lhasa alone, outnumbering Tibetans two to one. In *Tibet Transformed* (ICT 1994), it is reported that Lhasa's total population is at least 200,000. Of this figure, the three security forces (People's Liberation Army, People's Armed Police, Public Security Bureau) are estimated at 50,000 to 60,000, approximately equal to the estimated number of Tibetans. In addition to Chinese security personnel, however, there are approximately 90,000 other Chinese. The report concludes that in Tibet's capital, the Tibetan people constitute only about one-third of the total population.

CHINESE IRREGULARITIES IN REPORTING DEMOGRAPHIC DATA

Following the invasion of Tibet, the Chinese realigned national boundaries redrawing and redefining regions and incorporating much of Tibet into neighbouring Chinese provinces. Today China refers to Tibet as the so-called 'Tibet Autonomous Region' ('TAR'). 'TAR' accounts for less than half of Tibet's territory prior to 1949 and corresponds roughly to the central Tibetan province of U-Tsang. A large proportion of Amdo, Tibet's north-eastern province, is now administrated as Qinghai province, with parts of Amdo also falling into western Gansu and Sichuan provinces. Finally parts of Kham, Tibet's southeastern province, have been subsumed into the Chinese provinces of Yunnan and Sichuan. As a consequence, terminology and descriptions of what constitutes Tibet are confused and Chinese propaganda statements are deliberately vague and ambiguous. This serves the Chinese cause well. Even today, much of the world is unaware of what constitutes the nation of Tibet in precise historical and geopolitical terms.

Population Statistics

While statistical tables and comparisons between early estimates and population figures from the 1982, 1987, 1990 and 1995 censuses are interesting and provide an indication of general trends, Chinese figures and categorisations vary with political requirements and remain unreliable. In the early years of the PRC under-reporting of Tibet's population was caused by lack of competence and difficult physical conditions including insurgencies. The official figure of just over one million for the entire Tibetan population was unreasonable. Census figures in 1953 and 1964 for 'TAR' were still based on estimates. The intensely politicised atmosphere of the 1960s and 1970s made "correct" responses a factor of survival; general disorganisation made totals unverifiable. Precision in the early 1980s suffered from this legacy. Whilst the 1995 census was far more professional, political sensitivities would still seem to preclude full transparency. Data is no longer available that shows unbiased information such as Chinese backwardness (scant availability of modern services or equipment in poor areas) or tabulations on an ethnic basis (infant mortality by ethnic group) reveal neglect, deterioration of conditions or discrimination against minorities (Statistical Yearbook of China et al 1995).

Ethnicity

The official view of the PRC is that all Chinese belong to a single ethnic group, overlooking the considerable differences, linguistic and otherwise, that exist between Cantonese, Fujianese and, northern and inland Chinese to name but a few. There is a marked emphasis on the high number and diversity of the PRC's 55 minorities. The former Republican government under Chiang Kai-shek identified only five ethnic groups — the Manchu, Mongolians, Muslims, Tibetans and Chinese. The passage from five to 55 was achieved through official creation and re-definition of "nationalities". The Hui (8.6 million) were formerly included among the Muslims(TIN 1998d). Their identity as a people was a Maoist creation: the term Hui and its variants formerly applied to any Chinese Muslim. In Amdo many Hui consider themselves Tibetan Hui or "Bo Hui" and call others "Gya Hui" or Chinese Hui. This is also reported in the 'TAR', but the sub-categories are not given official recognition.

Some of the "nationalities" have emerged by subdividing larger groups. Among the people formerly not considered different from Tibetans, the Tu (191,000) who live mainly in Haidung and in Gansu, were mostly Tibetan Buddhists. Among Tibet's renowned spiritual teachers of the past, some would now have to be classified as non-Tibetan Tu. Nor were the Qiang (198,000) formerly seen as different. The Moinba (7,500) and Lhoba (2,000) are very close politically and culturally and many of the Naxis (278,000) belong to the Bon, Tibet's pre-Buddhist belief-system; the rest are Buddhist. Taken together, these 700,000 non-Chinese, residing on Tibetan territory would arguably constitute additional users of Tibetan-language schools, Buddhist temples and other non-Chinese cultural institutions (ICJ 1997).

Taken together, these 700,000 non-Chinese, residing on Tibetan territory would arguably constitute additional users of Tibetan-language schools, Buddhist temples and other non-Chinese cultural institutions.

Official Exclusions

Military personnel, civilians working in military establishments, technical and professional staff brought in under official projects, workers registered elsewhere and who have resided in a place for less than a year, and those who entered Tibet before 1 July 1985 are not included in official figures. Additionally, neither are Chinese born in Tibet included, nor are dependants of Chinese workers. A recent addition to the exclusion list has been the self-employed. Official sentiment labels the "self-employed" as "seasonal migrators". A census that excludes so many people raises serious questions about legitimacy and credibility. By way of further example, in the second half of the 1970s Chinese workers employed within the leather industry were categorised under the heading of "military personnel" and so excluded from the official count.

Military Personnel

Despite the easing of Sino-Indian tensions and the signing of an agreement to reduce troops along the Indo-Tibetan border, China's security presence in Tibet has increased in recent years. Construction and modernisation of military and para-military facilities in both urban and rural areas have escalated. The report *Tibet Transformed* (ICT 1994) makes reference to Chinese area planning maps for Lhasa that show a number of sites designated as "special use" zones. Visual inspection of these sites, supported by photographic evidence, reveals that they are PLA bases, PAP camps, or other security facilities including prisons and other detention centres. The report adds that estimates for military personnel in the 'TAR' alone have reached up to 400,000.

The exact number of security personnel for all Tibetan regions ebbs and flows depending upon the perceived needs of the authorities. While there is some indication that the number of PLA personnel in Tibet may be decreasing following the trend in China, as Beijing downsizes its total military forces, eyewitnesses consistently report that the number of PAP personnel in Tibet is steadily increasing. The report quotes a knowledgeable source:

PAP arrive by plane from Chengdu in greater numbers than those leaving. There are far too many regular troop rotations. Their trucks, sedans and Land Cruisers, often marked with a "WJ" on the license plate, are everywhere in Lhasa. Every important town or city has a PAP garrison now. Smaller PAP units are now being established in many of the towns. Tibetans understand clearly why they are there. The PAP is taking over where the PLA left off.

Seasonal Migrators — Floating Population

Population numbers are further escalated with the introduction of a "floating population" from among several million unskilled and semi-skilled Chinese now drifting from rural areas to cities and towns in search of work throughout China. The mechanisation of agriculture and general industrialisation has made many workers surplus to requirements in China. Many such people are enticed to Tibet by higher salaries. The Chinese authorities now appear to accept that widespread migration is an unavoidable consequence of economic reform. However, the general intention of the Chinese government is to prevent large numbers of migrant workers from settling in urban areas. As a result, the floating population is encouraged to move to the northern and western regions.

In large cities like Beijing or Shanghai, migration is perceived as a grave social and economic problem and measures to limit the influx of the floating population have been introduced. In Tibet, migration by Chinese into the region is encouraged and welcomed under the pretext of enabling "economic development". With the prospect of unemployment spiralling in China the future does not bode well for Tibet.

LESSONS FROM HISTORY

If the present Chinese policy is successfully implemented, Tibetans will, before long, be reduced to a small and insignificant minority in their own country. This has been the case of the Turkic peoples of Eastern Turkestan and the Mongolians of Inner Mongolia. In Eastern Turkestan (Xinjiang) the Chinese population has grown from 200,000 in 1947 to six million in 1993, surpassing the five million native Uighurs (*The New York Times* 1985).

A comment made by Deng Xiaoping in 1993 on the subject of problems in Eastern Turkestan is a portent of things to come in Tibet. Referring to the "splittist" activities of the Uighurs, Deng noted "It is fortunate that in the past 40 years we have made population proportions such that splittists can't really do much".

In the wake of the Chinese colonisation of Inner Mongolia, Chinese now outnumber the Mongols by 25 million to 2.5 million in the Inner Mongolian Autonomous Region (AFP 1992). In a call to the United Nations for support, the Inner Mongolian People's Party (IMPP) condemned the PRC's policy of forcible assimilation of the Mongol population of Inner Mongolia by suppression and destruction of the Mongolian language and culture. A representative of the IMPP reported to the UN in 1998 that:

> The People's Republic of China and the Chinese Communist Party (CCP) have carried out a policy of genocide against the Southern Mongolian Nation. In the course of 50 years of Chinese occupation, over 1,000,000 Mongols have been killed by the CCP, and more than 800,000 Mongols have been imprisoned and tortured. Today, in 1998, the Chinese Government and the CCP continue their policy of annihilating the ethnic identity of the Southern Mongolians. They have used unspeakable kinds of torture to intimidate the Southern Mongolians. They have beaten, burned and maimed our people, and abused our women.

A third example may be seen in Manchuria where three million Manchus have been reduced to an insignificant minority; they are outnumbered by 75 million Chinese (AFP 1992). Such overwhelming numbers have led to the cultural, social and economic decimation of these peoples.

Orchestrated social ostracism, eviction and denial of housing, school admission or employment; expulsion from school or work unit, culminating in official investigation and detention with withdrawal of political rights have been, and remain, the fate of Tibetans who openly criticise or oppose the government.

Tibetans have a distinct history, language, culture and traditions. Despite 50 years of occupation, the Tibetan people refuse to be conquered and subjugated by China. ■

CHAPTER SIX

MINERALS AND MINING

Our ancestors viewed the earth as rich and bountiful, which it is.
Many people in the past also saw nature as inexhaustibly sustainable,
which we now know is the case only if we care for it.

His Holiness the 14th Dalai Lama, 5 June 1986
An Ethical Approach to Environmental Protection

THE MINERAL resources of Tibet are high in quality and rich in quantity and variety. This fact had been known to Tibetans for several centuries, yet they did not exploit the resources for economic gain or for any development — mainly due to their profound adherence to the principle of harmony between man and nature.

However, after the invasion of Tibet by China in 1949, things began to change dramatically. In fact, one of the prime reasons that lured China to invade Tibet was to gain access to its rich mineral wealth. The Chinese Government started exploiting the pristine and rich natural resources of Tibet from as early as 1956 (Namgyal 1995). Since then Beijing has sent hundreds of geological prospecting teams to the plateau with great expectations of finding more mineral deposits. In the areas of Amdo, Kham and U-Tsang thousands of geological maps have been plotted.

Today there are more than 126 identified minerals in Tibet with significant reserves of the world's deposits of uranium, chromite, boron, lithium, borax, and iron (DIIR 1992). Further, reserves of corundum, vanadium, titanium, magnesite, sulphur, mica, cesium, rubidium, arsenic, graphite, lepidolite and potash are some of the largest in both Tibet and China. Besides there are globally significant reserves of copper, gold, silver, zinc, oil and gas and other minerals on the plateau. Yulong Copper Mine at Chamdo and Norbusa chromite mine in Lhoka are some of their kind in Tibet (Namgyal 1995).

By the 1960s, the Chinese government realised that mining in Tibet is advantageous to the economy and the industries requiring mineral resources. Besides, China's past dependence on international markets for ferrous and non-ferrous ores and metals had cost it dearly in foreign exchange. As a result China started investing huge sums of money in Tibet from a variety of sources including the central and provincial treasuries and foreign investors.

Consequently, several mining projects in Tibet were launched in China's Eighth (1991-1995) and Ninth Five Year Plan (1996-2000). Many of the major schemes in the so-called "43 Development Projects" and "62 Development Projects" are directly related to the development and speeding up of the mining industry in Tibet. All these mining developmental areas are concentrated on potential mineral deposits that are sure of generating remarkable returns to the economy.

The material requirements of modern industrial economies are enormous, as are the environmental impacts of such consumption. The acceleration of mineral extraction has created unprecedented environmental and social problems in Tibet, yet China continues to emphasise that the development and expansion of Tibet's mineral industry is to facilitate economic growth. The Chinese government's ongoing process of building mining as the pillar industry of Tibet's economy (*Tibet Daily* 1996) and the recent revamping of mining laws and other provisions for attracting foreign

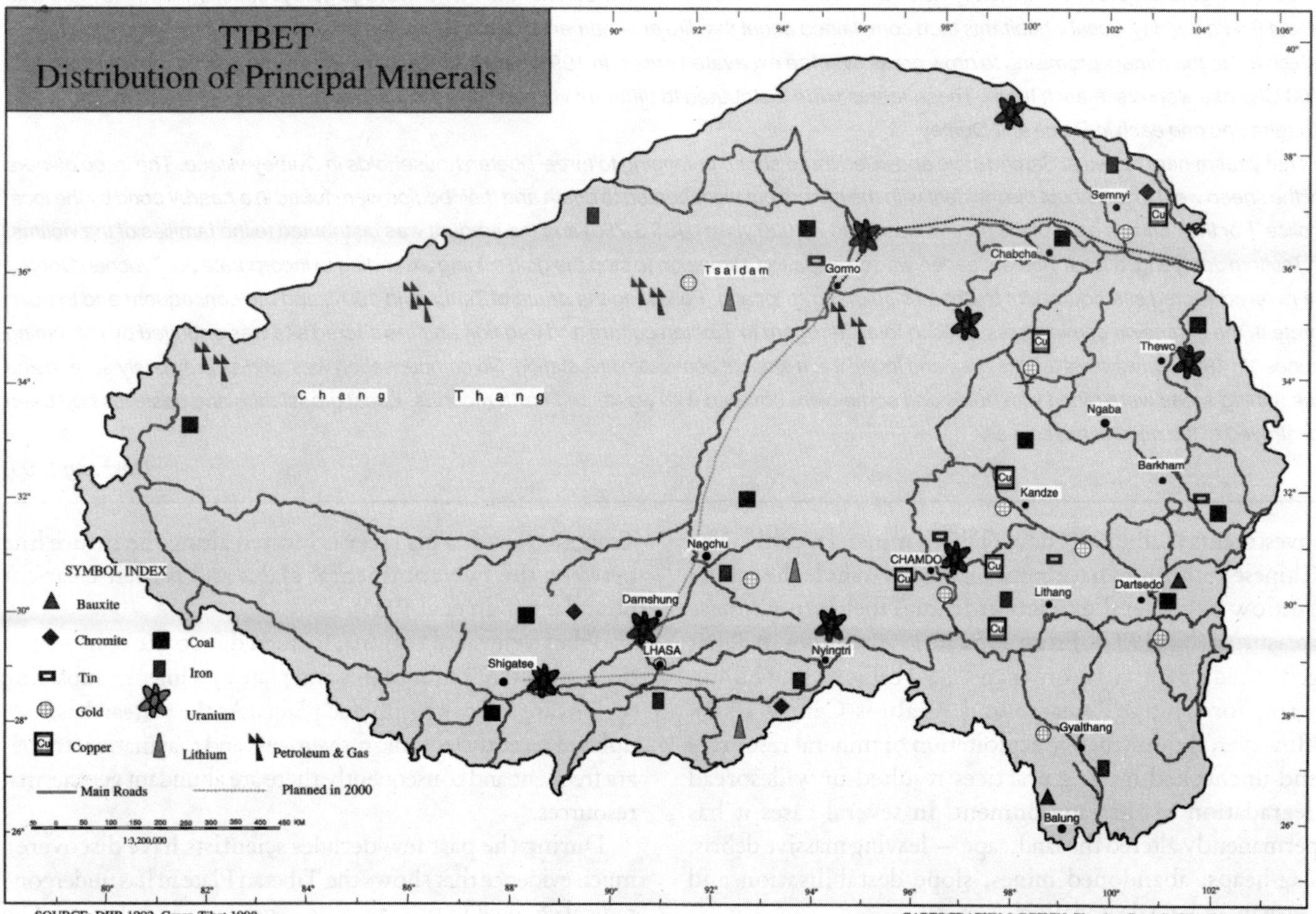

SOURCE: DIIR 1992, Green Tibet 1998

CARTOGRAPHY & DESIGN: Planning Council, CTA, Dharamsala-2000

Note : See colour map at the end of the book

How gold mining led to desecration of a sacred site — and deaths

According to testimony given by former government official, Dawa Dorjee, on 2 February 1999, between 1988-89 about 500-600 Chinese Muslim gold miners arrived at Sercherkhok, Trindu County, Jyekundo (Ch: Yushu) in Tsongon region and started mining. But following protests by local Tibetans who are mainly nomads the activity was halted. In 1991, another batch of around 100 Chinese gold miners arrived with mining exploration rights issued from the Qinghai Mining Bureau; subsequently the Trindu County officials licensed the prospectors to explore the area. Tibetans in the locality were ordered to provide food, accommodation and travel arrangements. Several Chinese geologists arrived and the exploration team estimated the minimum size of gold deposits in the region to be at least eight tons.

In 1994, a gold ore processing factory was constructed to the southwest of Sercherkhok. The average gold production from the mine was about 9.5 kg per day. Local inhabitants then complained about the dire environmental damage caused by such mining practises in the region which led to the miners promising to grow grass over the excavated areas. In 1995, nine additional mining teams arrived with not less than 100 Chinese workers in each team. These teams were distributed to different villages; three in Sarchu (Gushee), two each in Dama and Tongha and one each in Dutoe and Dumey.

That year miners based at Sarchu stole and killed three sheep belonging to three Tibetan households in Dumey village. The three owners of the sheep went to talk about the incident with the miners but were beaten to death and their bodies were found in a nearby pond by the local police. For their crimes each of the miners was fined 70,000 yuan (US$ 8,750) and the amount was distributed to the families of the victims.

Tsultrim Jamyang, a local Tibetan leader, waged a spirited campaign to stop the gold mining extending to incorporate Jo Gyuchen Dongra (a revered sacred site equivalent to Lhasa's Jokhang to locals). Following the death of Tsultrim in 1997, and the consequent end to open protest, the extension of mining resumed in total disregard to Tibetan culture and tradition and the sacred site was engulfed by the mining zones. In 1998, Dawa revisited the area and found it in a state of complete devastation. No compensation was paid as previously agreed and the mining areas were pitted with holes and some were covered with waste and earth mounds. Local grasslands and pastures had been destroyed to the point of no recovery.

Dekhang 1999.

investments (Lally 1997) drain Tibet's mineral wealth. The Chinese authorities have constantly tried to hide the capital outflow of mineral extraction from Tibet into Chinese treasuries (ICJ 1997). From 1952 to 1990 mining in Tibet generated a profit of more than US$ 2 billion (15.4 billion yuan) for China (Research and Analysis Centre 1991). However, the destructive exploitation of mineral resources and unchecked mining practices resulted in widespread degradation of the environment. In several cases it has permanently altered the landscape — leaving massive debris, slag-heaps, abandoned mines, slope destabilisation and permanent land degradation.

GEOLOGICAL EVOLUTION

The present geomorphological features of the Tibetan Plateau were formed as a result of intense upheaval during the last 40-50 million years and therefore constitute the youngest macromorphological unit in the world (Molnar 1998). According to the theory of plate tectonics, the uplifting of the plateau resulted from a collision between two continental plates, the Eurasian and the Indian Plates. The Indian Plate moved northward, sliding under the Eurasian Plate and prompting its edge to rise and form a belt of ultra-basic rocks and mixed rocks in the valley of the Yarlung Tsangpo River. This river is located along the suture line between the two continental plates and is their clear-cut boundary (Ren et al 1985).

Tibet's elevated regions, formed due to the continental drift, are today's mountains and plateau while the subsiding regions are today's basins and plains. As the plateau has been uplifted recently tectonic movements and magmatic activities are frequent and consequently there are abundant geothermal resources.

During the past few decades scientists have discovered much evidence that shows the Tibetan Plateau has undergone radical changes in topography, vegetation and climate. The recent discoveries of giraffe fossils at 4,500 metres above sea level in Driru County and three-toed fossils at 4,100 metres in Kyirong County, U-Tsang, infer that the land of Tibet was once much lower than it is today and that the climate was once hot and humid (Ren et al 1985). According to a *Radio Peking* report of 20 January 1997 fossils of dinosaurs were unearthed in the mountains in Tibet, some dating back 160 million years.

The intense uplifting of the mountain systems along the margins of the plateau has effectively blocked humid currents from entering and has turned the interior of the plateau into an arid region. Therefore, intense and extensive uplifting since the Neocene Period has been the leading factor in creating the physiographical features of the Tibetan Plateau (Ren et al 1985). Most importantly, the geological processes of uplift and subduction by which Tibet was formed have endowed it with considerable mineral reserves.

Outdated technology results in wasted minerals

A RICH HISTORY

Since medieval times minerals have played diverse roles in the lives of Tibetans. Minerals are used as vital ingredients in Tibetan phamaceutical preparations. Many religious objects and household and farm implements were made from minerals. Precious metals like gold, silver and copper were used largely in monasteries and nunneries and for ornamentation. Some of the metals mined in Tibet — particularly gold — were traded with India, Nepal, China and other neighbouring countries and so Tibet gained worldwide fame as a major repository of important minerals. Its name in Chinese, Xizang, means "Western Treasure House".

Tibetans never initiated modern large-scale mining schemes since there were sufficient raw minerals on the surface of the earth to meet demands. Another reason that contributed to the preservation of the plateau's mineral resources was the unique Tibetan approach to ecology. The centuries-old symbiosis between nature and religion led Tibetans to live in harmony with their land; this can be attributed largely to their profound faith in the principle of interdependence among living and non-living entities.

In the 1920s, Khenrap Kunsang Mondrag prospected parts of Dakpo and Lhoka in Central Tibet and found large reserves of petroleum ...the government did not grant permission for extraction on the ground that it would affect the ecosystem of the region.

Tibetans believed that mining the natural resources would diminish the strength of the land, invite the displeasure of the deities who are the guardian of minerals and therefore bring harm to society (Atisha 1991). Another factor that has helped to preserve the country's rich mineral resources was the Tibetans' deliberate disinterest in mining for fear of the government imposing heavy taxes (Shakabpa 1984). In certain cases where mining was considered imperative, rituals were performed to appease the deities who were believed to be the "owners of the land". Rituals like *sangsol* (incense offering) and the occasional performance of purification rites of objects and the environment helped the Tibetans continue to preserve and conserve their environment.

The first Tibetan metallurgist to use large quantities of minerals was probably Thang Thong Gyalpo (1361-1485). He was a *mahasiddha* (great accomplished one), a spiritual master, a talented iron bridge builder and a great theatrical performer. During his several spiritual journeys through Tibet and other countries he realised that building bridges, stupas and images was an integral part of his commitment to the *bodhisattva* ideal (a person who generates an aspiration to attain enlightenment for the sake of sentient beings). It is also believed that during his engineering work he coerced local demons, *nagas* (mythical water spirits with half human and half serpent physiques) and spirits to abandon their destructive activities; they eventually vowed to refrain from obstructing boats and help in building bridges (Gyatso 1991).

Thang Thong Gyalpo's first iron bridge was known as Yuna Chaksam (Yuna being the village name and Chaksam referring to the iron bridge), which is situated in the upper Kyichu valley north of Lhasa. The historic iron chains still exist and span about 30 metres, but modern steel cables stabilise the bridge today (Kahlen 1993). In all, he was said to have built 58 bridges (Gyatso 1991) and his discoveries of iron ore, developing smelting techniques and constructing iron chain suspension bridges, were attributed to the tradition of Buddhist teachings. Thus his engineering feat contributed to his elevation to the status of a realised master. To avert plagues, Thang Thong Gyalpo once built a stupa from lime and performed elaborate rituals to appease the local spirits, and repeated these rituals when his bridge-building required large quantities of iron.

Since that time, no record or evidence of mining has been heard of in Tibet — with two exceptions. In 1900, gold extraction was carried out near Mapham Tso (Lake Manasarover) in Western Tibet. However, following an outbreak of smallpox the Tibetan government stopped the mining because the epidemic was attributed to the wrath of the presiding deity of the region. In the 1920s, Khenrap Kunsang Mondrag prospected parts of Dakpo and Lhoka in Central Tibet and found large reserves of petroleum. He had been one of four students sent by the Thirteenth Dalai Lama to Britain to study where he majored in mining engineering (Shakabpa 1984). On finding the reserves, however, the government did not grant permission for extraction on the ground that it would affect the ecosystem of the region (*Tibetan Bulletin* 1992c).

The discoveries of huge reserves of various minerals, some of which are among the largest deposits in the world, catapulted the Chinese to dub Tibet the 'Treasure Bowl Awaiting Development'.

LARGE-SCALE MINING TODAY AND TOMORROW

Large scale modern mining began in Tibet only after China took full control of the country following the Fourteenth Dalai Lama's escape in 1959. Since then many areas have been surveyed and prospected by several Chinese government scientists. Their discoveries of huge reserves of various minerals, some of which are among the largest deposits in the world, catapulted the Chinese to dub Tibet the "Treasure Bowl Awaiting Development".

Some of the geological expeditions carried out since then in Tibet were the Tibetan Plateau Expedition in 1957, the Sino-French Expedition in 1983, the Sino-German Expedition in 1984 and the Sino-British Geo-traverse Expedition in 1985 (Tsundue 1994). In the 'TAR' and Eastern Tibet, 1:1 million and 1:200,000 geological maps have been worked out respectively (Namgyal 1995). The interest in mining in Tibet looks as though it will continue for long in the future as geological explorations tend to bring further successful results. In the Ninth Five Year Plan (1996-2000), China planned to invest nearly US$1.25 billion (10 billion yuan) in prospecting and developing mineral resources in Tibet's central and western regions (Norwill 1997).

Extraction from Norbusa Chromite Mine in Lhoka, Central Tibet, leaves the landscape permanently scarred

As with any colonised country of the world, the objective of developing the mineral and mining industry in Tibet was to exploit its rich mineral wealth for economic gains. In the 1960s, when systematic and large-scale mining in Tibet really began, the expansion of the Chinese presence and their development of infrastructure supported it. China launched an aggressive marketing campaign to kick-start the Tibetan economy with money being invested in infrastructure and with future plans to invest in forestry, trade and mining industries (*Xinhua* 1996a). In 1992, China accorded 'TAR' "Special Economic Zone" status and encouraged foreign investment by offering favourable tax terms. China has also undertaken construction of the costly US$ 6.2 billion Tibet-China rail link from Gormo (Ch: Golmud) to Lhasa, which will aid transportation of natural resources from the plateau to China and will encourage Chinese settlers into Tibet.

Chen Kuiyuan, on 17 December 1999, confirmed that the 'tapping of potential mineral resources to develop superior industries in Tibet is one of the main strategic policy decisions on the great development of Tibet'.

Since the inception of large-scale mining industries in Tibet, huge quantities of minerals were transported to China to help build its economy. These minerals were consumed largely by mineral-based industries and the surpluses were exported to other countries. In recent years, the expansion of Chinese markets in the international arena has further accelerated the growth of the mining industry in Tibet, with unprecedented investments from multinational companies and assistance from international aid agencies. As the industrialisation of China is heavily dependent on a huge consumption of resources and energy (NORAD 1997), Tibet's mineral reserves have become all the more important. The extraction and processing of these reserves is thought to be one of the principal reasons for opening up of the economy and road network, and for the undertaking of major development projects such as the controversial Yamdrok Tso hydropower project (DIIR 1992).

Norbusa Chromite Mine

Location:	*Lhoka, 3,700-5,000 metres above sea level, along the Yarlung Tsangpo River.*
Rank:	*Largest chromite mine in Tibet.*
Revenues:	*More than US$ 1.5 million annually.*
Deposit value:	*First class deposit in the world with more than 57 per cent chromite oxide. Potential value US$375 - 500 million. Expected to yield US$ 3.75 million annually.*
Output:	*Current output 130,000 per annum. Scheduled to produce 50,000 tons per year from 2000. In 1992, the mine represented 50 per cent of the total industrial output in 'TAR'. In 1991-95, the mine produced 450,000 tons of chromite ore.*
Recognition:	*In 1987 a special conference was held in Hunan, China, on the enormous prospects of the mine. In 1989 the mine was incorporated into the Five Year Plan and considered one of the most important developmental projects in "China".*

TIN 1998c, Tibetan Review 1998a, China's Tibet 1996.

With the ongoing expansion and development of Tibet's mineral industry, China plans to raise the 'TAR's' economic growth rate to 10 per cent per annum. This is driven by the acute shortage of mineral resources in China to satisfy its increasing demands. China today is the world's second largest consumer of mineral products and its demand for raw minerals has been growing fast, particularly for major non-ferrous minerals that are virtually exhausted. Seven out of 15 key minerals for China's industrial use were due to run out last decade (DIIR 1992). Moreover, by the year 2020, China's demand for various kinds of minerals will be more than double the present level. Many experts believe that the growing demand for mineral resources in China will make it necessary to develop and further expand mineral extraction in Tibet (*Xinhua* 1997b).

However, despite the significant increase in mineral output in the past four decades of mining in Tibet, the mining sector is still at a prospective stage. Hurried development and the improper implementation of mineral extraction methods in Tibet has seen most of the mining enterprises plagued by numerous problems that include low efficiencies in recovery, production, and utilisation. Likewise, the use of outdated mining technologies and lack of efficiency in the process of extraction has not only hampered the development of mining industry, but also has led to an unprecedented wastage of resources.

Despite the above problems, Chinese authorities are keen to make mining one of the pillar industries in 'TAR' with the ambitious target to treble the Gross National Product from that of 1995 (*Tibet Daily* 1996). Most of the resources are concentrated in Tsaidam Basin, Nagchu, Golok, Chamdo, Chang Thang, Kandze and Lhoka. However, the other regions of Tibet should not be neglected while speaking of minerals because the overall distribution of valuable reserves is throughout the plateau's three traditional provinces.

Today mineral extraction forms the largest economic activity in the industrial sector in Tibet. The growth of the mining sector is estimated at an annual rate of 30 per cent in the Ninth Five Year Plan (*Tibetan Review* 1998a). According to Dhondup Namgyal, the then Director of the TAR Mining Bureau in Lhasa in 1995, experts believe the mineral resources in Central Tibet area are worth US$ 81.3 billion in market value. Given the difficulty in obtaining information about mining operations in Tibet, however, the figures quoted officially are likely to represent only a small proportion of the true extent of extraction. The further large-scale development of mineral industries in Tibet is rising. The Regional Secretary, Chen Kuiyuan, in Tibet Regional Economic Work Forum, held in Lhasa on 17 December 1999, confirmed that the "tapping of potential mineral resources to develop superior industries in Tibet is one of the main strategic policy decisions on the great development of Tibet" (*Tibet TV*, 1999).

A RUNDOWN OF RESERVES

Chromite

Chromite reserves in Tibet are the largest in today's political China and the reserves in 'TAR' alone make up 40 per cent of what China claims as its national reserve. Chromite is the main material used to produce special steel and stainless steel. The now-exhausted Shar Lung mine in Nagchu region produced more than 60,000 tons of chromite ore between 1978 and 1979. From 1980 to 1985 the mine produced 300,000 tons of the ore, which had a value of around US$ 11 million (Research and Analysis Centre 1991).

Kandze, Kham, is a land strewn with gold reserves. Though much of the mining is kept secret, in 1986 China earned US$ 1.5 million from the sale of gold mined in Kandze. In Dechen County, Kham, gold is collected from the river.

Norbusa Chromite Mine in Lhoka is the largest of its kind in Tibet. The mine's potential value is predicted at about US$ 375-500 million (*Tibetan Review* 1998a) and contains more than 57 per cent of chromite oxide, rated as one of the top chromite deposits in the world (DIIR 1996b). In the 1980s, Norbusa mine produced a revenue of more than US$ 1.5 million (*China's Tibet* 1996). In 1992, the mine represented 50 per cent of the total industrial output of all industrial enterprises in 'TAR', and the total extraction of chromite between 1979 and 1989 was worth US$ 34 million. The construction of the mine was a key state project in the Eighth Five Year Plan (1991-95), with a total investment of US$ 10.7 million (DIIR 1996b). The production of 190,000 tons of chromite in those five years has paid more than US$ 3.25 million in tax to the 'TAR' (Waiser 1998).

With more profit in producing ferrochrome than metallurgical chromite, and with the increasing output of chromite in Tibet, the authorities produced their first batch of ferrochrome alloy in 1990. This demand is mainly driven by the stainless steel industry and this inexorable trend looks set to continue. By the end of last century the annual production of ferrochrome alloy is expected to reach 5,000 tons (*Xinhua* 1998a).

Yulong Copper Mine

Location:	*Jomda County, Chamdo, 'TAR'. Area 1,870 sq km 400 km long and 30-70 km wide.*
Rank:	*Largest and most valuable mine in Tibet. One of the largest copper mines in the world.*
Revenue:	*US$ 2.5 million profit annually.*
Deposit:	*7.14 million tons.*
Output:	*Production capacity 20,000 tons. Expected output by 2010 is 100,000 tons per year.*
Prospects:	*Shortage of copper in China increases pressures on this mine. The copper reserves at Yulong will begin to run out in 20 years time. As a result, the whole of this mining belt is being explored for other reserves.*
Foreign interest:	*Site visits conducted by Cyprus Amax, USA and BHP, an Australian conglomerate.*

Tibetan Review 1997b, Xinhua 1997a, TIN 1997e.

Copper

The 'TAR' has potential copper reserves of 13 million tons with proven reserves of 8.85 million tons. The region contains 14.4 per cent of "China's" copper reserves, which make up the third largest reserves and the largest porphyry copper belt in "China". Yulong Copper Mine in Jomda County, Chamdo, 'TAR', is among the largest mines of its kind in the world with an area of 1,870 sq km. The mine has a reserve of 7.14 million tons (*Xinhua* 1997a) and "with further investment and exploration around the region, this copper belt has tremendous significance in reducing China's foreign exchange expenditure and increasing Tibet's national income", states the internal document "The Specialist Plan for the TAR" (TIN 1997e).

Despite China's remarkable growth of copper production from 386,600 tons in 1980 to more than 1.1 million tons in 1997, the country was unable to meet its demand of 1.3 million tons in 1997. Therefore, China has opened up seven projects with big investments to curtail its copper imports. Two of the projects are located in Tibet, namely the Yulong Copper Mine in Chamdo and the Sashithang Copper Mine in Tsolho, Amdo. Both these mines are included in the Ninth Five Year Plan (1996-2000) with an investment of US$ 1.62 million and US$ 27.5 million respectively. The Sashithang mine has proven copper reserves of 230,000 tons. The operation of these mines in Tibet will help China ease its copper shortage in the market (TIN 1997d).

According to many geologists Tibet is perhaps the last and the largest oil belt on the continents...similar to the oilfields in the Persian Gulf and the Karakorum in Central Asia.

Other copper mines in Tibet, such as the one in Mongyon Hui County, Tsochang, Amdo also have rich reserves and good quality copper. Extraction at Mongyon Copper Mine started in 1958, exporting of copper started in 1983, and nowadays it is the chief source of income for people living in that area. Copper reserves in Machen County in Golok are considered to be 545,000 tons and in Norbusa Copper Mine at Chusum, Lhoka, the Chinese authorities have an investment of US$ 6.81 million (Research and Analysis Centre 1991).

Gold

Tibet has abundant gold reserves, particularly in Amdo as indicated by the following discoveries. On 22 July 1983, three farmers found 3.5 kg of natural gold rock in Yaradu, Wulan County (Research and Analysis Centre 1991) and in another incident a lump of natural gold weighing 6.57 kg was found in Amdo in 1996 (*Tibetan Review* 1997a). Hungjintai Gold Mine in Matoe, Golok, located at an altitude of 4,670 metres is the highest gold mine in the world. The production of gold in Amdo region in 1991 was over 200 kg (DIIR 1992) and in 1995 it reached 827.5 kg (TIN 1999a). Kandze, Kham, now incorporated into Sichuan Province, is a land strewn with gold reserves. Though much of the mining is kept secret, in 1986 China earned US$ 1.5 million from the sale of gold mined in Kandze (Research and Analysis Centre 1991). Tawo County, Kandze, alone had gold deposits of 22 tons, according to *Radio Lhasa* on 23 September, 1985. In Pongtsa-rawa, Dechen County in Kham, gold is collected from the river.

In the 'TAR', the Nagchu area has reserves of 10.1 tonnes of alluvial gold. Bengna Zhuangbu Gold Mine in Shentsa County, Nagchu, which started production in 1997, is the largest gold mine in the region. The mine is one of the highly publicised "62 Development Projects" in the 'TAR'. It is estimated that the mine will produce an annual average of 450,000 cubic metres of ore, and 386.6 kg of gold, with an annual net profit of US$ 1.56 million (*Zhongguo Xinwen She* 1997).

Laoran Mountain, Maodou, Markham in Kham, produces more than 100 kg of gold annually and due to gold content at a shallow depth the mine is expected to form large-scale gold deposits in the near future.

In the 'TAR', an aggregate 14.225 tons of deposits was discovered in six gold mining zones in 1993. In 1994, the production of gold in the region was 13.527 kg, which was an increase of more than 360 per cent from 1993. In 1995, there were 148 gold mines zones in the 'TAR' (*Tibet People's Broadcasting Station* 1995) with substantial gold reserves at 100 sites (Namgyal 1995).

Chinese Police Gold Hunt Continues

A special gold exploration team under the Chinese People's Armed Police has discovered two gold mines in the Nagchu region of Tibet that are believed to have high quality ore. The inspectors have also discovered signs of gold reserves in various other parts of Tibet. The two mines, according to an armed police officer, will soon be transferred to the local government, in accordance with the law.

Xinhua 1999e.

Oil and Gas

According to many geologists Tibet is perhaps "the last and the largest oil belt on the continents". The region has favourable geology for oil formations: The stratum are of the Mesozoic and Cenozoic periods and similar to the oilfields in the Persian Gulf and the Karakorum in Central Asia (*Xinhua* 1997c). Tsaidam Basin in Amdo — an area of 220,000 sq.kms, almost the size of Britain — and Chang Thang are the two major oil deposit zones in Tibet.

Tsaidam Basin has oil reserves of 42 billion tons and natural gas reserves of 1,500 billion cubic metres in 22 deposits (*Tibet Daily* 1998b). With China currently consuming 22 billion cubic metres of gas a year, Tsaidam's estimated reserves of 1,500 billion cubic metres would supply the Mainland's current need for up to seven years. Gas has been identified as the most practical and transferrable non-polluting energy to serve China's southern and eastern coastal boom cities in future and Tibet's Tsaidam gas fields are earmarked as the primary supplier. A pipeline is due to take Tsaidam gas to Lanzhou in 2002 — the first phase in a mammoth network to finally in corporate Xinjiang, Kazakh and Siberian gas fields. Since Chinese exploration started in 1954, more than 23.5 million tons of oil has been extracted from Tsaidam. Once the exploitation is fully implemented, the basin's potential economic returns are valued at US$ 1.9 billion (*China Daily* 1997b). One of the basin's operating oil fields has been verified as having 31 layers 69.9 metres thick, and another well had a proven 13 layers 43.4 metres thick (*China Daily* 1998a). Since the late 1980s the basin had been producing over one million tons of crude oil annually. In 1997 the production of oil and gas was 1.5 million tons annually and is scheduled to double by 2001, with projections showing 10 million tons a year by 2005 (*China Daily* 1997a). At the end of 1999 Qinghai Oilfield was expected to top 1.9 million tons, which is 130,000 tons more than the same period of 1998 (*Tibetan Review* 2000).

After years of oil exploration in Chang Thang, the first deep oil deposit — with 200 million tons — has been found in Lhunpula Basin. The basin is also stated to have a proven deposit of 1.5 million tons of oil (*Xinhua* 1997c). In 1999 another discovery in the same region found higher oil reserves of three million tons. According to several Chinese scientists, the total reserve in the basin is predicted to contain up to 10 million tons of oil. China National Star Petroleum Corporation plans to build at least one field with an annual capacity of 50,000 metric tons in the basin (*South China Morning Post* 1999b).

The basin is situated at an altitude of 4,700 metres above sea level and it is located 300 km northwest of Nagchu in Northern Tibet. An excellent quality oil field of 6 sq km was found in the region, with four prospective first grade oil gas zones, and one second prospective grade of oil zone. Excellent conditions for the formation of oil were determined in the region with three potential gas zones and 22 structured zones. The achievement of the prospecting team in the region was considered as a major breakthrough in oil discoveries. Many Chinese scientists predict that the region will become the major oil reserve base in the 21st century (*Xinhua* 1997c).

Tsaidam Potash Plant

Location:	*Tsaidam Basin, Amdo.*
Rank:	*Largest salt lake and potash reserve in the world.*
Revenue:	*US$ 8.75 million annually.*
Deposit:	*97 per cent of "China's" entire potash reserves. 150 billion tons of salt, sufficient to feed the global demand for edible table salt for 10,000 years. 60 billion tons of sodium and potassium chloride.*
Output:	*Qinghai Potash Fertiliser Plant began production in 1988. Capability of producing 0.2 million tons per year. Yearly production of potash 800,000 tons. Production reached 350,000 tons in 1997. Planned to increase production to one million tons by year 2000.*
New Project:	*The plant will soon be expanded as a joint venture project between the Chinese Ministry of Chemical Industries and Israel Chemicals with a budget of US$ 544 million. It will start working in 2000.*

Lafitte *1998a, Tibetan Review 1997c.*

Uranium

Tibet has the world's largest deposits of uranium. By 1990 more than 200 uranium deposits were discovered in Tibet, according to a *China Daily* report on 28 May 1990. The actual size of the uranium resources on the plateau is closely guarded by the Chinese government, but the location of the resources are indicated by the presence of the former Ninth Academy, which was involved in nuclear weapons development, around the eastern mountainous shores of Lake Kokonor (DIIR 1992). The largest uranium mine is in Thewo, Kanlho

(Gannan) Tibetan Autonomous Prefecture, Gansu Province (Chutter 1998). Known mines of uranium include Tsaidam Basin and Thewo in Amdo and Yamdrok Tso and Damshung, near Lhasa (Dekhang 1998).

Apart from mining uranium in Tibet, the Chinese also extract strontium which is used for nuclear missile cladding (Chutter 1998). A deposit of over 18 million tons of radioacitve strontium was discovered at Tsaidam in 1994 according to *Xinhua*. Official said the deposit was near the surface and easy to extract (*Reuters* 27 January 1994). The concentration of plutonium in the deep salt lakes of Tsaidam Basin is another major discovery in Tibet; however its extraction is unknown. The salt lakes also contain well known, large and accessible quantities of lithium which has many industrial applications such as its use as a raw material for nuclear fusion weapons (Slesser 1998). The lithium deposits in Tsonub, Amdo and the 'TAR' represent nearly all of "China's" known lithium resources (*Beijing Review* 1998a) and the total lithium deposits in Tibet are considered the largest in the world (Waiser 1998).

Cesium

A quarter of the world's cesium deposits (27.6 per cent) are discovered in Tibet (TIN 1991) and, according to an announcement made by the Chinese Academy of Geological Science, the deposit discovered in 'TAR' is estimated to have a value of as high as US$ 6.48 billion. This rare metal is mainly used in military and hi-tech applications, e.g. atomic clocks and high-energy solid fuel. (*Keji Ribao* 1999).

IMPACTS AND HAZARDS

"Of all the economic activities in the world's mountains, nothing rivals the destructive power of mining"

World Watch Paper 1995

For the existence and development of human society it is necessary to conserve the environment and to simultaneously meet man's demand for materials through the continuing exploration of mineral resources. However, to a varying degree, mining activities have changed the original state of the environment and created potential dangers for both ecological and social systems. Therefore, the continued development of human society depends on the attitude of the mineral industry towards achieving ecologically sustainable development of this sector.

The scale of mineral extraction in Tibet is rapidly expanding with China's industrialisation and modernisation programmes. Mining activities quite obviously impose considerable impacts on the natural environment, but these practices in Tibet have jeopardised not only its natural endowments but also its people. Moreover, as the mineral and energy potential in Tibet is vast and underdeveloped, China will continue to invest heavily in mineral exploration to meet its increasing domestic demand and to reduce its foreign debt. Given these pursuits, further degeneration of the environment is inevitable, which makes the issue of mineral extraction in Tibet of serious concern.

Since the Chinese invasion of Tibet, the use of mineral resources has been unprecedented. The activities have evidently profited the Chinese immensely, as has been revealed by the enormous quantities of production and the increasingly huge investments in the mining sector. This acceleration continues. But the process of extraction has paid little attention to the impact of mining. As a result, despite the generation of huge revenues in fuelling China's economic growth, mining activities have failed to produce real benefits for Tibetans as the majority still live in impoverished conditions.

The increasing practise of unchecked mining activities has not just damaged but permanently altered the shape of the plateau's landscape. Despite protests by locl people, vast areas of pastures have been turned into mining zones.

Natural Resources

Environmental impacts of mining are largely unreported by the Chinese authorities in Tibet. The extensive mining activities have led to the destabilisation of fragile mountain slopes, degradation of pastures, increased rates of sediment in river catchments, deforestation and other perils. The constant treatment of Tibetan natural resources as if inexhaustible, and the extraction of minerals, has also resulted in water contamination and air pollution. In many areas the pressure on local mineral resources has been mounting each year, further impoverishing the region.

The increasing practise of unchecked mining activities has not just damaged but permanently altered the shape of the plateau's landscape. Despite protests by local people, vast areas of pastures have been turned into mining zones. The once-99 per cent pastoral land of Tsalung, Diru, Kham, is today completely transformed into a mining zone (TIN 1997b). Nomads and farmers from Nagchu, Central and Eastern Tibet, raised

Sacred Mining Ground

The hill behind the famous Trachen-Ma Temple in Riwoche, a village in Kham, Eastern Tibet, is considered sacred by Tibetan Buddhists. It is also rich in uranium, a material the Chinese military wants. When miners were brought in to dig up the hill Tibet's leaders protested to Beijing. After their concerns were ignored they rioted.

A tense incident ensued in which three uranium surveyors' jeeps were set on fire and Chinese soldiers occupied Riwoche and rounded up villagers for interrogation.

The saga of Riwoche is one of the better-known clashes over Tibet's natural resources. As deforestation and indiscriminate hunting wipe out the region's terrestrial ecology, Tibet's occupiers are beginning to look underground — to Tibet's rumoured veins of gold and other valuable minerals. Already, some 60,000 itinerant Chinese gold miners have flooded into Amdo forcing out 17,000 nomadic herdsmen and destroying vast tracts of rich grazing land.

The Chinese have also tapped Tibet's coal and borax, and are beginning to mine for the region's so-called strategic minerals; iron, copper,

Ackerly 1990.

objections when gold mining in their regions was taking a heavy and destructive toll on their pastoral land — but to no avail.

In the gold-rich Serta County, Kandze, Kham, gold mining has devastated the subsistence of the nomads who have lived in the region for centuries. According to a former inhabitant of the region, Jigme Sonam, the Chinese authorities have ordered the evacuation of the Serta area for mining without any monetary or social compensation to the nomads. The land was confiscated under the pretext that it belongs to the "motherland" (TCHRD 1997b).

Vast tracts of rich grazing land were destroyed and more than 17,000 nomads were forced to start a new livelihood when a huge uranium deposit was discovered in Riwoche, Kham in 1990 (Ackerly 1990). In the mineral-rich Amdo Province, extraction and industrialisation have disrupted some 76 per cent of the valley's 16,000 sq.km area resulting in soil erosion and water loss (*Xinhua* 1996b).

The impact of mining on water resources in Tibet has long been an issue, not only for Tibetans but also for neighbouring countries since the headwaters of Asia's major rivers originate from Tibet. Therefore increased pollution and siltation of rivers affects downstream countries. An example of water contamination comes from a 1997 refugee report which states that during the processing of gold near Mt. Mekong Shaklung in Kungri, Machen County, Amdo, mercury residue used for the extraction of gold from ore was discharged directly into a nearby river (Bidhartsang 1998). Similar pollution was witnessed at Lang Gio Uranium Mine in Gansu Province, where liquid mercury, a product used in the processing of uranium, was dumped into the Machu (Yellow River). Half the lakes on the relatively less-developed Yunnan-Guizhou plateau — including Jangtsa Tso (ch: Dianchi), one of Tibet's largest fresh water lakes — were seriously polluted by August 1999 from 100 tons of waste liquids being released daily from 1,042 industrial enterprises including petrochemical, metallurgical, power and building materials sectors. These industries consume 15,000 tons of coal per annum (*Xinhua* 18 August 1999).

Lhasa residents' concern about the ever-increasing dust pollution being caused by cement factories describes the growing air impurity of the region (*Xinhua* 1998c) and highlights the reckless attitude of the authorities. Further, Tibet's industrial water treatment is the worst in China, and the percentage of industrial solid wastes in water resources in Amdo are the highest of any province in China (*The World Resources* 1998).

Human Health and Animals

Hundreds of thousands of litres of untreated, polluted water caused by mining in Tibet pour into major rivers like the Yangtze each day. At the same time, dozens of ferro-silicon, iron, steel, aluminium and silicon carbide plants are releasing their daily dosage of thick poisonous smoke (ICT 1993). All this is hazardous to human health and life. Uranium mining has been linked to illness among the local people, thought to be caused by exposure to radon gas or from drinking water contaminated by mine tailings (ATC 1998). Deaths, injuries and human and animal birth deformities in nearby mining processing are some of the direct effects of the state of mining in Tibet (ICT 1993).

In a village in Ngaba, Amdo, at least 35 people died after drinking water polluted by waste from a nearby uranium mine. One village near a uranium mine in the township of Chongtsa had mysterious illnesses. The victims died within a few hours of developing a fever, followed by a distinctive form of diarrhoea. The trees adjoining the mine also began to dry up (TIN 1992).

Gonpo Dhondup, who escaped from Tibet in 1987, stated at the 1992 World Uranium Hearing in Salzburg, Germany on 14 September, 1992 that in Amdo Province areas surrounding uranium mines have experienced decreasing crop yields and the increasing deaths of domestic animals and fish. He also cited mysterious illnesses among humans including skin and eye diseases, and births of deformed babies. At Thewo, site of the largest uranium mine in Tibet, more than 50 Tibetans and their domestic animal died between 1987-91 from mysterious illnesses. Corpses of both humans and animals turned blue after death. At this uranium mine waste is allegedly collected and stored in a stone structure 40 metres high before being released into the Dukchu Karpo river which is used for drinking water supplies (Dekhang 1998). The use of cyanide and mercury in the extraction and processing of some of the minerals in Tibet, especially gold and the generation of toxic wastes and dust particularly in open cast mining, (DIIR 1992), have been identified as the causes of loss of vision, hair, skin ulceration, respiratory problems and destruction of nervous systems and bone structures (Free Tibet Campaign 1997).

Population Transfer

Another major problem arising from mining in Tibet is the settlement of an increasing number of Chinese into Tibetan regions in the form of labour, technicians and others. This mass migration has created extra pressures on the plateau's dwindling natural resources, intensified ethnic tensions, and is leading to the marginalisation of Tibetans in their own country. During gold rush periods in Amdo and in northern 'TAR', tens of thousands of Chinese migrated into the area and additional thousands of Chinese were recruited by the government (*Xizang Ribao* 1994). Plans for building several towns to accommodate half a million migrant workers in Tibet in April 1996, are in the process with each proposed town set to house about 100,000 workers (Chan 1996).

Economic incentives in the form of three to four times the rate of standard pay, tax breaks and lower interest loans, plus subsidies from Beijing totalling US$ 125 million a year, are provided to attract and encourage more Chinese settlers and workers into Tibet (Chu 1999). Subsidised truck fuel and machinery costs, and improved infrastructure, are some of the benefits made to increase the Chinese presence in Tibet. In addition to the legal mining of Tibet's mineral resources, the potential adverse environmental effects are compounded by widespread illegal mining. Fights among the illegal miners for the best spots of gold in the region are common, often leading to several deaths. According to Gonpo, who was a participant at the Tibet People's Consultative Conference in Lhasa in May 1995, "there are over 12,000 miners unlawfully extracting gold in Gansu, Amdo and districts of Nagchu in the TAR" (DIIR 1996b). It is presumed that the number of illegal mining operations, especially for gold, are more common in the Tibetan regions outside 'TAR'. Both farmers and nomads in these areas have raised serious objections to the heavy extraction of minerals and the consequent destruction of pastures.

> **Fortune Seekers' Disregard for the Environment**
>
> *In many resource-rich areas in remote regions of western (Tibet) or southern China, a motley assortment of local fortune seekers, officials, police, People's Liberation Army and security force members – with no regard to the environment – mine gold and other deposits. These illegal miners extract high-grade gold deposits, taking only the 20-30 per cent of the oxidised surface ore that is easily processed. This practice makes the remaining ore, which requires more advanced mining processes to extract, much less attractive to exploit. Gold obtained in this manner is frequently smuggled out of China, but what is left in the ground is no longer recoverable, resulting in a double loss of national equity.*
>
> US Embassy 1996a.

Kabukye Rinpoche was arrested, tortured and imprisoned for six years for expressing his opposition to the Chinese government's gold mining operation near his monastery.

Forced Labour

With increasing prospects and advantages in Tibet today more and more Chinese are migrating there resulting in social unrest and ethnic conflicts. Chinese nationals run

Tibet Drained for the Benefit of China

Tibet's rich mineral resources — such as gold, copper, iron, uranium, coal, oil, borax, mica, natural gas, natural salt, etc. — are being exploited. Similarly, our ancient forest reserves are denuded, our once free — roaming wildlife and livestock are being exploited for the benefit of China. Today our country is completely impoverished.

Kashag Speech, Tibetan Government-in-Exile, 10 March 2000

most of the work in the mineral sector. Local participation and employment in mining enterprises has remained minimal and any direct benefit to Tibetans from such industrial development is insignificant. The use of forced labour, particularly prisoners, in State-run mining and in building infrastructure in Tibet continues to prevail despite heavy international pressure. For instance, a tungsten mine near Xinduquiao uses about 800 prisoners through the so-called "reform through labour programme" of China (TIN 1995). Tibetan individuals and families often have to work in adjacent mines as demanded by authorities. Failing to turn up for work results in fines and doubling the amount of work next time, and often these labourers are not paid. The deaths of many thousands of peasants from 12-15 hour stints of forced labour in the deserts and mountainous regions of Eastern Turkestan (Xinjiang) are kept secret (*Golos Vostochnogo Turkestana* 1997).

The revamped mining laws do not provide any solution for the effective and efficient running of mining activities. Rather, the focus still remains on encouraging further exploration and extraction of mineral resources.

The use of forced labour is banned under the International Labour Organisation's Conventions number 29 and number 105. Convention 29 describes forced labour as "work extracted from persons under the menace of penalty and for which the individuals have not offered voluntarily". Convention 105 is concerned with the banning of forced labour as a "means of political coercion or as punishment for political views, as a method of mobilising and using labour for purposes of economic development or as a means of racial, social, national or religious discrimination". Clearly, the use of Tibetan and Chinese prison labour violates these conventions.

Social Unrest and Conflicts

Despite the potentially severe impacts of mining on people and the environment in the form of contamination of drinking water or disruption of livelihood, these affected peoples often have very little meaningful input into decision-making processes about whether a mine will be constructed or not. Environmental protests by local people have been ignored and crushed; many individuals have been subjected to severe punishments, often leading to longterm imprisonment and torture.

In 1991, Phuntsok Chosang and Gyatso pasted posters for the third time to protest the building of roads into their hometown Meldro Gongkar, 'TAR', for the transportation of minerals from Thalung Mine in Gyama to China. Subsequently locals in the mining area also raised objections to the operation of the mine because it uses toxic materials and dynamite in blasting the area. According to Phuntsok the mine has caused severe ecological imbalance in the form of soil erosion, frequent rainfall and hailstorms and many wild animals, birds and farm animals have died from the toxic gases released. But the authorities ignored their pleas and both Phuntsok Chosang and Gyatso were imprisoned, tortured and put in solitary confinement for 13 days and nights (TCHRD 1997a).

The disregard for sacred places and for the sentiments of residents caused by mining operations in many places in Tibet is another growing concern. Opposition by local Tibetans and monks to the extraction of minerals at nearby sacred places of worship had led to harsh torture and imprisonment. In a mining protest near Nubsur Monastery in Serta, Kandze in Kham on 10 June 1996, monastery headman Kabukye Rinpoche was arrested, tortured and imprisoned for six years for expressing his opposition to the Chinese government's gold mining operation near his monastery (TIN 1998b).

FUTURE ALTERNATIVES

The development of mineral industries is inevitable for the overall development of Tibet's economy. For years the utilisation of Tibet's mineral resources has been hampered by bureaucratic restrictions, legal uncertainties, illegal mining activities, lack of capital and poor infrastructure. It is, therefore, important to mitigate mining activities through effective government action and policies that propel sound development. The challenge is not to stop development, but to meet development needs of the Tibetan people in a sustainable way.

Effective Legislation

The mineral resources law has an important role to play in promoting rational use as well as in conserving the mineral resources. It was only in August 1986 that China formulated its first mineral resources law, which came into effect in October the same year. But the exploration and extraction of mineral resources in Tibet had already started in 1956. In those three decades both the government and private miners took a huge toll of the fragile environment and the Tibetan people.

Nonetheless, in order to curtail the serious problem of illegal mining and to bring order to many mining localities, China amended its first mining laws on 29 August 1996. This revised law came into effect on 1 January 1997 and is known as the Mineral Resources Law of the "Chinese government" and consists of seven chapters and 53 articles. Though most of the old laws were retained, much of the revamped law has been designed to facilitate modernisation of the mining sector, and to attract increased foreign investment by introducing market mechanisms.

Given the nature of Tibet's topography, mining should not be practised in fragile areas, on mountain slopes, ecologically significant habitats, forests and croplands. Large-scale mining in mountainous regions should be banned and instead small-scale mining for basic minerals implemented, which can be allowed under appropriate safeguards and restrictions. The cost of site restoration and damage should be borne by the mining agency under law. Mining of uranium and other radioactive minerals should be halted, especially near rivers and lakes.

As stated in Article 10 of the Mining Law, "the State should give due consideration to the interests of those areas and make arrangements favourable to the areas' economic development and to the production and livelihood of the local minority nationalities". So far the mining industries in Tibet have benefited Tibetans marginally. The statistics of a United Nations Development Program report on Tibet shows a clear fall of life expectancy, a drop of post-school employment, and a decrease in literacy rate to 31 per cent (ICJ 1997).

Legislation should adhere to strict environmental safeguards and rules and deal with each of the main resources separately, i.e. water and air would each have a separate legislation. The establishment of policies and the implementation of laws should be followed strictly to foster economic growth in a sustainable way.

Proper Implementation of Rules

The situation of mineral resources in Tibet is still quite chaotic and the mining laws and regulations are still in evolution. This can be attributed mainly to the ineffective regulation and unsound legal system. For instance, mining is practised in places specified as a "no mining area" under Article 20 of the Mining Law. Chinese government collect fees by issuing mining rights on public and private lands, but the Tibetans receive no benifits as compensation for encroaching on their ancestral land. Exploration and mining rights issued by the Ministry of Geology and Mineral Resources are not made for public viewing, as stated in the law. The revamped mining laws do not provide any solution for the effective and efficient running of mining activities. Rather, the focus still remains on encouraging further exploration and extraction of mineral resources.

Tibetans should be provided technical knowledge and training to develop appropriate skills rather than directly appointing Chinese workers and overseers.

Following the changes, the government should ensure effective environmental protection, proper legislation, and the monitoring and enforcement of mining laws. Two relevant examples where effective legislation is urgently required are with respect to hazardous wastes and to stop illegal mining. Legislative standards should be developed to indicate environmental bottom lines for such basic issues as water and air quality and acceptable noise levels. Mining agencies should be held subject to these sound environmental commitments, not just on paper but in reality. In addition, environmental fees for the excessive release of pollutants should be applied to small-scale mining activities also.

The authorities should not propose the confiscation of land in the name of the "motherland". Jurisdictional disputes are another obstruction preventing speedy, effective approvals. Clear divisions on authorities should be established at the district and village level to prevent government red tape. Illegal activities and corruption of all kinds should be handled with heavy punishments. If it is a problem to deal within the established structure, a new agency directly appointed from the higher level could be given the *charge de force* to handle the situation. Other improvements needed include transparency of information dissemination between the government and the public. More research and comparative studies on similar small-scale mining operations should also be conducted.

Technical Upgrading

Due to the use of outdated technologies and equipment in mining activities most of the mines in Tibet suffer from a lack of structure optimisation. The backwardness of technology has resulted in low efficiency in recovery, production and utilisation of the mineral resources. Minimal safety standards, wastage of resources and poor economic returns in most mines are some of the constant problems. Underdevelopment of transportation infrastructure is another issue that remains inadequate in most of the mining areas.

The introduction of appropriate technology is required to minimise environmental damage and improve economic returns. Proper development of technical standards in small and large size production units and providing skills training in the mining sector are just a few changes that can be made to generate better returns.

The unregulated mining sector in Tibet is leading to the dilution of Tibetan culture and traditions by encouraging a further influx of Chinese settlers and also causing social conflicts.

Participation of People

Environmental Impact Assessments of mining areas should be conducted and the results made available for public viewing before starting any mining projects. It is recommended to allow and encourage the public, especially local communities, to participate in the environmental aspect of mining activities. For example, a Public Hearing or a round table conference can be held prior to the issue of a mineral title by the relevant mining management agency.

Mining agencies and authorities should have proper co-ordination with local people and they should inform the public about the developments and proceedings of the mine. Efforts should be made to encourage the increased participation of Tibetans at all levels. In this way a positive bond can be established which can help with the smooth running of mines with public support. Strict supervision and checks on mining methods should be made known to the public, to ensure safety and prevent environmental damage. Direct benefits to Tibetans should be provided whenever mining is done in their territory. This can be in the form of provision of jobs, social securities and social welfare schemes. All workers in mines should be treated equally regarding job placements. Tibetans hold only about 10 per cent of the mining jobs in Kham and less than 20 per cent in Amdo and U-Tsang, with the rest of the jobs going to Chinese settlers (DIIR 1992). Tibetans should be given preference over other nationals.

Check Human Pressures

The influx of a large number of Chinese workers into Tibet, especially miners, creates serious social and ecological problems. Therefore, mining developments in Tibet — as with all development projects — should discourage Chinese population transfer. Necessary steps should be taken to halt "migrational skilled workers" over the border. Tibetans should be provided technical knowledge and training to develop appropriate skills rather than directly appointing Chinese workers and overseers.

Large proportions of the Chinese settlers in Tibet are illegal miners. The government should take necessary steps to stop illegal mining and the random exploitation of mineral resources. These miners should be punished according to mining laws and must be deported to their native towns.

Foreign Investment

With its vast untapped mineral potential, Tibet may be the last truly great frontier in today's mining world. The mineral exploitation in Tibet has generated considerable returns to China. This activity has been expanded and promoted as one of the key pillar industries to increase economic growth. Several important changes to the mining laws have been made to attract foreign investment and consequently various investment channels are now open.

In the past a few foreign companies have been involved in mining in Tibet despite varying difficulties. Some have shown great respect and care for the Tibetan people and some have engaged in jeopardising Tibet's environment by focussing solely on economic gains. The industrialisation of Amdo, for instance, has attracted a total foreign investment of US$ 400 million, which includes US$ 70 million in foreign loans from aid agencies (Lafitte 1998a).

How much of these so-called developmental projects have benefited the Tibetans is understandable as the real income and standard of living of Tibetans still remains low. On the other hand, both the investors in Tibet and the Chinese government have profitably pocketed from these businesses. The current pattern of development has marginalised Tibetans and excluded them from effective participation, which is an intrinsic aspect of any sound development. The livelihood of most of the Tibetans who live in small rural communities has been neglected, receiving little of the investments (ICJ 1997).

The Tibetan Government-in-Exile has already issued guidelines for foreign aid and investment in Tibet. These are explained in depth in Chapter Nine of this report.The guidelines are offered to foster, not hinder, development. In fact, they encourage thoughtful, patient and sensitive developments devised specifically to enable Tibetans to participate fully in the development of their own land. Agencies and investors in mining enterprises in Tibet must be prepared to not only adhere to these guidelines, but in addition ensure they conform to relevant international conventions and treaties and also to the regulations and laws of China.

Decisions by investors in Tibet directly will in future affect the plateau's ecology and the livelihood of Tibetans. It therefore becomes important to consider the local issues thoroughly by building safeguards projects to ensure social development to the Tibetan populace. Proper social, cultural and environmental impact assessments should be done before launching any major mining operations in Tibet. Low priority should be given to massive infrastructure projects such as real estate, intensive mining and resource exploitation, the construction of heavy industries and large dams.

While such projects may be of minimal benefit, or often of no benefit whatsoever, to Tibetans, they more immediately benefit the Chinese who — without any mandate — speak for, exploit and control the Tibetan people. Therefore, mining companies need a far-sighted strategy with clear statements on ethical principles and a commitment to sustainable development — a concept which has a social as well as an environmental dimension.

CONCLUSION

Tibet's unique geological evolution led to the formation of abundant minerals and natural resources. For centuries these resources were not exploited since traditional beliefs prescribed that extraction of minerals would diminish the land's fertility, upset the presiding deities and harm society. Moreover, there were then no major commercial industries and factories so the mineral resources of Tibet were basically kept intact in a flourishing, natural and peaceful environment.

However, after the Chinese invasion of Tibet the scenario completely changed. In the name of "liberation" and "developing Tibet" China exploited the natural resources with little benefit trickling into Tibet and down to Tibetans and the lion's share of the income going to China to the tune of billions of dollars on the international markets.

China's haphazard mining practices continue to affect the fragile ecology of the Tibetan plateau. These include the destabilisation of fragile mountain slopes, the pollution of major river systems, degradation of agriculture and pastoral lands, deforestation, air pollution, not to mention that diminishing mineral resources lead to the impoverishment of the Tibetan region. Besides ecological concerns, the unregulated mining sector in Tibet is leading to the dilution of Tibetan culture and traditions by encouraging a further influx of Chinese settlers and also causes social conflicts.

Therefore, the Chinese government and associated mining enterprises working in Tibet must urgently address the limitation of current mining practices in Tibet and should achieve ecologically and socially sustainable development. The infiltration of Chinese settlers in the guise of miners should be halted as this new invasion has already jeopardised the quality of life of the Tibetans in their own land. Effective enforcement of regulations and technical up-gradation, as outlined, are some steps that need to be taken. In addition, greater emphasis needs to be placed on the short and long term consequences of mining on the environment, public health, safety and most importantly consider the wishes of Tibetans themselves. ■

CHAPTER SEVEN

NUCLEAR THREATS

We must first work on the total abolishment of nuclear weapons and gradually work up to total demilitarisation throughout the world ... we can then hope to see in the next millennium a year by year decrease in the military expenditure of the various nations and a gradual working towards demilitarisation.

His Holiness the 14th Dalai Lama, New Millennium Message, January 2000.

TIBET holds a unique position among the countries of the world. Not only does its territory cover the highest plateau on the planet, but also Tibet, alone among all nations, chose to abandon the path of aggression and military technology to pursue instead the creation of a society devoted to spiritual development and peace. Following the philosophy of the Buddha, Tibetans created spiritual universities where thousands of people were trained.

The most basic principle of Buddhism is *ahimsa* (non-violence); one should help others whenever possible and avoid causing any harm. So traditionally, the Tibetan Government kept only a small army. The well-armed and the massive Chinese army invaded Tibet in 1949.

Nuclear weapons, which can destroy all life forms and turn our beautiful green planet into a barren dust-bowl, are the antithesis of Buddhist philosophy. They can kill indiscriminately and continue killing over thousands of years. His Holiness the Dalai Lama poignantly asks, "We know that in the event of a nuclear war there will be no victors because there will be no survivors. Is it not frightening to contemplate such inhuman and heartless destruction? And is it not logical that we should remove the cause of our own destruction when we know it and when we have both the time and means to do so?"

It is especially disturbing for Tibetans to report that their motherland, once dedicated to the peaceful development of the human mind, has become the storehouse of Chinese nuclear weapons and a place for dumping radioactive waste. On top of this China, for financial gain, has reportedly been encouraging foreign countries to ship their toxic waste to Tibet.

This chapter brings to light some of the information available regarding the nuclearisation and militarisation of the altar of the earth — Tibet — and to explain why this is especially critical for the countries "downstream". In fact, we are all "downstream" from Tibet.

NUCLEAR WEAPONS

Nuclear weapons are explosive devices developed by harnessing the potential of atomic nuclei. Nuclear weapons get their destructive power from the transformation of matter in the nucleus of an atom into energy. They include missiles, bombs, artillery, shells, mines and torpedoes. The weakest nuclear weapons are far more destructive than the most powerful conventional weapons. The atom bombs dropped during World War II in Hiroshima and Nagasaki were nuclear weapons.

This Chapter Aims To:

- Document the development of nuclear weapons on the Tibetan Plateau
- Bring to light China's destructive military activities in Tibet and their impact on the environment
- Create global consciousness about the effects of the

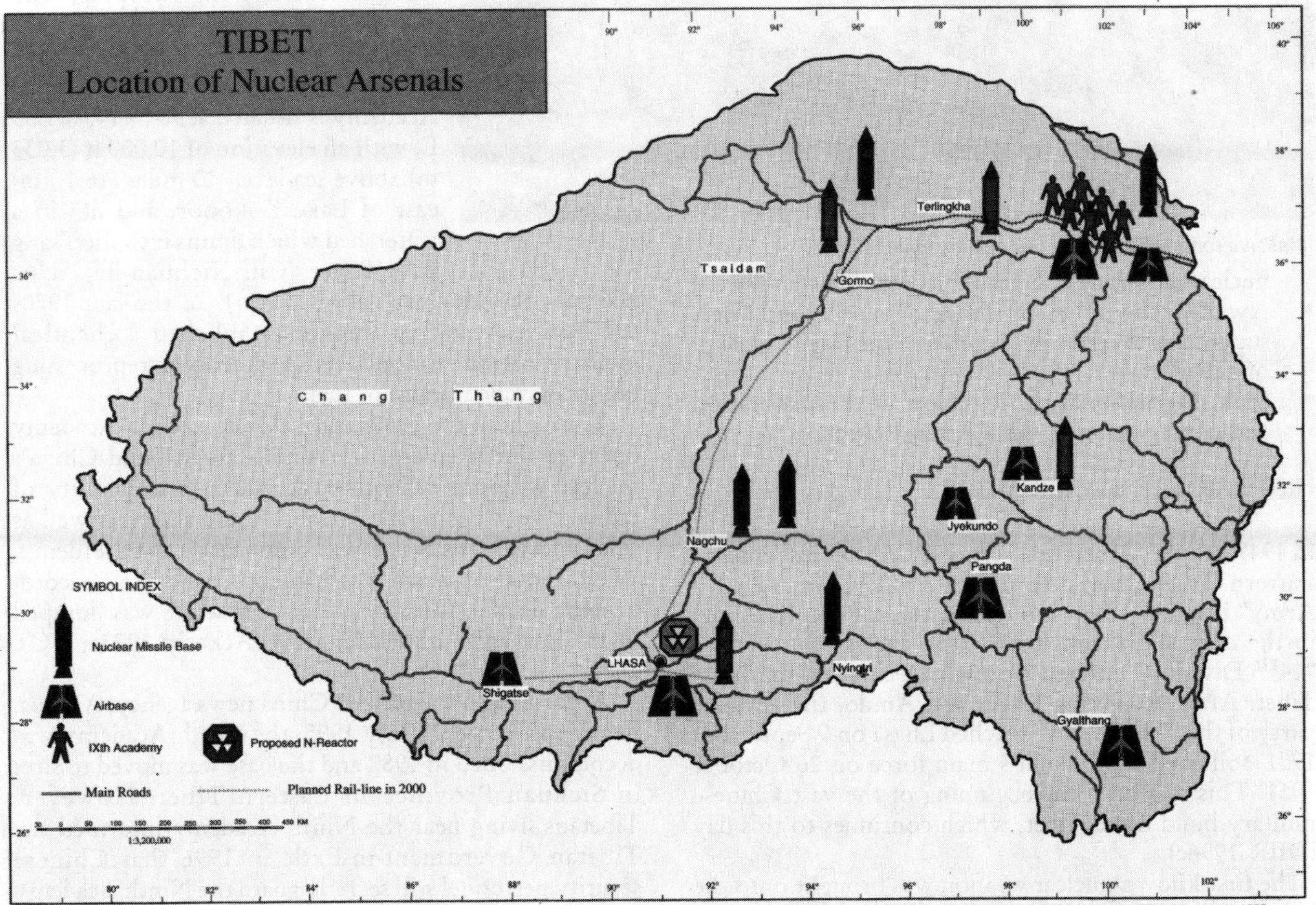

SOURCE: DIIR 1993 CARTOGRAPHY & DESIGN: Planning Council, CTA, Dharamsala-1999

Note : See colour map at the end of the book

Massive road networks access military installations

nuclearisation and militarisation of the Tibetan Plateau

- Awaken the spirit of Tibetan people and their supporters to restore and conserve the fragile ecology of Tibet
- Seek international participation in the restoration and conservation of the Tibetan Plateau.

HISTORICAL DEVELOPMENT

In 1949 People's Liberation Army (PLA) soldiers entered Eastern Tibet. In the spring of 1950, China's "18th Army" invaded Tibet through Dartsedo (Ch. Kanding) in the east, and through Amdo in the northeast. The "14th Division" entered through Dechen in southeast Tibet. After occupying Kham and Amdo, the advance party of the "18th Army" reached Lhasa on 9 September 1951, followed by the unit's main force on 26 October 1951. This was only the beginning of the vast Chinese military build up in Tibet, which continues to this day (DIIR 1996c).

The first known nuclear weapon was brought onto the Tibetan Plateau in 1971 and installed in the Tsaidam (Ch. Qaidam) Basin in northern Amdo (Ch. Qinghai). China is currently believed to have 17 secret radar stations, 14 military airfields, eight missile bases, at least eight ICBMs, 70 medium-range missiles and 20 intermediate range missiles in the whole of Tibet (DIIR 1998; DIIR 1996c).

The Ninth Academy

The Northwest Nuclear Weapons Research and Design Academy, known as the "Ninth Academy" or "Factory 211," was built by the Ninth Bureau of the Chinese Nuclear Production Establishment in the early 1960s to produce China's early nuclear bomb designs. It is China's top secret nuclear city located in Tsojang (Ch. Haibei) Tibetan Autonomous Prefecture in Amdo, 100 km west of Siling (Ch. Xining).

The construction of the Ninth Academy was approved by the late Chinese leader, Deng Xiaoping, who was then the General Secretary of the Central Committee of the Chinese Communist Party. The Ninth Academy is situated at 36.57 N, 101.55 E, with an elevation of 10,000 ft (3,033 m) above sea level, 10 miles (16.1 km) east of Lake Kokonor, and lies in a watershed which drains into the Tsang Chu River (Ch. Xichuan-he). This becomes the Machu (Yellow River). In the late 1970s the Ninth Academy further established a chemical industry institute to conduct experiments on reprocessing highly enriched uranium fuels.

Throughout the 1960s and 1970s, the Ninth Academy operated under emergency conditions to build China's nuclear weapons capability. An unknown quantity of radioactive waste in the form of liquid slurry as well as solid and gaseous waste was dumped by the Academy. The disposal of waste was haphazard and their record-keeping dismal. Initially radioactive waste was dumped in shallow and unlined landfills (Ackerly 1993a; ICT 1993).

According to the official China news agency, *Xinhua*, in a report dated 20 July 1995, the Ninth Academy was decommissioned in 1987 and the base was moved to sites in Sichuan Province in Eastern Tibet. However, Tibetans living near the Ninth Academy informed the Tibetan Government-in-Exile in 1996 that Chinese security personnel still secretly guard the Ninth Academy around the clock.

A direct railway line connects the Academy with Lake Kokonor, the largest lake on the Tibetan Plateau. Nuclear waste experts believe that radioactive waste was also dumped into the lake. A reliable report from a Chinese man whose father was a nuclear scientist in Lanzhou, Gansu, states that in 1974 there was an accident leading to nuclear pollution of the lake (ICT 1993). The Ninth Academy is located on marshy land allowing polluted water and radioactive particles to easily seep into the groundwater, which flows into Lake Kokonor.

How Lake Kokonor sprang to life

Lake Kokonor is called Tso Ngonpo (Blue Lake) by Tibetans. Legends originating from Tibetans living around the lake have it that Gar Tongtsen, the famous minister of great king Songtsen Gampo of Tibet (7th century), visited the lake with his son. At that time Gar was blind and his son was very thirsty. Gar knew the area well. He told his son to drink water from a sacred spring in the Tso Ngonpo region and to then seal the source of the spring with a rock after quenching his thirst. However, his son forgot his father's words and, over many days, water overflowed continuously from the spring to create the present-day lake. Both Gar and his son prayed to Guru Rinpoche for help. Guru answered their prayers and stopped the overflowing spring with a huge clod of earth, thereby creating an island in the middle of the lake. These days the island is home to a variety of bird species and is popularly known as the Birds' Island.

Lake Kokonor is sacred to Tibetans. Throughout history they have protected the natural beauty and sanctity of this lake through sustained spiritual practices and ecological respect. The principle lama of Rebgong Monastery in Amdo, Je Kalden Gyatso, has explained: "Today the island at the centre of Lake Kokonor is called the abode of *Maha Dewa* (Lord Shiva). It has historical connections with Tibet's great king Songtsen Gampo and also Guru Rinpoche (Padmasambhava). It is the abode of *klu* (beings who inhabit water bodies) and *jangchub sempa (bodhisattvas)*. It is a pilgrimage site for many kings and saints" (Palbar 1994).

Anti-Frigate Missile Centre at Drotsang

A new missile production centre is located at Drotsang (Ch. Ledu; 36.05N, 102.5E), 63 km east of Siling. The secret code number of this centre is 430. It was originally set up in 1986 and was massively expanded in 1995. It is a surrogate of the Ninth Academy and has been producing anti-frigate missiles which are being tested in Lake Kokonor (Chutter 1998).

Land-Based Nuclear Warheads

When Major-General Zhang Shaosong, the Political Commissar of the PLA in Tibet, was asked point-blank whether there were nuclear weapons in Tibet by the BBC's Mark Braine in 1988, he replied, "Whether there are nuclear weapons in Tibet or not, it is up to the authorities to decide." And he smiled (Kewley 1990).

Tsaidam's Nuclear Missile Launch Sites

The Ninth Academy was ready to produce nuclear weapons by 1971. The first batch of nuclear weapons manufactured at the Ninth Academy was reportedly brought to Tsaidam Basin and stationed at Small Tsaidam (Ch. Xiao Qaidam) and Large Tsaidam (Ch. Da Qaidam) in the extreme northwest of Amdo province (Ch. Qinghai). Tsaidam Basin is known to be one of most advantageous deployment sites for China because of its high altitude and isolation. China established the nuclear missile deployment and launch site for DF-4 missiles in the Tsaidam Basin in the early 1970s. The Large Tsaidam site located in northern Tibet (37.50N and 95.18E) has two missiles stored horizontally in tunnels near the launch pad. Fuel and oxidizers are stored in separate tunnels with lines to the launch pad (Fieldhouse 1991).

According to various reports, a launch site for Dong Feng Four (DF-4) missiles, which are equivalent to Russia's CSS-2, was built in Tsaidam. These missiles, located at Large Tsaidam and Small Tsaidam (37.26N, 95.08E), are reported to have a range of over 4,000 km placing the whole Indian sub-continent within striking distance.

The DF-4 is China's first intercontinental ballistic missile. During the 1970s its range was extended from 4,000 km to 7,000 km allowing the modified version now deployed on the Tibetan Plateau to target Moscow and the rest of the former Soviet Union (Fieldhouse 1991).

The Small Tsaidam site in Northern Tibet is presumably organised in a similar way to the Large Tsaidam deployment and launch site. The missiles were moved to these sites on the Tibetan Plateau in 1971 (Lewis & Xue 1988). According to diplomatic sources informing the International Campaign for Tibet (ICT) in Washington DC, nuclear missiles are stationed in Small Tsaidam and are only moved to Large Tsaidam in times of emergency.

Terlingkha Nuclear Missile Launch Site

Another nuclear missile launch site is located at Terlingkha (Ch. Delingha; 36.6N, 97.12E), 217 km southeast of Tsaidam. It houses DF-4 and Inter-Continental Ballistic

Laser Weapons Testing

Wary of United States' plans in Asia, China is developing a range of missiles and laser-weapons that can shoot down incoming missiles. China in late August 1999 conducted live tests of laser weapons in secret locations in the mountainous regions of Amdo (Ch. Qinghai) and Central Tibet instead of its normal testing ground in InnerMongolia because of the thin air environment favourable for the tests. Atmospheric interference sometimes cripples the destructive power of lasers. The PLA is conducting laser weapons research as part of its Theatre Missile Defence Development Programme. The latest test indicates that Beijing is now capable of using laser-weapons to intercept missiles flying at low altitude. The airborne laser system uses lasers to destroy the guidance system of missiles, causing them to fall harmlessly to the ground, unlike the traditional anti-missile defence system which strikes attacking missiles while airborne.

The Indian Express *16 November1999.*

Missiles (ICBM). Terlingkha is the missile regiment headquarters for Amdo which consists of four associated launch sites. The organisation of the sites are similar to Large Tsaidam (Chutter 1998; ICT 1993).

New Long Range Missile Division

A new nuclear missile division has also been established on the Tibetan Plateau on the border between Qinghai and Sichuan provinces, in the Tibetan province of Amdo. Four CSS-4 missiles are deployed here, which have a range of 8,000 miles (12,874 km), capable of striking the United States, Europe and anywhere in Asia. Amdo Province is home to four Chinese nuclear missile launch sites, two at Tsaidam, one at Terlingkha and one at the border between Amdo and Sichuan Province (Chutter 1998).

Underground Base at Nagchuka

In the 1970s numerous reports surfaced regarding the stockpiling of nuclear weapons. These reports also confirmed that in 1970 missile base construction work had started about 10 miles (16.1 km) north of Nagchuka (Ch. Nagqu), in the 'Tibet Autonomous Region' and that there was a considerable build up of Chinese military personnel in the area.

On 14 October 1987, an article in the Sydney-based national newspaper *The Australian* reported the presence of nuclear missiles at Nagchuka. Subsequently, the Australian Nuclear Disarmament Party, in a press release dated 28 October 1987, expressed its grave concern over the intermediate-range ballistic (IRBM) and medium-range missiles (MRBM) stationed in Nagchuka.

Tashi Chutter's book, *Confidential Study on Deployment of Chinese Occupational Force[s] in Tibet,* published in 1998 confirms that there are nuclear missiles permanently stationed at Nagchuka. The missiles are housed in underground complexes beneath Risur mountain, 25 km southeast of Nagchuka. The Risur site has reportedly been developed by the Chinese government for two major reasons; to provide an alternative to the Lop Nor nuclear test site in Eastern Turkestan (Ch. Xinjiang) and to store as well as test China's upgraded air defence missiles and nuclear weapons. Nagchuka is reported to have the largest airforce unit stationed at any secluded site.

Rocky Funnels House Missile Base

Like the Risur site, another missile base is located at Tagho Mountain (Tib. Horse-Head Mountain) in the remote valley (32.15N, 89.42E) of Pelok, which lies to the east of Nyima Dzong under Nagchuka administrative division of 'TAR'. Missiles possibly of a nuclear nature are reportedly stored in the underground rocky tunnels of Tagho Mountain. The entire region is described as a desolate desert where only military vehicles are allowed to enter (Chutter 1998).

Underground Missile Storage Near Lhasa

Dhoti Phu is located 3.5 km to the northwest of Drapchi Prison and one kilometre to the west of Sera Monastery. It came into existence between the late 1960s and 1970s. It was observed that occasionally 20 to 25 trucks loaded with elongated objects wrapped in canvas cloth were seen entering the storage site. The movement of these vehicles took place only at night. The sophisticated underground storage complex of Dhoti Phu reportedly contains missiles known as *di dui kong* (ground-to-air) and *di dui di* (surface-to-surface). In Lhasa during Chinese Army Day (1 August), a number of missiles of these types were displayed to the public on missile guiding vehicles (Chutter 1998).

Missiles Complex in Kongpo

A large underground missile storage facility is located near Payi Town in Nyingtri (Ch. Nyingchi) region of Kongpo,

'TAR' under the secret code number 809 (Ch: Pa Ling Jue). It is controlled by the Chengdu Military Logistic Division. Supplies are brought in by the 17th, 18th and 20th Transport Regiments from Chengdu and some supplies are also brought in from Lhasa. A few low ceilinged barracks were noticed near the foothill of a mountain in Payi where there is an entrance leading to an underground storage complex. Long convoys of military trucks belonging to the transport regiments have been observed entering the storage facility. When fresh supplies arrive at the facility, storage complex drivers replace the regular drivers inside the complex.

It is reported that ground-to-air and surface-to-surface missiles are stored at this site. During mock military exercises a large number of such missiles are taken out of this complex. At one time about 80 missiles were observed. They were mounted on 20 trucks, each truck carrying four missiles. Each missile measured about one and a half times the length of the trucks and some had fins. During these exercises, missiles were launched vertically and horizontally to hit pre-arranged targets (Chutter 1998).

Airbases with Nuclear Weapons

There are three types of aircraft in China currently available for nuclear bombing missions: the Hong-6 bomber, the Hong-5 bomber, and the Qian-5 attack jet. The Hong-6 has a combat radius of over 3,000 km and can reach targets in the former Soviet Union and India. The Hong-5 has a combat radius of 1,200 km (Fieldhouse 1991).

During the 1960s and 1970s the three main military airbases in Tibet were in Lhasa, Chabcha and Golmud. During the 1960s, Chabcha and Golmud airfields were used as refuelling stations for Chinese aircraft on their way to Tibet and the Indian border. The Gongkar airfield, located 97 km southwest of Lhasa, has been the main military airfield and the main supply centre for the Chinese forces in the border area.

At Shigatse military airport, four or five IL-28 bombers were deployed with some jetfighter aircraft. Military transport aircraft such as the AN-32 and the Russian made IL-18 were noticed in frequent operations at the airport. Every autumn, these bombers carried out bombing exercises at a place known as Logma Thang, 50 km west of the airport. During the rest of the year the aircraft practice flight manoeuvring exercises (Chutter 1998).

A classified Pentagon report quoted by *The Washington Times* states that missile launch complexes in Jianshui, near the China-Vietnam border and at Datong in Amdo

AIRFIELDS ON THE TIBETAN PLATEAU

S.No.	Name	Location	Altitude (ft.)	Type
1	Chabcha	25 km south of Lake Kokonor	10,006	secret military
2	Damshung	162 km from Lhasa	13,123	abandoned
3	Gangtsa	north of Lake Kokonor	11,601	minor
4	Gongkar (Gonggar)	97 km southeast of Lhasa	11,709	civil & military
5	Gormo (Golmud)	15 km northwest of Gormo	9,275	civil & military
6	Gyalthang	184 km from Dechen	9,000	civil
7	Jyekundo	northeast 'TAR'	12,831	abandoned
8	Kandze(Kanze)	NW Sichuan, Kanze Prefecture	11,070	abandoned
9	Lhasa	10 km north of Lhasa	14,091	military
10	Pangta (Bangda)	south of Chamdo	14,107	civil & military
11	Shigatse	40 km east of Shigatse	12,037	military
12	Siling (Xining)	south of Siling city	7,211	civil & military

Sources: (Chutter 1998; Dekhang 1998; ICT

China's explosive plans for the Yarlung Tsangpo and Yangtze

According to a report by Xinhua, *dated 30 November 1997, within a few years China will divert a part of the Yarlung Tsangpo River and Yangtze River into Lop Nor by using nuclear explosions. This, they say, will turn the desert region into a lush green area, which will then be suitable for human habitation. Xinjiang's Lop Nor covers a land mass comparable to North Korea.*

The main proponent of this project, Hu Zuxue of the Chinese Academy of Sciences, says that since Tibet is at an altitude higher than Lop Nor, the headwater of the two rivers can be diverted to Lop Nor through tunnels drilled through the Kunlun mountain range dividing them. The Kunlun range is one of the largest mountain ranges in the world. The Xinhua *report said that nuclear explosions must be used to drill tunnels thousands of kilometres long through this range. The radiation fall out and reduction of water flows to neighbouring countries are only two of the anticipated dangers of such a nuclear explosion. These major environmental disasters do not concern China.*

For over 40 years Lop Nor has been one of the most secret and sensitive regions of China. It was the main production site of nuclear weapons and most of China's nuclear tests were carried out here. The vast deserts of the region are uninhabitable. Diverting water into this nuclear waste-laden region will lead to the leaching of radioactive wastes into all the regions where the diverted river waters flow.

Yarlung Tsangpo (the Brahmaputra) flows through extensive areas of Tibet, India, and Bangladesh before emerging into with the Bay of Bengal. It has a total length of about 2,896 km. The Brahmaputra accounts for 20 per cent of the total water resources of India. Since this river is tightly linked with the economic development and environmental stability of these South Asian countries, sooner or later interference in its headwaters will lead to a major international dispute. Water — not oil — is set to be the political commodity of the 21st century.

---

are equipped with CSS-2 and CSS-5 launchers that can hit targets which cover "most of India". Other targets include Russia, Japan and Taiwan, as specified in a classified study prepared by the National Air Intelligence Centre (NAIC). According to the NAIC report, China now has about 40 CSS-2 re-fire capable launchers at six field garrison and launch complexes. The launchers at Datong missile garrison can target Russia as well as India. The CSS-2 training sites have also been observed by US spy satellites in nearby Haiyan.

Tibet and its people, because of their 'crime' of not being represented at the United Nations, continue to suffer humiliation as many countries of the world indulge in double-talk about international norms of good conduct.

Russia is selling 100 advanced artillery systems with precision guided shells to China in secret arms deals, including modern aircraft, destroyers and other high-tech arms. China purchased some 50 SU-27 flanker warplanes from Russia and has plans to purchase 250 more of the jets by 2005. The SU-27s will be fitted with AA-11 air-to-air missiles, a very effective radar guided rocket with electronic counter-measure pods (*The Tribune* 5 July 1997).

It is evident that China is modernising its nuclear weapons and developing multiple warhead missiles. The Chinese now have intercontinental nuclear capability. Intercontinental ballistic missiles can reach most of the USA, according to General Habiger, Commander of the US Strategic Command.

General Habiger added that China's new intercontinental ballistic missiles (ICBM) include the DF-31, a road-mobile missile with a range of more than 4,500 miles (7,242 km), and a second new ICBM with a range of more than 7,000 miles (11,265 km) (*The Tribune* 3 April 1998).

China continues to violate the Nuclear Test Ban Treaty of 1963. It exploded an underground nuclear device at Lop Nor test site in Eastern Turkestan (Xinjiang), directly north of Tibet, on 17 August 1995, and thereafter it exploded two nuclear bombs on 8 June 1996, and 29 July 1996. China has so far exploded 45 nuclear bombs since its detonation of an atomic bomb in 1964 at Lop Nor. China's 45th nuclear explosion of 29 July 1996 came just a few hours before delegates sat down to negotiate the final stage of the Comprehensive Test Ban Treaty (CTBT) at the United Nations Conference on Disarmament in Geneva.

China has land, sea and air-based missiles, nuclear missiles on submarines, and it continues to develop various smaller nuclear warheads. These nuclear warheads are loaded onto a multiple warhead missile, thereby greatly enhancing its ballistic capability. China's total nuclear power is estimated to be 16,000 times greater than the atomic bomb dropped on Hiroshima (20,000 kilotons of TNT) which killed 140,000 people in Japan. Yet China claims it needs more tests to ensure the safety of its nuclear devices (DIIR 1996a).

CNN World News on 7 April 1998 announced that France and the United Kingdom ratified the Comprehensive Test Ban Treaty (CTBT) to prevent international nuclear proliferation for a nuclear-free world. China is one of the nuclear states in the world, along with the US and Russia, who are yet to ratify the CTBT. China signed the Nuclear Non-Proliferation Treaty in 1992.

However, no matter what is signed or declared on the international stage, China evidently does not comply or yield ground. No country dares to upset the Asian giant for fear of losing its lucrative trade. Tibet and its people, because of their "crime" of not being represented at the United Nations, continue to suffer humiliation as many countries of the world indulge in double-talk about international norms of good conduct. These nations continue to ignore nuclear proliferation on the Roof of the World.

RADIOACTIVE WASTES

Radioactive wastes are chemical wastes which contain their own unique blend of hundreds of distinctly unstable atomic structures called radio-isotopes. Each radio-isotope has its own lifespan and potency for giving off alpha, beta and gamma rays. These rays can cause cancer and other diseases in human beings and animals; most frightening of all, radiation emitted by radioactive wastes can cause genetic mutation resulting in birth defects in human babies. Scientists have not discovered any foolproof way to permanently contain radioactive wastes, and currently-spent fuels from power plants are stored in dry castes, which must be kept cool. One spoonful of plutonium powder is enough to destroy the population of a large city.

Since Tibet is sparsely populated by 'minority nationalities' and is far removed from Beijing, the Chinese consider it as a perfect site to dump poisonous nuclear wastes.

A Dumping Ground for Nuclear Waste

The Vienna Declaration of the World Conference on Human Rights, 1993, articulated that, "Illicit dumping of toxic and dangerous substances potentially constitutes a serious threat to human rights, life and the health of everyone."

The Basel Convention, signed in 1992 by various countries and to which China is a signatory, and the subsequent Basel Ban, adopted as an amendment to the convention in September 1995, prohibit trade in hazardous wastes from industrialised to non-industrialised countries. At the fourth Conference of Parties (COP-IV) held in Kuching, Malaysia, between 23-27 February 1998, China supported no changes to the Basel Ban to stop certain developing countries from benefiting from trade in recyclable hazardous waste. Although this is a step in the right direction, China's own record of waste disposal on the Tibetan Plateau is dismal, to say the least.

On 18 February 1984, *The Washington Post* reported that China had tentatively agreed to store up to 4,000 tons of radioactive waste from European nuclear reactors in the remote Gobi Desert in exchange for US$ 6 billion. Since then this was to take place over the next 16 years.

In the fall of 1988, news began circulating among Tibetans that Tibet was to be used as a nuclear dumping ground for Western Europe. According to His Holiness the Dalai Lama, a signed document offered evidence that the Chinese government was planning to dump foreign nuclear waste in Tibet (Weisskopf 1984).

In 1991, Greenpeace reported that the city officials in Baltimore, Maryland, USA, had secured a tentative agreement with China to ship 20,000 tons of the city's toxic sewage waste to Tibet in exchange for payment of US$1.44 million. The brokers for the shipment were California Enterprises, and Hainan Sunlit Group, a Chinese government agency. The latter stated that such shipments did not require government approval according to China's import rules, and guaranteed that the sludge would not be shipped back to the USA. Greenpeace noted that the import document described the shipment as "*heni*", which means "river silt" in Chinese. Greenpeace protested that "urban sewage is not river silt". In the United States, sludge from urban sewage treatment plants are chronically laced with toxic pollutants. In Milwaukee, USA, such use was linked to outbreaks of amyotrophic lateral sclerosis. Due to international pressure the above shipment of waste to Tibet did not take place.

His Holiness the Dalai Lama, while participating in a meet-the-press programme, organised by the Karnataka Union of Working Journalists in Bangalore in India, said he had authentic information that China had set up a nuclear weapons factory in Tibet. He said that China had stationed a half-a-million-strong military force in Tibet, which indicated that the situation in the occupied territory was potentially explosive (*The Statesman* 21 January 1992).

China's Nationalities Affairs Commission issued a document through *Xinhua* on 18 April 1991 stating that

A display of military might behind the Potala

allegations of nuclear pollution from the deployment of nuclear weapons and nuclear waste in Tibet were "totally groundless". However, the same news agency had admitted that nuclear wastes were dumped in Tibet. On 19 July 1995 it reported that there was a "20 square metre dump for radioactive pollutants" in Tsojang (Haibei) Tibetan Autonomous Prefecture near the shores of Lake Kokonor. The report claimed that the military nuclear weapons facility (Ninth Academy), that produced the waste, had maintained an "excellent" safety record during its 30 years of operation, and that there had not been "any harm to the environment" and "no one at the base ever died of radiation".

The report did not give details as to how the nuclear waste was initially contained or how it is being managed. It did however quote You Deliang, spokesman for the China National Nuclear Corporation (CNNC), as saying that China spent a large amount of money from 1989 to 1993 to "strictly supervise the environmental conditions of the retired nuclear weapons base".

Chinese government propaganda even went to the extent of saying: "Haibei Prefecture moved its capital from Menynan county to the site of the retired nuclear plant, only one month after the area passed a state examination in June, 1993. Atom Bomb City (Ninth Academy) has since been serving the economic prosperity of the people" (*Xinhua* 19 July 1995)

A 1993 report, Nuclear Tibet, published by the International Campaign for Tibet, documented reports by a Tibetan doctor, Tashi Dolma, of abnormally high rates of diseases in the nearby towns of Reshui and Ganzihe. She also treated children of nomads who grazed their animals adjacent to the "Ninth Academy" or "Factory 211," nuclear base, seven of whom died of cancer within five years.

Shallow land burial techniques for nuclear waste, considered obsolete in the West, were deemed "sufficiently safe" for implementation in China. On the proposed site for High Level Waste (HLW), Chinese officials said that China had a very wide distribution area and it would be easy to find a site (UNI 1988). Since Tibet is sparsely populated by "minority nationalities" and is far removed from Beijing, the Chinese consider it as a perfect site to dump poisonous nuclear wastes.

According to a *Reuter* report dated 10 November 1993, China was building its first radioactive waste disposal centre in the arid western province of Gansu. Further, it had planned three more in southern, southwestern and eastern China under its ambitious schemes to boost nuclear power to make up for a projected annual shortage of some 150 million tons of coal by 2000 and 1.2 billion tons by 2050. The Gansu disposal centre would have an initial disposal capacity of 60,000 cubic metres of radioactive waste, which would expand to 200,000 cubic metres. CNNC spokesman, You Deliang, said costs are estimated to be at least 100 million yuan (US$ 12.5 million).

Taiwan's nuclear experts went to Beijing to attend a symposium billed as an "ice-breaker for atom splitters". China offered a dumpsite for Taiwan's stockpile of radioactive waste (*Far Eastern Economic Review* 25 March 1993) but, according to *AFP* on 28 May 1997, Taiwan snubbed the offer by China to take their 60,000 barrels of nuclear waste.

LOCAL IMPACTS

Dumping of nuclear wastes on the Tibetan Plateau will directly affect the lives of people and the health of the environment in both the short-term and over millions of years. For example, the half life (time it takes to lose half of its radioactivity) of uranium (U^{238}) is 4,500 million years. Therefore, harmful radiation emitted is a health hazard for millions of years to come and can lead to a number of deadly diseases including cancer and leukaemia. Radioactivity also affects the DNA of living cells causing genetic disorders and deformities that can be passed from generation to generation in humans, animals and plants.

The fission of U^{235} produces many other radioactive isotopes, such as strontium 90, cesium 137 and barium 140. These wastes remain radioactive and dangerous for about 600 years because of the strontium and cesium isotopes.

Plutonium and others remain radioactive for a million years. Even in small amounts, plutonium can cause cancer or genetic (reproduction) damage in human beings. Larger amounts can cause radiation sickness and death. Plutonium is so carcinogenic that one pound (0.5 kg) of it evenly distributed could cause cancer in every person on earth (Caldicott 1997). Safe disposal of these radioactive wastes is one of the problems that remains unsolved by world scientists, even today.

People, Animals and Plants Contaminated

Gonpo Thondup, who escaped from Tibet to Dharamsala in India in March 1987, visited two nuclear weapons production departments code-numbered 405 in Kyangtsa and 792 in Thewo, Amdo region. His statement was presented by Tsewang Norbu at the World Uranium Hearing in Salzburg, Germany, on 14 September 1992. It reads: "The effects of experiments and waste from 792 and 405 have been devastating. Before 1960, in this region of Amdo harvests were plentiful and domestic animals healthy. Now the crop yield has shrunk and people and animals are dying mysteriously, and in increasing numbers. Since 1987 there has been a sharp rise in the number of deaths of domestic animals and fish have all but vanished. In the years of 1989 and 1990, 50 people died in the region, all from mysterious causes. Twelve women gave birth in the summer of 1990, and every child was dead before or died during birth. One Tibetan woman, Tsering Dolma (aged 30), has given birth seven times and not a single child has survived."

Gonpo Thondup added that, "The people living near departments 405 and 792 have experienced strange diseases they have never seen before. Many local people's skin turned yellowish and their eyesight has been affected seriously. Local populace reported strange memory losses and many babies are born deformed. The people of the area are desperate, and can only turn to religion and local doctors, who have no knowledge of the uranium mines or of the nuclear plants nearby."

There is consistent evidence that China's nuclear programme has caused the regular loss of human lives. According to Tibet Information Network (TIN) in a News Update of 11 September 1992, at least 35 Tibetans living near uranium mines died within a few hours after developing a high fever and distinctive diarrhoea in Ngaba region in Sichuan Province.

In 1984 villagers from Reshui and Ganzihe villages, located close to the Ninth Academy in Amdo, reported strange diseases to the Tibetan doctor, Tashi Dolma and her medical team. However, the Chinese authorities would not allow the medical team to follow up these reports. Dr. Tashi worked at Chabcha hospital in Tsolho (Hainan) Tibetan Autonomous Prefecture, directly south of the nuclear city (Ninth Academy), where she treated the children of nomads whose cattle grazed near the Academy. These children developed cancer which caused their white blood cell count to rise uncontrollably. An American doctor conducting research at the hospital reported that these symptoms were similar to cancers caused by radiation after the Hiroshima and Nagasaki atom bombings in 1945. In addition, there have been numerous reports of unexplained deaths and illnesses amongst this nomad population in recent years.

In September 1992, the International Campaign for Tibet fact-finding team found that meat from the area had been banned from stores by the Chinese authorities. However, poor Tibetans often ate the contaminated meat, either out of ignorance or economic constraint.

DEATHS NEAR THEWO URANIUM MINE

Name	Age	Year of Death
Yilkhok	60	1987
Tsering Samdup	17	1987
Tashi Dolma	43	1987
Soton	80	1988
Rinzin Dolma	28	1988
Majing Tsering Norbu	60	1988
Kyolbo	46	1988
Detruk	60	1988
Arikmo	23	1988
Lhagyal	60	1989
Tsering Dolma	40	1989
Tashi Dolma	52	1989
Phuntsok Dhondup	58	1989
Rigan	?	1990
Abe	50	1990
Sonam Gyatso	60	1991
Chopakyap	23	1991
Ugyen Kyi	70	1991
Pema Tso	34	1991
Paltso	40	1991
Achak	50	Not known
Dolma	48	Not known
Yulkhor	80	Not known
Gedun Ther	92	Not known

URANIUM MINING

Uranium mines are located in several regions of Tibet, including Damshung, north of Lhasa; Tsaidam Basin north of Gormo (Ch. Golmud); Yamdrok Tso, and Thewo (3338N, 10245E) in southern Amdo, 254 km from Tsoe under Kanlho (Ch. Gannan) Tibetan Autonomous Prefecture in Gansu Province. The uranium deposits at Thewo in Kanlho Tibetan Autonomous Prefecture are known to be the largest in Tibet. The processing of uranium takes place four km southwest of Thewo. Apart from mining uranium in Tibet, the Chinese also extract strontium which is used for nuclear missile cladding (Chutter 1998).

At the uranium mine at Thewo, poisonous waste water is allegedly collected and stored in a stone structure 40 meters high before being released into the local river, which the people use for drinking. Tibetan refugees escaping to India report the following results from the mining:

Since Tibet is the fountainhead of water for most of South and Southeast Asia, the impact of headwater pollution on the social and economic fabric of millions of people living downstream would be disastrous.

- More than 50 Tibetan residents of Thewo died between 1987-91 from mysterious illnesses
- Domestic animals die mysteriously and the cause of illness is unidentifiable
- Trees and grasses wither
- The Jampakok River is polluted; the water is black and smells putrid. This river merges with Dukchu Karpo (Ch. Palungjang River).

A list of 24 Thewo residents who mysteriously died was part of the information provided to the Tibetan Government-in-Exile's Environment Desk. Witnesses said that before they died, all the victims experienced a high fever, then shivering cold; after death, their skins had a bluish hue. Animals also turned blue or black after death and their organs appeared burnt.

Vanya Kewley, a BBC reporter who visited the Chinese missile base at Nagchuka in 1988, interviewed several people living in the area. In her book *Tibet: Behind the Ice Curtain* a man called Kelsang said: "Many people have seen and heard movements and noises. Most people here have seen missiles coming from China and many travellers have seen movements of missiles at different places."

He further said: "As a result of the situation here, animals are getting strange diseases and dying. Some people are dying and children are being born deformed. In many places, water is contaminated and undrinkable. The moment you drink it, you get ill or get diseases that we never had before. People get ill and go to different hospitals. They don't get better and the doctors don't tell us what it is and then we have to keep quiet about it."

Prison Labour at Nuclear Missile Sites

During the 1960s and 1970s, prisoners including political prisoners were used to build China's nuclear infrastructures. In Amdo huge prison labour camps (*laogai*) are consistently placed next to nuclear missile sites. Next to the Terlingkha silos is the "Delingha Farm", which is one of the three largest labour camps in China today with a prison population estimated at 100,000.

The two nuclear missile sites in central Amdo, Large Tsaidam and Small Tsaidam, also have sizeable labour camps alongside them. Prominent human rights activist and former Chinese political prisoner, Harry Wu, reports that labour reform camps in Amdo use prisoners to excavate radioactive ore. In addition, prisoners are forced to enter nuclear test sites in order to perform dangerous work. Common and political prisoners are also used in nuclear facilities in Lanzhou, Gansu Province (ICT 1993).

The International Campaign for Tibet confirmed in 1993 that prison labour was used in the building of nuclear installations at Lop Nor, the Ninth Academy and Lanzhou.

TRANS-NATIONAL IMPACTS

Most toxic disposal sites on the Tibetan Plateau have minimal, if any, safety standards. The effects of harmful radioactive pollutants dumped anywhere on the plateau will be felt far beyond its borders, particularly because it is the source of Asia's ten major river systems and numerous tributaries. It thus commands massive interdependent ecological zones which share weather and climatic anomalies.

Atmospheric Pollution

The nuclear waste pollution of the Tibetan Plateau, besides having local effects, also has trans-national implications. The high altitude winds (jet streams) that blow over the Tibetan Plateau may carry nuclear pollutants from Tibet across the globe to affect other countries; no boundary can be built to control air pollution. The Tibetan Plateau is seismologically an active region. Consequently, serious accidents at nuclear power and weapons production plants can endanger the lives of people and the health of the environment. When the disaster occurred at the Chernobyl nuclear power plant in the former Soviet Union in 1986, radioactive dust from the plant travelled 950 miles (1,529 km) in all directions, resulting in irreparable damage to people, property and the environment (Chitkara 1996).

Ground Water and Soil Contamination

Pan Ziqiang, Director of the Safety Department of the state-run National Nuclear Industry Corporation, is quoted as saying that so far all of China's nuclear wastes have been put in concrete basement facilities which are safe for only about 10 years.

Luo Guozhen of the State Environmental Protection Bureau says that 1,200 people were injured by radioactivity between 1980 and 1985 and about 20 died. He said managers who ignored regulations on handling radioactive waste were partly to blame for radioactive leaks (*Sunday Morning Post* 1989).

Due to weathering, radioactive and other military wastes buried in the ground in concrete containers will seep out and contaminate ground water sources that are normally used for drinking and agricultural purposes. Ground water makes up a significant share of China's water resources.

Reports from Tibet confirm that underground water supplies in Amdo have been diminishing at a rapid rate. One of the main sources of drinking water, underground aquifers, are impossible to clean once contaminated. Therefore, any pollution at all, especially radioactive contamination of ground water, is of great concern (Chitkara 1996).

River Pollution and Flooding

Radioactive waste randomly disposed of near water bodies will pollute rivers, lakes, and springs. Since Tibet is the fountainhead of water for most of South and Southeast Asia, the impact of headwater pollution — especially by nuclear or industrial toxic waste — on the social and economic fabric of millions of people living downstream would be disastrous. Countries including China, Pakistan, India, Bangladesh, Burma, Thailand, Cambodia, Laos, Bhutan, Nepal, and Vietnam will be drastically affected and forced to alter their livelihood. This will certainly

CHINA'S CURRENT MILITARY EXPANSION

Equipment	Cost US$ million	Numbers purchased	Year purchased
Su-27 fighter (and weapon packages)	1,000	26	1992-93
S-300PMU surface-to-air missile system	1,000	8	1994 and 1995
877EKM and 636 'Kilo' submarines	600-700	4	1994
Su-27 (and weapon packages)	710	22	1995
Su-27 production license	450		1995
Su-27 assembly production	1,500-2000	200	1998-2015
Sovremenny class destroyers	800-1000	2	1997
2S23 Nona-SVK self-propelled gun mortar system	45	1997	
A-50 airborne early warning and control aircraft (Joint Russian-Israeli-UK project)	250 (options on 3 more worth $750m)	1	1997

Source: *Jane's Defence Weekly* 10 December1997

cause terrible suffering to everyone dependent on these rivers for their subsistence.

Massive deforestation of the Tibetan Plateau largely contributes to the siltation of the downstream rivers and the increasingly destructive flooding that occurs each year. Rivers such as the Brahmaputra, Yangtze, Yellow River, Salween, Sutlej, Indus, Mekong and others may also carry nuclear-related waste from uranium mines in Tibet. These rivers finally flow into the Arabian Sea, Bay of Bengal and the South China Sea. The global scale of such an environmental catastrophe is truly frightening.

Between 1985 and 1994 36,000 hectares of Chinese farmland suffered annually from topsoil loss, especially along the Yangtze and Yellow Rivers, both of which originate from Tibet. Erosion has caused river beds to rise several meters higher than the surrounding farmland, thereby increasing the incidence of flooding. Since 1990, China's major rivers have flooded large tracts of land almost every year (UNDP 1997). More than 1,600 people drowned due to flooding of the Yangtze River in July 1996. The flooded river waters have affected one in 10 Chinese (*FEER* 1996).

> *India's defence expenditure on the Himalayas is 50 to 60 million rupees per day. China's defence expenditure may be even more. It costs China four times more to feed and clothe a soldier in Tibet than in China. And the cost of the nuclear arms race between China and India is beyond our simple calculation. It benefits neither Chinese or Indians peasants who constitute over 80 per cent of their respective populations.*
>
> Norbu 1999

In an extensive survey of China's major river basins, carried out in 1994, only 32 percent of the river water was found to meet the national standards for drinking water sources. Large segments of the Chinese population have to rely on polluted sources for drinking water, though estimates differ considerably (UNDP 1997).

At the "Endangered Tibet" Conference in Sydney on 28 September 1996, His Holiness the Dalai Lama said, "Five years ago, a local Tibetan from the Dingri region of southern Tibet told me about a river that all the villagers used for drinking. There were also Chinese living in the area. The Chinese residents belonging to the People's Liberation Army were informed not to drink the water from the river as it was polluted by a factory upstream, but local Tibetans were not informed. The Tibetans still drink the polluted water. This shows some sort of negligence going on. This obviously is not because of lack of awareness, but due to other reasons."

INTERNATIONAL TENSION

Beijing has unresolved territorial disputes over land or sea borders with countries ranging geographically from India and North Korea to Indonesia, not to mention its outright claim to Taiwan. Beijing's official 1996-97 defence budget was US$ 30.27 billion and over the last 10 years China's defence budget shows a net increase of 12 to 20 percent (Kanwal 1999). China has 9,200 tanks, 51 submarines, 55 destroyers and frigates, 870 patrol and coastal crafts, and 5,845 combat aircraft (*FEER* 13 April 1995).

The Nuclear Weapons Data of 1994 brought out by the US Natural Resources Defence Council had estimated China's nuclear arsenal at 450 warheads, of which about 300 were physically deployed. An autumn 1995 study in the US *Strategic Review* had estimated the delivery capability of China's strategic triad as consisting of: four Inter-Continental Ballistic Missiles (DF-5A also known as CSS-4) capable of hitting targets in the US, Russia, and Europe; Intermediate-Range Ballistic Missiles (an unknown quantity of DF-4, also known as CSS-3 and about 50 DF-3A also known as CSS-2) capable of hitting Russia and India; about 25 to 50 mobile missiles (DF-21 also known as CSS-6) with a range of 1,800 km; an unknown quantity of tactical missiles (DF-15 also known as M-9) with a range of 600 km; Submarine-Launched Ballistic Missiles (JL-1 also known as CSS-N-3) with a range of 1,700 km, and a limited number of aircraft capable of nuclear delivery such as the H-5 and H-6 bombers and the Q-5 attack aircraft.

In addition, according to the *Strategic Review*, China was further developing DF-31 with a range of 8,000 km, DF-41 with a range of 12,000 km and JL-2, and a submarine-launchable version of DF-31. China's new small nuclear missiles will very likely equip DF-31 and DF-41 (Fischer 1999). It was also developing H-7, a twin-jet, twin-seat all-weather strike and interdiction aircraft capable of nuclear delivery (*The Hindu* 12 October 1998).

China has 120 TU-16 bombers that have a 3,100 km range and has deployed the S-3000 surface to air missile (*The Tribune* 11 June 1998). China is indeed a nuclear power to be reckoned with.

China admitted that it has powerful nuclear arms. "We have developed a limited number of strategic nuclear arms for the sake of breaking the nuclear monopoly, opposing blackmail, containing a possible nuclear attack

©Department of Security, CTA

Surface-to-surface Chinese missile being tested in an unidentified region of Tibet

and creating a peaceful environment for China's construction," Yang Guoliang, commander of the Second Artillery Force (SAF) of the People's Liberation Army was quoted as saying by the official Chinese media (*The Times of India 1997*).

A new Central Intelligence Agency (CIA) report says that 13 of China's 18 long-range strategic missiles have single nuclear warheads aimed at cities in the United States. Quoting an intelligence document sent to top policy-makers in advance of Secretary of State Madeleine Albright's visit to Beijing on 30 April 1998, *The Washington Times* said the 13 CSS-4 missiles aimed at the US — with a range of more than 8,000 miles (12,874 km) — indicate that China views the United States as its major strategic adversary (*The Indian Express* 2 May 1998).

China has been supplying missiles and other weapons technology to client countries including Russia, Iran, Syria, and Pakistan. In fact, in recent years China has become the fifth leading weapons supplier in the international arms market, ranking behind the other four Permanent Members of the Security Council of the United Nations, thereby threatening global peace and security.

TENSION BETWEEN INDIA AND CHINA

Tibet was the traditional buffer state between the two Asian giants — India and China. However, after its occupation by China, this neutral zone of peace collapsed. It escalated tension between the two, which culminated into the Sino-Indian war in 1962. China defeated the Indian army and is now occupying the Aksai Chin range in Northern India, which is claimed by India.

According to a report submitted by American author John F. Avedon to the US Senate Foreign Relations Committee on 17 September 1987, "One quarter of China's 350-strong nuclear missile force is in Tibet." Subsequently, the Australian Nuclear Disarmament Party in a press release on 28 October 1987 expressed its grave concern and stated that "nuclear missiles are reported to be deployed as follows: 70 medium-range, 20 intermediate-range at Nagchuka, ICBM base at Nyingtri, Kongpo and Powo Tramo and nuclear reactors at Golino. Deployment of the above nuclear missiles in Tibet could be aimed primarily at India" (*The Times of India* 1988).

India has long accused China of threatening nuclear attack. This had led China's late Prime Minister, Zhou Enlai, to respond that if China really wanted to destroy India he would gather 100 million Chinese in Tibet and order them to urinate downhill — washing India into the ocean. Zhou's remark underlines the Himalayas' enormous strategic importance. All of India's great rivers rise in the Himalayas (Margolis 1997)

India's rapid development of a nuclear arsenal, a powerful navy and tactical and medium-ranged missiles, has heightened tensions between Delhi and Beijing. Intelligence sources say India's new intermediate-range missile, the "Agni," has been designed to fire nuclear warheads at Chinese targets as far away as the major industrial centres of Chengdu, Lanzhou, Xian and Wuhan. A longer range 5,000 km version capable of hitting Beijing is under development. India's security sources say "Agni" is a counter-force weapon against Chinese missiles pointed at north India from the Tibetan Plateau (Margolis 1997).

China supplied over 50 M-11 missiles to Pakistan between 1992 and 1994. It also supplied 5,000 ring magnets for the uranium enrichment facility for making nuclear bombs at Kahuta in 1995. Pakistan stored the M-11 missiles in canisters at its Sargodha airbase and has been constructing a missile factory using Chinese equipment. This illicit trade was clearly a violation by China of the Nuclear Non-Proliferation Treaty which it signed in 1992. In 1997, Pakistan announced that another missile, the Hatf-III, which is actually a Chinese M-9 had been successfully test-fired (*India Today* 20 April 1998).

According to Indian defence experts, China has supplied technology know-how to Pakistan to produce surface-to-surface ballistic missiles called "Ghauri". Pakistan successfully tested its "Ghauri" missile as a counter measure to India's "Agni" on 6 April 1998. Air Commander Jasjit Singh, Director of India's Institute of Defence Studies and Analysis, said, "Obviously Pakistan is in the process of legitimising its missiles programme as indigenous even though it has Chinese help, " (*The Times of India* 1998). The "Ghauri" missile of Pakistan is nothing but a primitive CSS-5 (DF-21) sold by China to Pakistan, reported the Indian daily *The Tribune* on 15 April 1998.

China is strengthening its defence by elongating runways at 11 airbases in Tibet. This will enable Chinese bombers to take off with the maximum payload possible and hit targets deep inside Indian territory. Between 1992-93 China acquired 24 Russian-made Sukhoi-27 long-range multi-role fighters. These high technology aircraft have a combat range of about 3,000 km which are much superior fighters in terms of radius of action, payload and fuel efficiency to the Indian Jaguars and Mig-27s. The former Air Chief Marshal of India, S.K. Kaul went on record to state that China posed the primary long-term strategic challenge to India (*The Times of India* 1996).

The Defence Minister of India, George Fernandes, has reportedly declared that China is India's "potential threat number one" and has said that India is surrounded by Chinese military and naval activity. He further said China had its nuclear weapons stockpiled in Tibet right along India's borders and that there had been a lot of "elongation" of military airfields in Tibet where the latest versions of Russian-made Sukhoi (SU-27) combat aircraft were going to be stationed. "And this happened in the last six months," he added (*The Tribune* 4 May 1998).

India tested three nuclear devices on 11 May 1998 followed by two tests on 13 May at Pokhran in Rajasthan. Many experts believe this is in response to the Chinese military build-up on the Tibetan Plateau. The Prime Minister of India, A.B. Vajpayee, in a confidential letter addressed to the President of the United States, Bill Clinton, dated 11 May 1998 said, "We have an overt nuclear weapons state on our borders, a state (China) which committed armed aggression against India in 1962...To add to the distress that country has materially helped another neighbour of ours (Pakistan) to become a covert nuclear weapons state."

India refuted China's condemnation of its tests by pointing out that China had already conducted 45 nuclear tests (*The Times of India* 18 May 1998). The tension between India and China is boiling and at an all-time high.

INTERNATIONAL ACTION

Saving the environment of the Tibetan Plateau guarantees the purity of major rivers that originate from it to form the life-blood of millions of people downstream in Asia. Chinese nuclear weapons production, nuclear tests and waste dumping endangers the lives of millions of people in Asia. Before it is too late, grassroots and international actions must be taken to educate the Chinese and global community as to the disastrous consequences of deployment of nuclear weapons and dumping of toxic nuclear waste on the Tibetan Plateau.

SOME ACTION CAMPAIGNS COULD INCLUDE:

- Writing letters to your parliamentarians, state representatives, and to the United Nations expressing concern over the nuclearisation and militarisation of the Tibetan Plateau.
- Organising street demonstrations, concerts, talks, conferences to transform Tibet into a demilitarised zone.
- Calling upon China and other nations with nuclear weapons to begin negotiations immediately on a Nuclear Weapons Convention,

which would prohibit and eliminate all nuclear weapons by the next century.

- Join Abolition 2000, and other global lobbying networks, to work to to create a nuclear-free world (email: wagingpeace@napf.org).

SIX STEPS CHINA AND OTHER NUCLEAR STATES MUST TAKE TOWARDS A NUCLEAR-FREE WORLD

- Pursue earnestly the goal of abolition of nuclear weapons
- Make strategic reduction of nuclear arsenals time-bound
- Increase transparency and international accountability of nuclear weapons and waste
- Ban production and sale of weapons of mass destruction
- Enforce international embargoes and sanctions against treaty breakers
- Educate the public and government officials about the dangers of nuclear weapons

CONCLUSION

The Tibetan Plateau has been militarised and weaponised by China in pursuit of its own myopic designs without any consideration for the lives and well-being of the Tibetan people and their environment. Given the poor record of Chinese nuclear waste management and the lack of advanced technology to contain nuclear wastes, the implications in nuclearising the Tibetan Plateau for Tibet, China, and its neighbours is truly alarming.

Militarisation of the Tibetan Plateau with its attendant pollution is an important regional and global issue because it is the source of major river waters for India, China, Nepal, Bhutan, Pakistan, Burma, Bangladesh, Thailand, Cambodia, Vietnam and Laos. Upsetting the ecological balance of the high Tibetan Plateau also affects the jet streams that blow over it, and this in turn is found to be irreversibly linked with the environment of the whole Asian continent and the disturbance of global climatic patterns.

The altar of the earth — the Tibetan Plateau — must be saved from a nuclear holocaust for the survival of mankind. This responsibility falls on the Chinese government, Tibetans and the international community equally. We must act before it is too late. His Holiness the Dalai Lama has championed non-violence and proposed to the government of China that they turn Tibet into a Zone of Peace as stated in His Five Point Peace Plan (see Appendix 4), announced on 21 September 1987 in Washington DC, USA. But to no avail.

India's Defence Minister, George Fernandes, during the August 1989 International Convention on Tibet and Peace in South Asia said, " If Tibet becomes a zone of peace, free from Chinese troops and nuclear weapons, there will be no reason for India to maintain a large army on the Himalayan heights. This would immediately enable both India and China to reduce their military expenditure and use the money thus saved for economic development"(Fernandes 1991).

China has vowed time and time again that they are a no-first-use nation and that they are on record as being strongly in favour of nuclear abolition (Butler 1998). The head of the Chinese delegation at the Second Session of the Preparatory Committee for the 2000 Review Conference of the Parties to the Treaty on the Non-Proliferation of Nuclear Weapons (NPT) in Geneva on 27 April 1998, Sha Zukang, called for a convention on a total ban of nuclear weapons to be concluded at an early date like the conventions banning chemical and biological weapons (*Xinhua* 27 April 1998). China on 23 July 1999 declared publicly its endorsement of a treaty to maintain Southeast Asia as a nuclear-weapons-free zone, making it the first major military power to do so (*Inside China Today* 1999a). These are positive signs.

As an initial act of goodwill the government of China must first de-militarise the Tibetan Plateau and declare Tibet a Zone of Peace. It should restore Tibet to its traditional status as a neutral buffer state between the two most populous nations in the world — China and India. Such an action would not only benefit Tibet, China itself and its neighbours, but also the whole Asian continent and the millions of people across the globe. Moreover, such a concrete initiative will help foster a more friendly and compassionate world for all our children to live in and to share with all other sentient beings. ■

CHAPTER EIGHT

HUMAN RIGHTS AND THE ENVIRONMENT

The human right to development also implies the full realisation of the right of people to self-determination, which includes, subject to the relevant provisions of both International Covenants on Human Rights, the exercise of their inalienable right to full sovereignty over all their natural wealth and resources.

UN Declaration on the Right to Development, 1986

THE PURPOSE of identifying the human rights components of environmental degradation on the Tibetan Plateau is to illustrate the strengths created by bridging these two disciplines. Both conceptually, and as applied, their merging can be a more potent tool than either discipline working in isolation.

This chapter firstly describes the development of environmental human rights in international law, and then explains the environmental dimension of particular human rights and how these concepts apply in the context of Tibet. This chapter then outlines and analyses several instances of environmental harm on the Tibetan Plateau and their human rights implication. Topics include China's food policy in Tibet, destruction of rangelands, mining, deforestation and despoliation of sacred places. Each situation is described and analysed through the lens of environmental human rights.

HOW ENVIRONMENTAL HUMAN RIGHTS CAME INTO INTERNATIONAL LAW

The United Nations Stockholm Declaration on the Human Environment (1972) stands as a landmark decision in the development of the link between natural environments and human rights in international law. Principle 1 outlines the earliest explicit recognition on an international level of a human right to "adequate conditions of life, in an environment of a quality that permits a life of dignity and well-being" (Report of the UN Conference on the Human Environment 1979). In 1989, the UN Sub-Commission on Prevention of Discrimination and Protection of Minorities (hereafter referred to as the Sub-Commission) was first called upon to study the relationship between the environment and human rights. There was already a substantial body of international and regional law that recognised the environmental dimension of human rights. The United Nations Commission on Human Rights endorsed the appointment of a Special Rapporteur on Human Rights and the Environment to guide the Sub-Commission's investigation of the area (Popovic 1996). The Sub-Commission's four reports to the United Nations Commission on Human Rights over as many years progressively established the legal basis and human need for environmental human rights (Aguilar and Popovic 1994).

During the Sub-Commission's consideration of the concept, debate over the existence and definition of environmental human rights flourished and became the subject of at least five major international conferences. Commentators have explored the precedent in international and regional laws for environmental human rights. Some have questioned whether such environmental rights should be expressed only through the environmental dimension of established human rights, or whether there should be adoption of a separate human rights instrument (Shelton 1991). Others have called for measures to create and codify environmental rights in new legal instruments. Still others have been critical of the new prominence given to environmental rights in the human rights discourse (Gormley 1990).

This level of attention and healthy debate over a legal precedent for the expansion of human rights to encompass an environmental component is not new in human rights law. Almost 20 years of drafting debates preceded the UN Convention on Economic, Social, and Cultural Rights. The Convention took another 10 years from the time it was opened for signature until it took effect. Even with regard to what is now considered a cornerstone of human rights law — the Universal Declaration of Human Rights of 1948 — many commentators at the time doubted the feasibility of reaching any meaningful consensus and urged that far more modest goals be set. The same observation can just as easily be made now, over 40 years later, regarding the development of environmental human rights law.

The Sub-Commission's work since 1989 has advanced the discussion on the links between the natural environment and human rights. Under the able leadership of the Sub-Commission's Special Rapporteur, Fatma Zohra Ksentini, this five-year effort produced tangible results. Firstly, its report established that there is ample precedent for environmental human rights in international, regional and national law. Secondly, the report thoroughly explored environmental dimensions of established human rights; thirdly, situations that visibly demonstrate the inadequacy of existing environmental laws and human rights instruments to meet the needs of victims of environmental harm were identified and explored. And fourthly, a Draft Declaration of Principles on Human Rights and the Environment was drafted by an international group of leading experts on human rights and international environmental law on the recommendation and invitation of the Sub-Commission.

Regardless of whether the Draft Declaration ultimately becomes binding international law, or whether it only serves as a model from which to incorporate environmental rights into existing human rights laws, it currently serves an important purpose. The Draft Declaration presents environmental human rights in a comprehensive yet succinct statement.

There are five thematic sections to the Draft Declaration in addition to its Preamble: (1) the universality of human rights; (2) substantive rights; (3) procedural rights; (4) environmental duties; and (5) special considerations in the Declaration's implementation. The following discussion analyses violations of human rights and environmental rights in Tibet through the lens of the Draft Declaration.

THE ENVIRONMENTAL DIMENSION OF HUMAN RIGHTS

"All human rights are universal, indivisible, interdependent and interrelated" (Vienna Declaration and Programme of Action 1993). The indivisibility, interdependence and global applicability of all human rights are one of the defining characteristics of environmental human rights. The Preamble to the Draft Declaration places environmental human rights in context by recognising their sources in international law and in the universality and interdependence of all human rights. The Draft Declaration's Preamble also describes the indivisibility of environmental human rights by stating that:

> **Human rights violations lead to environmental degradation and that environmental degradation leads to human rights violations.**

Part I of the Draft Declaration affirms the universality of all human rights and their interdependence with peace, security, and an ecologically sound environment (Principles 1 and 2). It also establishes the applicability of the universal norm of non-discrimination to environmental human rights (Principle 3), and highlights their unique emphasis on protecting inter-generational equity (Principle 4).

The indivisibility, interdependence and global applicability of all human rights are one of the defining characteristics of environmental human rights.

SUBSTANTIVE HUMAN RIGHTS

The Rights to Life and Health

The interdependence of human rights and environmental rights is nowhere more fundamental than the right to life's dependence on environmental conditions. The right to life is protected in Article 3 of the Universal Declaration of Human Rights, and in Article 6(1) of the International Covenant on Civil and Political Rights. Principle 5 of the Draft Declaration declares "the right of all persons to be free from pollution and all kinds of environmental degradation which may threaten life, health, livelihood, well-being or sustainable development." Principle 6 expresses "the grounding of human survival in healthy ecosystems and the maintenance of biological diversity." The realities of human exploitation of the environment make the link between life and environmental protection obvious; more than two million deaths globally can be directly attributed to pollution.

Similarly, the right to health cannot be fully realised in degraded or hazardous environments. For example, the worldwide thinning of the ozone layer may cause an additional 300,000 cases of skin cancer and 1.7 million cases of cataracts annually. Articles 25(1) and 23(1) of the Universal Declaration of Human Rights, and articles 12(b) and 7(b) of the International Covenant on Economic, Social, and Cultural Rights, firmly enshrine the right to health as well as safe and healthy working conditions as fundamental human rights (International Covenant on Economic, Social, and Cultural Rights 1976). In the Draft Declaration, the environmental dimensions of the established human rights to health, food, safe and healthy working conditions, and adequate housing are declared in Principles 7-11.

The obvious link between health and the environment has been recognised by human rights bodies such as the Committee of Experts that reviews compliance with the European Social Charter (European Social Charter, Oct. 18, 1961). This Committee has recognised that the Social Charter's right to health requires special attention to air and water pollution, dangerous radioactive materials, noise pollution and food contamination.

The Right To Be Free From Hunger

Food security is also a human rights issue. It is recognised in article 25(1) of the Universal Declaration on Human Rights, and declared in article 11 of the International Covenant on Economic, Social and Cultural Rights as the fundamental right of everyone to be free from hunger. Food security is threatened by many different kinds of environmental abuses, which can affect affluent nations and developing nations alike. Contamination of food by pesticides or air- and water-borne toxins, declining harvests due to desertification and salinisation, and loss of food-crop biodiversity are just a few ways in which environmental degradation endangers the fulfilment of this basic human right.

China's agricultural policies in Tibet have resulted in numerous violations of the fundamental human right to be free from hunger.

One of China's first acts was to begin to institutionalise its agricultural policy. Its aims were two-fold: to 'modernise' the 'backward' Tibetan subsistence farmers on the one hand, and to feed Chinese settlers moving into Tibet on the other.

Undermining Food Security

One of China's first acts upon gaining military control over Tibet was to begin to institutionalise its agricultural policy. Its aims were two-fold: to "modernise" the "backward" Tibetan subsistence farmers on the one hand, and to feed Chinese settlers moving into Tibet on the other. China imposed far-reaching collectivisation programmes under which farmers and nomads were stripped of their lands and their herds. Tibetans were subsequently reorganised into communes and brigades (Longworth and Williamson 1993).

In Tibet barley is the traditional crop because it is well suited to the short growing season and the harsh, high-altitude conditions of the Tibetan Plateau. The Tibetan food staple of roasted barley flour or *tsampa* is eaten plain or mixed in butter tea. However, the Chinese-imposed "communes" required farmers to grow hybrid wheat varieties, often referred to as winter wheat, which were ill-suited to the harsh conditions of the plateau and therefore dependent on intensive application of artificial fertilisers and pesticides (TWA 1996).

The results were disastrous. Tibet experienced two intense periods of widespread famine; the first recorded in over 2000 years of Tibetan history. From 1961 to 1964, and again from 1966 to 1976 during the Cultural Revolution, more than 340,000 Tibetans starved to death (DIIR 1996). The forced collectivisation of agriculture was ultimately abandoned as a Chinese policy after the historic visit of Hu Yaobang, then Communist Party General Secretary, to Tibet in 1980 (Peatfeld 1995). Hu Yaobang made strong recommendations for reform. Among these were exempting Tibetan farmers from compulsory sales to the government as well as ending the taxation of Tibetan herders (Schwartz 1995). Although many of Hu Yaobang's sweeping recommendations were never fully implemented, Tibetans did regain more control over their own lands (*ibid*). Hu Yaobang was ultimately demoted from his powerful position as General Secretary for his criticism of Chinese policies in Tibet (TYC 1995).

By the mid-1980s, there was a huge Chinese settler population in Tibet as a result of Beijing's aggressive population transfer programme. "A well-researched and credible estimate puts the Chinese population in Lhasa, including the Hui (Muslims), at 110,000 and in the 'TAR' at 250,000-300,000, including military and police and the "floating" population" (ICJ 1997). The number of Chinese settlers in the eastern areas of the Tibetan Plateau, in Kham and Amdo, numbered in the millions. One of the greatest obstacles to

China's full control of Tibet was emerging: how to feed the Chinese who were encouraged to settle there (Ackerly 1993).

The cost of feeding Chinese settlers in Tibet is staggering. According to the UN World Food Programme, almost the entire budget of the historic Amdo region (Ch: Qinghai) is spent on importing grain. At the same time, over 70 per cent of that province's budget is composed of subsidies from the central government (Forbes & McGranahan 1992). Although the cost for long-haul truck transport into Lhasa valley has been calculated at 0.7 yuan (US$ 0.0875) per kg of grain, one kg still costs only 0.45 yuan (US$0.0563) in Lhasa markets. Continued government subsidies for grain help to explain a market price that is half of the transportation costs alone (Liu 1992). By the 1980s, Chinese central government subsidies to the 'Tibet Autonomous Region' had risen to 97 per cent of the total industrial and agricultural output of the region (DIIR 1992). Annual subsidies to Chinese urban settlers in Tibet through the 1980s was approximately US$128 per person (*ibid*). Meanwhile, the price of locally-grown barley, the staple Tibetan food, was left to market forces, making it almost twice as expensive to purchase as the wheat and rice trucked in to feed Chinese migrants from thousands of kilometres away.

The cost of feeding Chinese settlers in Tibet is staggering. According to the UN World Food Program, almost the entire budget of the historic Amdo region (Ch: Qinghai) is spent on importing grain.

Within six years of the liberal reforms initiated by Hu Yaobang in 1980, production of wheat in Tibet's main agricultural belt was restored to pre-1960 levels through so-called government intervention (Schwartz 1991). Tibetan farmers were then, and still are, compelled to sell the bulk of their production to the government, after which they often have little left for home consumption, barter or market sales.

The Chinese government pays a fixed price for the wheat produced by Tibetan farmers, which is well below actual value. Furthermore, these profits are used to offset huge government losses on imported grains such as rice and additional wheat for Chinese consumers. Tibetan rural householders interviewed by one researcher all reported that compulsory sales to the government are a burden rather than a source of income, and that it would be impossible to evade the required production quotas of wheat. This coercive and compulsory government sales practice forces Tibetan farmers to be commodity producers against their will, and prevents them from realising an income from market sales.

China's second tactic to increase wheat production in Tibet has been to lobby international aid organisations to invest. This avenue has been highly successful. In the name of improving conditions for rural Tibetan farmers, several large-scale aid projects have been launched to increase wheat production and "modernise" both Tibetan agriculture and its traditional rural economy. Benefits of this "modernisation" will be realised primarily by Chinese settlers in Tibet. International aid agencies have financed China's agricultural policies that directly undermine Tibetan subsistence and food security.

One of the most significant international aid projects began in 1989 in the Lhasa valley's prime agricultural belt in collaboration with the UN World Food Programme (WFP). Not only does the project involve millions of dollars of aid money itself, but it is intended to serve as a model for equally large-scale aid projects in three other agricultural valleys in Tibet (Forbes & McGranahan 1992). In addition to this aid project in Lhasa valley, the WFP has funded two other agriculture development schemes in Amdo. The WFP is spending US$ 5.5 million on one of its projects in Amdo, the Agriculture Development Through Irrigation Project (no. 3557), in funding approximately 40 per cent of the scheme.

Such agricultural development projects, launched with the legitimacy of international approval, are aimed at increasing commodity grain production and moving Tibetan farmers from subsistence-based production to market production. This exposes Tibetan farmers to price fluctuations and increases their dependence on imported machinery, materials and irrigation supplies (Peatfeld 1995). It also further undermines the traditional Tibetan economy of self-sufficiency. The UN officials involved in the project have never seriously questioned the underlying logic of growing wheat within the project area as a means to reduce the huge grain imports into the region.

The Right to a Secure Food Supply

Under the added pressure of a new and largely urban Chinese settler population, which is in many regions greater than the Tibetan population, China's agricultural policy violates Tibetans' substantive human rights. The most obvious violation is that of the right to adequate food. Principle 8 of the Draft Declaration declares that all persons have the right to safe and healthy food adequate to their well being. China's policy of "modernising" agriculture in Tibet comes at the expense of eliminating traditional subsistence farming and a self-sufficient rural economy.

An agricultural policy intended to provide only for the needs of Chinese settlers at the expense of rural Tibetans literally leaves Tibetans hungry.

Principle 5 of the Draft Declaration, regarding the right to a healthy livelihood, is also violated by China's agricultural policy. Principle 5 provides that "all persons have the right to freedom from pollution, environmental degradation, and activities that threaten livelihood, well-being, or sustainable development within, across or outside national boundaries." The burden of state procurement imposed on Tibetan farmers, and the coercive policies required to make Tibetan farmers grow wheat crops which are dependent on large inputs of expensive and soil-depleting chemical fertiliser ill-suited to agricultural conditions of the high plateau, effectively violates Principle 5.

Tibetan nomadic peoples have an undeniable right to live in a manner which nurtures their traditional practices. The right to travel, the right to move their herds in an unrestricted fashion, and the right to treat their animals and rangelands in their own traditional manner are all undeniable rights.

Intrinsic Cultural Rights

Many cultural rights have roots in environmental protection. This link is especially vivid for local peoples and subsistence pastoralists as well as farmers whose specific relationship with their land defines the essentials of their cultural life. As one Indian leader stated to the UN Working Group for Indigenous Affairs:

> [O]ur principal and fundamental struggle is for the land, our territory and natural resources . . . Our defence of the land and natural resources is for the cultural and human survival of our children.

Article 27 provides ethnic, religious, or linguistic minorities with the right to enjoy their own culture. In addition, the right to freely participate in the cultural life of the community is protected in article 27(1) of the Universal Declaration of Human Rights, and in article 15(1)(a) of the International Covenant on Economic, Social and Cultural Rights (recognising the right to take part in cultural life).

The pastoral nomads of Tibet are actively being denied the right to their cultural practices through Chinese government policies. Most important is the increasing commercialisation of Tibet's rangelands which, as noted previously in the Agriculture Chapter, presents the antithesis of the nomadic lifestyle. A principle of environmental rights in the Draft Declaration is that "all people have the right to the sustainable use of nature and natural resources for cultural and spiritual purposes". In its 1998 report, the International Commission of Jurists (ICJ) commenting on the destruction of Tibetan rangelands, notes:

> The degradation of the [Tibetan] grasslands is the most pervasive environmental impact of the era of Chinese control of Tibet, and the impact which most threatens the sustainability of Tibetan civilisation.

Tibetan nomadic peoples have an undeniable right to live in a manner which nurtures their traditional practices. Central to these practices is the state of the environment in which they live and depend upon for their basic needs. The right to travel, the right to move their herds in an unrestricted fashion, and the right to treat their animals and rangelands in their own traditional manner are all undeniable rights.

Environmental rights and human rights are so closely linked in the Tibetan nomadic lifestyle that they cannot be separated.

Prior to China's military build-up in Tibet, no commercial mining took place on the Tibetan Plateau — for uranium or otherwise — despite Tibet's many extensive and valuable mineral deposits. One reason for this was the Tibetans' firm belief that mining disturbs and weakens the strength of the earth and that this would also disturb the local spirits associated with that place. Ultimately this was believed to bring harmful effects to the people living there as described in the mining chapter.

An incident involving uranium mining near the town of Riwoche, in the Chamdo region of the Tibet, was reported in 1989 that further illustrates the connection between the denial of cultural rights and environmental degradation. There was a hill behind the Trachen-Ma Temple in Riwoche that had always been regarded as a sacred site by Tibetans. When miners were brought in to begin excavation for a uranium mine, villagers protested to the Chinese authorities — but to no avail (Ackerly 1990). The report states that a tense incident ensued in which three surveyors' jeeps were set on fire and subsequently Chinese soldiers occupied the town and rounded up villagers for interrogation.

The authoritarian Chinese governance effectively denies Tibetans their culture and spiritual practices based on their relationship with the land as guaranteed in Principle 13 of the Draft Declaration.

The Right to Preserve Sacred Sites

Principle 13 also includes the right to preservation of unique sites consistent with the fundamental rights of persons or groups living in the area. This is closely linked to the notion of cultural and spiritual practices mentioned above. Sacred sites such as forests, lakes, mountains and rivers are to many peoples a source of religious inspiration, places of pilgrimage, and the focus of many rituals. In Tibet sacred natural places abound. Mount Kailash, one of the better known sites, is sacred to Hindus and Buddhists alike. Others such as Lake Kokonor and Yamdrok Tso have special significance to Tibetans and once despoiled by invasive human intervention are easily defiled.

A sacred lake, river or grove cannot be partially sacred whereby certain aspects may be exploited for utilitarian requirements. In a sacred grove, all the plants are sacred; likewise a sacred mountain cannot contain a mining district and retain its sacredness. All over Tibet places which have religious significance to local peoples are being desecrated by Chinese "development" projects, effectively denying local people's right to their own religious practices.

Environmental rights and human rights clearly converge where sacred natural sites are concerned. This claim, which is echoed by indigenous peoples worldwide, is substantiated in Tibet where both Buddhist and traditional Bon religious practices incorporate natural phenomena as part of their spiritual traditions. The continued and blatant lack of respect towards Tibetan religious practices by the Chinese administration is well known. The Chinese occupation of Tibet has resulted in numerous well-documented human rights abuses and, as the above examples show, numerous less well-known violations of environmental rights. Destruction of sacred landforms through mining processes are the most obvious. Deforestation and pollution of rivers and lakes is subtler but equally damaging to the sacred aspect that directly impinges upon people's well being and sense of place.

The destruction of sacred places is a direct violation of human rights. The fact that in Tibet many of these sacred sites are natural entities further strengthens the link between environmental and human rights.

In a sacred grove, all the plants are sacred; likewise a sacred mountain cannot contain a mining district and retain its sacredness. The destruction of sacred places is a direct violation of human rights. The fact that in Tibet many of these sacred sites are natural entities further strengthens the link between environmental and human rights.

The Right to Self-Determination

Denial of the human right to self-determination is closely linked to environmental degradation. Article 1 of the International Covenant on Civil and Political Rights declares unequivocally that "all peoples have the right of self- determination." Article 1 explains that "by virtue of that right they freely determine their political status and freely pursue their economic, social and cultural development". The Covenant's right to self-determination includes environmental sovereignty, stated as a peoples' right to "freely dispose of their natural wealth and resources... and in no case may a people be deprived of their own means of subsistence".

Denial of the right to self-determination is interwoven with the exploitation of a nation's natural resources. The Sub-Commission's Special Rapporteur found that the political and economic subjugation that exists in occupied territories and formerly colonised countries creates social conditions under which extreme environmental degradation is unchecked. During the course of the Sub-Commission's study, environmental degradation and resulting human rights abuses relating to the denial of self-determination included intensive exploitation of raw materials and products that upset ecological balances, wastage of non-renewable energy sources, establishment of polluting and high-risk industries, and pauperisation of rural areas (Sub-Commission Final Report). The Preamble to the Draft Declaration recognises the right to self-determination and its relation to sustainable development: "The environmental dimension of the right to self-determination lies at the heart of the economic exploitation that inures to the benefit of the dominating force".

PROCEDURAL HUMAN RIGHTS

The Universal Declaration of Human Rights recognises that procedural aspects of human rights are as important to full realisation of human rights as substantive protections such as the right to life and health. Denial of the fundamental rights of freedom of association, of opinion and expression, and of the right to take part in government, are denials of basic human rights without which protection of substantive human rights are called into question.

The Universal Declaration of Human Rights codifies these procedural rights in Article 8 (effective remedy); Article 19 (freedom of opinion and expression); Article 20 (freedom of association); Article 21 (right to take part in government); and Article 26 (right to education). Articles 2(3), 19, 21, 22, and 25 of the International Covenant on Civil and Political Rights set forth these same procedural guarantees as fundamental human rights. Similarly, Part III of the Draft Declaration sets out the procedural aspects of human rights necessary for the full realisation of environmental rights.

These rights are enabling rights. They make it possible for people to contribute actively to the protection of their environment. Likewise, in many situations the absence of respect for these rights ensures that environmental degradation is not only more likely to occur, but it is likely to be on an irreversible scale which may threaten the rights of future generations.

Denial of the fundamental rights of freedom of association, of opinion and expression, and of the right to take part in government, are denials of basic human rights. Not only are Tibetans denied any public opinion on development issues, but also are severely punished if they attempt to make any protest.

The environmental dimension of these procedural human rights constitute the essential building blocks of environmental protection. The following section of this report provides a striking illustration of the degree to which substantive environmental human rights violations follow in the wake of violations of these procedural guarantees.

The Right to Freedom of Expression

Principle 16 of the Draft Declaration guarantees the right to hold and express opinions, just as Article 19 of the Universal Declaration of Human Rights guarantees the right to freedom of opinion and expression. The denial of the fundamental human right to the freedom of expression under China's repressive administration of Tibet is exemplified in the story of Phuntsok Chosang, a Tibetan who protested mining near his village, Meldro Gongkar in Gyamo Shang.

Phuntsok Chosang pasted wall posters in his village in 1990 protesting China's plans to build roads to service a new mine in Gyamo Shang in Central Tibet some 73 km east of Lhasa. Over the following year Phuntsok put up posters twice more that were openly critical of China's mining operations. One poster declared that "Chinese should not exploit our natural resources". Within three months Phuntsok was taken from his home, arrested, placed in solitary confinement, beaten, and had iron rods jammed into his mouth during daily interrogations (TCHRD 1997a).

The implications of such treatment are that not only are Tibetans denied any public opinion on development issues, but also are severely punished if they attempt to make any protest.

The Right to Environmental Information

Principle 15 of the Draft Declaration guarantees the right to environmental information. Because the foreign press are not permitted to operate in Tibet, and due to travel restrictions on Western travellers, compounded by reprisals against Tibetans observed speaking to any Westerner on such subjects, it is exceedingly difficult to obtain accurate information about conditions in Tibet. As a result, some of the most valuable information available comes from Tibetans who fled Tibet and are now living in exile in Tibetan settlements in India and Nepal.

Dolma Kyap, a nomad who arrived in India from Amdo in 1996, described how large groups (sometimes as many as 1,700 people at a time) of Chinese Muslims from a distant Chinese city would come several times each year to cut trees in a forested area known as Kagya (Kyap 1996). Dolma Kyap did not know why the Chinese Muslims were allowed to cut the trees and take them back to China. She then described how the People's Liberation Army, who supposedly "guard" the forest and would shoot and kill any Tibetan who cut down a tree, also felled trees and loaded them onto trucks bound for China. Dolma Kyap noted:

> We are all very worried about the forests being finished, but when we see the Chinese people cutting the forest we can do nothing. If we fight, they shoot us. If we were to tell the Government officials about the Chinese Muslims coming to cut the trees, they would do nothing. My father remembers the Chinese Muslim people coming each year since 1958 and my grandfather said that when he was young, every place in Kagya was covered with trees; now there are no trees left in places that used to be thick forest.

China's military domination facilitates the use of Tibet for its development of nuclear weapons. Tibetans do not have the right to information regarding any aspect of China's nuclear programmes. Tibetans from villages near Lake Kokonor, when interviewed by International Campaign for Tibet observers, said that they were extremely unhappy about the military complexes, but that they did not know anything about their use for nuclear weapons (Kyap 1996).

The inability to get information out of Tibet about the health and living conditions of Tibetans in such areas prevents any thorough investigation of China's practices. In July 1991, for example, a small protest was reported that took place in Xining by 30 Tibetans who had travelled from the area near Lake Kokonor. Their slogans read: "Return our snowlands. Give us back our grasslands. We are dying of hunger". The conditions that sparked the protest remain unknown *(South China Morning Post 1992)*.

According to eye-witness reports, about 40 students of Lhasa Teachers' Training School gathered at their school on 4 October 1998 with banners and a one-page petition and were on the verge of taking to the streets of the city when the police arrived and stopped the procession. The police also banned the students from distributing their petition addressed to the Chinese government and the general public. The petition was a mildly worded plea for better environmental protection. Tibetan Government-in-Exile received a copy of the petition from a newly arrived Tibetan refugee on 29 December 1998 (DIIR 1999a).

The roots of the discriminatory practices can be traced to the denial of Tibetans' civil and political rights, and the denial of their right to self-determination.

The Right to Take Part in Decision-Making

Principle 18 of the Draft Declaration provides for the right to "active, free, and meaningful participation in planning and decision-making activities".

Tibetans' lack of control over the destruction and use of their forests is perhaps most poignantly best exemplified by the reports — confirmed by surviving prisoners — that over 1,000 political prisoners from the notorious labour camp of Powo Tramo in the 'TAR' were forced to cut down old-growth trees. Areas that used to be thick forests are described by observers as completely barren and bleak (TCHRD 1998).

Jamyang, imprisoned by the Chinese after objecting to the arrest of his brother, fled Tibet and was interviewed in 1999 Dharamsala. He explained:

> **In my home region in Kham there are thousands of [Chinese] people who cut down trees. The trees were very good, really tall and big. Now, if a Tibetan cuts a tree, he will be imprisoned.**

A Western observer travelling in Kham in 1999, passing through miles of clear-cut forests and logging trucks, saw notices attached to the few trees left standing alongside the road stating that Tibetans were not allowed to cut trees (DIIR 1999). The discrimination and lack of any avenue to participate meaningfully in decision-making means that Tibetan control over natural resources or for that matter forest policy in Tibet is a distant dream.

CONCLUSION

In Tibet, violation of the human rights to express opinions, exchange information, associate with others, as well as to participate meaningfully in decision-making, has created conditions under which extreme environmental degradation is unchecked. China's repressive administration is able to exploit Tibet's native forests on a massive scale for its own benefit. Industrial clear-cutting has already claimed about half of Tibet's virgin forests to feed China's enormous demand for wood and paper. China has capitalised on several centuries of uninterrupted forest growth, pocketing an estimated US$54 billion from this trade between 1959 and 1985 alone. Denial of the Tibetan peoples' right to self-determination through prolonged military repression has given China free reign over the once-abundant native forests of the Tibetan Plateau.

China's use of Tibet for nuclear weapons development, nuclear waste disposal, and uranium mining has violated Tibetans' human rights to life, health, traditional livelihood and religious practice. The fate of environmental activists such as Phuntsok Chosang, who was imprisoned and tortured for over a year for putting up posters protesting China's plans to mine near his village, demonstrates Tibetans' enforced silence over decisions affecting the environment. China's use of Tibet for its nuclear programme illustrates once again the connection between substantive human rights violations, environmental degradation, and the violation of Tibetans' civil and political rights.

Food security on the Tibetan Plateau is also an environmental human rights issue. Its agricultural policy in Tibet is an important component of China's strategy to absorb Tibet into "modern" China. The goals and implementation of China's agricultural policy violates Tibetans' right to be free from discrimination in decisions that affect the environment. The roots of the discriminatory practices can be traced to the denial of Tibetans' civil and political rights and the denial of their right to self-determination.

The violations of the basic human rights to adequate food and traditional livelihood that result even from international aid projects intended to improve the agricultural productivity of the Tibetan Plateau are testimony to the inter-relatedness of substantive human rights and the procedural rights of access to information, freedom of expression and participation in decision-making. These human rights violations demonstrate the fallacy of China's human rights record in Tibet.

The principles of the UN Sub-Commission on Prevention of Discrimination and Protection of Minorities' Draft Declaration on Human Rights and the Environment present the essential elements of the human rights violations stemming from environmental degradation on the Tibetan Plateau during the 51 years of China's military repression of Tibet. The Draft Declaration provides an invaluable tool for understanding the relationship between denial of basic civil rights and freedoms and the resulting substantive violations of fundamental human rights to life, health, traditional livelihood and adequate food. The global language of human rights standards helps to clearly focus the impact of environmental degradation in Tibet.

The visibility of massive deforestation, extensive destruction of rangelands, nuclear proliferation, the creation of haphazard mining zones, despoliation of sacred natural sites sheds light on the human rights violations across the plateau that would otherwise be difficult to assess and measure. The principles of the Draft Declaration describe, in the global language of human rights, the limits there should be on environmental degradation that are otherwise without standards in Tibet.

Drawing the connection between human rights violations and environmental harm provides another tool for responding to the dynamic nature of human rights and further developing the relevance of human rights law in a rapidly changing world. ■

CHAPTER NINE

GUIDELINES FOR INTERNATIONAL DEVELOPMENT PROJECTS AND SUSTAINABLE INVESTMENT IN TIBET

The right to development is an inalienable human right by virtue of which every human person and all peoples are entitled to participate in, contribute to, and enjoy economic, social, cultural and political development, in which all human rights and fundamental freedoms can be fully realised. The human right to development also implies the full realisation of the right of peoples to self-determination, which includes... the exercise of their inalienable right to full sovereignty over all their natural wealth and resources.

Article 1, UN Declaration on the Right to Development, 4 December 1986

THESE GUIDELINES were compiled by the Tibetan Government-in-Exile (TGIE) to foster sustainable development in Tibet[1] that will enhance the capacity of the Tibetan people to fully participate in the development of their land and to control the use of their natural resources. These Guidelines seek to encourage active international engagement that will improve the Tibetan people's quality of life and to address the existing imbalances in the development of Tibet.

Through responsible development and investment, the international community has the ability to make a major, positive impact on the lives of the Tibetan people. Throughout Tibet today, resources for promoting local businesses, education, and healthcare are extremely limited.

The socio-economic situation in Tibet is on par with some worst areas in the third world.

While the specific needs of the Tibetan people in Tibet may vary from region to region, all Tibetan communities are disadvantaged. We therefore encourage the involvement of the international community in sustainable development and prodective investment in all regions inhabited by Tibetans.

Despite living in economically and socially depressed conditions, Tibetans have attempted to build schools, monasteries, initiate development projects and develop their own enterprises (such as textile, carpet, handicraft manufacturing, dairy and grain processing). But it has been difficult for the majority of Tibetan communities to benefit from and expand these projects because they have received little or no assistance from the Chinese government, and they have very limited access to capital. Furthermore, rural infrastructure is very poor and prohibits development.

By providing the resources necessary for the Tibetans to be actively involved in their own development, and to become business and civic leaders in their communities. International organisations and individuals can play a critical role in empowering the Tibetan people to become self-sufficient and to protect Tibet's unique way of life.

HISTORICAL BACKGROUND

Ever since 1949, even though the Chinese government initially made some efforts to improve the standard of living of the Tibetan people, China's development strategy was largely geared towards imposing the People's Liberation Army-led administrative superstructure, and later, towards assimilating Tibet into the People's Republic of China.

From 1950 until 1979, economic and structural measures such as co-operatives and communes were introduced in Tibet. These measures disregarded Tibetan culture and traditions: nomads were forced to be sedentary farmers; pasturelands became arable lands; winter wheat replaced native barley (Tibet's staple foodcrop); and huge state taxes were imposed to achieve unreasonable regional production targets. All these measures resulted in declining productivity, the degradation of grassland, and foodgrain shortages unknown in the history of Tibet.

The then Chinese Communist Party General Secretary, Hu Yaobang, recognised this decline in conditions of the Tibetan people at the First Work Forum on Tibet in 1980. As a result, the Household Responsibility System (HRS) was introduced, reversing the policies of the previous 30 years. By the end of 1982, decollectivisation was implemented and more social and religious freedom was granted in Tibet. Living conditions began to improve as the revenue and taxation systems were decentralised.

However, the positive impact of the HRS was short-lived because the emphasis was placed on Tibet's integration with China rather than on local self-sufficiency. Tibet was providing China's rich coastal region with energy, minerals and timber. In return, Tibet was receiving Chinese "skilled" settlers who brought "technical, managerial and business skills" to the region and helped open Tibet's market for Chinese manufactured goods. This massive influx of Chinese settlers further marginalised the Tibetan people, economically and socially.

In 1984 the Chinese government initiated 43 development projects, following up with 62 additional projects in 1994. These projects aimed to "develop the Tibetan economy and society" in Central Tibet. However, these initiatives did not result in the development of any significant Tibetan-run projects. Instead they have mainly benefited Chinese urban dwellers and strengthened China's control over Tibet. For example, the projects initiated in 1984 alone brought 60,000 Chinese into Tibet, causing 30,000 Tibetans from 18 work units to lose their jobs. Rural areas in Tibet still have no access to electricity, education, healthcare and safe drinking water facilities.

LONGTERM GOALS FOR TIBET'S DEVELOPMENT

The priority of the Tibetan Government-in-Exile is for the Tibetan people to be able to achieve their optimum economic and cultural potential. Thus, His Holiness the Dalai Lama has sought to enter into negotiations with the Chinese government in order to achieve a settlement, which would grant Tibetans genuine autonomy within the framework of the People's Republic of China.

As a political solution to Tibet is being pursued, international aid and development agencies, as well as investors, can and should be involved in raising the standard of living for the Tibetan people and in assisting Tibetans to become self-reliant.

BASIC PRINCIPLES:

- To enhance the capabilities of Tibetans to meet the needs of the present generation without compromising the needs of the future.
- To transform the whole of Tibet into a zone of peace with a democratic society.
- To create a future economic system based on a non-violent and equitable society.
- To restore and conserve Tibet's extensive, fragile resource base and the environment.
- To reverse the process of marginalisation of Tibetans in Tibet and empower Tibetans to take control of developing Tibet.
- To support not only the economic well-being of Tibetans, but also their social, cultural, spiritual and environmental welfare.

AID AND INVESTMENT GUIDELINES

- All development projects should be implemented only after conducting a thorough need-assessment of the Tibetan people through field visits and interviews.
- All development initiatives should be preceded by cultural, social and environmental impact assessments.
- Development projects should foster self-sufficiency and self-reliance of Tibetans.
- Projects should promote accountability of the development agencies to the Tibetan people and active participation of Tibetans in all project stages.
- Projects should respect Tibetan culture, traditions and the vast Tibetan knowledge and wisdom about their landscape and survival techniques.
- Agencies should have a local presence at all stages of the project to ensure that the intended target group benefits.
- Tibetan should be used as the working language of projects. It will be important for the development project staff to know the Tibetan language.

Prioritised Areas for Aid and Investment

Given the vast needs of the Tibetan people, we would like to highlight the following priorities for international development and investment programmes in Tibet:

1 Education

- Provide increased opportunities for primary, secondary and tertiary education in rural areas, including the building of schools;
- Provide adequate teaching materials in Tibetan to promote spoken and written Tibetan language;
- Develop learning centres for Tibetan language, culture and traditions to ensure the survival of Tibet's unique way of life;
- Provide professional training and skill development for Tibetans, preferably in the Tibetan language;
- Provide pre-service and in-service teacher training;
- Develop adult-literacy programmes;
- Provide opportunities for Tibetan language media, including television, radio and print.

2 Culture and Traditions

- Restore and protect Tibet's sacred places, historical monuments, and institutes of learning;
- Develop Tibetan cultural and traditional schools of learning;
- Preserve Tibetan relics and manuscripts; and
- Promote Tibet's unique arts and crafts, such as *thangka* painting, wood carving, metal crafts, handicrafts, music and dances.

3 Healthcare

- Establish primary healthcare centres in villages;
- Train doctors and health workers;
- Provide essential medicines and vaccination to the rural areas;
- Train village health workers in primary care and first aid;
- Ensure safe drinking water and decent rural sanitation;
- Develop community healthcare action programmes and publications to prevent diseases, especially infectious diseases such as tuberculosis; and
- Preserve and promote Tibetan medical knowledge.

4 Environment and Biodiversity

- Train Tibetans in sustainable management of natural resources;
- Protect and rehabilitate vulnerable ecosystems;
- Prevent water, air and land pollution;
- Pursue reforestation programmes and cultivation of medicinal plants;
- Protect rare species of animals and plants;
- Promote environmental education and awareness;
- Develop eco-friendly tourism; and
- Promote culturally sensitive ecological research and information sharing.

5 Agriculture

- Encourage sustainable crop farming;
- Ensure basic food needs and alleviate Tibetan poverty;
- Promote ownership of land by Tibetans;
- Create water conservation and irrigation programmes;
- Promote agro-forestry and soil conservation techniques;
- Promote use of appropriate technology in agriculture;
- Encourage use of renewable energy sources such as solar and wind; and
- Promote agro-based local enterprises.

6 Pastoral Nomadism

- Prevent grassland and pasture degradation;
- Protect and improve winter grazing-land;
- Provide emergency relief and humanitarian aid;
- Create veterinary and animal disease prevention facilities;
- Support skill training in livestock breeding and improvement;
- Provide training in agricultural management;
- Give training in modern dairy processing and preserving techniques;
- Provide small-scale hydropower for rural Tibetan communities;
- Strengthen the traditional economy and livelihood of rural Tibetans; and
- Facilitate marketing of traditional products.

7 Employment Enhancement

- Promote rural-based vocational skills, education and training;
- Introduce self-help and small development

enterprises;

- Support projects which provide business management and entrepreneurial training to achieve self-reliance;
- Develop Tibetan-run charitable organisations which can more effectively articulate the needs of their local communities;
- Provide access to information, training, funding sources and project facilities for Tibetans;
- Provide loans and credit facilities for Tibetan-run businesses;
- Promote youth entrepreneurship; and
- Promote cooperation among Tibetan communities.

8 Business Development

- Encourage business and development projects run and managed by Tibetans;
- Spur sustainable economic growth in Tibet;
- Provide equity, credit and forms of guarantee for Tibetans in order to encourage business initiatives;
- Provide information about business projects and economic sectors in the Tibetan language;
- Provide details on privatisation issues, such as how to start an independent business;
- Offer business plan development assistance;
- Provide assistance in locating soft funding for technical, environmental, community development and training work related to projects.

CONCLUSION

With international development assistance and investment, the Tibetan people have the potential to become economically self-sufficient and to preserve their unique way of life. While their needs are great, coordinated international involvement can have a major impact on Tibetans' standard of living.

We strongly believe that the Tibetan people must be intricately involved in their own development. They must be consulted at all project stages and be allocated key roles in the design, implementation and supervision of projects.

We encourage international development agencies to coordinate and cooperate with each other by sharing information and resources. Furthermore, we encourage those who are interested in helping Tibetans inside Tibet to seek the views of the Tibetan people, particularly His Holiness the Dalai Lama and the TGIE. For obvious reasons, any formal involvement of the Tibetan leadership in exile may not be acceptable. However, it is critical that the views of the Tibetan people, and the exile leadership, be taken into full consideration. This will ensure that the Tibetans are the primary beneficiaries of development and investment in Tibet and that they will have the ultimate say in their own development.

Lastly, we encourage agencies and individuals interested in helping Tibetans in Tibet to keep the TGIE apprised of their activities, progress and difficulties.

A FINAL NOTE OF CAUTION

We request that all individuals and agencies working in Tibet make efforts to ensure that their participation in Tibet does not:

a) Deplete natural resources; with little or no benefit to the Tibetan people.
b) Facilitate the erosion of Tibetan culture and traditions.
c) Facilitate the migration and settlement of non-Tibetans into Tibet.
d) Negatively affect the sustainability of Tibet's ecosystems.
e) Transfer ownership of Tibetan land and natural resources to non-Tibetans.
f) Operate projects without the participation of affected Tibetans.
g) Facilitate large-scale, capital intensive, and commercial projects.

For further information and for discussion of specific project proposals contact:

Environment & Development Desk
Department of Information & International Relations
Central Tibetan Administration
Dharamsala-176215 H.P. India
Tel: +91-1892-22510/22457/24662
Fax: +91-1892-24957
E-mail: ecodesk@diir.gov.tibet.net
website: www.tibet.com

[1] Tibet comprises the three provinces of Amdo, Kham and U-Tsang (called *Cholka-sum* by Tibetans), with a total area of 2.5 million sq. km. It includes the present day 'Tibet Autonomous Region', Qinghai and other Amdo areas incorporated into the Chinese provinces of Sichuan and Gansu, and major parts of Kham taken by Sichuan and Yunnan. China today acknowledges only the so-called Tibet Autonomous Region (1.2 million sq. km) founded in 1965 as "Tibet".

APPENDIX 1

A MESSAGE FROM HIS HOLINESS THE 14TH DALAI LAMA FOR THE NEW MILLENNIUM

1 JANUARY 2000

MANY people seem to be excited about the new millennium, but the new millennium in itself will be nothing special. As we enter into the new millennium things will be the same; there will be nothing unusual. However, if we really want the next millennium to be happier, more peaceful and more harmonious for humankind we will have to make the effort to make it so. This is in our hands, but especially in the hands of the younger generation.

We have had many experiences during this century — constructive as well as extremely destructive ones. We must learn from these experiences. We need to approach the next millennium more holistically, with more openness and farsightedness. If we are going to make the right kind of efforts to make the future of the world better, I believe the following matters are of great importance.

1. While engaging in material progress and taking care of physical well-being we need to pay equal attention to developing peace of mind and thus taking care of the internal aspect of our being.

2. Along with education, which generally deals only with academic accomplishments, we need to develop more altruism and a sense of caring and responsibility for others in the minds of the younger generation studying in various educational institutions. This can be done without necessarily involving religion. One could therefore call this 'secular ethics', as it in fact consists of basic human qualities such as kindness, compassion, sincerity and honesty.

3. This past century in some ways has been a century of war and bloodshed. It has seen a year by year increase in defense spending by most countries in the world. If we are to change this trend we must seriously consider the concept of non-violence, which is a physical expression of compassion. In order to make non-violence a reality we must first work on internal disarmament and then proceed to work on external disarmament. By internal disarmament I mean ridding ourselves of all the negative emotions that result in violence. External disarmament will also have to be done gradually, step by step. We must first work on the total abolishment of nuclear weapons and gradually work up to total demilitarisation throughout the world. In the process of doing this we also need to work towards stopping the arms trade, which is still very widely practiced because it is so lucrative. When we do all these things, we can then hope to see in the next millennium a year by year decrease in the military expenditure of the various nations and a gradual working towards demilitarisation.

Human problems will, of course, always remain, but the way to resolve them should be through dialogue and discussion. The next century should be a century of dialogue and discussion rather than one of war and bloodshed.

4. We need to address the issue of the gap between the rich and the poor, both globally and nationally. This inequality, with some sections of the human community having abundance and others on the same planet going hungry or even dying of starvation, is not only morally wrong, but practically also a source of problems. Equally important is the issue of freedom. As long as there is no freedom in many parts of the world there can be no real peace and in a sense no real freedom for the rest of the world.

5. For the sake of our future generations, we need to take care of our earth and of our environment. Environmental damage is often gradual and not easily apparent and by the time we become aware of it, it is generally too late. Since most of the major rivers flowing into many parts of South-east Asia originate from the Tibetan Plateau, it will not be out of place to mention here the crucial importance of taking care of the environment in that area.

6. Lastly, one of the greatest challenges today is the population explosion. Unless we are able to tackle this issue effectively we will be confronted with the problem of the natural resources being inadequate for all the human beings on this earth.

We need to seriously look into these matters that concern us all if we are to look forward to the future with some hope. ■

APPENDIX 2

SPEECH OF THE KASHAG

THE CABINET, TIBETAN-GOVERNMENT-IN-EXILE, ON THE 41ST ANNIVERSARY OF THE TIBETAN NATIONAL UPRISING DAY, 10 MARCH 2000

TODAY is an unforgettable day in the history of Tibet. Forty-one years ago, on this day, the people of Tibet gave up their lives to unitedly resist the systematic destruction of their race, religion, culture and political freedom by foreign invasion.

In 1949 the Chinese communist forces marched into Tibet and gradually, against all the canons of international law, forcibly occupied the entire country. Since then, over the past 51 years, the Tibetan people have suffered inhuman brutality and repression, resulting in the death of over 1.2 million Tibetans and destruction of over 6,000 monasteries and nunneries. The Chinese communists have also destroyed or plundered Tibet's cultural artifacts and family wealth, which our people had created and preserved for many generations. Tibet's rich mineral resources — such as gold, copper, iron, uranium, coal, oil, borax, mica, natural gas, natural salt, etc.— are being exploited. Similarly, our ancient forest reserves are denuded, our once free roaming wild life and livestock are being exploited for the benefit of China. Today, our country is completely impoverished.

Particularly, since the start of the so-called "democratic reforms" in eastern and western Tibet in 1955-1956 and the whole of the country in 1959, China has taken a number of steps to wipe out Tibetan identity and characteristics as they are seen to represent conditions for "splitting" Tibet from China. Referring to this in his 70,000-Character Petition submitted to the Chinese Premier in 1962, the late Panchen Lama said, "Innumerable religious objects (in the so-called Tibet Autonomous Region) were consigned to flames and rivers, some were destroyed and melted down. Monasteries, nunneries, *mani* cairns, stupas, etc. lay in ruins as if a mad elephant had run amok among them. Religious scriptures were used as manure. Many *thangkas* and scriptures were cannibalised to make shoe soles."

The Panchen Lama went on to say, "Before democratic reforms, there were more than 2,500 large, medium and small monasteries in Tibet. After the democratic reform, only 70 or so monasteries were kept in existence by the government. This was a reduction of more than 97 per cent. ... In the whole of Tibet in the past there was a total of about 110,000 monks and nuns. Of those, possibly 10,000 fled abroad, leaving about 100,000. After the democratic reforms were concluded (sometime in 1960), the number of monks and nuns living in monasteries and nunneries was about 7,000, which is a reduction of 93 per cent."

Sometime in 1993 China started the "patriotic reeducation" campaign in Tibetan monasteries and nunneries. Under this campaign, the authorities fixed the minimum age for those who could join monasteries and nunneries. Banning the photos of His Holiness the Dalai Lama, the "reeducation" campaign forces monks and nuns to discard the Panchen Lama recognised by His Holiness the Dalai Lama, accept the one appointed by the Chinese government, and to denounce His Holiness the Dalai Lama and his followers as an impediment to stability and development in Tibet. Thousands of monks and nuns have been expelled from monasteries and nunneries, and sent to prison for resisting the "reeducation".

Qualified spiritual figures, commanding the respect of people, are subjected to false charges, imprisoned and prevented from pursuing their spiritual practice. In the past, Tibet University in Lhasa taught some subjects in the Tibetan language. Later, the authorities forced the university to teach even those subjects in Chinese. The Tibetan-language schools opened by monasteries, spiritual figures and fairly well-to-do Tibetan individuals are forced to close down or nationalised on the charges of promoting Tibetan nationalism and splittist tendencies.

In February 1989 Hu Jintao, the then Secretary of the Tibet Autonomous Regional Communist Party, circulated an internal document within the communist party. Observing that religion and religious figures enjoyed too much importance, the document recommended downgrading the importance of religion and religious figures as a condition for decisive implementation of the Party policy toward Tibet. On 20 November 1998 Chen Kuiyun, Secretary of the Tibet Autonomous Regional Communist Party, held an exclusive meeting of Party leaders. The meeting discussed the strategy to destroy the Tibetan religion and culture. Addressing the meeting, Chen identified religion as the fundamental weapon of splittists and impediment to stability. "Therefore, what should we do to destroy Buddhism in Tibet?" Chen spelled out the following three initial strategies: a) Use of force and coercion to destroy religion; b) Propagation of the Marxist-Leninist ideology to erode faith in Buddhism among the masses; and c) Promotion of economic and cultural development to erode faith in Buddhism among the masses.

In another meeting, Chen Kuiyun stated openly that "reactionary sentiment is directly related to knowledge of the Tibetan language and literature". This clearly shows that China is implementing a policy to destroy the distinctive identity of the Tibetan people. From the Tibetan people's point of view, this is intolerable. The international community should pay serious attention to this.

Last year, in 1999, China celebrated a number of anniversaries: the 40th Anniversary of the "democratic reforms" in Tibet, the 34th Anniversary of the establishment of the "Tibet Autonomous Region", etc. During these celebrations, the Chinese leaders announced that they had brought earth-shattering political, economic and cultural developments in Tibet, whereby China built schools, health facilities and roads where there had been none before. "Democratic reforms", Chinese leaders announced, ended the feudal serfdom in Tibet and made the "formers serfs and Tibetan masses" the masters of their own destiny. The Chinese announcement also talked about millions of yuan spent on the development of Tibet's agriculture, animal husbandry, forest, industry, telecommunications, public transport system, etc.

But in reality, it has become questionable in the international community as to whether the development programmes were indeed aimed at the benefit of the Tibetan people. According to our findings, and as known to all, all these developments benefit the PLA personnel, Chinese cadres, their families, and Chinese immigrants in Tibet. As a matter of fact, they are the intended targets of these developments. Similarly, China is making efforts to reduce the Tibetans into a minority in their own homeland and to completely sinicise Tibet.

As for having made the "former serfs" masters of their own destiny, this is just a crude propaganda to deceive the international community. In reality, the Tibetans do not have the freedom to practice their religion, express their thoughts or even to move from one place to another. Far from being masters of their destiny, the Tibetans have no right even over their own lives; they live in constant fear of Chinese security forces.

If the Tibetans had indeed become masters of Tibet and were leading a happy life, why are the authorities afraid to hold a referendum in Tibet? More particularly, why are the authorities afraid to allow free movement to international media persons, tourists and official delegations during their visits to Tibet?

In 1980 Hu Yaobang, the then secretary of the Chinese Communist Party, visited Tibet on a fact-finding mission. In order to give genuine autonomy to the so-called Tibet Autonomous Region, Hu decided to repatriate 85 per cent of Chinese officials to China and replace them with Tibetans. Subsequently, many Tibetans were appointed to leadership positions at the prefectural and county levels. But around 1993 the Chinese government discovered that the Tibetan cadres held nationalistic feelings. Since then, all the Tibetan officials, except for a couple or so, have had their jobs changed. Today, most of the Party secretaries and administrators above the county level are Chinese.

The much-vaunted health care and education facilities in Tibet are concentrated in urban centres and intended for the PLA personnel, Chinese officials, and Chinese settlers in Tibet. In rural areas, where the Tibetan population predominates, schools either do not exist or are so basic that they do not provide meaningful education, have no qualified teachers or material facilities. Small wonder that a large number of young Tibetans leave their families behind in Tibet and risk hazardous journeys across the Himalayas, some even losing their limbs to frostbite or dying on the way, so that they can receive meaningful education in the exile Tibetan community. To date, 12,307 young Tibetans have escaped Tibet to join schools in exile. Health care facilities are almost non-existent in rural Tibet.

It is remarkable that even the Tibetan lamas, whom the Chinese authorities try to cultivate for political reasons, escape from Tibet as they are unable to reconcile themselves to the repressive Chinese activities. This clearly shows that the Chinese claim of religious freedom, education facilities and developments in Tibet is mere propaganda. If the Chinese statements and announcements on the improved situation in Tibet were true, then there would be no reason for all these Tibetans to leave behind their beloved families, homes and monasteries and escape to a foreign land at great risk to their lives.

In all the three provinces of Tibet, oppression, suppression, exploitation, racial slight, brutality, torture and death have become part of the Tibetan people's daily life. Tibetans do not even have the right to express their views freely. Nevertheless, they have retained unwavering commitment to the cause of Tibet. With increasing determination and effort, they continue to resist the Chinese government's deceptive designs, coercion and brutality. These brave Tibetans serve as a source of inspiration not only to their compatriots in exile, but also to Tibet Support Groups and governments. As a result of their determination, the cause of Tibet has become an important international issue now.

In order to bring genuine democracy to future Tibet, His Holiness the Dalai Lama has issued a charter and a constitution. Within the limitation of the exile situation, the Tibetan Government-in-Exile functions democratically. His Holiness the Dalai Lama and his exile government look after the livelihood, education and health care of the Tibetan people. The Tibetans in exile have the opportunities that are not available to people of many free countries, let alone those of Tibet. Although China continues to destroy the religion and culture of Tibet, all the Tibetan spiritual lineages flourish in the Tibetan exile community, from where Tibetan Buddhism, with its precepts of peace, compassion and morality, has spread to almost all parts of the world.

It has been over two decades since His Holiness the Dalai Lama initiated his Middle Way approach to bring about a mutually-beneficial solution to the issue of Tibet. However, the Chinese leadership has consistently stalled negotiations by repeatedly putting forward unreasonable and irrelevant preconditions. Obviously, the Chinese leadership is bidding for time in the hope that the issue of Tibet will die as time passes. This is, of course, a shortsighted, unrealistic and empty dream.

The issue of Tibet is not as simple as the Chinese leaders seem to think. It is a universal fact that the struggle of a nation and its people will go on for many generations. More particularly, Beijing cannot ignore changes in China and the international political scene, just as it cannot ride roughshod over the determination and efforts of the Tibetan people and the international community's interest in and support for the plight of Tibetans.

The present approach of the Chinese leaders to the Tibetan issue is a recipe for unending problems and regrets to China. Therefore, we urge the Chinese leadership to consider seriously the long and short-term interests and give a responsible response to the open-minded overture of His Holiness the Dalai Lama. We urge the Chinese leadership to recognise the importance of this issue for the mutual benefit of Tibet and China.

I would like to take this opportunity to fervently make the following requests to the international community:

1. The situation inside Tibet is as dangerous as a fire pit under a layer of ashes. We request governments, parliaments, organisations, media and individuals to visit Tibet frequently to seriously study the urgent situation there and educate the international community.

2. The identity of Tibet, with over 2000 years of history and rich culture, is facing the threat of extinction at the hands of the Chinese government. We request the international community to take concrete actions under international law to reverse this situation.

3. We request the international community to put pressure on the Chinese government to release the young Panchen Lama and other Tibetan political prisoners.

I take this opportunity to thank the Indian government and people, parliaments, organisations, intellectuals, media, the general public, students and Chinese people, who have shown concern and caring attitudes to the people of Tibet.

With my prayers for the long life of His Holiness the Dalai Lama and the fulfillment of all his wishes.

Sonam Topgyal, Kalon Tripa ■

APPENDIX 3

NATIONAL PUBLIC HEARING ON TIBET'S ENVIRONMENT

REPORT PREPARED BY THE TIBETAN YOUTH CONGRESS CENTREX, DHARAMSALA

A PUBLIC Hearing that focussed on Tibet's changing environment was organised by the Tibetan Youth Congress and held on 16-17 November 1998 at Lhakpa Tsering Memorial Hall, Gangchen Kyishong, Dharamsala, India. Delegates were invited from all departments of the Tibetan Government-in-Exile (TGIE), institutions, monasteries and nunneries, non-governmental organisations, and local schools were represented by both teaching staff and students.

The Hearing was chaired by Thupten Lungrik, Vice-Chairman of the Assembly of Tibetan Peoples' Deputies (Tibetan Parliament-in-Exile), co-chaired by Tempa Tsering, Secretary, Department of Information and International Relations (DIIR) and coordinated by Pema Lhundup, General Secretary, Tibetan Youth Congress (TYC). Panel members presiding over the hearing were Tsultrim Palden Dekhang, Head of the Environment and Development Desk, DIIR, and Karma Yeshi, Vice-President, TYC.

AIMS AND OBJECTIVES

The Hearing was convened with the aim of obtaining and understanding public opinion on issues relating to Tibet's environment through a forum in which issues of concern could be identified and prioritised. Recommendations would then be developed as a means to moving forward. In order to encourage discussion and promote the exchange of ideas, the Hearing was divided into a number of sessions with both group and open discussions.

A secondary purpose was to create public testimonials to attach to the National Report on Tibet's Environment and Development being prepared by the Environment and Development Desk, DIIR.

The Report was being prepared for submission to the United Nations and international governments as a testimony to the environmental conditions in Tibet before and after the Chinese invasion.

The language of the Hearing was Tibetan and the focus on five specific issues:

1 Environmental practices in Tibet prior to the Chinese invasion
2 The Tibetan environment from a religious perspective
3 The destruction of Tibet's environment under China
4 The importance of sound environmental practices in Tibet
5 Actions and recommendations to save Tibet's environment.

SPEAKERS AND TOPICS DISCUSSED

Environmental Practices in Tibet Prior to the Chinese Invasion

Rev. Thonsur Lobsang Tenzin, Private Office of His Holiness the Dalai Lama, arrived in 1980 in Dharamsala. Before his escape into exile the speaker was arrested and imprisoned in Tibet for 19 years and six months.

It is important for us all to understand that prior to the Chinese invasion, Tibet had constituted and made provision for land use systems and management, both endorsed by Boshung Gandhen Phodrang (Tibetan Government) under the leadership of the Dalai Lama and respected by the populace. Thus, whilst the concept of environmental protectionism is a relatively new global phenomenon, the people of Tibet have always had an inherent respect for the land. Much of this traditional concern was based on religious beliefs; these in turn played a fundamental part in the formation of social values and state policy. As early as the 17th century, in the Water Horse Year (1642), His Holiness the Great Fifth Dalai Lama, Ngawang Lobsang Gyatso, sought to protect the environment. In the tenth month of every year, a Decree for the Protection of Animals and the Environment (Rilung Tsa Tsik) was issued in his name: this environmental law forbade the killing of all creatures and consequent misuse of the land.

One of the decrees issued by the Thirteenth Dalai Lama states: "From the first month of the Tibetan calendar to the 30th of the seventh month ...nobody will hurt, let alone kill, the different birds of the air, animals of the hills and forest, fish and otter of the water. In fact, nobody, noble or humble, should do violence to or harm any animal of land, water or air, no matter how big or small."

Under the government's Sonam Lekhung (Office for Agriculture) regulations were in place for managing and monitoring land use. Private land was not allowed to stand fallow. If poor irrigation or topography made land unusable, government assistance was provided to upgrade the area and ensure it became productive. Land irrigation and cultivation was, and still is, forbidden during the holy month of Saka Dawa — the month in which the Lord Buddha attained enlightenment. This acknowledges that many insects and worms are killed during the tilling process and so the regulation is out of respect for Buddhist tradition.

There was an office overseeing the vast pastures in northern Tibet, but there were no special rules and regulations governing these lands. Animals and human beings had the freedom to move to any grassland areas as they pleased. However, each group of nomads living in particular regions had their own rules and regulations (Tsa Thang Drik Shi).

The Destruction of Tibet's Environment Under China

Ngawa Tsegyam, Assistant to the Representative of H.H. the Dalai Lama in Taipei, Taiwan and former Director, Research and Analysis Centre, TGIE. He escaped into India in 1992 after three years of imprisonment in Tibet. Ngawa Tsegyam has travelled extensively, visiting many countries to speak on China's abuse of human rights and to present the true picture of Tibet under Chinese rule.

The years immediately after the Chinese invasion must represent a landmark in environmental destruction. Prior to 1949 the Tibetan landscape was pure and virgin; pollution, waste, killing — all these were unheard of. Wildlife Conservation Decree was the guiding principle; people were praying and working within a framework that protected the lives of their religious leaders, deflected disease, saved the land from crop failure and the people from starvation. This system successfully protected both the people and their land for centuries.

With the Chinese invasion came a brutal assault on Tibet's natural resources. The Chinese arrived with a master plan: almost immediately they divided the land, creating 70 districts from the three existing provinces of Amdo, Kham and U-Tsang. Then they initiated large-scale logging and environmental desecration.

In 60 out of the 70 newly-created districts, which cover an area of 250,000 km^2, the Chinese commenced logging operations. And all the timber was transported to China. No regard was paid to Tibetan wishes or possible environmental consequences. By 1967 the destruction was so complete in the district of Kanze that there was extensive flooding in the region after repeated appeals to halt operations had been ignored by the Chinese authorities. The resulting disaster affected thousands of people; homes were lost, families displaced and crops destroyed.

More recently the Chinese have introduced a new threat to Tibet's ecology and people, unheard of in the country's history: nuclear waste. Large tracts of land in Northern and Central Tibet have been assigned as "nuclear dumps". This waste disposal service was provided by China to governments and organisations which would rather not store such dangerous and politically sensitive materials in their own countries: A service that pays no regard to the wellbeing nor safety of Tibet and Tibetans.

It is ironic that a country which evolved on Buddhist principles that protects all life forms is now home to a huge number of animals and plants being hunted or poached to the verge of extinction. The giant panda, snow leopard, golden monkey, wild yak, Asiatic black bear, and black-necked crane are some rare and endangered wildlife species. Wild animals and birds have vanished through the destruction of habitat or been slaughtered by indiscriminate hunting and the wildlife trade.

The Importance of Sound Environmental Practices in Tibet

Tenzin Phuntsok Atisha, Representative of His Holiness the Dalai Lama in Taiwan. He, has an M.Phil. from Panjab University, India, and is the former Head of the Environment and Development Desk. He was one of the Tibetan delegates at the Earth Summit held in Rio de Janeiro, June 1992.

The limited demands of the Tibetan lifestyle placed minimal hardship on the vast lands of Tibet and with little inclination for hoarding material wealth the huge reserves of mineral resources have remained untouched for thousands of years. For centuries Tibetans have lived in harmony with their environment; an environment that links Tibet with the rest of Asia and the world.

Tibet is Asia's principal watershed and is the source of its major rivers, including the Machu (Yellow River), Drichu (Yangtze), Senge Khabab (Indus), Macha Khabab (Karnali), Langchen Khabab (Sutlej), Yarlung Tsangpo (Brahmaputra), Zachu (Mekong), Gyalmo Ngulchu (Salween), Bhumchu (Arun) and others. Some 90 per cent of Tibet's river runoff flows from Tibet to other countries. The significance of this rests with the fact that the areas irrigated by these rivers support around 47 percent of the earth's human population.

As the "Roof of the World", Tibet significantly influences atmosphere and weather conditions over Asia. Stable summer conditions over the Tibetan Plateau act as a forcing mechanism for the South Asian monsoon that brings rain to the Indian subcontinent. Scientists are beginning to establish that changing land-use patterns on the plateau will influence the flow of jet streams in the upper troposphere. This in turn may lead to a delay and weakening in the stable pattern of summer monsoons. From a global perspective it is believed that the behaviour of jet streams over Tibet correlates with the occurrence of weather anomalies in the rest of the world.

Whilst these links are complex, it can be safely said that a stable environment is not just important for Tibet but for Asia and the world as well.

The Tibetan Environment from a Religious Perspective

Geshe Kelsang Damdul, Deputy Director, Institute of Tibetan Buddhist Dialectics, Dharamsala. He has an MA in history from Himachal Pradesh University and a Geshe (doctorate) degree from Drepung Loseling Monastery in Tibetan Buddhism. He has visited Tibetan communities to lecture on religion and ecology and has also travelled widely, lecturing on Tibetan Buddhism.

Tibetans have always respected the cycle of nature, seeking to learn and understand its nuances and rhythms. Buddhism, which was introduced to Tibet in the sixth century, has played an important role in this respect. A general taboo against exploiting the environment was a direct result of Buddhist knowledge and belief of the inter-relationships between human beings, plants, animals, as well as the non-living elements of nature such as the sunshine, sky, mountains, valleys, lakes and rivers. This close relationship between religion and nature meant that the simple yet effective principles that maintained balance in the natural world became a part of daily life. After living like this for hundreds of years, it is in fact difficult for a Tibetan to differentiate between the practice of religion and concern for the environment.

The Tibetan way of life restricts the killing of any sentient being. Children are taught from birth that all life is sacred. I find that there is a great difference between the ethos of environmental workers in the West and Tibetans. In the West, the dominant motivation stems from a desire to save the environment for the benefit of human beings. But, from a Tibetan Buddhist perspective, the desire to protect the environment is borne out of compassion towards all living creatures.

GROUP DISCUSSIONS

Participants were divided into four groups with discussion focussing on the deteriorating environmental situation in Tibet. A number of common thoughts, issues and concerns emerged:

1. Stop continued deforestation
2. Stop dumping of nuclear waste
3. Stop extensive mining
4. Increase protection of wildlife
5. Recognise of endangered species
6. Stop population transfer
7. Protect of traditional nomad lifestyles
8. Protect of Tibet's spiritual heritage.

OPEN DISCUSSION

This presented a forum to debate how to protect Tibet's environment from further destruction at the hands of the Chinese. A number of suggestions emerged:

1. Regional Environmental Conference to be called by TGIE as a platform for building awareness amongst neighbouring countries about current Chinese environmental practices and their regional implications
2. TGIE to establish a global "Tibet Eco Awareness Day" as a means of increasing public education on Tibet's environment
3. Establish guidelines for agencies operating in Tibet to ensure Tibetans are the true beneficiaries of development initiatives
4. Greater availability of literature relating to Tibet and environmental destruction, developed as a medium of building global awareness
5. Use of international law to protect Tibet's environment and to force China to uphold the many Covenants and Global Agreements to which it is signatory
6. A call to the United Nations to send representatives regularly into Tibet to document environmental and development changes
7. Develop environmental education programmes in Tibetan communities, especially in schools.

ANCILLARY HEARING

Pokhara Tibetan Refugee Settlement

A Public Hearing on Tibet's Environment was held in Pokhara, Nepal on 24 October 1998. The meeting was conducted by the Regional Tibetan Youth Congress, Kathmandu, and the four regional chapters of Pokhara, and was coordinated by Dechen Tsomo, Finance Secretary, TYC. Camp Leaders of the Pokhara settlements and members of government and non-governmental organisations of the region attended the Hearing.

The meeting concluded that there was an urgent need for an increase of literature on Tibet's environment and the global implications for China's destruction of the Tibetan Plateau. Material should be widely available and have two areas of focus:

1 The implications of environmental destruction and thus the need for environmental protection

2 Documented evidence of Tibet before and after the Chinese invasion, demonstrating to the world the Chinese contempt and disregard for the environment and Tibet.

Darjeeling Tibetan Refugee Settlement

A one-day Public Hearing on Tibet's environment was held in Darjeeling on 29 November 1998 by the Regional Tibetan Youth Congress, under the coordination of Pema Gyatso, Information Secretary of the Central Executive Committee. The meeting was attended by presidents of the north-eastern regional branches of TYC — Gangtok, Kalimpong, Shillong, Miao, Tezu, Rawangla, Kurseong, Oodlabari, Salugara, Mirik and Darjeeling — together with members of the public.

The gathering of over 60 people considered Tibet's environment before and after the Chinese invasion. Two points were resolved:

1 Appeals by all organisations present will be made to the United Nations calling for an end to the Chinese exploitation and destruction of Tibet's environment

2 Study teams will be created to research and document environmental changes in Tibet since the Chinese occupation. Video footage is sought that can be used to solicit support from the United Nations.

CONCLUSION

The Dharamsala Hearing concluded on the afternoon of 16 November with a speech by TYC President, Tseten Norbu. Concluding remarks were also made by Tsultrim Palden Dekhang, Head of the EDD, and Pema Lhundup, General Secretary, TYC, on the importance of environmental awareness among Tibetans and how they can move forward to save Tibet's fragile ecology, not only for the benefit of Tibet but for the whole world. ■

APPENDIX 4

FIVE POINT PEACE PLAN FOR TIBET BY HIS HOLINESS THE 14TH DALAI LAMA

ADDRESS TO MEMBERS OF THE UNITED STATES CONGRESS, WASHINGTON, D.C., SEPTEMBER 21, 1987

THE world is increasingly interdependent, so that lasting peace — national, regional, and global — can only be achieved if we think in terms of broader interest rather than parochial needs. At this time, it is crucial that all of us, the strong and the weak, contribute in our own way. I speak to you today as the leader of the Tibetan people and as a Buddhist monk devoted to the principles of a religion based on love and compassion. Above all, I am here as a human being who is destined to share this planet with you and all others as brothers and sisters. As the world grows smaller, we need each other more than in the past. This is true in all parts of the world, including the continent I come from.

At present in Asia, as elsewhere, tensions are high. There are open conflicts in the Middle East, Southeast Asia, and in my own country, Tibet. To a large extent, these problems are symptoms of the underlying tensions that exist among the area's great powers.

In order to resolve regional conflicts, an approach is required that takes into account the interests of all relevant countries and peoples, large and small. Unless comprehensive solutions are formulated, that take into account the aspirations of the people most directly concerned, piecemeal or merely expedient measures will only create new problems.

The Tibetan people are eager to contribute to regional and world peace, and I believe they are in a unique position to do so. Traditionally, Tibetans are a peace-loving and non-violent people. Since Buddhism was introduced to Tibet over one thousand years ago, Tibetans have practised non-violence with respect to all forms of life. This attitude has also been extended to our country's international relations. Tibet's highly strategic position in the heart of Asia, separating the continent's great powers— India, China and the USSR — has throughout history endowed it with an essential role in the maintenance of peace and stability. This is precisely why, in the past, Asia's empires went to great lengths to keep one another out of Tibet. Tibet's value as an independent buffer state was integral to the region's stability.

When the newly-formed People's Republic of China invaded Tibet in 1949/50, it created a new source of conflict. This was highlighted when, following the Tibetan national uprising against the Chinese and my flight to India in 1959, tensions between China and India escalated into the border war in 1962. Today large numbers of troops are again massed on both sides of the Himalayan border and tension is once more dangerously high.

The real issue, of course, is not the Indo-Tibetan border demarcation. It is China's illegal occupation of Tibet, which has given it direct access to the Indian subcontinent. The Chinese authorities have attempted to confuse the issue by claiming that Tibet has always been a part of China. This is untrue. Tibet was a fully independent state when the People's Liberation Army invaded the country in 1949/50.

Since Tibetan emperors unified Tibet, over a thousand years ago, our country was able to maintain its independence until the middle of this century. At times Tibet extended its influence over neighbouring countries and peoples and, in other periods, came itself under the influence of powerful foreign rulers— the Mongol Khans, the Gorkhas of Nepal, the Manchu Emperors and the British in India.

It is, of course, not uncommon for states to be subjected to foreign influence or interference. Although so-called satellite relationships are perhaps the clearest examples of this, most major powers exert influence over less powerful allies or neighbours. As the most authoritative legal studies have shown, in Tibet's case, the country's occasional subjection to foreign influence never entailed a loss of independence. And there can be no doubt that when Peking's communist armies entered Tibet, Tibet was in all respects an independent state.

China's aggression, condemned by virtually all nations of the free world, was a flagrant violation of international law. As China's military occupation of Tibet continues, the world should remember that though Tibetans have lost their freedom, under international law Tibet today is still an independent state under illegal occupation.

It is not my purpose to enter a political/legal discussion here concerning Tibet's status. I just wish to emphasise the obvious and undisputed fact that we Tibetans are a distinct people with our own culture, language, religion and history. But for China's occupation, Tibet would still, today, fulfil its natural role as a buffer state maintaining and promoting peace in Asia.

It is my sincere desire, as well as that of the Tibetan people, to restore to Tibet her invaluable role, by converting the entire country—comprising the three provinces of U-Tsang, Kham and Amdo — once more into a place of stability, peace and harmony. In the best of Buddhist tradition, Tibet would extend its services and hospitality to all who further the cause of world peace and the well-being of mankind and the natural environment we share.

Despite the holocaust inflicted upon our people in the past decades of occupation, I have always strived to find a solution through direct and honest discussions with the Chinese. In 1982, following the change of leadership in China and the establishment of direct contacts with the government in Peking, I sent my representatives to Peking to open talks concerning the future of my country and people.

We entered the dialogue with a sincere and positive attitude and with a willingness to take into account the legitimate needs of the People's Republic of China. I hoped that this attitude would be reciprocated and that a solution could eventually be found which would satisfy and safeguard the aspirations and interests of both parties. Unfortunately, China has consistently responded to our efforts in a defensive manner, as though our detailing of Tibet's very real difficulties was criticism for its own sake.

To our even greater dismay, the Chinese government misused the opportunity for a genuine dialogue. Instead of addressing the real issues facing the six million Tibetan people, China has attempted to reduce the question of Tibet to a discussion of my own personal status.

It is against this background and in response to the tremendous support and encouragement I have been given by you and other persons I have met during this trip, that I wish today to clarify the principal issues and to propose, in a spirit of openness and conciliation, a first step towards a lasting solution. I hope this may contribute to a future of friendship and cooperation with all of our neighbours, including the Chinese people.

This peace plan contains five basic components:

1 Transformation of the whole of Tibet into a zone of peace;
2 Abandonment of China's population transfer policy which threatens the very existence of the Tibetans as a people;
3 Respect for the Tibetan people's fundamental human rights and democratic freedoms;
4 Restoration and protection of Tibet's natural environment and the abandonment of China's use of Tibet for the production of nuclear weapons and dumping of nuclear waste;
5 Commencement of earnest negotiations on the future status of Tibet and of relations between the Tibetan and Chinese peoples.

Let me explain these five components:

- 1 -

I propose that the whole of Tibet, including the eastern provinces of Kham and Amdo, be transformed into a zone of *"Ahimsa"*, a Hindi term used to mean a state of peace and non-violence.

The establishment of such a peace zone would be in keeping with Tibet's historical role as a peaceful and neutral Buddhist nation and buffer state separating the continent's great powers. It would also be in keeping with Nepal's proposal to proclaim Nepal a peace zone and with China's declared support for such a proclamation. The peace zone proposed by Nepal would have a much greater impact if it were to include Tibet and neighbouring areas.

The establishing of a peace zone in Tibet would require withdrawal of Chinese troops and military installations from the country, which would enable India also to withdraw troops and military installations from the Himalayan regions bordering Tibet. This would be achieved under an international agreement which would satisfy China's legitimate security needs and build trust among the Tibetan, Indian, Chinese and other peoples of the region. This is in everyone's best interest, particularly that of China and India, as it would enhance their security, while reducing the economic burden of maintaining high troop concentrations on the disputed Himalayan border.

Historically, relations between China and India were never strained. It was only when Chinese armies marched into Tibet, creating for the first time a common border, that tensions arose between these two powers, ultimately leading to the 1962 war. Since then numerous dangerous incidents have continued to occur. A restoration of good relations between the world's two most populous countries would be greatly facilitated if they were separated as they were throughout history by a large and friendly buffer region.

To improve relations between the Tibetan people and the Chinese, the first requirement is the creation of trust.

After the holocaust of the last decades in which over one million Tibetans - one sixth of the population - lost their lives and at least as many lingered in prison camps because of their religious beliefs and love of freedom, only a withdrawal of Chinese troops could start a genuine process of reconciliation. The vast occupation force in Tibet is a daily reminder to the Tibetans of the oppression and suffering they have all experienced. A troop withdrawal would be an essential signal that in the future a meaningful relationship might be established with the Chinese, based on friendship and trust.

- 2 -

The population transfer of Chinese into Tibet, which the government in Peking pursues in order to force a "final solution" to the Tibetan problem by reducing the Tibetan population to an insignificant and disenfranchised minority in Tibet itself, must be stopped. The massive transfer of Chinese civilians into Tibet in violation of the Fourth Geneva Convention (1949) threatens the very existence of the Tibetans as a distinct people. In the eastern parts of our country, the Chinese now greatly outnumber Tibetans. In the Amdo province, for example, where I was born, there are, according to Chinese statistics, 2.5 million Chinese and only 750,000 Tibetans. Even in the so-called Tibet Autonomous Region (i.e. central and western Tibet), Chinese government sources now confirm that Chinese outnumber Tibetans.

The Chinese population transfer policy is not new. It has been systematically applied to other areas before. Earlier in this century, the Manchus were a distinct race with their own culture and traditions. Today only 2 to 3 million Manchurians are left in Manchuria, where 75 million Chinese have settled. In Eastern Turkestan, which the Chinese now call Xinjiang, the Chinese population has grown from 200,000 in 1949 to 7 million, more than half of the total population of 13 million. In the wake of the Chinese colonisation of Inner Mongolia, Chinese number 8.5 million, Mongols 2.5 million.

Today, in the whole of Tibet 7.5 million Chinese settlers have already been sent, outnumbering the Tibetan population of 6 million. In central and western Tibet, now referred to by the Chinese as the "Tibet Autonomous Region", Chinese sources admit the 1.9 million Tibetans already constitute a minority of the region's population. These numbers do not take the estimated 300,000 to 5 00,000 troops in Tibet into account, 250,000 of them in the so-called Tibet Autonomous Region.

For the Tibetans to survive as a people, it is imperative that the population transfer is stopped and Chinese settlers return to China. Otherwise, Tibetans will soon be no more than a tourist attraction and relic of a noble past.

- 3 -

Fundamental human rights and democratic freedoms must be respected in Tibet. The Tibetan people must once again be free to develop culturally, intellectually, economically and spiritually and to exercise basic democratic freedoms.

Human rights violations in Tibet are among the most serious in the world. Discrimination is practiced in Tibet under a policy of "apartheid" which the Chinese call "segregation and assimilation". Tibetans are, at best second class citizens in their own country. Deprived of all basic democratic rights and freedoms, they exist under a colonial administration in which all real power is wielded by Chinese officials of the Communist Party and the army.

Although the Chinese government allows Tibetans to rebuild some Buddhist monasteries and to worship in them, it still forbids serious study and teaching of religion. Only a small number of people, approved by the Communist Party, are permitted to join the monasteries.

While Tibetans in exile exercise their democratic rights under a Constitution promulgated by me in 1963, thousands of our countrymen suffer in prisons and labour camps in Tibet for their religious or political convictions.

- 4 -

Serious efforts must he made to restore the natural environment in Tibet. Tibet should not be used for the production of nuclear weapons and the dumping of nuclear waste.

Tibetans have a great respect for all forms of life. This inherent feeling is enhanced by the Buddhist faith, which prohibits the harming of all sentient beings, whether human or animal. Prior to the Chinese invasion, Tibet was an unspoiled, wilderness sanctuary in a unique natural environment. Sadly, in the past decades the wildlife and the forests of Tibet have been almost totally destroyed by the Chinese. The effects on Tibet's delicate environment have been devastating. What little is left in Tibet must be protected and efforts must be made to restore the environment to its balanced state.

China uses Tibet for the production of nuclear weapons and may also have started dumping nuclear waste in Tibet. Not only does China plan to dispose of its own nuclear waste but also that of other countries, who have already agreed to pay Peking to dispose of their toxic materials.

The dangers this presents are obvious. Not only living generations, but future generations are threatened by China's lack of concern for Tibet's unique and delicate environment.

- 5 -

Negotiations on the future status of Tibet and the relationship between the Tibetan and Chinese peoples should be started in earnest.

We wish to approach this subject in a reasonable and realistic way. In a spirit of frankness and conciliation and with a view to finding a solution that is in the long-term interest of all: the Tibetans, the Chinese, and all other peoples concerned. Tibetans and Chinese are distinct peoples, each with their own country, history, culture, language and way of life. Differences among peoples must be recognised and respected. They need not, however, form obstacles to genuine cooperation where this is to the mutual benefit of both peoples. It is my sincere belief that if the concerned parties were to meet and discuss their future with an open mind and a sincere desire to find a satisfactory and just solution, a breakthrough could be achieved. We must all exert ourselves to be reasonable and wise, and to meet in a spirit of frankness and understanding.

Let me end on a personal note. I wish to thank you for the concern and support which you and so many of your colleagues and fellow citizens have expressed for the plight of oppressed people everywhere. The fact that you have publicly shown your sympathy for us Tibetans has already had a positive impact on the lives of our people inside Tibet. I ask for your continued supporting this critical time in our country's history. Thank you. ■

APPENDIX 5

AN EXCERPT ON WILDLIFE CONSERVATION FROM A GENERAL DECREE ISSUED BY HIS HOLINESS THE 13TH DALAI LAMA

FROM the first month of the Tibetan calendar to the 30th of the seventh month, except tigers, leopards, bears, hyenas, rats and *rishu*, nobody will hunt, let alone kill the birds of the air, the animals of the hills and forests, fish and otter of the water... in fact any animals dry (land) or wet (water), no matter how big or small. Nobody, however noble or humble, should do violence to them or harm them.

All the district officials and governors, instead of exerting all their energy for private gain, should see that these laws are fully and completely enforced.

From the Potala Palace, 1901.

His Holiness the 13th Dalai Lama of Tibet (1876-1933)

APPENDIX 6

WILDLIFE CONSERVATION DECREE ISSUED IN 1944, BY TAGDRA RINPOCHE, REGENT OF TIBET

FOR the health of His Holiness the Dalai Lama, for the sake of the Dharma and for the benefit of all sentient beings, the village heads, officials and governors of all districts of Tibet are commanded to prevent the killing of all animals, except hyenas and wolves. The fish and otters of the water, animals of the hills and forests, the birds of the air, all animals endowed with the gift of life, whether great or small, must be protected and saved. Governors must see that the contents of this decree are carried out fully.

Since the Iron Dragon Year [1940], the Tibetan Government has decreed that in each and every village and town in Tibet on the 8th, 15th and 30th day of each month no domestic animals shall be killed. In addition, during the entire first and fourth months of the year, people shall refrain from slaughter, as well as the 4th day of the 6th month, the 22nd day of the 9th month, and the 25th of the 10th month. On these dates no domestic animal should be slaughtered for the purpose either of selling or eating its meat. All governors and officials of each district must see to it that this injunction is faithfully observed in all the regions of the Land of Snow.

In the past numerous decrees have been issued on this subject; however, there has been no sincere attempt made by the concerned governors and district leaders to implement the contents of these decrees. As a result of the inefficiency of the governors and district officials, Nechung Chogyal [the state oracle] has stated in a trance this summer that the hunting and environmental decrees must be more strictly enforced in all districts of Tibet.

Consequently, the Tibetan Government is taking more effective steps to see that these decrees are enforced. If the Tibetan Government hears of, or if the concerned governors report, individuals who consider these decrees as routine and continue to violate them, whether that person is of high or humble status, they will be punished according to the law of the land. If the law breakers are caught, not only they but the governors of the district where this law is broken will be punished.

It is possible that during winter months there will be mass slaughter of cattle. If one cannot survive without either selling or eating meat, such killing is permissible. If one can live without selling meat, the killing of yaks and other domestic animals should be avoided and district officials must make sincere attempts to look into the matter.

All officials of Tibet and the public must obey and respect the Ten Moral and Sixteen Civil Codes of Conduct. Everyone must obey the essence of the five principles of hunting and environmental protection laws first proclaimed in the Earth Dog Year [1896] and all the similar laws and decrees of the ancient kings of Tibet and the successive regents, supported by the Kashag, and know and carry out the responsibilities due to every individual.

28th day of the seventh month
of the Wood Monkey Year [1944]

INTERNATIONAL INSTRUMENTS SIGNED OR RATIFIED BY CHINA

International Instruments	Signed	Ratified A: Acceded Ac: Accession At: Acceptance
Convention on Biological Diversity (CBD)	11 June 1992	5 Jan 1993
Convention on International Trade in Endangered Species (CITES) of Wild Fauna and Flora		18 Jan 1981 (Ac)
RAMSAR Convention on Wetlands	1992	
United Nations Convention to Combat Desertification	14 Oct 1994	18 Feb 1997
United Nations Framework Convention on Climate Change (UNFCCC)	11 June 1992	5 Jan 1993
Kyoto Protocol to the United Nations Framework Convention on Climate Change	29 May 1998	
Vienna Convention for the Protection of the Ozone Layer		11 Sept 1989 (At)
Montreal Protocol on Substances that Deplete the Ozone Layer		14 June 1991 (At)
London Amendment to the Montreal Protocol		14 June 1991 (At)
Basel Convention on the Control of Transboundary Movements of Hazardous Wastes and Their Disposal		17 Dec 1991
Rotterdam Convention on Prior Informed Consent Procedure for Certain Hazardous Chemicals and Pesticides in International Trade	24 Aug 1999	
The Chemical Weapons Convention	13 Jan 1993	25 April 1997
Comprehensive Nuclear-Test-Ban Treaty (CTBT)	24 Sept 1996	
Convention on Nuclear Safety	17 June 1994	9 Apr 1996
Convention on the Prohibition of the Development, Production, Stockpiling and Use of Chemical Weapons and on their Destruction	13 Jan 1993	25 April 1997
Convention on Early Notification of a Nuclear Accident	26 Sept 1986	10 Sept 1987

Cont.

International Instruments	Signed	Ratified A: Acceded Ac: Accession At: Acceptance
Convention on Assistance in the Case of Nuclear Accident or Radiological Emergency	26 Sept 1986	10 Sept 1987
Convention on the Physical Protection of Nuclear Material	26 Oct 1979	10 Jan 1989 (A)
International Convention on the Elimination of All Forms of Racial Discrimination (CERD)	31 Mar 1996	29 Dec 1981 (Ac)
Convention on the Elimination of All Forms of Discrimination Against Women (CEDAW)	17 July 1980	4 Nov. 1980
Convention on the Rights of the Child (CRC)	29 Aug 1990	2 March 1992
Convention on the Prevention and Punishment of the Crime Of Genocide	20 July 1949	18 Apr 1983
Convention against Torture and Other Cruel, Inhuman or Degrading Treatment or Punishment (CAT)	12 Dec 1986	4 Oct 1988
International Convention on the Suppression and Punishment Of the Crime of Apartheid		18 Apr 1983 (Ac)
International Covenant on Civil and Political Rights	5 Oct 1998	
International Covenant on Economic, Social and Cultural Rights (ICESCR)	27 Oct 1997	
United Nations Educational, Scientific and Cultural Organisation Convention concerning the Protection of the World Cultural and Natural Heritage (World Heritage Convention)		12 Dec 1985

REFERENCES

Ackerly, John. 1993a. A poisonous atmosphere: Nuclear installations on the Tibetan Plateau. In *China Human Rights Forum*, Spring 1993, Washington D. C., USA, pp. 4-8.

Ackerly, J. 1993b. Wheat wars: How Tibet's fate is being decided behind the headlines. In *Tibetan Review*, 15 November, New Delhi, India.

***AFP* (*Agence France Press*). 1992.** China denies Asia Watch report on Inner Mongolia. 2 April, Paris, France.

***AFP*. 1997.** Three experts propose construction of giant dam in Tibet. 5 September, Paris, France.

***AFP*. 1998.** China's flood spreads to Tibet. 29 August, Paris, France.

***Agenda 21 For Sustainable Agricultural Development In Tibet Autonomous Region*. 1996.** Government of China publication, September, Beijing, China, p.67.

Aggarwal, S.K., G. Singh, and S. Inderjeet. 1993. *The Degrading Environment* (*Cause for global concern*). Commonwealth Publishers, New Delhi, India.

Aggarwal, A., and S. Narain. 1999. Dying wisdom: Rise, fall and potential of India's traditional water harvesting systems. In *State of India's Environment: A Citizen's Report*, no.4, Centre for Science and Environment, New Delhi, India.

Aguilar, A. F., and P. Neil. 1994. Lawmaking in the United Nations: The UN study on human rights and the environment. In *Review Of European Commission And International Environmental Law*, p. 197.

Alford, D. 1992. *Hydrological Aspects of the Himalayan Region*, ICIMOD (International Centre For Integrated Mountain Development), Occasional paper, no. 18, Kathmandu, Nepal.

American Society of Civil Engineers. 1996. Hydroelectric pumped storage technology: International experience. The Committee on Hydropower, Energy Division, USA.

Amnesty International. 1995. Persistent human rights violations in Tibet. May, London, UK. p. 2.

Anandan, S., R. Joshi, S. Biswas, S. Prasad, M.S. Shanker, S. Menezes, A. Mukherjee, A. Sinha, and P. Shastri. 1998. Vegetable crisis. In *Outlook*, 9 November, New Delhi, India, pp. 57-62.

Anderson, A.H., S. Cooke and M. Wills. 1995. *New Majority: Chinese Population Transfer Into Tibet*, Tibet Support Group, London, UK.

Apte, Robert Z., and A.R. Edwards. 1998. *Tibet: Enduring Spirit Exploited Land*. Heartsfire Books, New Mexico, USA, p. 175.

***AP* (*Associated Press*). 1998.** Flood waters surge downstream. 30 August , Beijing, China.

Atisha, Tenzin P. 1991. The Tibetan approach to ecology. In *Tibetan Review*, February, New Delhi, India, pp. 9-14.

ATC (Australia Tibet Council). 1998. *China's Nuclear Activities In Tibet*, Factsheet 13, Melbourne, Australia.

Badmayew, Peter, V. Badmayew, and L. Park. 1982. *Healing Herbs, The Heart Of Tibetan Medicine*. Red Lotus Press.

Baker, M. J. 1998. The effect of community structure on social forestry outcomes: Insights from Chota Nagpur, India. In *Mountain Research And Development*, vol. 18, no. 1, International Mountain Society, Boulder, USA, pp. 51-62.

***Beijing Review*. 1980.** Zhou Enlai, Some questions on policy towards nationalities. Beijing, China, p. 6.

***Beijing Review*. 1998a.** 23 March, New Star Publishers, Beijing, China, p. 29.

***Beijing Review*. 1998b.** 21-27 December, Beijing, China.

Bengyi. 1995. Sixty-two aid projects in full swing. In *China's Tibet*, vol. 6, no.1, Minzu Press, Beijing, China, pp. 7-10.

Berkes, F., C. Duffield, and R.B. Singh. 1998. Local knowledge in the assessment of resource sustainability: Case studies in Himachal Pradesh, India and British Columbia, Canada.

Bian, Yaowu. 1987. *The Guide To The Development Of Western China: Qinghai Province.* China Science and Technology Press, Beijing, China.

Bidhartsang, Tashi C. 1997. Interview with Mr Rilu, 25 November, Environment and Development Desk, DIIR, Dharamsala, India.

Bidhartsang, Tashi C. 1998. Eyewitness accounts: Mining in Tibet. In *Green Tibet Annual Newsletter 1998*, DIIR, Dharamsala, India, pp. 28-32.

Bohm, Robert., C. Ge, M. Russel, J. Wang, and J. Yang. 1998. Environmental taxes: China's bold initiative. In *Environment*, September.

***BBC* (*British Broadcasting Corporation*). 1997.** Qinghai province gains economic strength. 28 May, London, UK.

***BBC*. 1998**. Flooding has spread to the upper reaches of the Yangtze. 30 August, London, UK.

Brown, L., and B. Halweil. 1998. China's water shortage could shake world food security. In *World Watch*, July/August, vol. 11, no. 4, World Watch Institute, Washington D. C., pp. 10-21.

Burang, Theodore. 1974. *Tibetan Art Of Healing.* Robinson and Watkins Books Ltd, UK, p. 117.

Butler, Lee. 1998. National Press Club Speech, 2 February, Federal News Service, Washington D. C., p.17.

Cai, Guiquan. 1997. Status of the wild yak in the Qinghai-Tibetan Plateau. In *Conservation And Management Of Yak Genetic Diversity: Proceedings Of A Workshop*, 29-31 October, ICIMOD, Kathmandu, Nepal, pp. 61-65.

Cai, Shiwen. 1993. China's environmental pollution and health problems. In *Water Pollution And Human Health In China*, CCICED Conference, The World Resources Institute, Beijing, China.

Caldicott, Helen. 1997. Nuclear Power Won't Fix Our Greenhouse. *Los Angeles Times*, 30 November, Los Angeles, USA.

Chan, V. P. 1996. Thousands of Han Chinese to work in Tibet mines. In *South China Morning Post*, 2 April, Hong Kong, China.

Chang, William Y.B. 1987. Large lakes of China. In *Journal of Great Lakes Research*, International Association Great Lakes Research, vol 13 (3) pp. 235-249.

Chellaney, Brahma. 1991. Regional proliferation: Issues and challenges. In *Nuclear Proliferation In South Asia: The Prospects For Arms Control*, Stephen Cohen (edit), Westview Press, Boulder, USA, p. 323.

Chen, J., and R.L. Edmonds. 1989. Population growth management and environmental degradation in China. In *Patterns of China's Lost Harmony: A Survey Of The Country's Environmental Degradation And Protection*, Routledge, London, UK, pp. 1-14.

Chen, Shi. 1987. The origin of Bird Island. In *China's Majestic And Richly Endowed Qinghai Plateau*, Qinghai People's Publishing House, Qinghai, China, pp. 73-74.

Chen, S., and M. Zhang. 1987. A paradise for birds. In *China's Majestic And Richly Endowed Qinghai Plateau*, Qinghai People's Publishing House, Qinghai, China, pp. 6-8.

Chen, X., and Z. Lin. 1992. Abnormal climate and its influence in the 1980s in Tibet. In *Chinese Journal Of Arid Land Research*, vol. 5, no.3, Beijing, China, pp. 241-248.

Cheng, Xuemin. 1994. Hydropower development in China. In *Civil Engineering*, vol.102, no.1, pp 22-33.

***China Daily*. 1997a.** Oil and gas exploration to speed up in west. 28 May, Beijing, China.

China Daily. 1997b. Qinghai taps potential of Qaidam Basin. 3 June, Beijing, China.

***China Daily*. 1998a.** Qaidam area reveals rich oil and gas. 10 March, Beijing, China.

***China Daily*. 1998b.** World's largest canyon, a biological treasure house. 24 October, Hong Kong.

***China Daily*. 1999a.** Aid needed to protect rivers. 19 April, Beijing, China.

***China Daily*. 1999b.** Water, soil conservation improved. 30 June, Beijing, China.

***China Daily*. 1999c.** Qinghai closes nature reserve. 30 December, Beijing, China.

China Daily Business Weekly. 1997. Power projects. 21 September, Beijing, China.

China In Brief. 1994. *The Protection and Development of Wildlife.* New Star Publishers, Beijing, China, p.23.

China National Committee On Large Dams. 1987. Large dams in China: History, achievements, prospects. In *China: Water Resources And Electric Power*, Beijing, China.

China Pictorial Publications. 1994. The plateau full of hope: The three rivers development project of Tibet. New Star Press, Beijing, China.

China's Tibet. 1996. Norbusa chromite mine in Tibet. Vol. 20, Minzu Press, Beijing, China.

Chitkara, M. G. 1996. *Toxic Tibet Under Nuclear China.* APH Publishing Corporation, New Delhi, India, p. 163.

Choephel, Norbu. 1983. *Folk Culture of Tibet.* Library of Tibetan Works and Archives, Dharamsala, India.

Choephel, Yeshi. 1976. *Tibet Under Chinese Communist Rule - A Compilation Of Refugee Statements 1958-1975*, DIIR, Dharamsala, India, pp. 121-125.

Chosang, P. 1997. *Tibetan Environment And Development News.* ICT, Washington D. C., USA.

Chu, Henry. 1999. Migrants diluting Tibet cities. In *Los Angeles Times*, 3 August, Los Angeles, USA.

Chutter, Tashi. 1998. *Confidential Study On Deployment Of Chinese Occupational Forces In Tibet*, India, Tashi Chutter (Independent Publication Ltd.), p.128.

Clark, Jennifer. 1999. Vicuna, the politically correct cashmere. 24 December, *Reuters*, Milan, Italy.

Cossor, E. 1998. Denial of educational rights. In *Seminar On Tibet: South East Asian Human Rights*, TCHRD, Dharamsala, India.

Cui, Ban. 1998. Scientific exploration of Yarlung Zangbo river grand canyon. In *Beijing Review*, March/April, Beijing, China, pp.21-22.

Dalai Lama. 1962. *My Land And My People.* McGraw Hill, New York, USA.

Dalai Lama. 1995. *On The Environment, Collected Statements*, Environment and Development Desk, DIIR, Dharamsala, India, p. 66.

Dekhang, Tsultrim P. 1996. Forestry in Tibet: Problems and solutions. In *Green Tibet Annual Newsletter 1995-96*, DIIR, Dharamsala, India, pp. 12-19.

Dekhang, Tsultrim P. 1997. Biodiversity of the Tibetan Plateau. In *Green Tibet Annual Newsletter 1997*, DIIR, Dharamsala, India, pp. 18-31.

Dekhang, Tsultrim P. 1998. Nuclear weapons on the Tibetan Plateau. In *Green Tibet Annual Newsletter 1998*, DIIR, Dharamsala, India, pp. 14-27.

Dekhang, Tsultrim P. 1999. Interview with Mr Dawa Dorjee. 2 February, Environment and Development Desk, DIIR, Dharamsala, India.

Dekhang, Tsultrim P. 2000. Clearcutting of forest in Thewo, Amdo, Tibet. Interview with Mr Dorjee Tsering. 17 January, Environment and Development Desk, DIIR, Dharamsala, India.

DIIR (Department of Information and International Relations). 1992. *Tibet: Environment And Development Issues*, Environment Desk, Dharamsala, India, p. 124.

DIIR. 1995. Introduction to Tibet's environment: Present conditions and protection measures. Second edition, Environment and Development Desk, Dharamsala, India, (in Tibetan), p. 97.

DIIR. 1996a. China snubs the world with nuclear tests. In *Green Tibet Annual Newsletter 1995-96.* DIIR, Dharamsala, India, p. 22.

DIIR. 1996b. Tibet chromite mine becomes China's largest. In *Green Tibet Annual Newsletter 1995-96.* DIIR, Dharamsala, India, p. 9.

DIIR. 1996c. *Tibet: Proving Truth From Facts.* Dharamsala, India p. 113.

DIIR. 1997a. Eyewitness account: A report from Tibet. In *Green Tibet Annual Newsletter*, DIIR, Dharamsala, India, p. 33.

DIIR. 1997b. Newsbrief. In *Green Tibet Annual Newsletter*, DIIR, Dharamsala, India. p. 33.

DIIR. 1998a. *Tibet's Environment: A Crucial Issue.* Environment and Development Desk, DIIR, Dharamsala, India, p. 11.

DIIR. 1998b. Where did Tibet's forests go? Dharamsala, India, p. 11

DIIR. 1999a. Police banned Lhasa students' procession and petition for cleaner Tibetan environment. In DIIR Press Release, 8 January, Dharamsala, India.

DIIR. 1999b. Stop! World Bank WPRP Dulan Project. In An open letter to the President of World Bank, Dharamsala, India, p. 2.

Derbyshire, E., and F. Gasse. 1996. *Environmental Changes In The Tibetan Plateau And Surrounding Areas*, London University, London, UK.

Dong, Shi. 1990. Water crisis in north China and counter measures. In *Beijing Review*, 8 April, Beijing, China, pp 27-29.

Dong, Z. 1985. Present situation of the forest administration in south-west regions of China and its role in river basin management. In *Proceedings Of The International Workshop On Watershed Management*, Chengdu. ICIMOD, Kathmandu, Nepal, pp. 53-57.

Dorje, Gyurme. 1996 (Reprinted September). *Tibet Handbook With Bhutan*, Footprints Handbooks, London, England. p. 768.

Dorje, Karma, and Tsering, Norbu. 1999. Tibet's democratic, economic reform viewed: Text of report. In *Xinhua New Agency*, 24 March, Lhasa.

***Down to Earth*. 1998.** Waters of woe. 30 September, Thomson Press, New Delhi, India.

Drengson, Alan. 1993. Remembering the moral and spiritual dimensions of forests. In *Clearcut: The Tragedy Of Industrial Forestry*, Earth Island Press, California, USA, pp. 21-22.

Du, Qing. 1987. Notes on the wildlife resources in the Qinghai-Tibet Plateau. In *China's Majestic And Richly Endowed Qinghai Plateau*, Qinghai People's Publishing House, Qinghai, China, pp. 45-55.

Edmonds, R. L. 1994. *Patterns Of China's Lost Harmony: A Survey Of The Country's Environmental Degradation And Protection*. Routledge, London, UK, p. 334.

***FEER* (*Far Eastern Economic Review*). 1995.** 13 April, Hong Kong, China.

***FEER*. 1996.** 8 August, Hong Kong, China.

Fernandes, George. 1991. Keynote address. In The International Convention On Tibet And Peace In South Asia, 12-14 August, National Committee for Tibet and Peace in South Asia, New Delhi, India, pp. 17-26.

Fieldhouse, Richard. 1991. *Chinese Nuclear Weapons: A Current And Historical Overview*. Natural Resource Defense Council, March, USA.

Fisher, Richard D, Jr. 1999. Heritage report on China's Zhuhai air show. In *The Heritage Foundation Web Exclusive*, www.huiheritage.org

Fleming, Robert. 1998. The extraordinary nature of the GA. internet.www.future.org/future-gener

Forbes, A., and C. McGranahan. 1992. *Developing Tibet? A Survey Of International Development Projects*. ICT, Washington D. C., USA.

Forney, Matt. 1999. The veil of Kashmir: How many died for the shawl? *The Wall Street Journal*, Europe, 25 October.

FTC (Free Tibet Campaign). 1996. Death of a sacred lake: The Yamdrok Tso hydro-electric power generation project of Tibet. London, UK.

FTC. 1997. Mining in Tibet, indigenous people and mining. London, UK.

***Geography of Tibet*. 1991.** Vol. I and II, People's Publishing House, Lhasa, China.

Geshe, Chekawa. 1996. Oral commentary on a 12th century text. Dharamsala, India.

Goldstein, Melvyn. 1989. *A History Of Modern Tibet 1913-1951: The Demise Of The Lamaist State*. University of California Press, Berkeley and Los Angeles, p. 898.

Goldstein, M., and C. Beall. 1990. *Nomads Of Western Tibet*. University of California Press, Berkeley and Los Angeles, p.191.

***Golos Vostochnogo Turkestana*. 1997.** The Chinese Economy: The Price Of Success. 16 October, China.

Gormley, W. P 1990. The legal obligation of the international community to guarantee a pure and decent environment: The expansion of human rights norms. In *Georgetown International Environmental Law Review*, pp. 85-96.

Grey, John. 1995. Modernise, or else! Building the new Lhasa. In *HIMAL*, Jan/Feb, Vol. 8, No. 1, Kathmandu, Nepal.

Grunfeld, A.T. 1987. *The Making Of Modern Tibet.* M.E. Sharp Inc., New York, USA, p. 277.

Gyatso, Janet. 1991. *A Literary Transmission Of The Tradition Of Thang Thong Gyalpo: A Study Of Visionary Buddhism In Tibet*, University of California, Berkeley, USA.

Harris, Richard B. 1995-96. Introduction: Perspectives on wildlife conservation in China and Taiwan. In *Chinese Environment And Development*, vol. 6, no 4.

He, Bochuan. 1991. The ecological crisis: A grim legacy. In *China On The Edge, The Crisis Of Ecology And Development*, China Books and Periodicals Inc., USA, pp. 24-29.

Hessler, Peter. 1999a. Tibet through Chinese eyes. In *The Atlantic Monthly*, Part I, 4 February, USA.

Hessler, Peter. 1999b. Tibet through Chinese eyes. In *The Atlantic Monthly*, Part IV, 7 February, USA.

Horgan, J. 1996. Peaceful nuclear explosions: China's interest in this technology may scuttle a test-ban treaty. In *Scientific American*, June, USA, pp. 9-10.

Huang, Shaojian. 1996. Recent progress in China's hydro development. In *Hydropower And Dams*, Issue 5.

***Inside China Today.* 1999a.** Daily briefs: China declares support for nuclear-free Southeast Asia. 28 July, European Internet Network Inc.

***Inside China Today.* 1999b.** Emergency appeal launched as Yangtze flooding death toll passes 400. 4 August, European Internet Network Inc.

***Inside China Today.* 1999c.** Chinese panda cubs arrive at Atlanta Zoo. 10 November, European Internet Network Inc.

ICT (International Campaign for Tibet). 1992. World government and the Chinese population transfer into Tibet. In *Tibet Press Watch*, Washington, D. C., December, p. 2

ICT. 1993. *Nuclear Tibet: Nuclear Weapons And Nuclear Waste On The Tibetan Plateau.* April, Washington D. C., USA, p. 64.

ICT. 1994. *Tibet Transformed. Pictorial Essay Documenting China's Colonisation Of Tibet.* Washington D. C., USA.

ICT. 1997. *New Dam Said To Make Electricity For Pump-storage Scheme.* Washington D. C., USA.

ICIMOD. 1986. Joint report of ICIMOD in Kathmandu and the Commission for the Integrated Survey of the Natural Resources in Beijing, Kathmandu, Nepal.

ICIMOD (International Centre For Integrated Mountain Development). 1988. *Agricultural Experiences In West Sichuan And Xizang China.* At a workshop organised by ICIMOD and Chinese Academy of Sciences, 6-10 October, Kathmandu, Nepal.

ICJ (International Commission of Jurists). 1959. *The Question Of Tibet And The Rule Of Law.* ICJ Publications, Geneva, Switzerland.

ICJ. 1997. *Tibet: Human Rights And The Rule Of Law.* ICJ Publications, Geneva, Switzerland, December, p. 370.

ICLT (International Committee of Lawyers for Tibet). 1992. *Population Transfer Into Tibet.* 19 September. California, USA, p. 11.

***International Herald Tribune.* 1993**. Burst dam kills 223 in China. 30 August.

IUCN (International Union For The Conservation Of Nature And Natural Resources). 1996. *1996 IUCN Redlist Of Threatened Animals*, Cambridge, UK, p.448.

***International Water, Power And Dam Construction Monthly.* 1994.** World news: Project progress in China. December, London, UK.

***International Water, Power and Dam Construction Monthly.* 1997.** World News: In Brief. November, London, UK.

***International Water, Power and Dam Construction Monthly.* 1998.** World News: Chinese hydro moves up a gear on the Yangtze river. March, London, UK.

***Jane's Defence Weekly.* 1997.** China: Major modernisation sees slimmer giant. 10 December, UK, pp. 24-32.

Jiang, Q., and R. Zhu. 1998. Protect the Yangtze our mother river: An open letter to the Chinese people. *The Journal of Human Rights in China*, September, New York, USA, pp. 32-34.

Jones, Dow. 1999. Report on China's 1999 employment: Outlook looks gloomy. In *Business And Finance*

Asia, 24 November.

Kahlen, Wolf. 1993. Thang Thong Gyalpo: A Leonardo Of Tibet. Proceedings of the International Seminar on the Anthropology of Tibet and the Himalayas. 21-28 Dec. Ethnological Museum of the University of Zurich, Switzerland.

Kanwal, Gurmeet. 1999. China's long march to world power status: Strategic challenge for India. In *Strategic Analysis*, vol. 22, no. 11, Institute for Defence Studies and Analysis, New Delhi, India.

***Keji Ribao*. 1999.** *Science and Technology Daily*, 31 July, Beijing, China.

Kent, A. 1998. The universal declaration of human rights and China. In *China Rights Forum: The Journal Of Human Rights In China*, Fall 1998, New York, USA.

Kewley, Vanya. 1990. *Tibet: Behind The Ice Curtain*. Grafton Books, London, UK, p. 396.

Lafitte, G. 1996. Upper Mekong: Ethnicity, identity and economy. In *Development Dilemmas In The Mekong Subregion*, Working Proceedings 1-2 October, ed. Bob Stensholt, published by Monash Asia Institute, Monash University, Clayton, Australia, pp. 39-44.

Lafitte, Gabriel. 1998a. Fertilisers. In *Foreign Investment In Tibet*, September, ATC, Melbourne, Australia.

Lafitte, Gabriel. 1998b. An end to the nomadic way of life? In *Tibetan Bulletin*, Oct/Dec. 1998, DIIR, Dharamsala, pp. 18-20.

Lafitte, Gabriel. 1999. World Bank Tsaidam population transfer project. In *Draft TIN Update*, 29 March, London, UK.

Lally, Michelle. 1997. Revamped law leads Chinese into new era. July/August, US Embassy, Beijing, China.

Lawrence, S.V. 1998. China: Seeing the green right. In *Far Eastern Economic Review,* 22 October, pp. 21-28.

Leckie, Scott. 1994. *Destruction By Design: Housing Rights Violations In Tibet*. Centre on Housing Rights and Evictions, Amsterdam, The Netherlands, p. 199.

Lewis, W., and L. Xue. 1988. *China Builds The Bomb*. Stanford University Press, USA.

Lhundup, Pema. 1976. *Tibet Under Chinese Communist Rule: A Compilation Of Refugee Statements, 1958-1975*, DIIR, Dharamsala, India, pp. 103-109.

Li, Bosheng. 1995. Biodiversity of the Qinghai-Tibetan Plateau and its conservation. ICIMOD, Discussion Paper Series no. MNR 95/3, Kathmandu, Nepal, p. 47.

Li, J., N. He, F. Kong, and L. Ross. 1988. Price and policy: The keys to revamping China's forestry resources. In *Public Policies And The Misuses Of Forest Resources*, World Resource Institute, Cambridge University Press, New York, USA, pp. 205-245.

Li, Mingsen. 1996. Richly endowed Amdo area in east Tibet. In *China's Tibet*, vol.7, no.2, Minzu Press, Beijing, China, pp. 44-45.

Li, F. Wang, and D. Yu. 1992. Farmers' strategies in the mountain areas of west Sichuan: China. In *Sustainable Mountain Agriculture*. Intermediate Technology Publications, Oxford, UK.

Li, Wenhua. 1993. Forests of the Himalayan-Hengduan Mountains of China and strategies for their sustainable development. ICIMOD, Kathmandu, Nepal, p. 159.

Liu, Yanhua. 1997. Dynamics of highland agriculture in Lhasa district, Tibet. In *Conservation And Management Of Yak Genetic Diversity*, Proceedings of a workshop, 29-31 October, ICIMOD, Kathmandu, Nepal, p. 28.

Li, Yuzhen. 1996. Hydro development in the Yangtze River Basin. In *Hydropower And Dams*, issue 5.

Liao, Dongfeng. 1997. Sixty-two aid projects: A boon for the Tibetans. In *China's Tibet*, vol. 8, no.4, Minzu Press, Beijing, China, pp. 7-11.

Long, R., and Ma, Yushou. 1997. Qinghai's yak production systems. In *Conservation And Management Of Yak Genetic Diversity,* Proceedings of a workshop, 29-31 October, ICIMOD, Kathmandu, Nepal, pp. 105-114.

Longrigg, C., and B. Rowe. 1991. Deforestation in western China and Tibet. In *Essential Environmental Materials On Tibet*, ICT, Washington D. C., pp.14-19.

Longworth, J., and G. Williamson. 1993. *China's Pastoral Region: Sheep And Wool, Minority Nationalities, Rangeland Degradation and Sustainable Development.* Australian Centre for International Agriculture Research, Canberra,

Australia, pp. 42-45.

Lowe, Justin. 1998. Environmentalists condemn deadly fashion trend for endangered species product. In *World Tibet News*, 3 December, Calgary, Canada.

Mao, Yu-Shi. 1998. *The Economic Cost Of Environmental Degradation In China: A summary.*

Margolis, Eric. 1997. Nuclear dangers in the high Himalayas. In *Inside Track On World News*, 11 August.

McCue, Gary. 1991. *Trekking In Tibet: A Traveller's Guide.* The Mountaineers, Seattle, USA. p. 304.

McCully, P. 1996. *Silenced Rivers: The Ecology And Politics Of Large Dams.* Zed Books, London, UK.

McRae, Michael. 1999. Trouble in Shangri-la: The siege of the Tsangpo. In *National Geographic Adventure Spring 1999*, pp. 97-106.

Menzies, N., and N. Peluso. 1991. Rights of access to upland forest resources in southwest China. In *The Journal Of World Forest Management*, vol. 6, pp.1-20.

Miehe, G. 1998. Assessment of naturally forested areas in Southern Xizang. Tibet's biodiversity: conservation and management. In WWF (World Wide Fund for Nature) China Programme International Workshop, September, Lhasa, Tibet.

Miller, Daniel J. 1997a. Conserving biological diversity in the HKH-Tibetan Plateau rangelands. In *Rangelands And Pastoral Development In The Hindu-Kush-Himalayas.* Proceedings of a Regional Experts' Meeting, 5-7 November, ICIMOD, Kathmandu, Nepal, pp. 47-52.

Miller, Daniel J. 1997b. Rangelands and pastoral development: An introduction. In *Rangelands And Pastoral Development In The Hindu-Kush-Himalayas.* Proceedings of a Regional Experts' Meeting, 5-7 November, ICIMOD, Kathmandu, Nepal. pp. 1-5.

Miller, Daniel J. 1997c. A photo essay of Himalayan and Tibetan pastoralism. In *Rangelands And Pastoral Development In The Hindu-Kush-Himalayas.* Proceedings of a Regional Experts' Meeting, 5-7 November, ICIMOD, Kathmandu, Nepal. pp. 58-140.

Ming, Wan. 1998. China's economic growth and the environment in the Asia-Pacific region. *Asian Survey*, April, vol. 38, no. 4, pp. 365-378.

Ministry of Forests: People's Republic of China. 1997. In *China-Forestry Development In Poor Areas Project.* Application and submission to the World Bank, 6 January, Beijing, China.

Molnar, P. 1989. The geologic evolution of the Tibetan Plateau. *American Scientist*, vol. 77, pp. 350-360.

Namgyal, D. 1995. Director of the Tibet Mining Bureau, Geological prospecting and mining in Tibet. In *China's Tibet* no. 5, Beijing, China, pp. 3-5.

NEPA (National Environmental Protection Agency). 1997. 1996 Report on the State of the Environment. Beijing, China, (Chinese language edition).

Netting, R. 1997. Unequal commoners and uncommon equity: Property and community among smallholder farmers. In *The Ecologist*, 27 January, pp.28-31.

NSP (New Star Publishers). 1994. *The protection and development of wildlife.* First edition 1994. China in Brief series, Beijing, China, p. 23.

***New York Times.* 1985.** A vast sea of Chinese threatens Tibet. 9 August. New York, USA.

Norbu, Dawa. 1999. Tibetan buffers good for both India and China. In *The Statesman*, 18 September, Calcutta, India.

NORAD (Norwegian Agency For Development Co-operation). 1997. *State Of The Environment, China 97.* Oslo, Norway.

Norwill, J. 1997. Mining in Tibet. Free Tibet Campaign, UK, p. 20.

Nyima, Paintog. 1996. Repolished pearl in Xigaze. In *China's Tibet*, vol.7, no.2, Minzu Press, Beijing, China. pp. 16-17.

O'Donnell, Lynne. 1999. Shawl casts pall over antelope. In *The Australian*, 23 October, Canberra, Australia.

Palbar, Tenzin. 1994. *The Tragedy Of My Homeland.* Narthang Publications, Dharamsala, India, p. 453. (Tibetan language edition).

***People's Daily.* 1998.** 31 March, Beijing, China.

Pomfret, John. 1998a. Despite floods China is running dry. In *The Washington Post*, October, Washington D. C., USA.

Pomfret, John. 1998b. In China, a battle to turn tide to save environment, but flood disaster highlights policy problems. In *The Washington Post*, November, Washington D. C., USA.

Popovic, N. 1996. In pursuit of environmental human rights: Commentary on the Draft Declaration of Principles on Human Rights and the Environment. *Columbia Human Rights Law Review*, pp. 490-491.

***Radio Lhasa* (Tibet People's Broadcasting Station). 1995.** 18 January, Lhasa, Tibet.

Rawling, C. 1905. *The Great Plateau.* Edward Arnold, London.

Reiter, Elmar. 1981. The Tibet connection. In *Natural History*, September, pp. 51-56.

Reiter, Elmar. 1993. Tibet and the earth's climate. In *Environment And The People of Tibet, the Third Pole:* Conference paper, 30 September - 1 October, Paris, France.

Rekhi, S., and K. S. Singh. 1998. The great onion disaster. In *India Today*, 9 November, New Delhi, India, pp.20-26.

Ren M., Renzhang, and H. Bao. 1985. *An Outline Of China's Physical Geography.* Foreign Language Press, Beijing, China, p. 471.

***Renmin Ribao.* 1994.** Three-river exploitation plan. 15 August, Beijing, China.

***Renmin Ribao.* 1995.** How armed police braved high altitude to build power stations of Tibetans. 18 September, Beijing, China.

Rennie, David. 1998. In *The Daily Telegraph*, 15 October, London, UK

Research and Analysis Centre. 1991. *Rich Minerals Of Tibet.* Department of Security, Dharamsala, India.

***Reuters News Agency*, 1994.** 27 January, London, UK.

***Reuters News Agency*, 1999.** China's northwest province joins hands to tap natural gas resources. In *Alexander's Gas & Oil Connections*, 15 October, London, UK.

Richardson, S. D. 1988. The forest economy of Tibet. In *Commonwealth Forestry Review*, vol. 67, no.3, pp. 253-62.

Richardson, S. D. 1990. *Forests and Forestry In China: Changing Patterns Of Resource Development.* Island Press, California, USA, p. 350.

Saunders, K. 1998. Birth control and population transfer in Tibet. In *Seminar On Tibet, South East Asia Human Rights*, TCHRD, Dharamsala, India.

Schaller, George B. 1994. *The Last Panda.* The University of Chicago Press, Chicago, USA p. 300.

Schaller, George B. 1997. *Tibet's Hidden Wilderness: Wildlife And Nomads Of The Chang Thang Reserve.* Harry N. Abrams Inc., New York, USA. p. 168.

Schaller, George B. 1998. *Wildlife of the Tibetan Steppe.* The University of Chicago Press, Chicago, USA, p. 373.

Schaller, George B. and B. Y. Gu. 1994. Comparative ecology of ungulates in the Aru Basin of northwest Tibet. In *National Geographic Research And Exploration*, vol. 10, no. 3, pp. 266-293.

Schwartz, R. 1993. International legal protection for victims of environmental abuse. In *Yale Journal of International Law*, USA, p.355.

Schwartz, R. 1995. The reforms revisited: The implementation of Chinese economic policy and the future of rural producers in Tibet. ICT, 1 November, Washington D. C., USA, pp. 4-8.

Science Press. 1990. Terrain map of the Qinghai-Xizang Plateau. Institute of Geography, Chinese Academy of Sciences, Zhonghua Printing House, Shanghai, China.

Shakabpa, W. D. 1984. *Tibet: A Political History.* Potala Publications, New York, USA, p. 249.

Sharma. P. 1988. China's chemical warfare manoeuvres. In *The Hindustan Times*, 9 October, New Delhi, India.

Shelton. 1991. Human rights, environmental rights and the right to environment. In *Stanford Journal of International Law*, USA, p.103.

Shen Dajun. 1995. Research on the rational use of water resources on the Lhasa river, Tibet. In *Modelling And Management Of Sustainable Basin-Scale Water Resource Systems*, July, Kathmandu, Nepal, pp. 151-156.

Slesser, Malcolm. 1998. *Macmillan Dictionary of Energy*, USA, pp. 166-177.

Smil, Vaclav. 1984. *The Bad Earth: Environmental*

Degradation In China. M.E. Sharpe Inc., New York, USA, p. 247.

Song, X., and J. Yao. 1998. Resources Exploitation And Conservation Of Qaidam Basin Under The Principle Of Sustainable Development. At the International Symposium on the Qinghai Tibet Plateau: Xining, July 24, China.

***South China Morning Post*. 1992.** Tibet's grassland under threat. 26 September, Hong Kong, China.

***South China Morning Post*. 1999a.** $300,000 fine for rare shawls dealer. 14 April, Hong Kong, China.

***South China Morning Post*. 1999b.** CNSPC breaks ice with Tibet's first field. 22 July, Hong Kong, China.

SEPA (State Environmental Protection Administration). 1999. *1998 Report On The State Of Environment In China*, 1 June, SEPA, Beijing, China.

Stockman, L., and P. Seibert. 1997. The Yamdrok Tso Hydropower Plant in Tibet: A Multi-Facetted And Highly Controversial Project. At the International Conference on Large Scale Water Resource Development in Developing Countries: New Dimensions of Prospects and Problems, 20-23 October, Kathmandu, Nepal.

Stoddart, L. A., A. D. Smith, and T. W. Smith. 1975. *Range management*. McGraw Hill, New York, USA.

Stone, P. 1992. *1992: The State Of The World's Mountains*. Zed Books, London, UK, p. 191.

***Sunday Morning Post*. 1989.** Mainland stores nuclear waste amid claims of ignorance. 6 August, Hong Kong, China.

Tenzin, Gendhun. 1998. Interview on 3 July, 1998, Environment and Development Desk, DIIR, CTA, Dharamsala, India.

Tewari, Manish. 1998. Waters of woe. In *Down To Earth*, 30 September, vol. 7, no. 9, Thomson Press, New Delhi, India, p.16.

Tharpa, Liushar Thupten. 1968. *Renmin Ribao*, 22 November 1959 quoting speech by Chairman Mao, Union Research Institute, Tibet 1950-67, Document 9, p. 45. Hong Kong, China.

***The Hindu*, 1998.** Pokharan II and Indo-US relations. 12 October, Madras, India.

***The Indian Express*. 1998.** Chinese missiles anti-US. 2 May, New Delhi, India.

***The Indian Express*. 1999.** Wary of American plan, China tests new anti-ship missile, laser weapon. 16 November, Chandigarh, India.

***The Statesman*. 1992.** China dumping N-waste in Tibet: Dalai Lama. 21 January, New Delhi, India.

***The Times Of India*. 1988.** Nuclear missiles in Tibet. 24 March , New Delhi., India.

***The Times Of India*. 1996.** Activities at airbases in Tibet cause concern. 17 July, New Delhi., India.

***The Times of India*. 1997.** China admits it has powerful N-arms. 23 July, New Delhi, India.

***The Times of India*. 1999.** When the fur flies. 22 December, New Delhi, India.

***The Tribune*. 1997.** Russia sells China hi-tech artillery. 5 July, Chandigarh, India.

***The Tribune*. 1998.** China threat number one. 4 May, Chandigarh, India.

The World Bank. 1997. Clear water, blue skies: China's environment in the next century. The World Bank, Washington D. C., USA.

The World Resources Institute. 1998. In *World Resources 1998-99: A Guide to the Global Environment*. Oxford University Press, New York, USA, p. 369.

'TAR' ('Tibet Autonomous Region') Economy Co-ordination Committee. *A Guide to Investment in Tibet*. Beijing, China.

***Tibet Daily*. 1994.** Tibet article urges 'correct' nationalities' views. 4 July, Lhasa, China.

***Tibet Daily*. 1996.** Mining in Zangbei. 4 December, Lhasa, China.

***Tibet Daily*. 1997.** 1996 TAR Environment Report. 27 June, Lhasa, China.

***Tibet Daily*. 1998a.** One river, two streams project. 27 January, Lhasa, China.

Tibet Daily. 1998b. Increase in daily output of natural gas reserve in Tsaidam Basin (in Tibetan), 31 July, Lhasa, China.

TIN (Tibet Information Network). 1991. *TIN News*

Update, 18 September, London, UK, p. 32.

TIN. 1992. Tibetans dying from uranium mine waste. *TIN News Update*, 11 September, London, UK.

TIN. 1995. *TIN Background Briefing Paper* no. 28, 28 December, London, UK.

TIN. 1996. River captured for new power station. *TIN News Update*, London, UK.

TIN. 1997a. Gold mining in Tibet. *TIN News Update*, January, London, UK.

TIN. 1997b. Testimony of a 25 year old from Diru, Kham. TIN News Update, February, London, UK.

TIN. 1997c. A poisoned arrow: The secret report of the 10th Panchen Lama. London, UK.

TIN. 1997d. CNNC opens seven mines to boost supplies. *TIN News Update*, 26 August, London, UK.

TIN. 1997e. Tibet seeks investments for major copper mine. TIN Unpublished Report, London, UK.

TIN. 1998a. More than 50 deaths in Tibet floods. *TIN News Update*, 3 September, London, UK.

TIN. 1998b. Harsh punishment for environmental protest. *TIN News Update*, 15 December, London, UK.

TIN. 1998c. *News review: Reports from Tibet.* March, London, UK. pp. 71.

TIN. 1998d. China floods force logging ban in Eastern Tibet. 26 August, London, UK. p. 3

TIN. 1999a. Section I: Pillar industries, A: Agriculture. In *TIN News Review No. 27- Reports from Tibet, 1998*, London, UK. pp. 59-64.

TIN. 1999b. Social evils: Prostitution and pornography in Lhasa. *TIN Background Briefing Paper* no. 31, London, UK. p. 26.

TIN. 1999c. Nomads killed in pasture fights. In *TIN News Update*, 21 June, London, England.

***Tibet People's Broadcasting Station.* 1995.** 18 January, Lhasa, China.

***Tibet TV.* 1991.** In Standard Chinese 1130 gmt, 21 December, Lhasa, China.

***Tibet Times.* 1999.** Destruction to Tibet's environment ignored by China. (In Tibetan). 30 June, Dharamsala.

***Tibetan Bulletin.* 1992a.** The de-greening of Tibet's grasslands. January/February, DIIR, Dharamsala, India, pp.18-20.

***Tibetan Bulletin.* 1992b.** Chinese agricultural chief defends land exploitation in Tibet. May/June, DIIR, Dharamsala, India, pp. 14-16.

***Tibetan Bulletin.* 1992c.** Tibetan approach to ecology. May /June, DIIR, Dharamsala, India, p. 29.

TCHRD (Tibetan Centre For Human Rights And Democracy). 1997a. Imprisoned for protesting environmental destruction in Tibet. In *Human Rights Update*, vol. 2, 30 April, Dharamsala, India.

TCHRD. 1997b. China's gold mining in Tibet. In *Human Rights Update*, vol. 2, 15 July, Dharamsala, India.

TCHRD. 1997c. China in Tibet: Striking hard against human rights. In *Human Rights Annual Report 1997.* Dharamsala, India. pp. 70-75.

TCHRD. 1997d. *The Next Generation: The State Of Education In Tibet Today*, Dharamsala, India. p. 13.

TCHRD. 1998. Details on Powo Tramo. In *Human Rights Update*, vol. 2, no. 8, 15 October, Dharamsala, India, p. 2.

TCHRD. 1999. Tibet: Crackdown on humanity. In *Annual Report 1998: Human Rights Violation In Tibet*, Dharamsala, India. p. 124.

***Tibetan Review.* 1997a.** China reports record mineral finds in Tibet. July, New Delhi, India.

***Tibetan Review.* 1997b.** Tibet to meet China's copper shortage. September, New Delhi, India, p. 7.

***Tibetan Review.* 1997c.** China exploits Qinghai's record mineral reserves. November, New Delhi, India, p. 5.

***Tibetan Review.* 1998a.** Tibet news, China to exploit Tibet's vast minefields. New Delhi, India, p. 4.

***Tibetan Review.* 1998b.** Deforestation and the Yangtze flood. September, New Delhi, India.

Tibetan Women's Association. 1996. *Cultivating Genocide: A Message To The World Food Summit*, FAO (Food and Agriculture Organisation), November, Rome, Italy, pp.13-17.

Tibetan Youth Congress. 1994. *Strangers In Their Own Country: Chinese Population Transfer In Tibet And*

Its Impacts. Dharamsala, India.

Tsering, Dawa. 1998. The threat from Chinese imperialism to Tibet's survival. In *Sino-Tibetan Dialogue Finding Common Ground.* At the Conference on Tibet: Tibetan Community in Europe and The Alliance for a Democratic China, London, UK.

Tsering, Tashi. 1996. The spiritual and cultural significance of Yamdrok Tso. In *Death Of A Sacred Lake: The Yamdrok Tso Hydro-electric Power Generation Project of Tibet.* Free Tibet Campaign, London, UK, pp.25-26.

Tsundue, Kunchok. 1994. *Change In Continuity In Tibetan Agriculture*, Ruhr University, Bochum, Germany.

Tsundue, Kunchok. 1999a. Revisiting the roots. In *Tibetan Bulletin*, January/February, DIIR, Dharamsala, India.

Tsundue, Kunchok. 1999b. Pastoral-nomadism of Tibet. *In Between Tradition And Modernisation, People And Rangelands Building The Future.* Proceedings of the VI International Rangeland Congress, 19-23 July, Queensland, Australia.

Umali, D.L. 1993. Irrigation induced salinity: A growing problem for development and environment. In World Bank Technical Paper, no. 215.

United Nations Centre For Human Rights. 1996. Fact sheet No. 16, The Committee on Economic, Social and Cultural Rights, p. 6.

UNDP (United Nations Development Programme). 1994. *Human Development Report 1994*, Oxford University Press, New Delhi, India.

UNDP. 1997. *The People's Republic Of China: Development Co-operation Report 1995*, June, Beijing, China, p. 322.

***UNI* (*United News of India*). 1988.** China plans to bury radioactive waste. 28 September.

US Embassy (United States Embassy). 1996a. A report on gold mining in China: Taming the wild west. May, Beijing, China.

US Embassy. 1996b. Grassland degradation in Tibetan regions of China - Possible recovery strategies. September, Beijing, China.

US Embassy. 1996c. Multidisciplinary approaches to assess grassland ecology and degradation in Tibetan regions of China - Impact on policy? September, Beijing, China.

US Embassy. 1996d. The Northwest Institute of Biology Beijing, China.

US Embassy. 1997. The environment enters the Chinese criminal code. May, Beijing, China.

US Embassy. 1998a. Illegal cutting of forests by local governments common. August, Beijing, China.

US Embassy. 1998b. Yangtze floods and the environment. 10 August, Beijing, China.

US Embassy. 1998c. Yet Central Government orders and laws are often ignored. August, Beijing, China.

United States Environmental Protection Agency. 1994. Extraction and beneficiation of ores and minerals. Technical Resource Document, vol. 4, Office of Solid Waste, USA.

UNPO (Unrepresented Nations And Peoples Organisation). 1997. *China's Tibet: The world's largest remaining colony.* In Report Of A Fact-finding Mission And Analyses Of Colonialism And Chinese Rule In Tibet, The Hague, The Netherlands, p. 83.

Verghese, B. G. 1990. Waters of hope: Integrated water resource development, co-operation within the Himalaya-Ganga-Brahmaputra-Barak basin. Centre for Policy Research, New Delhi, India.

Waiser, Khedup. 1998. Chinese development trends in Tibet. In *Green Tibet Annual Newsletter 1998*, DIIR, CTA, Dharamsala, India, p. 47.

Wang, Hai. 1984. Qinghai – a treasure province. In *China Reconstructs*, January, Beijing, pp.30-33.

Wang, Hongchang. 1993. *Deforestation And Dessication In China: A Preliminary Study.*

Wang, X., and N. Bai. 1991. *The Poverty Of Plenty*, Macmillan, London, UK.

Wangdu. 1998. Urgent need of the conservation of wildlife in Tibet. In *China's Tibet*, Issue 9, vol. 33, Beijing, China (in Tibetan).

Weiskopf, Michael. 1984. China reportedly agrees to store western nuclear wastes. In *The* Washington Post, 18 February, Washington D. C., USA, p. 21.

Winkler, Daniel. 1996. Forests economy and

deforestation in the Tibetan prefectures of west Sichuan. *Commonwealth Forestry Review*, vol. 75, no.4, pp. 296-310.

Winkler, Daniel. 1998. Deforestation in eastern Tibet: Human impacts past and present. In *Development, Society And Environment In Tibet*. Proceedings of the 7th Seminar, International Association of Tibetan Studies (IATS), pp. 79-96.

Winkler, Daniel. 1999. Floods, logging, and hydro-electricity; the impact on Tibetan Areas. In *World Tibet News*, 27 January, Calgary, Canada.

World Bank. 1997. China. File://windows/desktop/webpages/DIIR Report/WBchina.htm. World bank group home, Beijing, China.

***World Journal*. 1998.** Kokonor Lake drying up. 14 May, T.W.Wang Inc., New York, USA.

WTN (*World Tibet News*). 1998. 28 August, Calgary, Canada.

World Watch. 1995. High priorities: Conserving mountain ecosystems and cultures. Paper no. 123, February, Washington D. C., USA, p. 35

WWF (World Wide Fund For Nature). 1998. Tibet's Biodiversity: Conservation And Management International Workshop, 30 August - 4 September, Lhasa, Tibet, p.42.

Wu, Ning. 1997. Conservation of yak biodiversity and its development potential in Western Sichuan, China. In *Conservation And Management Of Yak Genetic Diversity*. Proceedings of a workshop 29-31 October, ICIMOD, Kathmandu, Nepal, p. 220.

Wu, Sugong and Feng, Zuojian. 1992. Characteristics and utilisation and conservation of Tibetan biological resources. Proceedings of the first workshop of the Chinese Research Society of the Qinghai-Tibetan Plateau, Beijing Science Press, Beijing, pp. 29-89.

Wu, Xiutao. 1990. Hydropower construction in Sichuan. In *Modern Power Systems*, October.

Xiao, Hao. 1992. Water, more expensive than gold. In *China's Tibet*, vol.3, Minzu Press, Beijing, China, pp.18-19.

***Xinhua News Agency*. 1992.** Qinghai develops medium, small hydropower stations. 6 April, Beijing, China.

***Xinhua News Agency*. 1996a.** Tibet to expand mining industry. 22 January, Beijing, China.

***Xinhua News Agency*. 1996b.** 21 March, Beijing, China.

***Xinhua News Agency*. 1997a.** 1 August, Beijing, China.

***Xinhua News Agency*. 1997b.** 20 August, Beijing, China.

***Xinhua News Agency*. 1997c.** 15 October, Beijing, China.

***Xinhua News Agency*. 1998a.** 27 April, Beijing, China.

***Xinhua News Agency*. 1998b.** China: Tibet sets goal of 15 % growth. 2 July, Beijing, China.

***Xinhua News Agency*. 1998c.** Tibetans raise environmental protection concerns. 30 July, Beijing, China.

***Xinhua News Agency*. 1998d.** Southwest China province bans forest logging. 5 September, Beijing, China.

***Xinhua News Agency*. 1998e.** China reports Brahmaputra in Tibet facing threat. 17 September, Beijing, China.

***Xinhua News Agency*. 1998f.** Tibet's Yamzho Yumco power station operational. 19 September, Beijing, China.

***Xinhua News Agency*. 1998g.** Tibet: Water control project underway. 6 October, Beijing, China.

***Xinhua News Agency*. 1998h.** More forests saved after summer floods in China. 24 November, Beijing, China.

***Xinhua News Agency*. 1998i.** March, Beijing, China.

***Xinhua News Agency*. 1998j.** 5 June, Beijing, China.

***Xinhua News Agency*. 1999a.** 16 January, Beijing, China.

***Xinhua News Agency*. 1999b.** 14 March, Beijing, China.

***Xinhua News Agency*. 1999c.** 7 April, Xining, China.

***Xinhua News Agency*. 1999d.** 18 August, Beijing, China.

***Xinhua News Agency*. 1999e.** Chinese police gold hunters find 'high quality' mines in Tibet. 17 September, Beijing, China.

***Xizang Ribao*. 1994.** 5 February, Lhasa, China.

Xu, C., and B. Zhong. 1993. Yangtze exodus begins. *Panoscope*, no.37, London, UK.

Yan, Zhenzhong. 1998. Review of the three-river project (I). In *China's Tibet*, vol.9, no.1, Minzu Press, Beijing, China, pp. 16-19.

Yang, Y.P. 1986. Importance of the ecological balance of sub-alpine forest of West Sichuan. In *Tibet's Biodiversity: Conservation And Management*. Proceedings of WWF China Program International Workshop, September, Lhasa, pp. 41-44.

Yang Yichou. 1998. Scientific exploration in the Yarlung Zangbo grand canyon. In *China's Tibet*, vol. 9, no.5, Minzu Press, Beijing, China, pp. 40-45.

Yufan, Hao. 1992. Environmental protection in Chinese foreign policy. In *Journal Of NorthEast Asian Studies*, vol. 1, no. 3, pp. 26-46.

***ZDF Die Welt.* 1998.** A giant project on the roof of the world / effects on the environment feared – proponents want to prevent floods. 7 January, Save Tibet Austria.

Zhang, Chunguang. 1997. Fish resources in Tibet. In *China's Tibet*, vol.8, no.5, Minzu Press, Beijing, pp.38-40.

Zhang, Rongzu. 1989. Case study on mountain environmental management: Nyemo county (Tibet). ICIMOD Occasional paper, no. 13, ICIMOD, August, Kathmandu, Nepal, p. 76.

Zhang, Tianlu and Zhang, Mei. 1994. *The Present Population Of The Tibetan Nationality In China*. Beijing, China.

Zhang, Weiming. 1989. Synopsis of the west-route project of south-to-north water transfer from the Yangtze to the Yellow River. In *Taming The Yellow River: Silt And Floods*, Kluwer Academic Publishers, pp. 677-686.

Zhang, Weiping, et al., eds. 1994. *Twenty years of China's Environment Protection Administrative Management*. China Environmental Science Press, Beijing, China.

Zhao, Ang. 1992. The crisis of the forest industry in the Tibetan area of Sichuan and ways toward positive development. In *Economic Geography*, vol. 12, Changsha, China, pp. 55-61.

Zhao, Songqiao. 1992. The Qinghai-Xizang (Tibetan) Plateau: Its physical environment and economic development. In *The Chinese Journal Of Arid Land Research*, vol.5, no.3, Beijing, China, pp. 203-222.

Zheng, Q., and J. Wu. 1995. Numerical study on the dynamic and thermodynamic effects of the Qinghai-Xizang Plateau on the seasonal transition in the early summer in East Asia. In *Chinese Academy Of Meteorological Sciences*, vol. 9, no. 1, pp. 35-47.

***Zhongguo Xinwen She News Agency.* 1997.** 13 October, Beijing, China.

Zhu, Li. 1990. Protecting water resources. In *China Daily*, August, Beijing, China, pp. 10-12. ■

Printed at ARCHANA, Ph. : 431-1992, 432-2834

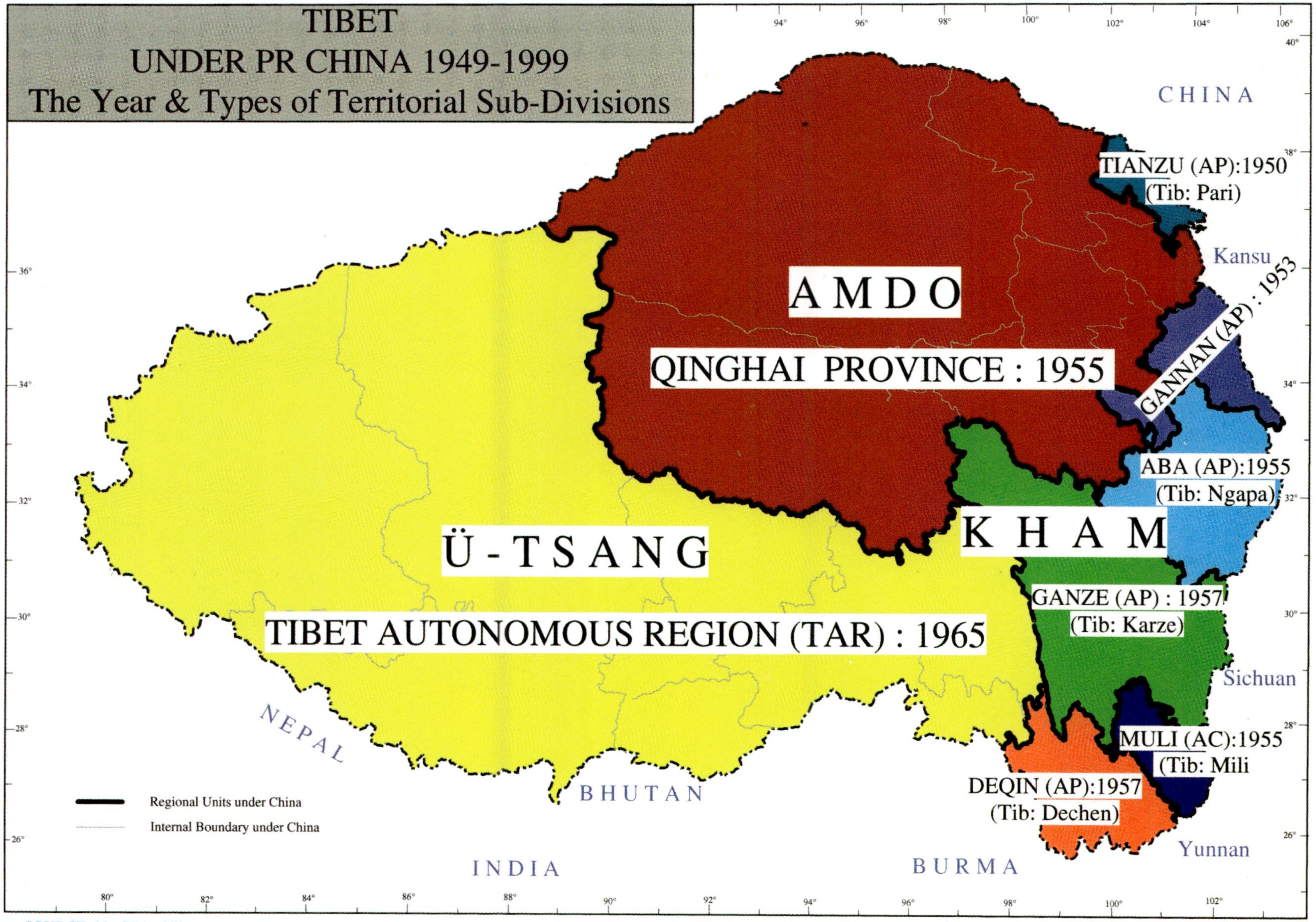

SOURCE: IO, CTA 1979

Digital-Cartography & Design: Planning Council, CTA, Dharamsala-2000

TIBET
Hydrographic System

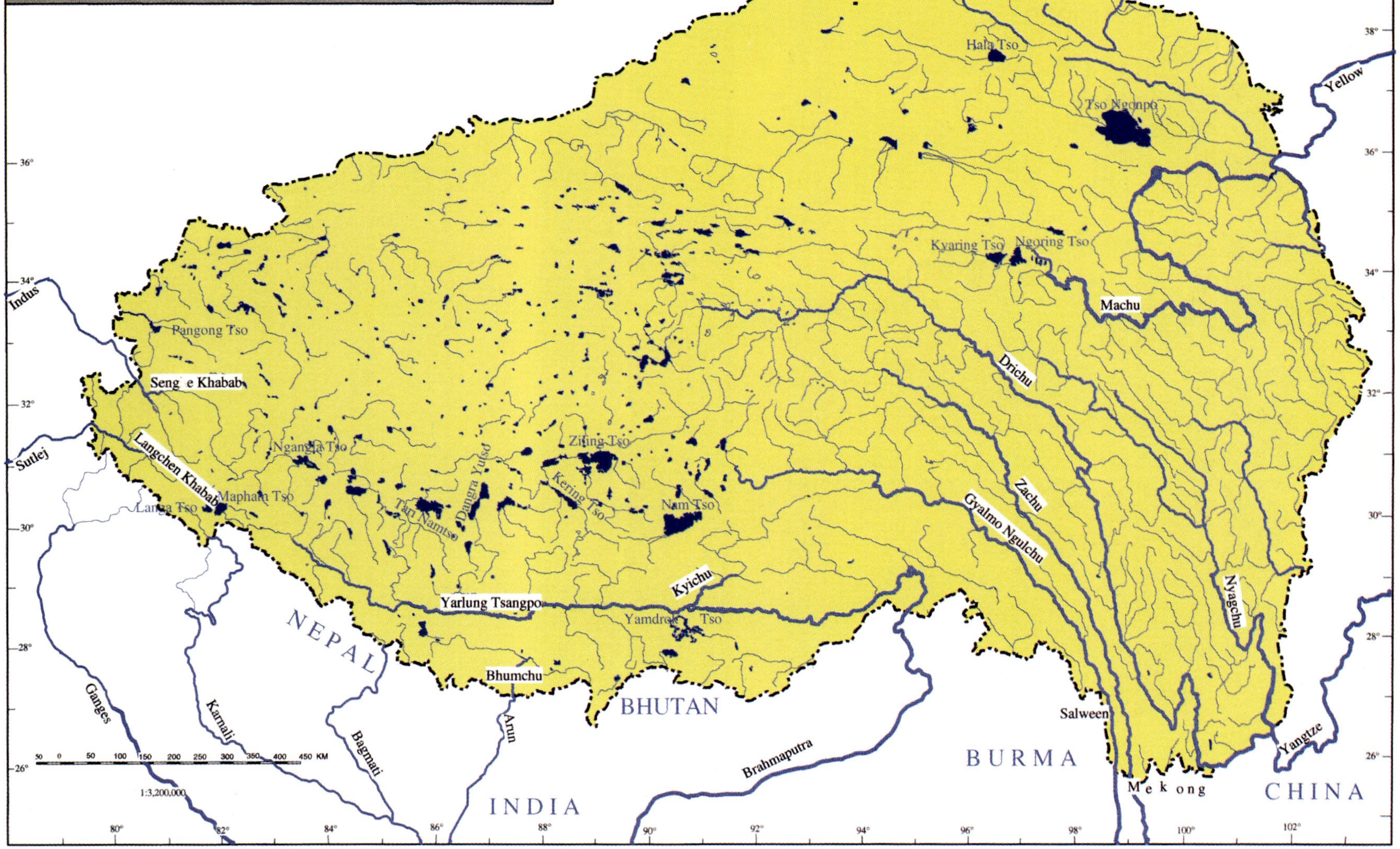

SOURCE: AMI 1998; Information Office, CTA 1979

CARTOGRAPHY & DESIGN: Planning Council, CTA, Dharamsala-2000

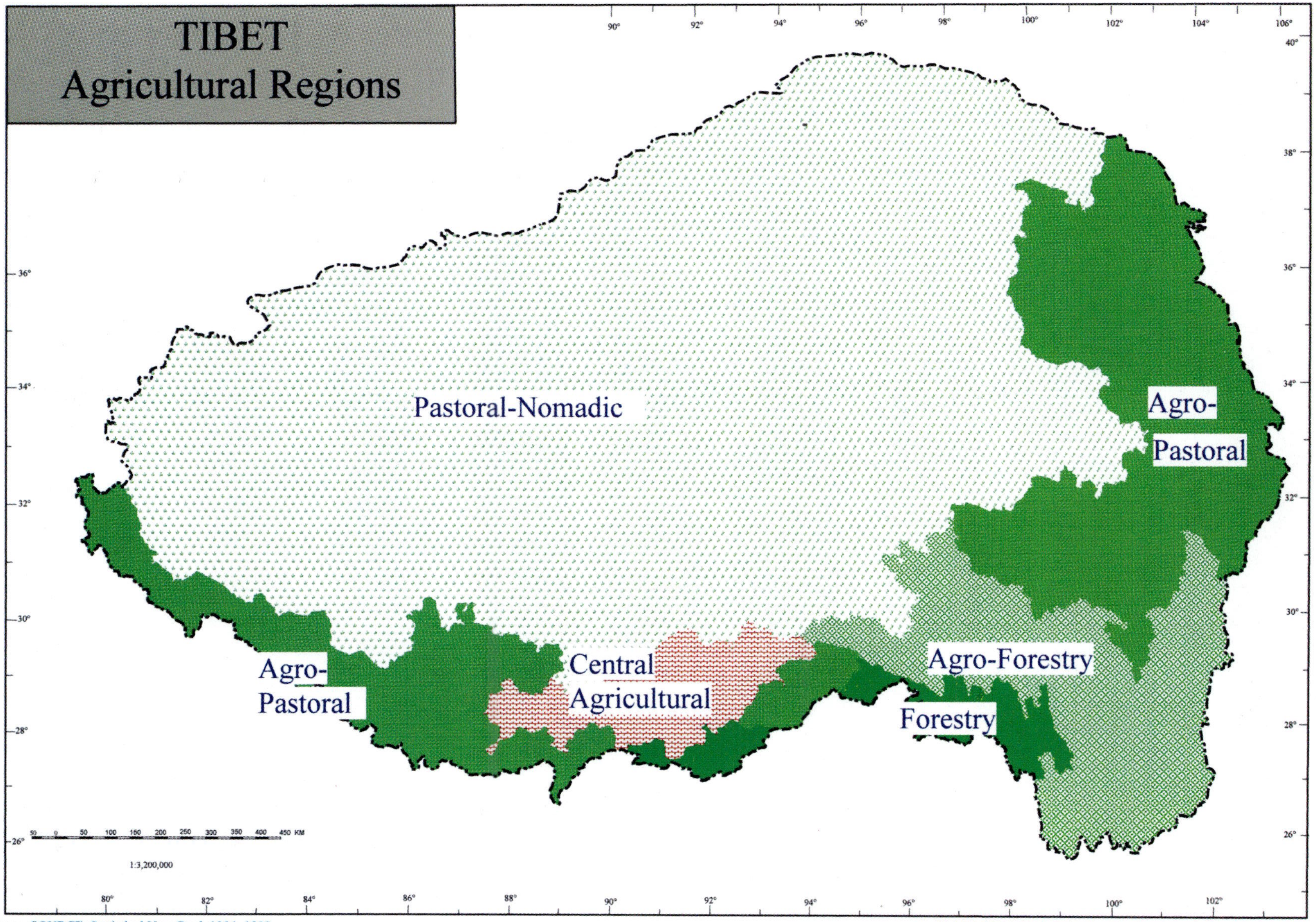

SOURCE: Statistical Year Book 1994; 1998

CARTOGRPAHY & DESIGN: Planning Council, CTA-2000

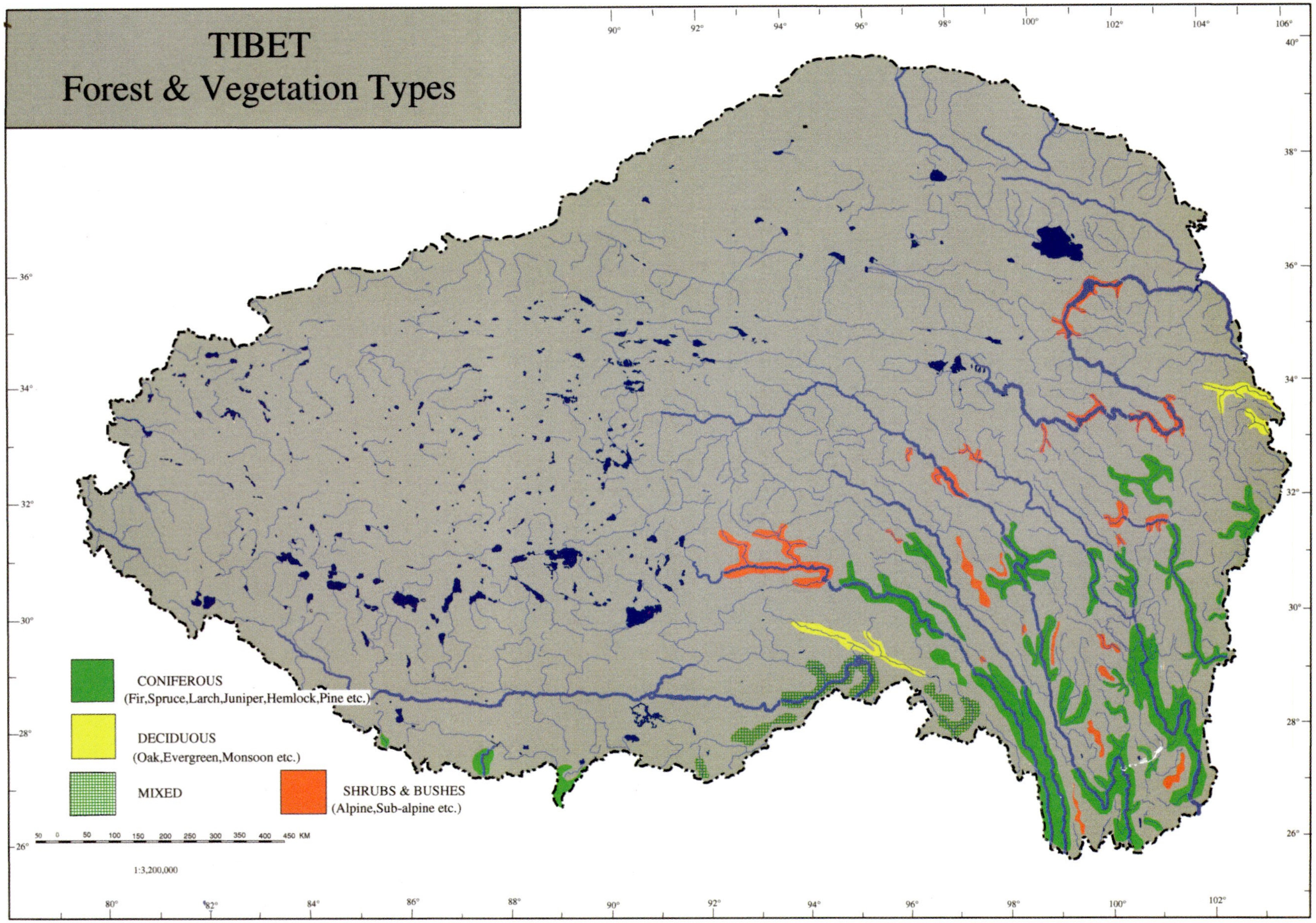

SOURCE: Wenhua 1993, Tsundue 1994

CARTOGRAPHY & DESIGN: Planning Council, CTA, Dharamsala-1999

TIBET
Distribution of Principal Minerals

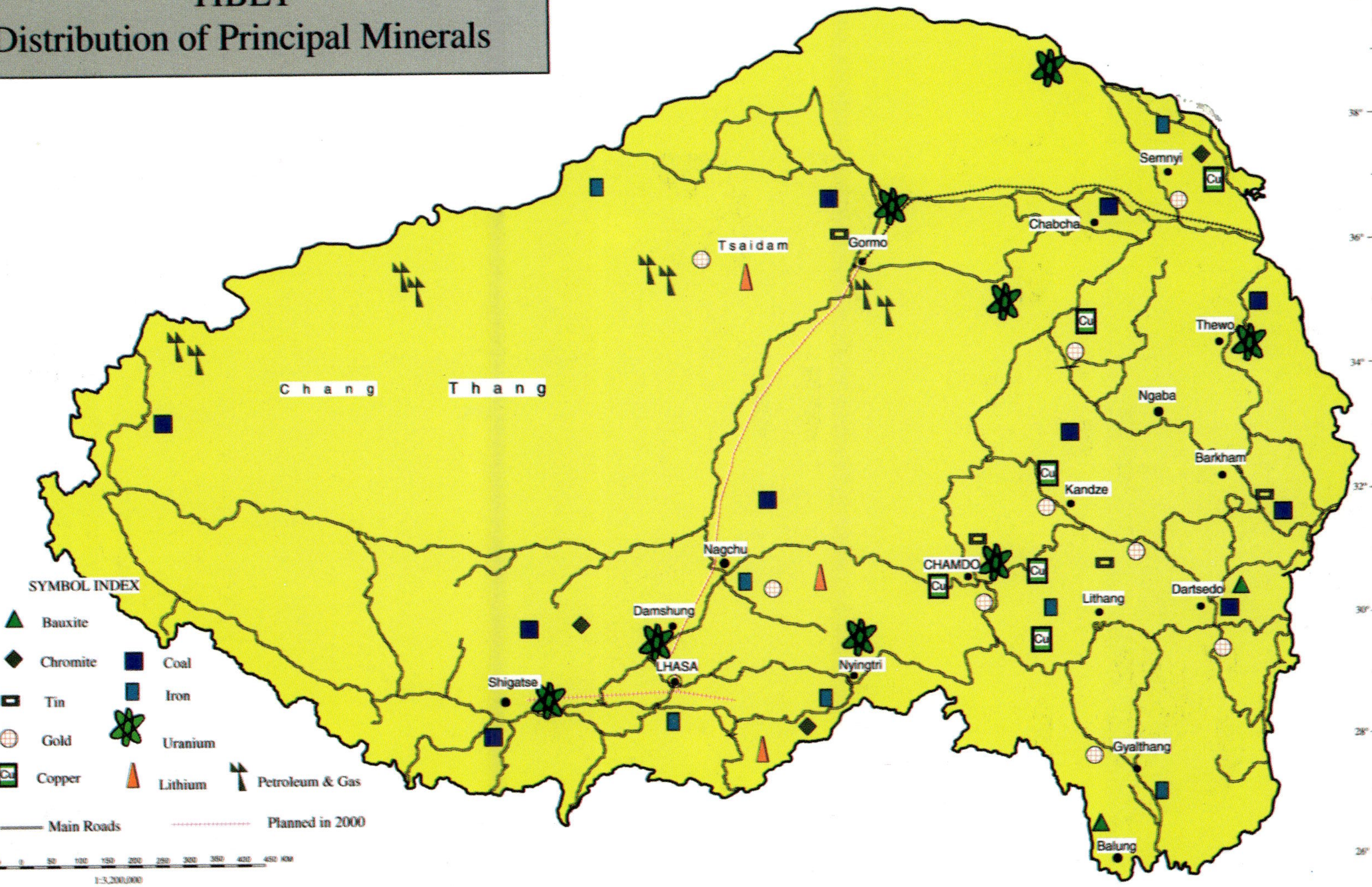

SOURCE: DIIR 1992, Green Tibet 1998

CARTOGRAPHY & DESIGN: Planning Council, CTA, Dharamsala-2000

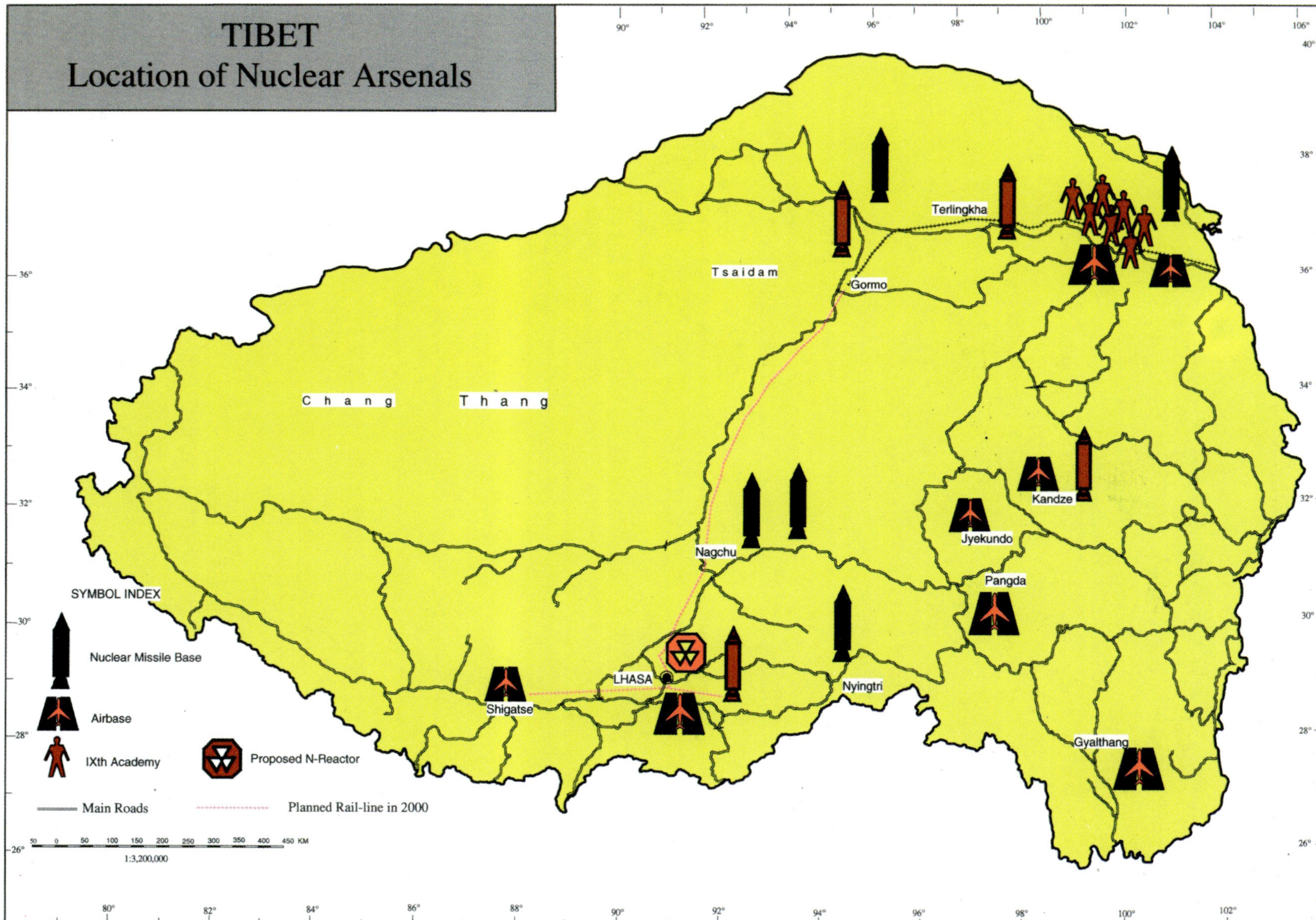

SOURCE: DIIR 1993

CARTOGRAPHY & DESIGN: Planning Council, CTA, Dharamsala-1999